NW

D0576902

‾ DUE

RECEIVED

JUN 0 2 2003

NORTHWEST RENO LIBRARY
Reno, Nevada

RECEIVED

A MURDER
IN
VIRGINIA

ALSO BY SUZANNE LEBSOCK

The Free Women of Petersburg

A MURDER IN VIRGINIA

SOUTHERN JUSTICE ON TRIAL

Suzanne Lebsock

W. W. NORTON & COMPANY
NEW YORK   LONDON

Copyright © 2003 Suzanne Lebsock

All rights reserved
Printed in the United States of America
First Edition

For information about permission to reproduce selections from this book,
write to Permissions, W. W. Norton & Company, Inc., 500 Fifth Avenue,
New York, NY 10110

Manufacturing by Maple-Vail Book Manufacturing Group
Book design by Mary A. Wirth
Production manager: Amanda Morrison
Composition by Molly Heron

LIBRARY OF CONGRESS CATALOGING-IN-PUBLICATION DATA
Lebsock, Suzanne.
    A murder in Virginia : Southern justice on trial / Suzanne Lebsock.—1st ed.
        p. cm.
Includes bibliographical references and index.
    ISBN 0-393-04201-4
1. Murder—Virginia—Lunenburg County. 2. Trials (Murder)—Virginia—
Lunenburg County 3. Criminal justice, Administration of —Virginia—Lunen-
burg County. I. Title.
    HV6533.V8 L43 2003
    364.15'23'09755643—dc21

W. W. Norton & Company, Inc., 500 Fifth Avenue, New York, N.Y. 10110
www.wwnorton.com

W. W. Norton & Company Ltd., Castle House, 75/76 Wells Street, London W1T 3QT

1 2 3 4 5 6 7 8 9 0

FOR

Kenneth L. Lebsock

Maxine Wells Lebsock

Richard P. McCormick

Katheryne Levis McCormick

CONTENTS

LIST OF
CHARACTERS

(Italics indicate people of known African descent.)

THE VICTIM

Lucy Jane Pollard—born Lucy Jane Fowlkes; married to farmer
Edward S. Pollard

THE ACCUSED

William Henry ("Solomon") Marable—sawmill hand from
North Carolina; married to *Fannie Marable*

Mary Abernathy—mother of nine; married to *Wilson Abernathy*, farmhand and tenant of Edward Pollard

Mary Barnes—mother of nine; farmhand for Edward Pollard;
married to farmhand *Joseph Barnes*

Pokey Barnes—laundress; the Pollards'neighbor; daughter of
Mary and Joseph Barnes

David James Thompson—storekeeper in Finneywood

OTHER MEMBERS OF THE BARNES FAMILY:

Rosa Barnes—daughter of Mary and Joseph; Pokey's younger sister

Rena Barnes—daughter of Mary and Joseph; Pokey's younger sister

Mary Elizabeth ("Lizzie") Bragg—daughter of Mary; Pokey's older half sister

Martha Ann Barnes—Pokey's young daughter

OTHER MEMBERS OF THE FINNEYWOOD
THOMPSON-PETTUS FAMILY:

Mattie Lee Thompson—David James Thompson's wife

Martha Ann Pettus Thompson—mother of David James; trial witness

J. H. H. (Herbert) Thompson—David James's older brother and business partner

Lucius M. Pettus—the Winking Man; David James Thompson's half brother

W. W. ("Bill") Pettus—David James Thompson's half brother and business partner

Nell H. Pettus—wife of Bill Pettus

MEMBERS OF THE FORT MITCHELL THOMPSON FAMILY:

Frances Thompson Pollard—Edward Pollard's first wife, deceased

William G. ("Bill") Thompson—Owner of farm immediately north of Edward Pollard's; Frances Pollard's son; Edward's stepson, neighbor, and enemy

David Jennings Thompson—William G. Thompson's son

Vincent ("Dump") Thompson—William G. Thompson's son

OFFICIALS AND ATTORNEYS:

William M. Bernard—Lunenburg attorney hired to aid prosecution

M. C. Cardozo—Lunenburg County sheriff

E. A. (Austin) Clements—constable

Samuel F. Coleman—judge, circuit court

Joseph Marshall Crute—judge, Prince Edward County court

J. H. Derbyshire—commanding officer, militia expedition to Lunenburg

Thomas Dickinson—Prince Edward County sheriff

J. F. Eubank— Lunenburg justice of the peace

Henry Wood Flournoy—attorney for the three women

Alexander Barclay Guigon—attorney for the three women

William Hodges Mann—prosecuting attorney

William E. Neblett—Lunenburg County commonwealth attorney

Charles Triplett O'Ferrall—governor of Virginia

George C. Orgain—judge, Lunenburg County court

Robert Goode Southall—prosecuting attorney

Asa D. Watkins—Prince Edward County commonwealth attorney

George Douglas Wise—lead attorney for the three women

OTHER SIGNIFICANT PLAYERS:

Edward S. Pollard—farmer; husband of Lucy Jane Pollard, the victim

Rosa Dixon Bowser—educator; president, Richmond Women's League

Joseph Bryan—publisher, *Richmond Times*

Marietta L. Chiles—schoolteacher; secretary, Richmond Women's League

Pattie Clements—wife of Constable Austin Clements; witness

Frank Cunningham—tenor; captain in the militia

Ellen Gayle—prime witness

H. C. ("Cass") Gregory—businessman; leader of the campaign to convict the women

Durelle J. Gregory—farmer; son of Cass Gregory; witness

Ben Knight—lived with Pokey Barnes; farmhand; witness

John Mitchell, Jr.—editor, *Richmond Planet*; leader of campaign to defend the women

William L. Royall—*Richmond Times* editorial writer; attorney for Solomon Marable

Lambert Welbers—Roman Catholic priest

PROLOGUE

L ucy Jane Pollard was murdered with an ax on a sticky June
afternoon in 1895, her body found just a few steps from her back
door in Lunenburg County, Virginia. Fifty-six years old, white,
and a farmer's wife, she had evidently been headed for the chicken
house to set hens when she came to her sudden, horrible end.

The alarm was raised by her husband, Edward S. Pollard, who
soon determined that a large sum of money was missing from the
house. A moderately prosperous farmer, Edward Pollard had risen
from next to nothing by hard work, by marrying up (three times), by
lending his earnings to neighbors at high rates of interest, and by
suing those who failed to pay him back on time. At seventy-two, he
did not rank among Lunenburg's most beloved citizens.

*Edward and Lucy Jane Pollard sat for this studio portrait,
probably taken soon after they were married in 1882.*

PHOTO COURTESY OF REGINALD H. PETTUS.

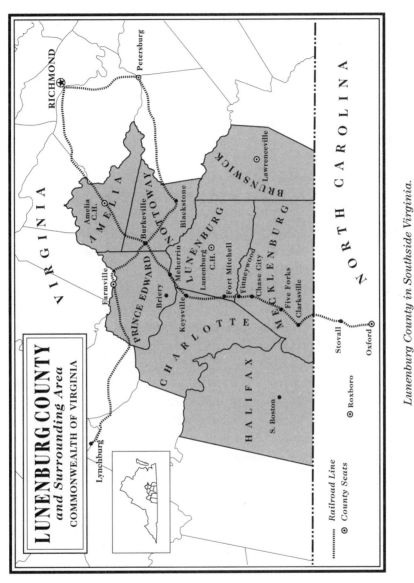

Lunenburg County in Southside Virginia.

MAP BY CONNIE SMITH.

In the hours after Lucy Pollard's death, hundreds joined the search for suspects and the missing money. After four days a posse arrested Solomon Marable, a lanky mulatto sawmill hand who had been spotted in the next county spending suspicious twenty-dollar bills. Marable admitted his presence on the Pollard place at the time of the killing, but he claimed that the crime itself was the work of three black women who had plotted the robbery and wielded the ax. The women—Mary Abernathy, Mary Barnes, and her daughter Pokey Barnes—were quickly apprehended and with Marable hustled out of the neighborhood to prevent a lynching. First to last, the three women insisted they were innocent.

In that place and time it was predictable that the men who controlled the criminal justice process would target black suspects. Almost everything else about the case defied prediction, beginning with the intense interest it generated outside Lunenburg County. Lunenburg was off the beaten path, tucked into the center of the Southside, the tobacco-growing region lying south of Richmond between the James River and the North Carolina border. Even by Southside standards, Lunenburg was rural. No railroads passed through it, except at the edges. Lunenburg had no newspaper and not a single settlement big enough to be called a town.

All the more cause for wonder at the phenomenal media spectacle touched off by Lucy Pollard's murder. Eighty miles away, in the capital city of Richmond, the Lunenburg case consistently made the front pages of all four daily papers. African Americans, alerted to the plight of the accused women by an energetic young editor named John Mitchell, Jr., followed the case from all over the United States. The Lunenburg case was a challenge for the military, a crisis for the governor, a puzzle for the courts. No fewer than eleven judges became involved, along with a host of less likely characters, including a Catholic priest, a committee of science-minded doctors, a locally famous tenor, and a woman who claimed to be a world-famous "manimorphologist." (It isn't in the dictionary; see Chapter 22.)

For eighteen months in 1895 and 1896 the Lunenburg case vied for space in the Virginia press with the nation's hottest political story of that era, the explosive third-party insurgency known as Populism, the ascendancy of free silver as the issue that swallowed all others, and the epochal presidential race of 1896, which ended with a Republican in the White House and the Populist dream in tatters. The rise and demise of Populism constituted one of the great dramas in the history of American politics, and it went on to dominate much of the written history of that time.[1]

Not so the Lunenburg case. Although it had bedeviled some of Virginia's most prominent politicians, engaged its best legal minds, and inspired some of the state's most creative investigative reporting, the case simply vanished after 1896. Neither participants nor historians wrote about it; nearly ninety years passed before the Pollard murder was mentioned in any published work of history.[2]

That long silence is especially perplexing given the importance of the issues that played out as the case evolved. Did justice stand a chance against the gathering forces of white supremacy? The late nineteenth century was a time of galloping racism all over the United States (in the North, Italians and Jews were among the many groups classified as distinct, inferior races), but the stakes were highest in the South, where 90 percent of black Americans still lived and where the meaning of emancipation remained a matter of continuous experimentation and struggle. Mary Abernathy and Mary Barnes, both in their forties at the time of Lucy Pollard's death, had married, worked, and brought up their children in freedom, but they had been born and raised as slaves, a reminder to us of how fresh the memories of slavery still were in 1895.

White people remembered too, of course, often with a profound sense of displacement and loss. In the 1890s a growing segment of influential whites took up the cause of white supremacy, seeking to take the vote away from black men, to dislodge black officeholders, to limit black economic and educational opportunities to whatever levels best served the interests of white employers, and to segregate everything that wasn't segregated already.

Although many white supremacists disavowed lynching, mob violence was in fact one of their most effective instruments. Lynching had been epidemic since the late 1880s; for the four people accused of killing Lucy Pollard, the most immediate issue was whether they would live long enough to get to trial. In Virginia, fortunately, the mob found a stubborn opponent in Governor Charles O'Ferrall. From his first moments in office in 1894 O'Ferrall pledged to put an end to lynching, "cost what it may, in blood or money."[3] Lunenburg was to be his biggest test.

The governor's intervention earned him the hot resentment of "the people" of Lunenburg, the vocal white men who normally got their way in the conduct of the county's affairs. Here was another epic conflict, the struggle for local autonomy in the face of the growing assertiveness of the state, a conflict that intensified ancient rivalries between the countryside and the city. All these issues were filtered through an unruly news business, itself torn between rising standards of objectivity and the awareness that sensationalism sold papers.

Six months after the death of Lucy Pollard, John Mitchell, Jr., wrote that the Lunenburg story "has presented a new phase at every step and a recital of its thrilling chapters sounds more like fiction than like reality."[4] Much of what happened was indeed extraordinary. Pokey Barnes, young, female, and unable to read or write, stood up in a courtroom and cross-examined witnesses like a seasoned attorney. A dozen white farmers risked their necks to head off a threatened lynching of their black neighbors. Time and again in the Lunenburg case, people acted bravely and against type. It would be a shame if the import of their actions were undermined by the suspicion that it was all a fabrication.

This book therefore is not a work of fiction, nor is it that brand of nonfiction that actually involves a truckload of invention on the author's part. This is decidedly a work of history, a tale from real life, and like life, it demands something of the reader. The Lunenburg case was populous and complicated, its sometimes dizzying action carried forward by scores of characters. In a work of fiction some of them would have to go; what novelist would clutter a story with eleven judges? In a novel the plot would be cleaner, the legal maneuvers less intricate, and at the end we all could experience the pleasures of resolution.

The narrative that follows, however, is history. I have tried to be meticulous in sticking to the evidence. I have not put words in people's mouths. I have not made up events or changed their order. The same goes for locations, weather, and objects. An old rope, a new spittoon—nothing appears here unless a document says it was there. Our story begins with one of those documented objects, a bell clanging out an alarm on a sultry evening in 1895.

A MURDER
IN
VIRGINIA

CHAPTER

1

"MURDER
MOST BRUTAL"

A t most hours of the day the southwest corner of Lunenburg County offered nothing special to the eye. But in the hour before dusk the landscape flooded with golden light, and for a time the woods and sandy fields lay placid and glowing. Every few hundred yards, smoke rose from the chimney of a farmhouse or cabin.

Off by itself in a stand of woods, about a mile and a half east of the village of Fort Mitchell, stood a two-story log house, since Christmas the home of Wilson and Mary Abernathy and seven of their children. On this warm June evening Wilson was just up from the field, where he had been coaxing young corn plants to grow in spite of the lack of rain. Mary sat on the porch, ample hips filling her big chair, her sleeves rolled up and dress unbuttoned at the throat.

She had finished mending Wilson's suspenders and now patched dresses while the younger children buzzed around the yard.

"You all keep still!" Wilson strained to make sense of the sounds coming from the direction of the sunset. "I think that's the boss."[1] Mary listened too, thinking at first that it was only Old Man Pollard calling his cows. But the hollering went on, and the farm bell rang and rang.

"That's him—" said Wilson, certain now that it was Edward Pollard, "hallooing like the horse might have kicked him."

Wilson asked Mary to follow, then sprinted down the path through the woods and soon was out of sight. Mary labored behind as fast as she could manage. A heavy woman and not long in the legs, she had gone about three hundred yards, halfway to the Pollard house, when she met Wilson running back with the news.

"Someone has killed Old Miss!" Wilson told her.

"Oh pshaw," said Mary, "surely that ain't so."

But when she got up into the Pollards' yard, she saw that it was so.

Mary Abernathy, mother of nine living children, was the last person known to have seen Lucy Pollard alive and the first to be arrested for the murder.

IMAGE FROM THE *RICHMOND TIMES*, 25 JULY 1895, COURTESY OF THE LIBRARY OF VIRGINIA.

*   *   *

BY THE TIME Mary Abernathy got there, ten or twelve people, some black, some white, were milling about, all of them shocked and trying to figure out what to do. Among them was Edward Pollard, gray-haired, gray-eyed, and stricken. "Auntie," he said to Mary, "someone has killed Lucy for my money." Six feet tall and sturdily built, Edward Pollard normally stood as straight as a post. But he soon crumpled to the ground beside the body of his wife and lay there weeping, his hand upon Lucy's face.[2]

The light grew dim, but the worst of Lucy Pollard's wounds remained all too visible. She lay on her back on thin grass and weeds, her feet pointing toward the northeast corner of the house only four or five paces away. Her eyes blared open. She had suffered multiple gashes on the left side of her face and head. Her left ear was almost chopped off, and her spectacles were knocked sideways, with one of the lenses punched out. Scattered on the ground nearby were about a dozen eggs, all broken and oozing. The dead woman's hands rested neatly on her breast, as though the killer had taken a moment to tidy up.[3]

On the eastern edge of the yard, about twenty feet from the body, stood a small woodpile. Mary Abernathy sat down on it to keep watch. Long after dark people still came, lanterns bobbing up the road and on footpaths through the woods. In the lamplight the newcomers could see for themselves how Lucy Pollard had been butchered. They had to be told about the other crime, the robbery. The murderer had stolen almost all of the Pollards' money. When Edward discovered his wife's body—so he told those who first answered his alarm—he shouted for help and gave two or three pulls on the farm bell. Then it came to him: He must have been robbed. He ran into the house, and sure enough, more than eight hundred dollars had vanished. After that he ran back outside and hollered and rang until the neighbors came.[4]

All night long he lay on the ground beside Lucy. Someone found a couple of old sheepskins for him to lie on, but it was a hard bed for a man in his seventies.[5]

Mary Abernathy stayed out there too, maintaining her post on the woodpile a few feet away. She had been trained for this, all the sitting up with sick children and burying the ones who died. Married at age twenty-one, now forty-seven, she had given birth to fourteen children. Nine were left; she had lost a set of twins and three other babies.[6] Nothing could prepare a person for the stunning brutality of Lucy Pollard's death, but Mary Abernathy knew everything there was to know about long vigils in the dark.

At about midnight she was questioned by three white men—the

justice of the peace, the constable, and a citizen named Cass Gregory, who had volunteered to help investigate. No, she said, she did not see Mrs. Pollard often. Her husband, Wilson, saw both the Pollards regularly, as he did general farmwork for Mr. Pollard on Monday, Tuesday, and Wednesday of every week. On the other days Wilson worked for himself, growing crops on land allotted him in exchange for those three days of labor. Mary herself did not work for the Pollards. From December, when they had moved to the Pollard place, until today, she had been up to the Pollard house only two or three times, once when she needed Miss Lucy to read a letter for her.[7]

But yes, she had been up to Pollards' earlier that day. Wilson was working on his own account when they heard the farm bell ring at an unusual hour. Wilson told her, if you please, go see what the boss wants. So she walked to the Pollards' house, and the first person she saw was Mary Barnes, working in the Pollards' garden. Then Mr. Pollard came out to the garden and asked what was up. Mary Abernathy told him that Wilson had sent her to see why the bell was rung. Mr. Pollard said he was ringing for his wife, not for Wilson. "Wilson knows that's not his name," Mr. Pollard said. "Four taps spells his name." Just then Mrs. Pollard came up from the neighbors' place, saying it was mighty warm. They got to talking about how to get bugs off greens. Mary Abernathy said she made her children bug them, but she had heard salt water was good.

Under arrest: Mary Barnes [right], mother of nine, worked for Edward Pollard as a field hand in the days before the murder. Her grown daughter Pokey Barnes [left], a young mother and a laundress, was the Pollards' nearest neighbor.

MARY BARNES IMAGE FROM THE *RICHMOND DISPATCH*, 13 SEPTEMBER 1895; POKEY BARNES IMAGE FROM THE *RICHMOND TIMES*, 25 JULY 1895. BOTH COURTESY OF THE LIBRARY OF VIRGINIA.

Mr. Pollard invited them all up to the house, where they sat down on the front porch and had a drink of fresh water, which Mary Barnes brought up from the spring. Then Mr. Pollard hitched his horse to a plow and led her out the front gate, and in a few minutes Mary Barnes followed him to the field with her hoe. That left Mary Abernathy and Miss Lucy at the house, and after a short conversation Mary walked back home. Later the bell rang again, and it kept ringing, and someone was hollering. Wilson ran to see what was the matter, and Mary followed. That was all she knew.

After the questioning Mary Abernathy was told to stay put. She had company, fortunately. Pokey Barnes had come and perched beside her on the woodpile at the yard's edge.[8] "Pokey" was a nickname, suiting her the way "Tiny" suits a big man, for she was quick, restless, and smart. She was a near neighbor, twenty-three years old, and on any other night would have had something interesting to say. But they had been told not to speak to anyone. This was a hardship for Mary Abernathy, for whom conversation was a comfort as well as an art.

*   *   *

DAYBREAK CAME AT five. In the house and barn and all around the yard, the people at the Pollard place began to stir, grateful to be moving. In the kitchen a crew of neighbors fired up Lucy Pollard's stove and fixed breakfast. As soon as it was light enough to see, little groups of men began walking over the farm, eyes to the ground, searching for clues. Other groups prepared to hunt as far and wide as necessary to locate the missing money and a suspect. Wilson Abernathy did not normally work for Edward Pollard on Saturdays, but this day he took a shovel to the orchard in front of the house and dug Lucy Pollard's grave. Edward Pollard would have a clear view to his wife's grave site from his front porch.[9]

The countryside stood out from the city in this way: Cities attempted to shelter their residents from the sordid and the horrible; they paid cops to carry away bleeding bodies, to sweep lunatics from the streets, to bring thieves and murderers to trial. City people avoided the sight of the most basic human tragedies and then turned around and accused country people of being simple.

The Pollard house. Lucy Pollard's body was found on the ground between the chimney and the tree nearest the house; a chicken house is visible in the background.

IMAGE FROM THE *RICHMOND TIMES*, 11 AUGUST 1895,
COURTESY OF THE LIBRARY OF VIRGINIA.

In places like Lunenburg, people had little choice but to own the tragedies that befell their neighborhoods. They had no police force. Virginia counties were divided into districts—six districts in Lunenburg—and in each the voters chose one lone constable and three justices of the peace. These men almost always had some other occupation, typically farming; their official duties were part-time and unpredictable. The justices held court just about anywhere—in churches, stores, houses—whenever something came up. Cases involving small debts and minor crimes were resolved on the spot. When a felony was suspected, the justice of the peace did not try the case but instead held a hearing to decide if the evidence sufficed to send the suspect to the grand jury and thence to county court. The constable meanwhile carried out the justice's orders, and like the justice, he was paid by the task: fifty cents for serving a summons, a dollar for an arrest. If the constable needed more muscle or firepower, he could call in the county sheriff, but the sheriff too was only one man.[10]

Inevitably justices and constables relied upon their neighbors. In the hours after Lucy Pollard's death, scores of people came to the Pollard farm. They made themselves look at the body. They stayed the night or returned at dawn. They cooked for Edward and one another, did the chores, and the men among them, whites and blacks both, felt it their duty to solve the crime—to search for evidence, recover the money, and bring the guilty to justice.

When the sun was an hour high, Constable Austin Clements tagged six white men for a coroner's jury, their task spelled out in the archaic syntax of the law, "to inquire upon the view of the body of Mrs. Lucy J. Pollard there lying dead, when, how, and by what means she came to her death."[11] Her body still lay in the yard. None of the six jurors who now inspected her injuries knew medicine, but it did not take doctors to figure out what had killed her.

Edward Pollard kept an old ax ready to hand, leaning against a white oak tree in the yard, a meat ax, sometimes called a pole-ax, made for butchering livestock. It had a blade on one side and on the other an oversize hammerhead, designed to stun the animal before the butchering began. After Lucy Pollard's murder the ax was found in its usual place against the tree, with blood on the blade.[12] A sharp side and a blunt one: The ax matched Lucy Pollard's wounds to sickening perfection.

The jury's work done, the body was carried into the house to be prepared for burial by a quartet of amateur undertakers—Mary Abernathy, two other middle-aged black women, and a white man named George Duffer. To Duffer fell the task of cleaning up Lucy Pollard's head, which was in even worse condition than they had thought. Her left jaw had been broken. Behind her ear the skull was crushed. Although the skin there was not broken, the entire back of her head was pulp. Duffer toiled at separating the hairs, freeing them from crusted blood. Edward Pollard watched for a time but finally could no longer stand it. He walked out of the room, telling Duffer to give it up.[13]

Mary Abernathy had fetched the tub and warm water and a cloth; now it was time for the women to wash the body. They eased

Lucy Pollard's calico off her left shoulder, which appeared to be broken. They also took a good look at the bruising. Even with all those fearful cuts on her face, it had at first been possible to hope that Lucy Pollard's death had been swift. Perhaps she had been struck from behind, knocked unconscious before she could know anything. But the deep bruises on her throat and around her wrists said otherwise.[14] Lucy Pollard had felt the grip of her killer. She may have seen her killer. She had struggled with her killer. Or killers.

The women finished washing Miss Lucy's body and clothed her in the best dress Edward had been able to find.

*   *   *

THAT WAS ANOTHER thing. The Pollard house had three rooms on the ground floor: the "big room," a narrow "little room" that ran along the side for storage, and a kitchen across the back. In a loft above the big room Lucy Pollard had stored their bedding and her clothes. Not until Edward went up to find something to bury her in did he think something else might be missing. Edward came down the narrow staircase worried that some of Lucy's dresses had been stolen, and maybe some bedclothes as well.[15]

But he couldn't be certain. Women knew their dresses intimately, could describe them down to the last tuck and buttonhole. They named them too: my black merino, my old calico, my green silk. Edward knew no names, nor could he remember the color or cut of any specific dress that might now be missing. He resorted to arithmetic; he had counted seven dresses, and he thought most ladies had more than that. The posses out searching for the stolen money would now look for dresses too, and bed linens, although they did not know exactly what to look for.

The money was another matter. Edward Pollard did not believe in banks, so the Pollards had locked up their cash, his and hers, in a small, old-fashioned liquor cabinet in the big room. Edward kept his money, eight hundred dollars on the nose, inside the cabinet in a sheepskin pocketbook. All of it was in twenty-dollar bills, divided into packets of a hundred dollars each and labeled with his name, the amount, and the date last counted. Lucy preferred gold coins. She kept them in a pouch, either two or three twenty-dollar pieces

(Edward could not remember which), plus a five-dollar piece and a one-dollar piece. Also missing were two gold bracelets and a gold chain. Edward had bought the chain himself and remembered it had cost fifteen dollars.[16]

The thief had left the empty money pouch and pocketbook in the liquor case. Edward had found the liquor case closed but unlocked, the keys in their customary hiding place in a little box in a drawer of the sideboard. At the foot of the bed a small trunk sat upon a table; the trunk still contained thirty-two dollars.[17] Aside from what his neighbors owed him, it was all the money Edward had left in the world.

Edward and Lucy Pollard had no children, and Edward insisted that he and Lucy were the only people who knew where they had kept their money. No leads there. Nor did forensic science help. Blood typing, fingerprinting: These would not be available for many years.

The search for physical evidence yielded just a few clues. Between the time Edward Pollard left for the field and the moment of the murder, Lucy Pollard had been busy. She had sewed five buttons on Edward's pants and marked thirty eggs with the number 15. Half the eggs were scattered about the yard near the body. In the yard also were three pools of blood, the largest in the spot where Lucy's head had come to rest. The two others, about eighteen inches from each other, were three feet from the corner of the house. Three hairpins turned up on the ground.[18]

This much was clear. They had the body—the "corpus delecti," as prosecutors loved to say. They also had a weapon and, if they could assume the killer had been out to get the Pollards' money, a motive.

One more thing: The last person known to have seen Lucy Pollard alive was Mary Abernathy. Twenty-four hours after the death of Lucy Pollard, Mary Abernathy was under arrest.

CHAPTER

2

CHASE CITY

One thing about the restaurant business in Chase City: You never knew who might walk into your place next. It was a bright, eye-blinking June morning, and before long Mary Wootten's kitchen would be sweltering. The turn in the weather would bring more customers, though, as the heat drove the prosperous people out of the bigger cities. Most went to the seashore or the mountains. But some of them, the sick especially, and the hypochondriacs, came to the gentler landscape of the Southside, where newly discovered mineral springs promised relief from whatever ailed them.[1]

In the middle 1890s the country as a whole was sunk in depression, the worst in living memory. But thanks to its mineral springs, Chase City, population 750, was growing and boosterish, with a new

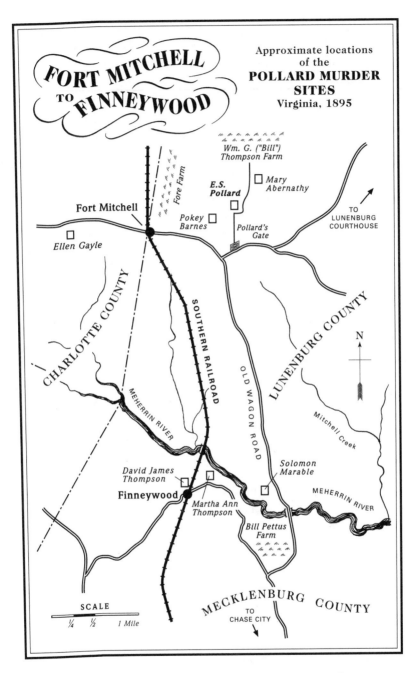

The neighborhood of Fort Mitchell and Finneywood.

MAP BY CONNIE SMITH.

wagon factory going up, a new fire engine on order, and a plan to pave Main Street. In high season the trains disgorged more people than the platform could hold.

So much the better for Chase City's women, some of whom made very decent livings providing visitors and workers with bed and board. Among them was Mary Wootten, a black woman with an entrepreneurial streak and a helpful twelve-year-old daughter named Jennie. Mary Wootten operated her restaurant in a two-story clapboard house with a rail fence around the yard. It was the morning after Lucy Pollard's murder, and although the Pollard farm was only eight miles away, Mary Wootten had not yet heard the news.[2]

She was therefore not alarmed when a tall young stranger entered her restaurant; she served strangers all the time, especially on Saturdays, when farmers and sawmill hands came to town for supplies and conversation. This particular customer was the color of ginger cake, his build slim, almost delicate. Not bad-looking either. A full head of hair. A black mustache. His shirt was dirty, though, and he wore a seriously dilapidated coat.

He sat down and ordered a big breakfast, fifty cents' worth. After eating, he offered Mary Wootten a twenty-dollar bill. Unable to change so large a bill, she sent daughter Jennie up Main to the Bank of Chase City. Jennie was soon back, counting out change to the man with the sorry coat. When he put the money into his pouch, Jennie spotted another twenty.

Mary Wootten later learned that the tall man's name was Marable. Floyd Clarke, a white merchant who ran a general store up the street, found out the name when Marable came into his store to shop and afterward asked him for help with a letter.[3] The man picked out a worsted dress and paid for it. He then chose a gingham dress, some white fabric, a shirt, and a man's suit, paying cash for each, one item at a time. Clarke was accustomed to this serial shopping, a practice of customers who knew little math and were wary of taking more than they could pay for.

While the man made his selections, a young fellow named Jones stuck his head in the door. "Mr. Clarke," he said, "have you heard of that murder near Fort Mitchell?" Clarke had, and was on the alert.

The railroad made it a cinch to get from the neighborhood of the murder to Chase City. The killer had only to board the southbound train at Fort Mitchell and get off two stops later, a trip of less than twenty minutes.[4] A person could walk it in under three hours.

The man buying things one at a time tried on a hat, studying himself in the mirror. After he bought the hat, he asked storekeeper Clarke to write a letter for him. "Dear Brother," he dictated, and Clarke began to write.

> I have written you several times telling you of the death of father, but have failed to hear from you. The money that father owed you he left with uncle. Uncle says he has spent some of the money but sends you $15 in this letter.
>
> OSBORNE MARABLE

Clarke addressed the envelope to a William Henry Marable in Finneywood, Virginia. Marable put in a ten-dollar bill and a five, and Clarke sealed it. But then Marable asked Clarke to unseal the envelope. Marable removed the ten, pocketed it, picked up his packages and the letter, and left the store, heading toward the post office.

Afterward Floyd Clarke thought it strange that this Marable had said not a word about the murder.

*   *   *

OVER THE NEXT twenty-four hours the people investigating Lucy Pollard's murder got a bead on the identity of the tall young man who dictated the letter under the name of Osborne Marable. "Osborne" Marable, they learned, was an alias. William Henry Marable, however, was their neighbor, a young mulatto man who had moved up from North Carolina a few months earlier. He lived near Finneywood and worked intermittently at a sawmill. No one ever called him by his real name. He went instead by the nickname Solomon, and he fitted perfectly the description of the big spender in Chase City. It must have been Solomon Marable who had eaten breakfast at Mary Wootten's, shopped in Floyd Clarke's store, and then mailed the letter to himself.

The investigation now moved forward on two tracks. Those out

William Henry (Solomon) Marable implicated Mary Abernathy, Mary Barnes, and Pokey Barnes in the murder and robbery, but changed his story many times.

IMAGE FROM THE *RICHMOND TIMES*, 25 JULY 1895, COURTESY OF THE LIBRARY OF VIRGINIA.

hunting for suspects began looking for Solomon Marable, who would be hard pressed to explain where those two twenties came from. At the Pollard place, meanwhile, authorities pressed ahead on a theory in the making that Lucy Pollard had been killed by a black woman or perhaps several black women. The day after the murder Justice of the Peace J. F. Eubank had ordered the arrest of three women who lived in the neighborhood of Fort Mitchell. Despite her reputation as a kind neighbor and a devout Christian, the prime suspect was Mary Abernathy. She claimed to know nothing of the murder, but because she was the last person known to have seen Lucy Pollard alive, the authorities wanted her in custody.

Next the constable arrested Pokey Barnes, the young woman who with Mary Abernathy had spent the night sitting up with the body. Pokey was twenty-three, a widow with one small child, and the Pollards' nearest neighbor. She lived about three hundred yards from the Pollard house, just across the double fence separating Edward Pollard's farm from that of the Fore family to the west. On the afternoon of the murder she had walked north along the fence in the company of friends who hoped to get cherries from the Thompson farm just north of Pollard's. By her own account, Pokey Barnes did not go all the way to the Thompsons'. Instead she and her friend Ellen Gayle turned back, retracing their steps to Pokey's house. When Ellen Gayle was questioned, she confirmed that she had been with Pokey the entire time.[5]

Could they have detoured to the Pollard house and pulled off the theft and the murder? On the bet that they had, the constable arrested both Pokey Barnes and Ellen Gayle.

While the arrests went forward, the searches yielded nothing. An abandoned house lying halfway between the Pollards' and the Abernathys' was thought to be a likely hiding place. Constable Austin Clements and Cass Gregory searched it as thoroughly as they could by lantern light, but came up empty-handed.[6]

All the while Mary Abernathy said emphatically that she had nothing to hide. On Saturday afternoon, roughly twenty-four hours after Lucy Pollard's death, she willingly led a search party to the two-story cabin she shared with her husband, Wilson, and their children. Single file, Mary Abernathy and the four searchers walked up the wooded path: Clements and Gregory again, with two other neighbors, one white and one black. The Abernathys' house was small, only one room upstairs and one room down; Clements thought it the most packed place he had ever seen. Her children watching, Mary Abernathy opened trunks and boxes, pulled out the contents, invited the men to search for themselves. They did find a piece of harness Clements thought belonged to him, but no suspicious dresses or bedding and no money.

It was the same at Pokey Barnes's house and everywhere else they thought to look. With the searches yielding nothing, the investigators might have rethought their approach. Instead they cut the groove deeper: Late Saturday the justice of the peace ordered the arrest of three more black women.

*   *   *

FANNIE MARABLE FINALLY had the Chase City depot in sight. She hurried down the tracks, struggling to hold on to her bundles and both babies. Johnny was only a few weeks old and didn't weigh much, but at fifteen months Henry was an armful. Fannie Marable was nineteen years old and a refugee from the uproar over Lucy Pollard's murder.[7]

Every few steps she cast an anxious glance back at her husband, Solomon, who paced in the doorway of Mary Wootten's restaurant. It was Sunday morning, two days after the murder, and Fannie and Solomon Marable had just walked six miles from their cabin near Finneywood. Before they set out, Solomon had refused breakfast. By the time they reached Chase City he was famished and had stopped at Mary Wootten's to get a lunch for the train.

Solomon had told Fannie to wait for him by the tracks, but she kept moving, propelled by fear and dreadful memories. The law had come after Solomon before. A year and a half earlier, in their old neighborhood in North Carolina, the body of a young black woman named Ida Marrow had been found in a pine thicket near a public road. The victim was only seventeen and well regarded in the neighborhood. She had been raped and strangled; even the white people clamored for a conviction.[8]

No one had seen anything, but Solomon admitted that he had been walking down that road at dusk. Fannie could only stand by as her husband of eighteen months was arrested, jailed, and tried for murder. Nearly thirty witnesses were called. After three days—a long trial by the standards of the time—the jury found the evidence insufficient to convict. Solomon went free. But Solomon and Fannie Marable were shadowed by the suspicion that he had in fact done the deed.

Their move to Virginia at Christmas had promised a fresh start. Solomon got work hauling timber, and Fannie came on a few weeks later, with one baby in arms and another on the way. But now Lucy Pollard was dead, their Virginia neighborhood bordering on crazy, and the authorities wanted Solomon for questioning.

Fannie had no idea what he would tell them. He had told her only that he had gone to Fort Mitchell on the day of the murder and to Chase City the morning after that. He had come home from Chase City at midday Saturday.

"Somebody been here looking for you as a witness," Fannie had told him. The two men seeking Solomon, both white, had been packing pistols. "They liked to scared me to death."[9]

"I don't know nothing about it," Solomon had said. "I ain't done anything to anybody." But he spent a good part of the afternoon standing in the door of their cabin, looking up and down the road.

In the late afternoon Solomon had gone out, saying he expected a letter from his father at the Finneywood post office. He had come home with no letter and with frightening news: Some whites claimed that all the colored people around there were going to be white-capped until they turned in the murderer. Whitecapping could mean any form of intimidation, from insults and threats to torture, arson, or murder. Toward evening two of Pokey Barnes's sisters came by; they too had heard rumors of whitecapping.

Alone in their cabin the Marables would be sitting ducks. With night coming on, Fannie quickly readied the little ones and set out with Solomon for her uncle's place, where they hoped to find safety in greater numbers. After that Solomon walked back to their cabin, intending to stay there by himself. Fannie had cried and begged him not to, but Solomon kept insisting he had done nothing wrong and had nothing to fear. He changed his mind shortly after dark when he heard horses pounding up the road. Snatching up his new clothes, he disappeared into the woods just as the horsemen pulled up at his door.

Solomon made his way west, to the place where the trains crossed the river. There he took off his old clothes, put on his new ones, and sat down on the ground beneath the railroad trestle. Eventually he slept, wrapped against the damp in his old coat. In the full light of morning he returned to the cabin. Fannie was already there with their little sons.

"Babe," Solomon said, "don't you want to go home today?"

"I want to go home," said Fannie. "You have been promising to send me home long enough. But you can do as you like about it."

Fannie didn't mean that last bit. She was already packing.

"You'd better send we all," she said, "and you stay here."

Solomon agreed. "Fix the children and let's go."

He had a plan: They would walk south to Chase City and catch the train there. Solomon would ride partway with Fannie, then return to face the music. Fannie and their boys would ride on to Bullocks, a village in North Carolina about twenty-five miles away.

Early that morning it had looked like rain, but now, as Fannie pushed on toward the Chase City train station, the sky had cleared and a dry, blasting wind blew at her back. She looked again and saw Solomon coming from Mary Wootten's, his sack of lunch in hand. Suddenly he struck a trot. "Halt!" someone yelled. "Halt! Stop that man!" Solomon dropped the sack and broke into a run, a dozen men in swift pursuit. Two bullets zinged over his head. When he got close to Fannie, he tossed her his money pouch and kept running. A barbed wire fence lay directly in his path. Solomon hurdled it and crashed into the woods. The fence stood four feet high, and by the time his pursuers picked their way through it, Solomon was gone.

In the commotion, no one paid any attention to Fannie Marable. She found two dollars in the money pouch. When the train came in, she climbed aboard with her babies and headed home.

*　　*　　*

By SUNDAY EVENING, forty-eight hours after the death of Lucy Pollard, six suspects were in custody. The seventh, Solomon Marable, was still on the loose. The fact that all the suspects were black surprised no one in Lunenburg, least of all Lunenburg's black people. White officialdom habitually tagged African Americans as criminals, especially in cases involving theft. Everything about larceny cases tended to be disproportionate: the likelihood of a black person's being charged, the swiftness of conviction, the harshness of the sentencing. Steal a chicken in Virginia (its value about fifteen cents), and the judge could put you away for six months. Break into the hen house, and you could be gone from three to ten years.[10]

Clearly more was at stake than the chicken. Contention over theft had a long history, reaching well back into slavery. In the grand scheme of things, of course, slavery itself was theft; in the eyes of the enslaved, almost everything that one group of human beings could take from another had already been stolen from them: their bodies, their children, their names. As their labor was expropriated daily, some slaves did not deem it a sin to take in turn property the master called his—a ham from the smokehouse, a spool of thread from the sewing basket. Slaves termed this taking. Masters called it stealing and complained about it incessantly.[11]

In slavery, appropriating the master's goods was partly a practical matter, a strategy used by some slaves to get enough to eat or wear. Had it ended there, the masters might not have minded as much. But taking was also an act of resistance to slavery itself, part of an elaborate mind game designed to undermine the master's sense of security and power.

In 1895 slavery was thirty years dead, but the struggle for security and power persisted, intense as ever. In the wake of emancipation, much was available to the freedpeople that had been closed to them as slaves. For the first time they could move freely from place to place. They worked for wages or a cut of the crop, and if the boss treated them like slaves, they could walk away. They could acquire property. They could marry, bring up their children as they saw fit, and sometimes send them to school. Abandoning the churches of their masters, they founded their own. They also turned willingly to politics, the men voting in numbers and electing some of their fellows to office.[12]

Almost everything the freedpeople experienced as gain, their former owners experienced as loss. Having to share political power hurt most—that and the refusal of black farmhands to work day and night. As individuals some former slaveholders bore up more gracefully than others, but as a class they felt robbed.

Any instance of larceny had the potential to hook into this troubled history, churning up anxiety about black people's taking what whites thought belonged to them.[13] So it was when Edward Pollard's house was robbed. Had some obvious trail of evidence led right to a white person's door, the authorities would likely have acted on it. Otherwise it went without saying that the suspects would be black.

But why would they be women? Amateurs all, the investigators worked from what they thought they knew. Dresses were missing, or at least Edward Pollard believed dresses were missing. In the folklore of the white South clothing was a woman's weakness, the theft of clothing a black woman's crime. Like white perceptions of theft in general, this one also went back decades, to a time when enslaved women were issued cheap, shapeless dresses and fought back by contriving to sew, borrow, buy, or take clothes that had color and style. After freedom came, black women retained a reputation for dressing beyond their means. Moreover, a high proportion of them washed clothes for a living, placing them under suspicion whenever a garment went missing.[14]

The investigators also considered the number of cuts on Lucy Pollard's face and head. Whoever murdered Lucy Pollard had swung the ax at least a dozen times. This too suggested a female perpetrator. Wouldn't a man have accomplished the killing with a single blow?[15]

The second round of arrests took place on Sunday, two days after the murder. Caught in the dragnet this time were Mary Barnes—the mother of Pokey Barnes—Pokey's younger sister Rena Barnes, and Polly Carter. Why Rena Barnes and Polly Carter came under suspicion was never explained. Mary Barnes, however, had been close to the scene. When Edward Pollard sounded the alarm, she had come running ahead of everyone else and was about to kneel by the body until Edward told her to run for help.[16]

During the four days preceding the murder Mary Barnes had been employed by the Pollards, mostly as a field hand for Edward.[17] She was a slight, wiry woman, just over five feet tall, with a high forehead and dark skin stretched tautly over prominent cheekbones. In many ways her life history paralleled that of Mary Abernathy. She was born in slavery, freed as a teenager in the general emancipation of 1865, married in 1871 to a farmhand, and she was the mother of nine living children. She was often referred to as Old Mary Barnes, though she was the same age as Mary Abernathy.

On the afternoon of the murder Mary Barnes had worked with Edward Pollard most of the time. After the interlude on the porch, when she brought a drink of cool springwater to the Pollards and Mary Abernathy, she had followed Edward Pollard out to the field with her hoe. Before she left the house, however, she was alone for a few moments with Mary Abernathy and Lucy Pollard.

Virginians did not hold court on the Sabbath, so the accused women, now six in number, would have to wait a day to learn their fate. On Monday Justice Eubank and the coroner's jury would reconvene at the Pollard house, question the suspects and the neighbors one more time, and at length make their recommendations.[18] If the evidence proved sufficient, the women would be delivered to Lunenburg Courthouse, sixteen miles away, to be jailed while they awaited trial.

This is how the race card was played in 1895. Within forty-eight hours of the murder of Lucy Pollard, six black women were arrested, even though no physical evidence linked any of them to the crime. Not one white person was questioned as a suspect. Not one white person's house was subjected to search.[19]

*　　*　　*

ALL DAY SUNDAY rumors flew. By midday it was all over Fort Mitchell that a male suspect had been captured in Chase City.

Mary Abernathy and Pokey Barnes were at dinner when they heard. Constable Clements had decided his prisoners were best kept away from the Pollard place, so on Sunday morning he had several guards escort them on foot to his own home, a two-story frame house on a farm about two miles away. Once at the Clements place the women passed the morning fixing a big Sunday dinner. Pokey caught the chickens but then thought better of plucking them lest she get chicken blood on her dress. They ate in shifts, the able-bodied white men served first. Then Mrs. Clements sat down with her elderly parents and her children. When all the white people were finished, Mary and Pokey sat down with Ellen Gayle and Phil Watson, who was guarding them in a neighborly sort of way.

While they ate, Mrs. Clements suddenly put her head in the dining room door. "You all be still," she said. "They have caught the rascal who got Mr. Pollard's money!"

Mary Abernathy clapped her hands and shouted, "Thank God! Thank God!" and fell out of her chair rejoicing.[20]

Constable Clements was quickly off to Chase City on horseback. Other men jumped on the train. At all the ferries and bridges north of Fort Mitchell, sentries abandoned their posts and headed south to join the army of citizens who would bring Lucy Pollard's killer to justice.[21]

Sooner or later they all learned the disappointing truth. By Sunday evening it was clear that Solomon Marable was their man, and he had been spotted that morning in Chase City. But he had taken off on those long legs of his and got away. As night fell, the three women prisoners at the Clements place prepared for bed. Mary Abernathy remained buoyant, even after hearing of Solomon's escape. She felt sure the searchers would catch up with him, and when they did, she would be in the clear.

But then Durelle Gregory arrived all in a sweat from the Pollard place. He had brought Mary Barnes with him, their way lit by a lantern. Durelle was a steady young man of twenty-five and an able farmer. He was Cass Gregory's eldest son and, like his father, had been active in investigating the murder.[22]

It looked bad at Pollard's. People had heard that Solomon Marable had been captured, and they had been gathering all afternoon, eager to see him brought low. When they heard of his escape, their mood turned ugly. Durelle Gregory thought Old Mary Barnes was unsafe at the Pollard place, and he wasn't sure the rest of the women were safe anywhere.

Gregory ordered the four women prisoners outside and with two other guards decided to take them to an abandoned house on his own farm. Every so often they stopped to listen for trouble. When they got within sight of the house, Gregory blew out the lantern. They all climbed over the fence, crept up to the house, and slipped in. Once inside, Gregory lit the lantern again and led the women upstairs. He put Mary Barnes and Pokey in one room and Mary Abernathy and Ellen Gayle in another. If he came up and tapped them in the night, they were to be ready to move out.

Their situation was critical. The women knew it, and by this time so did a considerable portion of the reading public in Richmond. The story broke in Sunday's *Richmond Dispatch*. "The neighbors are very much wrought up," said the *Dispatch*, "and a lynching is likely to occur before tomorrow morning."[23]

You could call that news. Or you could call it a script.

CHAPTER

3

FLIGHT

Eight hundred dollars was a lot of money, enough to buy a farm, even two farms. It could buy a stake in California or the Klondike, or two trips to Europe, or a pilgrimage to Palestine.[1]

Cass Gregory was fixated on the money, and this Monday morning he was headed in his buggy to Edward Pollard's to talk about it. Perhaps in flusher times the missing money would not have seemed so lustrous, but there had been a financial panic in 1893, and in its wake had come nationwide depression. Banks and businesses went under at double the normal rate; hardly anyone would fault Edward Pollard for thinking his money safer at home than in a bank. Farmers despaired at sinking crop prices and piled debt upon debt, provided someone would extend them credit.[2]

The dirtiest job in the county belonged to the sheriff, whose duty was to seize and sell the assets of men and women who could not pay their debts. On the first visit to a given farm the sheriff might get something—a cow, some implements, a crop just harvested. On his next visit he would likely come away with nothing. He would fold up the warrant, write, "No effects," on the back, and turn it over to the county clerk, who would tie it in a bundle and file it in the courthouse with hundreds of others just like it.[3]

From Edward Pollard's outer gate it was easy to see how someone might get away with murder. The house sat well back from the public road, about four-tenths of a mile up Edward's private road. Anyone passing by on the public road would be able to see the Pollards' roof, but nothing of the yard.

On this uncommonly chilly June morning, Cass Gregory was fretting over the notice on Pollard's gate. Edward had posted a sign offering 20 percent of the stolen money to anyone who recovered it. In Gregory's opinion, it wasn't enough. Lucy Pollard had been dead for nearly three days, and none of the stolen money had been accounted for, except the forty dollars allegedly in the possession of Solomon Marable. The longer this went on, the farther the money might travel. As a practical matter, Gregory would argue, people in outlying areas were more likely to join the search if Edward held out a larger reward.[4]

Gregory thought of himself as a practical man; at fifty-one he had experience in just about every sort of business a man in the tobacco belt could undertake. Agriculture he knew from a boy, having grown up on a farm about two miles east of Pollard's, but he preferred enterprises with bigger stakes and quicker returns. He had tried the timber business and, when he could get backing, took up the risky enterprise of buying and selling tobacco. During the previous season he had set up as a tobacco broker in Roxboro, twelve miles over the North Carolina line. Roxboro was still his residence, but the season had not been a success. Heavily in debt, Gregory was looking for opportunities elsewhere.[5]

Meantime the tobacco business gave Cass Gregory one thing no other man in Fort Mitchell had in abundance: free time. Almost everyone else kept dashing home to tend livestock. Hay needed mowing, winter wheat needed cutting, corn was due for replanting, and in every field and garden the weeds grew faster than the crops.[6] The tobacco-buying season, however, had ended in May and wouldn't begin again until late August. Cass Gregory, temporarily in Lunenburg to visit his son Durelle, had plenty of time.

He had also the look of a gentleman, fair-haired with high cheekbones showing above a neat beard. His build was trim. Above all, Gregory moved with quiet self-assurance. Taking charge came naturally to him, and other men readily granted him their confidence.[7]

Thus it did not seem strange when Gregory took a leading part in the investigation of Lucy Pollard's death, even though he held no office. Within hours of the murder Gregory was questioning Mary Abernathy and other potential suspects. That night he searched the abandoned house that stood halfway between the Pollards' and the Abernathys'. Then a neighbor piloted him to the Thompson farm, immediately north of Pollard's. They stopped too at the house where twenty-year-old Lula Knight lived with her parents. Lula Knight was engaged to Wilson and Mary Abernathy's son and had spent the afternoon at their house. At both stops Gregory questioned the residents at length. Afterward he went to the house occupied by the Pollards' nearest white neighbors and slept for an hour. At dawn he was back at the Pollard place looking for any clues that might turn up in the morning sun.[8]

Gregory stopped his buggy at Pollard's yard gate and scanned the crowd, looking for Edward. When Gregory finally spotted him, he asked for a word in private. The two men walked around to the back. Gregory opened.[9]

"I see you are offering twenty per cent for the recovery of the money."

"Yes," said Pollard, a plainspoken man.

"Can't you make it fifty?"

"No," Pollard said, "I will let the advertisement stand as it is."

"You won't give it?" Gregory asked again.

"No," Pollard repeated.

"I believe a dollar is your God. Good morning."

Gregory turned and took a few long strides into the back of Edward's house, then walked straight through to the front door and out to the gate. Without a word to anyone, he jumped into his buggy. The people gathered in Edward's yard turned their backs to the frigid wind and watched him speed away.

*　　*　　*

THE WIND BLEW all day Monday, cold and sobering. Among the men at Pollard's, the conviction grew that the fugitive Solomon Marable was the killer. In the morning a party of five men, two black and three white, had searched Solomon's cabin, returning with the news that the cabin had been abandoned, another indication of Solomon's probable guilt.[10]

By the time Justice Eubank convened the coroner's jury on Monday afternoon, the jurors were prepared to weigh the evidence with care. One by one the six accused women were taken into Edward Pollard's house to be grilled about the death of Lucy Pollard. Mary Abernathy said she was as clear of it as the angels. The other women proclaimed their innocence with equal vehemence, going over and over their movements on the day of the murder. The coroner's jury got nowhere.

After several hours, Justice Eubank, Constable Clements, and the six jurors walked out to a corner of the yard and formed a huddle. They were dog-tired but lucid enough to see that they did not have the evidence to bind any of the women over for trial. Eubank decided he had no choice but to let them all go. The constable walked over to the cornhouse where Mary Abernathy and Pokey Barnes had been waiting. "Mary and Pokey, you are excused and can go home."[11]

It was nearly sundown. Mary Abernathy went right home, but Pokey Barnes was afraid to. Her house was less than three hundred yards from Pollard's, and she did not want to be trapped if some provocation suddenly turned the men at Pollard's into a mob. So Pokey walked into Fort Mitchell, hoping to spend the night with the Hutsons, white people who would protect her.

When she got there, Pokey learned that the Hutsons already had overnight company, and there was no place for her to sleep. By this time it was completely dark. Pokey thought another white family named Taylor would take her in. Would Peter Hutson walk her down there? she asked. He'd already pulled off his shoes, Hutson said, but Mrs. Hutson told him he could put his shoes back on. "I done pull off my shoes," he said again.

"Oh, Pokey, you ain't afraid," Hutson went on. "I'll stand in the door and talk to you until you get to Mrs. Taylor's." Hutson talked her through the darkness, and for one more night Pokey was safe.[12]

*   *   *

THEY CAUGHT SOLOMON the next morning, Tuesday, June 18, 1895.

By afternoon the neighborhood of Fort Mitchell looked for all the world like 1861. On all the roads, armed men moved, solemn and expectant, in the direction of the Pollard farm. Edward Pollard sat in his big chair on the front porch, watching each little group come up his private road, down into the first sink, up again, and then down into the second. They looked like the mustering troops of the infant Confederacy, before there were matching uniforms or fancy flags. Carrying the rifles and shotguns they used for hunting, they rode if they could and walked if they had to, assembling in Pollard's front yard to wait for Solomon. It had not rained in the four days since the murder. Still visible in the grass near the chimney corner were the three spots where Lucy Pollard's blood had soaked into the ground.

The cavalcade bearing Solomon Marable approached slowly from the south, its progress visible for miles from the plumes of dust that drifted up over the treetops. Marable was on horseback, his arms pinioned behind him. He was guarded left and right, carried along in a column of fifty horsemen. At Pollard's yard gate the procession halted. Solomon appeared to be calm. Edward Pollard sat staring at Solomon, not moving.[13]

The search party had nabbed Solomon at a railroad siding about eight miles south of Chase City. Near Five Forks they spotted a tall man moving through a cornfield. When the man saw them coming, he ran toward the railroad siding and dodged under a boxcar. A young doctor from Chase City was the first to lay hands on him. The captive at first denied that he was Marable, but when some men who recognized him rode up, he admitted who he was. He at first denied any knowledge of the murder. Unarmed, he had nothing incriminating on him. He had ripped his pants when he hurdled the barbed wire fence in Chase City. Now he wore two pairs, his old pants covering the new.[14]

The posse had gone to Five Forks on a tip from a black farmer named Ben Daniel. Solomon had been on the lam for nearly forty-eight hours, not knowing where to go, stopping at the homes of black families to beg a bed or a meal. This day at about 6:00 A.M. he approached the home of Ben Daniel.[15]

The morning was chilly for summer, and Daniel invited him in, taking the stranger's hat and saying there would be breakfast shortly. Solomon introduced himself using his real name. Ben Daniel knew some of the North Carolina Marables; his friend Jeff Marable had a son named William Henry, whom Daniel had met long ago. Daniel hadn't seen him since, but he did remember that the boy had been dark, like his father.

"Why Henry, you don't favor yourself," said Daniel. "What make you so bright?"

The coincidence would have suited a second-rate novel. In fact two William Henry Marables had been born in North Carolina within a few months of each other.[16] Ben Daniel did not know this. Neither did Solomon, who tried to fake it.

"I been staying in a restaurant with Roger Jones in Oxford, North Carolina, that make me so bright."

Everyone in Daniel's family remarked on Marable's light complexion. This seemed to worry Solomon, and he asked for his hat. But Daniel persuaded him to stay for breakfast. They ate, and afterward Solomon brought up the murder.

"I heard two white gentlemen say when I got off the train at Jeffrey's Junction that a white lady had been killed up in the country somewhere, and they are looking for the murderer."

"What kind of man did they say he was?" Daniel asked him.

"They said he was a dark-complexioned, heavy-built, chunky man, with a beard coming down to the middle of his chest."

Daniel had heard something different, that the man they were looking for was tall, thin, and light-skinned. "Very much like you," he told Solomon.

Solomon dropped his head. "Well, that's what I heard," he said.

Then Solomon asked a question. "Do you think they would hurt this man if they caught him?"

Daniel wondered if he was sharing his breakfast table with a killer. "I reckon not," he answered, taking care to say nothing that might upset his guest.

Solomon said one thing more about the murder. He had heard the chunky man had held the lady still while three Negro women killed her.

After some further talk Solomon rose to leave. He was a contractor for the railroad, he said (another whopper) and was due at the junction to recruit section hands. Then he walked off singing.

Ben Daniel hardly knew what to make of this odd conversation, but he thought he'd better report it.

*   *   *

THE WOMEN DID it. So Solomon would say. A few of the people gathered at Pollard's knew more or less what was coming even before the cavalcade pulled up at Edward's gate. That morning, shortly after the search party had lashed Solomon to a horse and started for the Pollard farm, Solomon's captors told him he would be better off if he confessed. As they rode along, Solomon talked.[17] Instructions were then sent ahead to Fort Mitchell: Hold Mary Barnes. Hold Pokey Barnes. Hold Mary Abernathy.

It was too late, of course; the women had been released the previous evening. Now the whole process began again. Justice Eubank wrote out new arrest warrants for Pokey Barnes and the two Marys. He issued a warrant for Ellen Gayle as well, for the testimony given the previous day placed her in company with Pokey on the afternoon of the murder.

Constable Clements and three deputies fanned out to make the arrests. They soon learned that Mary Abernathy had gone off on foot to Rehoboth, a crossroads about eight miles to the east. One of the deputies turned his horse toward Rehoboth and rode after her. Two new rumors soon threaded the countryside. One, driven out by her guilty conscience, Mary Abernathy had fled the neighborhood the first chance she got. Two, Mary Abernathy had

absconded to Rehoboth in search of a more remote place to stash
the money.

The other three women were brought to Edward Pollard's yard,
where they sat wondering what on earth Solomon Marable was
going to say about them.[18]

*   *   *

IN THE YELLOW light of late day Solomon Marable stood on Edward
Pollard's porch and made a public statement. No professional
reporters were on hand, but a correspondent who sometimes sent
local news up to the *Richmond Dispatch* scribbled down Solomon's
words:

> On last Friday morning I was here on the farm to see some
> friends, and, while here, Mary Barnes, Mary Abernathy,
> Pokey Barnes, and [her sister] Rosa Barnes each told me
> they had something good in store for me. I asked what it
> was, and they told me to wait and see, and to come to the
> spring at twelve o'clock and wait until they came. I went
> to the spring at twelve o'clock and waited until four, when
> Mary Barnes came down after some water for Mr. Pollard,
> who was about ready to go out to the field. She said to me,
> "We will be ready for you soon." I then waited until about
> five o'clock, when Mary Abernathy and Pokey Barnes
> came running to the spring with their dresses up and their
> skirts and hands covered with blood. Mary Abernathy
> handed me a $20 note, and told me to use it, and say noth-
> ing about it. I took it and went home, and the next morn-
> ing went to Chase City, where I spent some of it, and they
> got after me and shot at me, and I ran. I did not know Mrs.
> Pollard had been killed, as they did not tell me why they
> were bloody.[19]

Solomon's captors pushed him into the house before the crowd
could react. There were easily two hundred people in the yard—
some thought four or five hundred—and more kept coming as the
light faded and the questioning proceeded inside.[20]

Solomon's story satisfied no one. The people in the crowd were

certain of his guilt; his old clothes had been found in the woods, not far from his cabin, and according to the latest rumor, they were covered with blood. Weeks later the truth would out: Solomon's clothing was stained only with turpentine, the badge of the sawmill worker. But this night the authorities were not letting anyone see the clothes, and the rumor of blood prevailed. The people waited for word from inside the house. Was anyone truly confessing? Did anyone say where the money was? The crowd grew impatient. They had ropes.[21]

Inside the house the accusers, the accused, the magistrates, and the guards assembled in the big room. One by one, Solomon Marable, Mary Barnes, Pokey Barnes, and Ellen Gayle told their stories. Edward Pollard stared at the prisoners as they gave their testimony in turn.[22]

The prosecution was fortified by the presence of an actual lawyer, William E. Neblett, the county's commonwealth attorney, who had come over from Lunenburg Courthouse to help Justice Eubank. It was the commonwealth attorney's job to prosecute criminals on behalf of the people of Lunenburg. Neblett was thirty-seven years old and facing his biggest case ever.[23]

At no time did Solomon mention Ellen Gayle as a participant in the conspiracy or the murder itself. With some reluctance, Justice Eubank set her free.[24] Solomon Marable, Mary Barnes, and Pokey Barnes were to be held for trial in county court.

Should they live so long. Austin Clements kept checking the yard, trying to gauge the mood of the roiling crowd out front. It was full dark, and the atmosphere felt more electric by the minute. He concluded that the suspects were not safe at Pollard's. The county jail would be safer, but it was sixteen miles away. The men in the big room came up with a plan. Austin Clements, constable and farmer, would now try his hand as an orator.

Clements stepped out on the front porch to address the crowd. He talked and talked some more. He explained in this way and that why the proceedings were taking so long, and he promised in one way and another that it wouldn't be too much longer.[25] His audience settled in, nineteenth-century people who measured the importance of an occasion by the length of the speeches.

While Clements was setting his new personal record for long-windedness, Peter Hutson moved quietly inside the house, motioning the prisoners to the back door. Pokey started to cry; she thought for certain they were being taken out to be killed. "Come on, Aunt Mary," Hutson said to Mary Barnes, "let's leave Pokey here and they will kill her."[26] At that Pokey pulled herself together. Directly behind the house, about a hundred feet away, was the lip of a deep ravine. They made a dash for it. A few steps down, and they could no longer be seen by anyone up at the house.

They made it to the bottom of the ravine. Sixteen of them—Solomon, the two women, and a guard of thirteen—crossed the spring branch and hiked up into the woods on the other side. Lunenburg Courthouse lay to the northeast, sixteen miles away by the most direct route. But who knew how far they would actually have to walk to get there? If they tried the main road, the captives were probably dead.

By the scant light of a crescent moon they kept moving, splashing through creeks and stumbling over roots, ducking into the brush whenever they thought they heard voices or horses. Part of the time they were able to pick up a footpath that linked one farmhouse to the next. Then they moved faster.

They dreaded crossing the one river too deep for wading. They expected to find the bridge guarded by men bent on lynching. Then what? Maybe those men would listen to reason. Maybe they would agree that it was stupid to kill the only people who knew where the money was. Maybe it would matter to them that Edward Pollard wanted the suspects spared. At Pollard's house, before they had sneaked out the back, Edward had been asked whether he wanted the prisoners given up to the mob. "Gadfoundit," he had said, "save them and maybe I'll get my money."[27] But the lynchers might not care if Old Man Pollard got his money.

The three captives and their band of protectors approached the bridge. It was empty—amazingly, blessedly empty. They hurried over, almost flying with relief, slipped back into the trees, and went on until it was nearly dawn, when they at last sat down, hidden in the woods that fringed the village called Lunenburg Courthouse. They waited for the sun—mobs rarely attacked in daylight—then rose and walked toward the courthouse in the clearing. From a distance it was beautiful, four white columns gleaming against red brick, and greenery all around. The deputy sheriff took the prisoners inside the jail and locked them up. He took the guards across the road and bought them breakfast.[28]

*   *   *

THE LUNENBURG COUNTY jail was forty feet long, one room deep, and two stories high. The second floor held two cells; below was a third cell, along with a room for the jailer. Built of brick, the jail was sturdy enough, most of the time, to keep unarmed prisoners in.[29] It was not designed to keep armed men out.

At eleven in the morning two deputies brought Mary Abernathy up from Rehoboth. Deputy Sheriff Bacon put her upstairs with Mary Barnes and Pokey. It was a peculiar reunion, not at all what Mary Abernathy had planned. She had started out on foot the previous day, headed east to Rehoboth with an apron full of little cabbage plants for her husband's sister Rachel. The day had been cool at first, but by midafternoon it was hot again, and Mary Abernathy took her time, marking her progress by the color of the soil. On the Pollard place the dirt was a nondescript grayish brown. Closer to Rehoboth the soil was deep red and, in the late-afternoon sun, positively glowing.

She had just sat down in Rachel's doorway when along came a white man named Charlie Harding, with a warrant for her arrest. Harding took Mary Abernathy to a neighbor's, where they gave her supper and guarded her through the night. After breakfast a justice of the peace conducted a hearing, and this time the outcome was not in doubt. Harding hitched up two horses, and Mary Abernathy took her last look at the red earth of Rehoboth.[30]

With Solomon Marable and the three women again in custody, the wrenching question was how to keep them alive until they could be tried. In another seven hours it would be dark, and the indications were sinister. One hundred men were said to be massed at Rehoboth, eight miles to the south. Through the middle of the day men sifted into Lunenburg Courthouse: fifty, sixty, seventy—a number unheard of on a weekday when no court sat and when crops needed attention.[31]

Deputy Sheriff Bacon organized an exodus. He hired five guards, some horses, and a wagon to transport the prisoners. The wagon was too small for a driver and four passengers; Bacon decided to leave Old Mary Barnes by herself in the Lunenburg jail. In Solomon Marable's telling, Mary Barnes had conspired to rob the Pollards, but she did not take part in the murder itself. Bacon thought she would be all right in Lunenburg.[32]

At four in the afternoon they rolled out of Lunenburg Courthouse, hoping to make the town of Blackstone for a night's rest; Bacon was exhausted, having not stretched out on a bed since the night of the murder. The following day they were to strike out for Petersburg, a city more than sixty miles from the scene of the crime.

Heavily armed and on double alert, the guards looked in all directions for signs of ambush, glancing into the wagon for signs of an escape attempt. They especially watched Solomon, who had earned his reputation as a fleet runner. Nothing had been left to chance; Solomon was handcuffed, his arms were tied down, and his ankles manacled. Neither Pokey Barnes nor Mary Abernathy had shown any disposition to run, and they were not handcuffed. The two were tied to each other, though, and after a while Mary Abernathy complained that the ropes hurt her. Bacon stopped and adjusted them. Mary told him he could hand the ropes over to her, and she would hang Solomon herself.[33]

At about dark they reached Blackstone, only to learn of a gathering crowd, possibly led by kinsmen of Lucy Jane Pollard's. Lucy Pollard was by birth a Fowlkes. As a child and a young woman she had lived in the upper end of Nottoway County, which bordered Lunenburg on the north. Blackstone lay at the lower end of Nottoway, but the Fowlkeses were a numerous tribe, and Lucy had cousins all over.

Blood out for blood: Bacon decided to keep moving. Guards and prisoners were suddenly wide awake, expecting an ambush at any moment. One guard told Pokey and Mary that if an attack came, he would turn them loose and they should make a run for it. Solomon, he said, wasn't going anywhere.

They had been told in Blackstone to put at least five miles between themselves and the town. Near a little place called Wellville, they finally stopped, making camp in the woods. The prisoners were kept in the wagon, dozing as they could. The guards surrounded the wagon and tried to stay awake. At dawn they started out again, stopping briefly at a stable lot to feed the horses and waking a storekeeper who sold them cheese and crackers. A full day's travel lay before them. It was another sunny, dusty day and hot again. Keeping to back roads, they met few people. At the end of the afternoon the steeples and smokestacks of Petersburg came into view.

They did not proceed directly to the city jail. Instead they went to a tobacco warehouse, while Bacon ascertained that the jailer was ready for them. Once assured that all was in order, Bacon took his charges out the back door of the warehouse and drove them to the jail. A crowd awaited them: not an ugly crowd this time, but a collection of the curious who strained for a glimpse of the prisoners.

The prisoners looked back in wonder. In Lunenburg they were murderers; in Petersburg, celebrities.

4

INDEPENDENCE DAY

A n odd holiday, the Fourth of July. Robert Allen, contemplative
and depressed, sat down to his diary. Allen was nearly eighty, a
justice of the peace and retired farmer who had lived his whole
life in Lunenburg County.

"This day was once celebrated all over and in every state of the
American union as the greate anniversary of American indepen-
dance," Allen wrote. For the first half of his life Robert Allen had celebrated the Fourth in the old Virginia style, with bells and cannon
fire, speeches and feasting. The war had changed that along with
everything else. Now the Fourth was about loss. "Since the infernal
mean unprincipled Yankees helped by the Brittish Government and
the whole outside world subdued the eleven Slave States and stole

all our slave property and robbed us of all our state rights, both of which was garanteed to us by the Constitution of the United States—we care nothing for such mockery & no longer participate in it as a general rule."[1]

M. C. Cardozo wasn't celebrating either. Cardozo, the new sheriff of Lunenburg County, instead traveled eighty miles to Richmond to see the governor, his mission to ask for troops to prevent mob violence when the trials opened in Lunenburg Courthouse. In the week after the murder, feeling in the county had understandably run high; Richmond's four daily newspapers all had claimed a lynching was imminent. Two more weeks had passed, with no sign that the bitterness in Lunenburg had abated. It was hot too, and still extremely dry. On two days the thermometer registered ninety-six degrees, what the locals called "blood hot."[2]

Cardozo had not bargained for this when he ran for sheriff just six weeks earlier. Cardozo's first name was Mordecai, a name he never used in public. He was forty-eight, a white man with a big mustache, and chairman of Lunenburg's mostly black Republican party. African Americans made up nearly 60 percent of Lunenburg's eleven thousand people, and had elections been fair, the Republicans would have won one office after another. But elections were seldom fair. In 1884 the state legislature, in Virginia known as the General Assembly, had rigged the system so that Democrats typically controlled the polling places. They might award a few minor offices to Republicans, even black Republicans; in Lunenburg custom decreed that the office of overseer of the poor go to a black candidate. For the more important posts, Democratic election judges usually "counted in" the nominees of their own minority party.[3]

Thus it was curious that M. C. Cardozo had run for sheriff as a Republican and still managed to unseat the incumbent, a Democrat who had held the office for twenty-eight years. Exactly how Cardozo pulled it off is not clear; it cannot have hurt that he had inherited most of the real estate in the village of Lunenburg Courthouse and that some of the county's most prominent Democrats owed him money.[4]

In any event, the greenhorn Cardozo now oversaw the biggest case anyone could remember. If he needed reminding, the Richmond press made it clear just how big. "One of the most diabolical murders ever committed in this section," said the *Times*. "Never was a more heinous crime committed on Virginia's soil," said the *Star*. Like schoolboys compelled to fill their slates with vivid prose, reporters piled on the adjectives. "Horrible," said the *State*, "dastardly . . . fearful . . . ghastly." "Most atrocious," said the *Dispatch*. Though slower to run the story, small-town papers chimed in as well; "peculiarly atrocious and daring," said the *Charlotte Gazette*.[5]

The trials were to begin in a week, when the county court opened for its regular July term. A sheriff lost face when he called in the military, in effect admitting he could not keep order in his own county. But the law was clear: The governor could send troops only if the local sheriff asked for them. So Sheriff Cardozo slipped into Richmond and made the request, with the backing of Lunenburg's commonwealth attorney and George C. Orgain, judge of the county court.

Sheriff and governor came swiftly to terms. Governor Charles O'Ferrall offered fifty soldiers. Cardozo countered with a request for double that number, fearing that fifty might be overwhelmed if a large mob intercepted them en route to the courthouse. A large mob was all too plausible; rumor had it that the people of surrounding counties were as riled as those in Lunenburg. Ultimately the sheriff and the governor compromised on two companies, a total of seventy to eighty men.

Sheriff Cardozo made a quick about-face and left for home without attracting the notice of Richmond's reporters, who did not yet recognize him. He was needed the next day in Fort Mitchell, where he was to begin to summon witnesses. Meantime his deal with the governor would be kept under wraps. Cardozo had been sheriff for only four days, but he had sense enough to see the advantage in surprise.

*　　*　　*

SHERIFF CARDOZO HAD good reason to place his faith in this governor. On the first day of January 1894 Charles Triplett O'Ferrall had roared into office, vowing in his inaugural address "to restore the supremacy of the law," no matter what the cost. The law, weakened since the middle eighties by an astonishing surge in lynching, was indeed fragile by 1894. By the time O'Ferrall took office, a lynching took place somewhere in the South every second or third day. Overwhelmingly the victims were black men. About one lynching in five involved a white man. Once in a very blue moon the victim was a woman.[6]

Going up against lynching was no job for the fainthearted. O'Ferrall had the self-confidence of a man who began his career as a boy wonder and who succeeded thereafter at almost everything he tried. As a youngster he had apprenticed with his father, the clerk of the Morgan County court, and when his father died, "Trip" O'Ferrall, age fifteen, was appointed to fill his father's place. A hundred years earlier, when precocity was in vogue, this sort of thing had happened often. A Washington or a Jefferson might hold office before he could shave, partly because he displayed talent, partly because membership in a ruling-class family trumped age. By the mid-nineteenth century, however, adolescent magistrates were a rarity. After serving out his father's term, O'Ferrall ran for a six-year term as clerk of the court. He was only seventeen, and as he later described it, the novelty of his campaign caught on "like fire in dry stubble."[7] He won his first election handily.

Two and a half years later the secession crisis catapulted O'Ferrall into a new career. Morgan County was a stronghold of Unionism (it soon became part of West Virginia), but Clerk O'Ferrall bucked the tide and went out of the Union with the greater part of Virginia, enlisting as a private in the Confederate cavalry. As a cavalryman he was both good and lucky. He was wounded eight times and once left for dead. By the time the war ended, however, he was back on active duty and a colonel.

In the decades after the war legions of male Virginians called themselves Colonel. O'Ferrall, however, was the genuine article, and that served him well when he discovered his passion for politics. It took awhile. O'Ferrall tried the hotel business, then became a lawyer and served a term as a judge. But nothing stirred him like a stump speech or a floor fight. He lost only one election, a race for Congress in 1872. Everything else he won: two terms in the Virginia House, five terms in Congress, and finally, in 1893, the governor's mansion.

At fifty-five Governor O'Ferrall had gone gray—his campaign literature called him the Gray Eagle—but he still had the look of a cavalry officer. His hair swept straight back from his face and flared full behind his ears. His mustache turned up at the tips; hair and mustache together gave the impression of perpetual forward motion. His eyes, however, were dark and mournful. O'Ferrall had seen a great deal of death early on, losing first his father, then comrades-in-arms, and then his first wife when their sons were still small. He was familiar with tragedy but not failure. This governor meant to end lynching in Virginia.

In Virginia, lynchings were not as commonplace as in Mississippi or Georgia, and some Virginians took pride in that. The growing numbers, however, were ominous: three lynchings in Virginia in 1888, seven in 1889, nine in 1892, and, in 1893, twelve.[8] Virginians also had to think about the lynching of Thomas Smith.

It happened in September 1893, only six weeks before O'Ferrall's election as governor. In Roanoke, a city of about twenty-five thousand, the lynch fever began in the usual way, with a white person allegedly wronged and a black man accused.[9] A country woman, Mrs. Henry Bishop, was selling produce in her market stand when she was beaten and robbed of $1.93 by a man she described only as

Governor Charles T. O'Ferrall, a resolute opponent of mob violence, sent troops to Lunenburg Courthouse to protect the suspects during their trials.

PHOTO COURTESY OF
THE LIBRARY OF VIRGINIA.

"tolerably black" and wearing a slouch hat. The police arrested Thomas Smith, an unemployed laborer from a nearby village. Mrs. Bishop could not identify Smith himself, but she thought she recognized his hat, and that was enough for the swelling mob.

Roanoke's mayor tried to uphold the law. He called up the local militia and all the members of the town's fledgling police force. But that made only thirty or forty men to repel a crowd numbering in the thousands. Failing to hold off the crowd with bayonets, Smith's defenders took cover in the jail. Then someone started shooting. Eight men soon lay dead in the street, and thirty others were wounded. In the pandemonium that followed, the police managed to smuggle Smith out of the jail and into the countryside. Deprived of their prey, the crowd took to looting, and some called for the lynching of the mayor, who had been wounded in the firefight.

It was never determined who started the shooting, nor was it clear how Thomas Smith came to be murdered after all. At three in the morning the police inexplicably returned him to town. On their way to the jail they were confronted by a dozen white men, who demanded that Smith be given up. The police turned him over. Smith soon hung from a hickory tree, his body sprayed with gunfire.

In the developing craft of lynching there were several genres, ranging from the quiet settlement of a private grudge to a full-scale spectacle with an audience of thousands.[10] With daylight on September 21, 1893, the lynching of Thomas Smith graduated to spectacle. Smith's body still hung there for all to see. A man cut off pieces of tree bark and Smith's clothing, offering them to spectators as souvenirs. Later that morning the body was transported to the riverbank, placed on a pyre, and burned. The audience for this final act was estimated at four thousand.

Georgia and Mississippi, it turned out, had nothing on Virginia; Virginians could lynch with equal determination and festivity. Virginians, moreover, did their share in the creation of a new, strikingly powerful mythology of lynching. White men lynched, or so went the suddenly conventional wisdom, because black men raped white women and girls. The crowd might rise up spontaneously—proud men brought to the boiling point by the "crime too horrible to mention"—or they might act more deliberately, their purpose to deter others from attempting such crimes. Either way, most white Americans took it on faith that lynching was a response to rape. To this, theorists both North and South added the idea of "degeneracy" to explain why lynchings had become so commonplace. Slavery, they claimed, had kept the natural criminal tendencies of Africans under control. Since emancipation, people of African descent—especially the younger generation—had all too frequently reverted to savagery.[11]

Those who had eyes to see understood the upsurge in lynching in a completely different way. In the Roanoke case Thomas Smith had not been accused of rape; anyone who kept track of the numbers knew that most lynchings involved not even a suggestion of sexual assault. Black southerners were lynched on suspicion of every imaginable crime, often for no crime, and sometimes because they had achieved too much to suit their white neighbors. Thus the minority interpretation: Lynching was an act of terror, meant to punish and intimidate black people, to compel them to knuckle under to white rule. The savages were the men—and sometimes women—in the mob.[12]

For Governor O'Ferrall meanwhile, only one thing was at stake: the rule of law. To O'Ferrall, lynching was not fundamentally about race or about protecting women. Lynching was the overthrow of legally constituted authority. In Roanoke, before the mob decided to burn the body of Thomas Smith, they had proposed to bury him—in the mayor's front yard. Lynching was anarchy, pure and simple, and O'Ferrall was going to stop it, "cost what it may."

So far so good. O'Ferrall had been governor for eighteen months when Lucy Pollard was murdered, and in that time not a single lynching had taken place in Virginia. O'Ferrall had first been tested in April 1894, when a black man in Staunton was accused of murdering a fourteen-year-old girl.[13] Common sense and the Roanoke riot suggested that local men could not be relied upon to defend potential lynch victims; O'Ferrall sent troops from Charlottesville and Harrisonburg, and a lynching was averted in Staunton.

Strategically, Lunenburg would be more difficult. Lunenburg Courthouse was a pretty little place, but the devil to get to. The courthouse had been plunked down in a meadow in the middle of the county, centrality the site's main virtue. There was no river to drive a mill or float the harvest to market. Consequently, no town grew up around the new courthouse, and later, when the age of rail came, there was no incentive to run a railroad line there.[14] No rail-road meant no telegraph. Sending troops to Lunenburg Courthouse was like sending them back to another century.

Moving the men would be clumsy and expensive. The soldiers would have to go by rail to Meherrin or Blackstone or Burkeville, and even if they chose the station nearest the courthouse, they would still have to cover the last sixteen miles on foot or by wagon, out of touch with their superiors in Richmond as soon as they left the train station. If they met trouble at Lunenburg Courthouse, they had no quick way to call for help and no swift means to get rein-forcements. Whatever the governor decided, he would have to get it right the first time.

*   *   *

THE ORDER CAME down on July 11. Governor O'Ferrall had decided upon two white infantry units from Richmond, Company A and Com-pany B, First Regiment, Virginia Volunteers. It was a Thursday, and when the call came, the men were scattered among work sites all over the city. Printer, painter, paperhanger. Clerk, cashier, harness maker. The roster of their occupations reads like a nursery rhyme. Decorator, excavator, grocer, molder, plumber, drummer. All were ordered to muster in at once. At the armory, James H. Derbyshire checked men in, checked equipment out. In ordinary times, he man-aged the Domestic Sewing Machine Company. In this hour he was a major in the infantry and the commanding officer of the expedition to Lunenburg. At 11:30 P.M. he ordered his men to form ranks, and marched them to Richmond's Southern Railway station, there to meet the increasingly famous Mary Abernathy, Solomon Marable, and Pokey Barnes.[15]

The three suspects were already in Richmond; earlier that evening Sheriff Cardozo had brought them from Petersburg by rail and parked them in the Second Precinct police station, where they were to wait until it was time to catch the midnight train for the Southside.[16] This was supposed to be a clandestine operation, but word dribbled out, and their arrival at the police station attracted an assemblage of rubberneckers, a reporter from the *Times*, and another from the *Dispatch*.

All the stories printed thus far had been submitted by amateurs, local clerks or attorneys who in their spare time fed local news to the big-city papers. Usually they wrote brief notices—of weddings, accidents, or crop conditions—and when the editor actually printed something they wrote, they were paid two dollars a column. A big story like the Pollard case taxed their talents, so the professional reporters of Richmond could perhaps be forgiven if they engaged in some journalistic one-upsmanship.[17]

The first thing the reporters noticed about Mary Abernathy was her size. One reporter estimated her weight at 250 pounds; "built on the rural wash-tub order," said the other. She was agitated at the prospect of returning to Lunenburg, and talkative. It was harder to get Pokey Barnes in focus. She was slight and young and wore a white cloth tied up on her head. According to one reporter, she was nut brown. The other described her as "very black." She said little, adding to her mystery.

Mary Abernathy spoke for them both. "She is very garrulous," the *Dispatch* man wrote, "and if given rope enough will probably convict herself." But try as they might, the reporters were unable to find any seams or inconsistencies in her story or in the few additions made by Pokey. Finding no evidence against the two women, the reporters resorted to innuendo. Mary Abernathy, said the man from the *Times*, walked with "a kind of swagger." Pokey Barnes, he added, wore "a careless sort of smile."

Solomon swaggered too. He stood with his hands jammed down in his pockets and hadn't shaved in two weeks. Better still, Solomon contradicted himself. Questioned by the officer in charge when he first arrived at the police station, Marable said that when Mary Abernathy and Pokey Barnes came running down from the house, they had no blood on their clothes. When he talked to the *Times* reporter, Marable said that there *was* blood on the women's clothes. Marable grew confused when the reporter confronted him with the contradiction.

Still more confusion emerged from Solomon's accounts of how the women had invited him to join their conspiracy. Solomon told the *Dispatch* that Mary Barnes had approached him two days before the murder. To the reporter for the *Times,* he said it was Pokey who had told him to come to the spring, that she had sent him a message the day Lucy Pollard was killed. When asked how Pokey had sent the message to him, Solomon had no answer.

All this should have cast at least a wee doubt upon the guilt of the women. But the *Dispatch* was ready to convict then and there. "Evidence against the prisoners is conclusive," the paper said, "and the three principals will likely be hung."

Shortly before midnight, the prisoners were loaded into the patrol wagon and taken to the railroad station, where they were placed in a coach with the waiting troops and handcuffed to their seats. As the train rumbled over the James River and into the South-side, it started to rain.

CHAPTER

5

SOLOMON ON TRIAL

T he train stopped at three in the morning. Sixty-five miles back was the city of Richmond. A half mile ahead lay Lunenburg County's northern border and the village of Meherrin, jumping-off place for the final leg to Lunenburg Courthouse. Major Derbyshire wanted to scout the place before he gave the order to disembark; he had been warned that a crowd might be waiting at the Meherrin station.

The spectators in fact numbered about fifty, none looking for trouble. Lined up at the station were a dozen two-horse farm wagons. The soldiers hoisted their gear into the wagons and waited. At daylight they moved out: seventy soldiers, the drivers, the sheriff, two guards, and, of course, the prisoners.

The morning was overcast, and the road a ribbon of mud, but at 9:30 A.M. the convoy reached Lunenburg Courthouse. It took only one glance to size up the entire village. A few houses lined the main road. Two general stores sold everything under the sun. There were two churches, a Masonic hall, and a public well distinguished by its creaky well sweep. Two small hotels bustled during court sessions and slumbered in between. Not immediately visible were the two saloons, one tucked in the basement of the Masons' hall and the other in back of Bacon's hotel.[1]

The court building itself stood out from everything else. In the 1820s public architecture ran to Roman revival, and Lunenburg had built itself a Roman courthouse, two and a half stories high, with a triangular white portico supported by four white columns. It would have been a thoroughly imposing building except for one unique feature: its exterior stairs. Under the portico, two ornamented wooden staircases swept up from the stone porch floor, meeting on a landing in the center.[2] Stairs were supposed to be inside a building, not out-

The Lunenburg court building in the village called Lunenburg Courthouse. The courtroom was on the second floor, reached by a unique exterior staircase.

PHOTO COURTESY
OF THE LIBRARY
OF VIRGINIA.

side. The soldiers might have been hard pressed to articulate the difference it made, but something about those stairs invited a person in, superimposing a kind of hominess on a structure that was otherwise stately and opaque.

Out back stood the brick jailhouse. The soldiers jumped out of the wagons, installed a line of pickets, and marched the prisoners inside. Solomon was placed upstairs in a high-security cell, with iron bars crisscrossed inside the walls and under the floor. Mary Abernathy and Pokey Barnes were locked up on the ground floor.[3]

They were greatly relieved to see Mary Barnes, Pokey's mother, who had been kept in the jail for three and a half anxious weeks. Also in the jail was Fannie Marable, Solomon's wife. Two days after the murder, when Solomon fled into the woods at Chase City, Fannie had gone by train and foot to her mother's place in North Carolina. There she'd settled in with the children, lending a hand with the washing and crops. Then, a week before the trials were to begin, Fannie too had been arrested for the murder of Lucy Pollard.[4]

No time for reunions: Solomon was needed in court. A ring of soldiers escorted him to the front of the courthouse and up the stairs to the packed courtroom on the second floor. Across the front of the room a rope separated the spectators from defendants and officers of the court. Solomon, still in handcuffs, was sent immediately into the jury room to testify before the grand jury. He was already under indictment for murder—the grand jury had acted before his return to Lunenburg—but no indictments had as yet been brought against the women. Three hours passed. When Solomon came out, the women were called in, one by one, and urged (to no avail) to testify against one another.[5]

Matters moved faster after Solomon's trial opened at 3:50 P.M. On the bench was fifty-eight-year-old George C. Orgain. A homegrown lawyer, Orgain (pronounced like the musical instrument) had hung out his shingle in 1860, interrupted his career to organize a company of infantry during the war, and come home after a brief and especially miserable campaign in the West. In 1883 he was elected commonwealth attorney and served in that post until appointed judge of the county court in 1892. In his private life he had a houseful of children and a big pile of debts. On the bench he looked solid and austere, the square planes of his face radiating authority. His hair, auburn gone to gray, tufted out at the temples. The tufts made little nests for the bows of his spectacles, which he preferred to wear on top of his head.[6]

Three reporters sat near the judge's bench, their jobs complicated by the isolation of Lunenburg Courthouse. After court adjourned, the reporters' handwritten stories had to be carried on horseback to the train station in Meherrin or Keysville. There the telegrapher broke the story into Morse code and sent it over the wires to Richmond or Petersburg, where the dots and dashes were reconstituted as prose, edited, and set in type. Whatever emerged in the newspapers was all the written testimony contemporaries had. It is all we have now; transcripts were made only when defendants could pay for them, and these defendants could not afford attorneys, much less transcripts.

Solomon sat alone at the defendant's table, his face smudged by a stubbly beard. He needed someone to defend him, but the lawyers were not exactly lining up. Solomon couldn't pay anything, and although members of the bar were morally obligated to defend the indigent, judges could not compel them to work for nothing. Judge Orgain collared the only attorney in the courtroom who was not already involved in the trial and urged him to take on Marable as a charity case, but the attorney begged off. The illiterate Solomon Marable would have to rely on his wits and whatever coaching the judge might offer him. And he was up against not one but two opposing lawyers. Edward Pollard had hired his own attorney, William M. Bernard, to assist with the prosecution.[7]

Solomon entered a plea of not guilty, and jury selection came next. Some of the men summoned for possible jury service were black, a legacy, it appears, from the brief but intriguing period when the Readjusters had run Virginia. Taking control of the General Assembly in 1879 and electing a governor two years later, this black-white coalition had scaled down the state's enormous debt—its central objective—and invested the savings in education. It had enacted other reforms as well, some operating most powerfully at the local level. Responding to black allies' proposals that mixed juries would produce fairer trials, some Readjuster-appointed judges began summoning black jurors. In Lunenburg this was still the practice.[8]

Jury selection, however, showed Solomon Marable to be completely out of his depth. Sixteen potential jurors were called, and it was then up to the defendant to scratch four of them. Solomon did not exercise this right, so his jury was chosen by lot. Two of the men chosen were black, ten white.[9]

The jurors settled into their chairs, and Commonwealth Attorney William E. Neblett delivered a brief opening statement. It was widely believed that Neblett had attained his office by fraud, putting him in step with half the officeholders in the Southside. Neblett could fling a platitude but was widely regarded as incompetent.[10] Solomon Marable, however, was to make it easy for him.

Having no attorney, Solomon presented his own opening argument. "All I have to say," he began, "is that I did not do the murder; but Mary Abernathy and Pokey Barnes done it.[11]

"I was standing about twenty-five steps from them, as nigh as I can come. I was there and Pokey Barnes hit her three licks, and Mary Abernathy she hit Mrs. Pollard with an axe and took them keys and gave them to Pokey Barnes. I throw myself upon your mercy. What I done they told me to come and do. I held her hands."

Judge Orgain broke in. "Whose hands?"

"Mrs. Pollard's," Solomon said.

A sensation rippled through the courtroom. Solomon was not aware of it, but he had just confessed to murder.

*   *   *

THE TRIAL COULD have ended right there, but the commonwealth attorney wanted a conviction for murder in the first degree, and for that he had to demonstrate both malice and premeditation. Fortu-

As commonwealth attorney for Lunenburg County, William E. Neblett prosecuted the suspects when the trials opened in July 1895.

IMAGE FROM THE *RICHMOND DISPATCH*,
28 NOVEMBER 1895, COURTESY OF
THE LIBRARY OF VIRGINIA.

nately for Neblett, the law favored the prosecution. Malice need not mean that the accused felt ill will toward his victim; a general wickedness or heartlessness would do. And premeditation need not involve a lengthy period of plotting; a momentary intent to rob or kill would suffice, and where there was intent, there was premeditation.[12]

Solomon's trial was also important as a dress rehearsal for the trials of the women, none of whom meant to confess. Because Solomon was the key witness against all three women, his performance on the stand was critical. From the prosecution's point of view, the remainder of his opening statement was promising.

"Mary and Pokey went into the house," Solomon went on. "When they came back they had something in their dress and gave me two pieces of money, two twenty-dollar notes, making forty dollars. Mary Abernathy said when she come away, 'I am the head of this money, and I'm going to hide it under the house until I get a chance to get it away from there.'" Solomon explained which house he meant, a vacant house halfway between Mary Abernathy's house and Pokey's. "I beg you all to have mercy on me for I am not guilty."

It was suppertime, but Judge Orgain allowed Neblett to call his first witness. Edward Pollard took the stand.[13]

A methodical man, Pollard laid out his story in an orderly way, beginning at noon on the day of the murder. Mary Barnes, who had been working for him that week as a field hand, was hoeing the garden. Austin Clements, the constable, had come to the Pollard farm for dinner. The two men ate in the big room, served by Lucy, whom Edward called Lou. He went on:

> After we had eaten, we all came back onto the porch, and, after my wife gave Mary Barnes her dinner, she joined us. She remarked to me that dog-days were rapidly approaching, and that she wanted to go over to Mr. Robertson's and get some eggs, with which to set some hens. I told her to go, and she said that she knew that I was going to ring for her before she had gotten rested. I assured her that I would not touch the bell until Mary Barnes had gotten through with the garden, and at the same time I ordered Mary to go out in the garden and resume her work. Lou went to Mr. Robertson's and Mr. Clements and I sat on the

porch and talked until two o'clock. I agreed to loan him
three barrels of corn, and he left telling me that he would
call for it in time to get back home before dark. I told him
that he would find me at work in the new ground, near the
middle gate.

The garden was only a few yards southeast of the house, easily
seen from the front porch.

"I then went out into the garden and helped Old Mary Barnes at
work, and at three o'clock I returned to the house to get some
snaps." Edward intended to replant snap beans in the spots where
his first crop had failed. "When I got to the house I rang the bell for
Lou and went out into the yard. There I heard somebody talking in
the garden, and looking in the direction of the noise I discerned Mary
Barnes at the corner of the fence talking to Mary Abernathy.

"What's up?" I hollered.

"Nothing," Mary replied, "but Wilson heard you ring the
bell at an unseasonable hour, and sent me to see what's
the matter."

"Wilson knows that's not his name," I replied. "Four
taps is his name."

I glanced behind Mary Abernathy at this time and
noticed that my wife was coming with her bonnet lying on
her basket of eggs, which was on her arm. As she came up
to Mary Abernathy, she remarked that 'twas mighty hot.

Lou then came into the house and I went into the garden to replant the snaps. I was in there some eight or ten
minutes when Mary Barnes came out of the gate to talk
further with Mary Abernathy. I remarked to Mary Abernathy that bugs were killing all of my greens, and asked
her what I could do for them. She said she made her
children pick the bugs off of her greens, whereupon
I remarked laughingly that I had no children to pick
mine off.

I then walked past the two Marys and went into the
house, and they followed me to the porch door. I told
Mary Barnes to go to the spring and fetch a bucket of
water, and as she reached the top of the hill on her return

the 3:56 train blew for Fort Mitchell. Mary placed the bucket of water on the shelf in the porch and both my wife and I, at her invitation, took a drink. I then invited Mary Abernathy to drink, and she took a tin cup and helped herself.

Thus refreshed, Edward readied his plow for the afternoon's next chore.

> I took a shovel point from under the table in the porch and prepared to take it to the field. In the meantime I told Mary Barnes to tote in Lou's stick wood, and after inviting Mary Abernathy to take a seat in the porch I went on to the field, telling Mary Barnes to follow me. As I got to the new ground I started to plow and very soon thereafter Mary Barnes rejoined me, leaving Mary Abernathy seated on the porch talking to my wife, who was in the big room.
>
> We plowed then until six o'clock, when I heard the empty wagon of Mr. Clements coming up the road, and I hastened to the house, walking straight in through the front gate, which I left open so Mr. Clements could drive in, and went directly into the porch, where I washed my hands, and without wiping them went hurriedly into the yard and to the corn house, where I unlocked the door just as Mr. Clements drove in through the gate.

Pollard's cornhouse stood west of his dwelling house and just a little south. After stepping off the front porch, he would have turned to his right, crossed the western half of the front yard, and walked about twenty-five long paces to the cornhouse door.

> We measured three barrels of corn, which Mr. Clements and his son filled in the corn house, and I emptied in the wagon. When we got the load Mr. Clements told his son to drive to the gate, and when he got there told him to smooth the corn down. Mr. Clements and I went directly into the house, and seating ourselves on the porch, I fixed up a bond for him to sign. I suppose this must have taken ten minutes, during which time the wagon was standing at

the gate and the boy was sitting therein. Mr. Clements went out, mounted the wagon, and drove off. I still sat at the table for some time, and going back into the house to put the papers away, when I came to the door he was just disappearing down the second bottom by the middle gate.

I called "Lou! Lou!" but receiving no answer, walked around to see where my wife was. [Edward stepped off the front porch, this time turning to his left.] Not until I reached the corner of the house did I see her. Then I made to her and put my hand on her and hollered. I then turned to ring the bell, and found that the wire was not on the porch as usual, but was thrown down on the ground. After ringing twice, it struck me that robbery was the cause of the murder, and I hastened back into the house, hollering all the time, "Oh! Oh!"

I noticed nothing strange or disarranged in the room, but went immediately to the oak case, where my money was kept. Finding it unlocked, I put my hand in and pulled out the two pockets, in which we usually kept our money. Both were empty, however, but were back in their place in the case.

I then ran back in the yard and pulled the bell violently, still hollering loudly, until the neighbors came. Mary Barnes was the first to come in the gate, but got no further, as I hollered to her, "Aunt Mary, my wife is murdered. Run to Mr. Robertson's and tell them!" She quickly obeyed, and I continued to ring and holler. Mr. Fore and Pokey Barnes were the next to come, and Wilson Abernathy next. Others followed soon thereafter.

The keys to the case from which the money was stolen were kept in the drawer of a sideboard, sitting next to the case. They were in their proper place, and the drawer was closed. There were three trunks in the room also. They had been unlocked with keys taken from the sideboard drawers, but they were all closed, and appeared, until opened by me, to be in perfect order.

The hour grew late; Solomon and the soldiers standing guard beside him were exhausted. Although the prosecution was not quite finished with Edward Pollard, Judge Orgain decided to call it a day. After Edward identified his old meat ax, court was adjourned.

Outside the courthouse the soldiers prepared for the onset of darkness. A makeshift infirmary was up and running in a vacant store and in fact had already been put to use by a local who needed stitches after spending his afternoon in the saloon instead of the court. The mess sergeant served up supper from his improvised field kitchen, and the pickets took up their posts, concentrating on the jail. Major Derbyshire covered the roads too, placing sentries two and a half miles beyond the village.[14]

This was not an excess of caution. After observing the trial, Robert Allen rode the four miles home to his farm and sat down to his diary. At seventy-eight Allen had turned his farm over to his son, but he still tended a truck garden and kept busy as justice of the peace. Allen's neighbors had elected him justice twenty consecutive times: He knew the law. He was also a man of principle, who might be expected to uphold the rule of law. On July 12, however, the diary said otherwise. "The said negroes have been kept in the Petersburg jail to prevent lynching and they are now being guarded . . . at a cost of more than $300 a day to the State of Va. and they should and ought to have been promptly lynched at once, for there is not the least shadow of doubt about the guilt of all four of them."[15]

Among those who rationalized lynching there was always this tinge of the mystical, a certainty that guilt could be known by intuition.

*   *   *

"JULY 13. CLEAR but very Smoky, no work being done on this farm today all the laborers went to court today to see and hear the Pollard murder trials."[16]

As Robert Allen understood it, the only way to make farming pay in this worn-out part of Virginia was to exact intense effort from his hands. Back when his farmhands were enslaved, Allen had driven them all year round; when ice or snow kept them out of the fields, he was apoplectic. Once free, however, his people had the nerve to go to court one Monday a month, rather than work his fields! It took Allen ten years to get used to the fact that his hands wanted to attend court on the same days he did. After that he'd settled into a state of cranky resignation.[17]

When court resumed at 10:00 A.M., Edward Pollard was back on the stand to clarify what had been taken in the robbery: eight hundred dollars in twenty-dollar bills, sixty-five to seventy-five dollars in gold, a one hundred-dollar bond on the Blackstone Female Institute, two gold bracelets, and a gold chain. He could not say with certainty that dresses or bedding had been stolen. The prosecution then brought on Rena Barnes, one of Pokey's younger sisters, who said that she had visited Solomon Marable's house the afternoon after the murder and spotted two bracelets along with some new clothing in a bundle on the bed.[18]

After Rena Barnes stepped down, Judge Orgain called a recess. The grand jury needed Solomon again. Indictments had come down the previous evening against Mary Abernathy and Pokey Barnes; both would face charges of first-degree murder. The case against Mary Barnes, however, was weaker since testimony thus far suggested that she had been working in the field with Edward when the murder was committed. The judge sent Solomon back to the jury room to be grilled on the role of Mary Barnes.[19]

When Solomon emerged from the jury room, the prosecution called Jennie Wootten, the twelve-year-old from the restaurant in Chase City. Jennie testified that Solomon was the man who came to her mother's restaurant and showed two twenty-dollar bills the morning after the murder.

Cass Gregory, who had set himself up as an expert on the case, came next; the prosecution let him take intellectual control of the trial. Gregory recounted the history of the crime, the condition of the body (which he had witnessed), and the pursuit and capture of Solomon Marable (which he had not witnessed). He produced a map of the Pollard place as well, explaining its key features to the jury.[20]

None of Gregory's words, however, was as important as Solomon's confession. Prosecutor Neblett skipped over the remaining witnesses and called the foreman of the grand jury. This, said the foreman, was what Solomon had told them:

> Mary Barnes told me to meet her down at the spring
> Thursday, and she would give me something. I met her at
> four o'clock on Thursday. She said she couldn't make it
> then, but told me to come back Friday, and she would fix
> it. I agreed to return, and went to the appointed place at
> the appointed time, and while I was kneeling, drinking
> from the spring, I thought I heard a kind of humming, and
> some one call me. I raised up and looked towards Mrs.
> Pollard's house. Then Mary Abernathy beckoned me to
> come there, which I did, and found Mary Abernathy and
> Pokey Barnes on Mrs. Pollard, and Mary told me to catch
> hold and help them.[21]

Neblett was smiling. The foreman went on.

> In my excitement I didn't know what to do but to catch
> hold of Mrs. Pollard by the throat and arm, and hold while
> the two women beat her over the head with an axe. Then I
> let loose my hold and went away. In a little while Mary
> Abernathy came running down to where I was standing,
> holding the skirts of her dress folded in her hand, and
> handed me two pieces of paper money, telling me to run
> on away. "Don't let anybody see you around here, and
> don't say anything about whar you got it." I took the
> money and went off, but didn't know what she wanted me
> to run for, because I hadn't done anything.

Although several more witnesses waited in the wings, the prosecution rested, utterly confident that Solomon would be found guilty.
The court then advised him of his right to defend himself. Solomon
called his wife, Fannie, as a witness; she assured the jury that Rena
Barnes was mistaken about seeing bracelets at their house.[22] Other
than that, Solomon did not know what to do, so he sat in the witness
chair and told his story again. But it was not the same story.

What would Solomon have said had he not just testified against
Mary Barnes before the grand jury? What he did say, according to the
Dispatch, was this:

> On the day before the murder Mary Barnes told me to
> meet her at the Pollard spring that evening, and if she did
> not come I was to come back at noon Friday and wait for
> her. About four o'clock Friday Mary Barnes came to the
> spring and said she would soon be ready for me. I did not
> know what she wanted with me. I heard someone call me
> about a half hour later. I went up to the back gate and
> stopped. I then saw Mary Barnes, Mary Abernathy, and
> Pokey Barnes standing in the yard talking. Mary Barnes
> went into the house and returned in a few minutes, and
> gave Mary Abernathy a key, or bunch of keys. Mary Barnes
> then went back through the house and out into a field in
> front of the house.[23]

Solomon might have looked dazed during much of the trial, but
he'd clearly listened to Edward Pollard. Edward had testified that
Mary Barnes had walked out to the field shortly after he did.
Solomon's new confession for the first time accommodated that
information. Edward had also stated that the keys were generally
kept inside the house and that they had been used to unlock the case
where the money was. Solomon's new confession also incorporated
this information about the keys.[24] It was also probably no coincidence that Solomon named Mary Barnes as a major player in the
crime just after the grand jury had questioned him specifically about
her movements.

Of course, as Solomon tailored his story to match Edward's, he
introduced new inconsistencies. But these were overshadowed by
the grisly specificity of what followed.

> In a few minutes Mrs. Pollard went out of the front door
> and came around the east side of the house. When at the
> southeast corner Mary Abernathy swung Mrs. Pollard
> around the waist. Pokey Barnes struck her over the head
> three times with a stick which knocked her down. Mary
> Abernathy then called to me at the gate, and I ran to their
> help, and while Mrs. Pollard was lying upon the ground I
> caught her hands in one of mine and put my other hand at
> her throat. While I was holding her in this manner she
> uttered low, gurgling sounds, and Mary Abernathy struck

her a number of times over the head with an axe. I then got sick at the sight and turned and walked off a few steps.[25]

Prosecutor William Bernard closed in, probing for one last piece. He reminded Solomon that he was under oath. Bernard then asked, "Did you not know *before* you went to the Pollard house that you were expected to aid in killing and robbing Mrs. Pollard?"[26]

Solomon hesitated and then admitted in a faltering way that he had known that "something serious" was going to happen.[27] That would pass for premeditation.

The judge told Solomon he could make a closing argument, but Solomon said nothing further except to ask if he could have his wife with him. Fannie Marable was accordingly escorted into the courtroom. Fannie herself was no longer a suspect; she had come off under questioning as untainted by any knowledge of the murder or the money. But what fate awaited her husband? Fannie sat beside Solomon, crying softly as each of the lawyers said his final piece.

Virginia lawyers had a legendary love of oratory, and closing arguments could go on for hours. Bernard and Neblett took only ten minutes each. Neblett spoke last. "When I look into the faces of this honest jury of law-abiding citizens, I know they will not let Virginia, the mother State of our Union and of Washington, Jefferson, Monroe, and a host of others, be polluted with the existence of such a scoundrel as sits there." Neblett pointed at Solomon. "But that this jury will render a verdict of murder in the first degree."[28]

The jury filed out at 3:25 P.M. They were back in nine minutes.

CHAPTER

6

QUICK WORK

July 13. One of the murderers trial was completed today—
Wm. Henry Marable (sometimes called Solomon Marable)
negro. And the jury say by their verdict that he is guilty of
murder in the first degree and must be hung. And *All the
people say, "Amen."*

— ROBERT ALLEN'S DIARY[1]

The punishment for first-degree murder was death by hanging.
Much as he wanted to see Solomon hang, the commonwealth
attorney requested that sentencing be delayed so that Marable
remained eligible to testify against the women. Judge Orgain agreed
and, as it was Saturday, moved toward adjournment. Mary Abernathy was brought into court and arraigned. She pleaded not guilty
and asked for time to procure counsel. Her trial was set for Monday
morning. IT WILL BE QUICK WORK, said the *Times*.[2]

The soldiers welcomed a Sunday of rest and relative peace. All
night Thursday they had been on the move to Lunenburg. The next
night half the men had been allowed to go to bed, only to be jolted
awake at 2:00 A.M. by gunshots that came from somewhere northeast

of the courthouse. The soldiers were at arms in a matter of seconds but did not find the gunfire's source.[3]

After Solomon was found guilty, everyone seemed less edgy, and Saturday night passed without incident. By midday Sunday the courthouse green was the picture of tranquillity, with the off-duty soldiers loafing about and the aroma of fried chicken wafting through the village.[4] Yet there was really no telling what some of the locals might try—in retaliation for the death of Lucy Pollard or out of sheer resentment of the military's presence.

Enter Captain Frank Cunningham. Major Derbyshire was the regiment's commander, but Captain Frank was its impresario, the master of morale, the chieftain of charm. Broad-shouldered and tall, the captain cut an impressive figure. He had strong, straight features, earnest eyes, and light brown hair parted just left of center. On either side of the part, a sweet little wave decorated his forehead.

Cunningham made his living as tax collector for the city of Richmond, but his genius was for sociability and song. In Richmond he was out nearly every night, if not at a militia drill, then at a rehearsal or a lodge meeting; he belonged to the Eagles, the Elks, the Odd Fellows, and half a dozen other fraternal orders. He was also on pace to sing at more funerals than anyone in human history. He sang at someone's funeral almost every day, often two funerals a day, black funerals as well as white, which earned him a reputation as a friend of black people. He even aspired to sing at his *own* funeral. The first phonographs had been developed in the 1870s; by the nineties the technology permitted Captain Frank the hope of recording his own best-loved funeral numbers, to be played when his time came.[5]

Cunningham was just the man to manage the queasy relationship

Militia Captain Frank Cunningham of Richmond
stood guard in the courtroom and soon afterward
raised doubts about the guilt of the accused women.

IMAGE FROM THE *RICHMOND TIMES*,
18 AUGUST 1895, COURTESY OF
THE LIBRARY OF VIRGINIA.

between citizens and soldiers. At forty-eight he was a good twenty years older than most of his inexperienced troops, who responded readily to his recreational schemes: baseball games, a beard-growing contest, a kangaroo court (which convicted several soldiers of felonious snoring). Cunningham's parade of amusements kept the soldiers busy and projected a heigh-ho joviality meant to disarm suspicious villagers.

Sunday passed without incident. It was not reported how the defendants slept that night.

*   *   *

COURT DAY. THE food vendors, black women all, arrived early Monday morning and set up in their customary places along the roads to the courthouse. Before long they opened for business, selling savory meat pies, gingerbread and sugar cakes, and cider sweet and hard. Not far behind came the spectators, hundreds altogether. The great crowd attracted horse traders, bill collectors, politicians, and salesmen (drummers, they were called), who offered everything from newfangled farm implements to miraculous medicines.[6]

The sheriff rang the courthouse bell at ten o'clock. Inside, the courthouse looked less impressive than from the outside. From the stains on the ceiling, Mary Abernathy could see where the roof leaked. The place hadn't been painted in ages. Several windowpanes were cracked or missing. And the carpet was something beyond disgusting, the repository of mud, manure, and everything that landed near but not in the spittoons.[7]

Beside Mary Abernathy stood William H. Perry, usually known as Judge Perry in recognition of his twenty-one years as judge of the county court. For the time being, he was Mary Abernathy's attorney. No love was lost between Perry and William Neblett, the commonwealth attorney. Less than two months earlier Neblett had run against Perry in one of the ugliest elections in recent memory. Although Perry had gotten more votes, Neblett had enough henchmen manning the polls to steal the election.[8]

Perry asked Judge Orgain to grant one of two motions on Mary Abernathy's behalf: to move the trial to some other county or, if this were not done, to import the jury from another county. But Perry had not done his homework. Several of his witnesses proceeded to sandbag Mary's case, arguing that an impartial jury could indeed be found within the county and that the military would protect Abernathy from harm. Orgain promptly denied both motions. Perry then withdrew from the case, unwilling to conduct a defense for the token payment the Abernathys were able to offer.[9]

So, like Solomon Marable, Mary Abernathy faced trial without counsel. She did not know how to read or write—none of the four suspects did—and she had never been inside a courtroom before. But she had the presence of mind to screen the jurors, examining them in turn and scratching four of them. She emerged with a panel of eight white men and four men of color.

As before, Edward Pollard took the stand first, and under prompting by the prosecution he told the same story. By the time he stepped down, it was midafternoon and hot—in the high eighties outside and warmer still in the stuffy courtroom. The prosecution called Solomon Marable to the stand.

As soon as Solomon opened his mouth, the reporters realized they were hearing a new story. So did Frank Cunningham, who had listened intently while standing guard during Marable's trial.

"Mary Barnes told me on Friday before the murder"—a week before the murder, Solomon meant—"that she had two women besides herself, and she wanted me to help them. My part was to keep Mrs. Pollard quiet, and Mary Abernathy and Pokey Barnes was to rob the house."

So there was a conspiracy! The object was robbery, and Solomon was in on it from the start. Solomon continued:

> Mary Barnes's part was to get the key to get the money and bring it to Mary Abernathy. She was also to get Mrs. Pollard out of the house, and I was to catch hold of her and keep her quiet.
>
> I did not intend killing her. When Mrs. Pollard came out I caught her by the hands and throat and held her just so she could not make a noise. As soon as I had hold of her, Mary Abernathy and Pokey Barnes ran in the house. They stayed in there about twenty minutes. When they came out I let Mrs. Pollard go. I did not want to kill her, for she

did not know me. She didn't see me until just as I caught
her. After I turned her loose, she tried to get up. Then
Pokey Barnes hit her three times with a stick. Then she
sorter shivered like and scrambled out. Then Mary Abernathy, who had an axe in her hand, hit Mrs. Pollard a good
many times. Then Mrs. Pollard died.

If Solomon was telling the truth this time, Lucy Pollard had experienced twenty minutes of terror before she was bludgeoned to
death. Solomon went on. "Afterwards we went to divide the money
at a place 'twixt Abernathy's house and an old, unused house on the
farm. The bargain was to let Mary Abernathy keep the money, and
give it out to each, so as to keep account."

Solomon was asked where Mary Barnes was while the robbery
and the murder took place. He explained that last piece of the plan:
"As soon as Mary Barnes gave the key to Mary Abernathy she was to
go to the field and keep Mr. Pollard from thinking anything was
wrong."

Marable's new confession was the centerpiece of the prosecution's case. Other witnesses were called—Cass Gregory returned to
describe the condition of Lucy Pollard's body—but the reporters
scarcely mentioned them, and the import of their testimony was not
at all clear.

Just one other witness got everyone's attention. Seventeen-year-
old Lula Knight often visited the Abernathys; she lived close by and
was engaged to Mary's son Willie. On the afternoon of the murder
she was at their cabin when Mary Abernathy returned from the Pollard house. Now, on the witness stand, Lula Knight told the court
that when Mary's littlest child saw her mother coming, she said,
"Mama look like she been fighting."[10]

This was hearsay—from a five-year-old no less—and any defense
attorney would have argued its admissibility. Mary Abernathy did not
know such a move was available to her.

*   *   *

MARY ABERNATHY'S DEFENSE centered on a straightforward denial
of Solomon's every allegation. She did go up to the Pollard house

that day, as Edward Pollard said, sent up by Wilson to see why the bell was ringing. She did chat with Mary Barnes in the garden, she sat on the porch for a time, and she stayed for a few minutes after Mr. Pollard and Mary Barnes went out to the field.

But she knew nothing about the crime. She did not see Pokey Barnes until after the murder. She hardly knew Solomon Marable. She never gave him money. The only serious money she'd had all year was five dollars, which her son sent her by registered letter, and she could account for all of it. The only money she'd had since the murder was two cents, which the jailer in Petersburg gave her so she could write home. As for the murder itself, she knew nothing. "I never had an axe in my hand in that yard in my life."

Mary Abernathy completed her defense by calling a string of character witnesses, "several respectable gentlemen" who testified to her previous good behavior.[11] There were undoubtedly respectable women who knew her better, but it might have damaged Mary's case to call them. To drag a white woman into court was an enormous imposition; for "ladies," the witness stand had a respectability rating only slightly higher than the gutter. Women in rural Virginia had only one official civic role: to sign petitions, for or against, when would-be saloonkeepers applied for licenses to sell liquor in their neighborhoods.[12] In other legal matters, the word of property-holding white men was valued above that of everyone else.

*   *   *

NOTHING IN MARY Abernathy's past marked her as a troublemaker. She had old-fashioned manners that put white people at ease. She had never been in trouble with the law, nor had her husband, Wilson, or any of their children. Considering the size of their brood, that was saying something.

Mary and Wilson began their recorded lives together in 1869, when they were married by a white Baptist minister. Wilson was just shy of his twenty-first birthday, Mary already twenty-one. The babies came quickly, Samuel in the year after their marriage and in the following year Willie. Their first daughter was stillborn. Mary was pregnant again within a few months and in 1874 delivered a healthy daughter, Amy. Hamp, a son, was born in 1876. Another son, born in the summer of 1877, died before he was named. Son Charner was born in 1879, so Mary and Wilson saw out the decade and their first ten years of marriage with a family of five children.[13]

After that seven more babies came. Three died, including a set of twins, but two sons and two daughters survived. In the 1880s, for the first time, the Abernathys enjoyed a modest prosperity. The farm economy had perked up some, and it helped that the older children worked in the fields. Mary did field work too when Wilson needed her. They had not yet accumulated enough to buy land, but they had property—two or three head of cattle, a few hogs, some household goods, a gun, and their single most valuable possession, a sewing machine worth twenty dollars. A few more years at this rate, and they might well join the growing number of former slaves who were acquiring small farms of their own.[14]

There were nine living children altogether, and not a bad one in the bunch. As the older children came of age in the 1890s, they married, legally and with the sanction of the Baptist church. The Abernathys were taxpaying, law-abiding, churchgoing folks, a model family among the respectable poor.

One more thing the character witnesses did not yet know: Mary Abernathy was pregnant again. She was not very far along, only twelve weeks or so, but she knew the symptoms.[15]

*   *   *

At 8:30 P.M., well after dark, Judge Orgain called a half hour recess for supper. At Gary's hotel and at Bacon's, the people sat elbow to elbow at long tables, passing steaming bowls and platters, eating fast and talking faster. Off by themselves in a private room, the jurors churned through the evidence. When they went back into court at 9:00 P.M., they asked to have Marable placed on the stand again. This was a blow to Neblett, the prosecutor, who had sent the jury off to supper hoping they would come back ready to convict.[16]

In the end Solomon made what nineteenth-century authors called an affecting scene. Neblett set it up. "You are soon to meet your God in judgment," said he, "and notwithstanding your hands are stained with human blood, by repentence you may gain forgiveness from God. But if you lie," Neblett declaimed, "and Mary Abernathy is hanged on a lie told by you, God will grant you no forgiveness, and no future reward, but will damn your soul."

Solomon sat for a moment. Then, with tears in his eyes, he spoke. He was barely audible, and the jurors leaned forward to catch his words. "I would not put the woman in it unless she was. She killed Mrs. Pollard with the axe. This is the truth, and nothing but the truth."[17]

The jurors exhaled as one and fell back in their chairs. Neblett was nevertheless uncertain of their intent and moved to adjourn until the next day, when he could produce one last witness.

Major Derbyshire monitored the proceedings with foreboding: nothing like the prospect of acquittal to trigger a lynching. Soon everybody would know that Neblett was faltering, that he did not get a verdict on the first day, that the jury was unsettled and the prosecution reaching. With Judge Orgain's assent, Derbyshire ordered his men to move the prisoners into the courthouse, a more defensible building than the jail.

Just before midnight the rains came. The soldiers stood at attention, got soaked, and peered between the raindrops for signs of night riders.[18]

*　　*　　*

TRIAL WAS SCHEDULED to resume at nine in the morning, but when the witness did not arrive, Judge Orgain adjourned the court until 2:00 P.M. Major Derbyshire dreaded a long recess almost as much as darkness. The people crowding the village had little to do but hang out in the saloons, laying bets on the guilt of Mary Abernathy. By the time court resumed, some would be drunk and obnoxious. Derbyshire procured a fast horse and sent a courier to Meherrin with instructions to telegraph the governor. Derbyshire wanted reinforcements without delay.[19]

Where Major Derbyshire saw a mob, Frank Cunningham saw an audience. He hastily organized a vocal concert, a peace offering to the citizens. The thicker the rumors of lynching, the more the soldiers and citizens improvised rituals to display mutual regard. The soldiers had dubbed their encampment "Camp Orgain" and patronized the two general stores. Some of the farmers let the soldiers ride their horses; others brought peaches and apples from their orchards. The regiment's medical staff gave free treatment to any Lunenburger who walked into the infirmary. In return, the women of Lunenburg Courthouse had presented the hospital corps with a flag of its very own.[20]

Finally, at four in the afternoon, a reluctant Pattie Clements rode up to the courthouse and was quickly placed on the witness stand. The commonwealth attorney set the scene. It was Sunday, June 16, two days after the murder. Mary Abernathy and Pokey Barnes were under arrest, held at the Clements farm. What, asked the prosecutor, did Mary Abernathy say to you on that day?

"She asked me if I reckoned if the persons who took the things from Mr. Pollard's house were to return them, and put them where he could get them, would Mr. Pollard let the matter drop."

And your reply?

"I told her I didn't know; that this was a very deep crime. Mary Abernathy was crying all the time."[21]

The implication of course was that Mary Abernathy knew exactly where the money was and might attempt to bargain the goods for her release. Had Pattie Clements pursued the point on that confused Sunday, she might have elicited critical information about the case. But she wanted to know nothing more. Dozens of self-appointed detectives were racing around Lunenburg, but Pattie Clements was not one of them. If she learned anything of significance, she feared she would be compelled to testify in court.[22]

Pattie Clements stepped down, and Mary Abernathy took the witness stand to rebut her testimony. "I asked that question out of curiosity," she explained. "I cried because I helped to shroud Mrs. Pollard, and I saw how she was butchered up, and I liked her."[23]

Judge Orgain called for closing arguments, the defense to go first. Mary Abernathy proclaimed her innocence one last time in a statement that took only a few seconds. The attorneys for the prosecution went on for a half hour each. Both went out of their way to put themselves on the side of innocence. "In my effort to prosecute the prisoner," said Bernard, "I pray that no wrong word may escape my lips, for God being my helper, I would not aid in the conviction of any innocent person for all the money in the universe." This was the oldest trick in the prosecutorial book. "It were better that ninety and nine guilty persons were acquitted," Bernard continued, "than one innocent person hung."[24]

The prosecutors laid out their strongest points: Marable's final, tearful testimony; Mary Abernathy's failure to provide an alibi; her question to Pattie Clements. Then there were the words attributed to Mary's young child, in Bernard's paraphrase, "It looked like she had been fighting, she was so bloody." This was shameless improvisation; no blood had ever been found on Mary Abernathy. But no matter, Bernard was building to a climax. "I ask you for a verdict of murder in the first degree. If you believe she is innocent, be men and say so. If she is guilty, be men, loyal to your country, your wives, and your defenseless children; be men, and say so."

The jury filed out, taking with them Judge Orgain's written instructions. Some were basic to all criminal cases: The defendant was presumed innocent until proved guilty; the burden of proof was upon the prosecution, which must demonstrate the guilt of the accused "to a reasonable and moral certainty"; if the jurors found themselves in a state of reasonable doubt, they must acquit. Judge Orgain's further instructions were specific to Mary Abernathy's case, and they were highly satisfactory to the prosecution. An accomplice to a crime, said the judge, was a competent witness. It was up to the jury to evaluate the credibility of Solomon Marable; if they found him credible, they could convict on his testimony alone. There was also the matter of the alibi. According to Judge Orgain, the burden of proving an alibi fell on Mary Abernathy.[25]

The jury began its deliberations at 6:10 P.M. but could not reach a verdict. At length Judge Orgain sent them over to Bacon's hotel to sleep on it. Weeks later it was rumored that a lone black juror had held out for acquittal that night.[26]

The situation was extremely dangerous. Major Derbyshire sent patrols to scout the countryside, many miles out.

* * *

IN THE MORNING an impatient crowd filled the courtroom. The day was clear and already hot when Judge Orgain again sent the jury out to deliberate.

They were not gone long. Mary Abernathy braced for the verdict. So did Frank Cunningham and the courtroom guard, wary but also more confident than before. The governor had responded swiftly to Derbyshire's call for reinforcements. Company C had arrived at 5:00 A.M.: thirty-six additional men with fourteen hundred rounds of ammunition. The soldiers now believed their forces sufficient to repel anything the locals might throw at them.[27]

The foreman read out the verdict. "We, the jury, find the prisoner, Mary Abernathy, guilty of murder in the first degree, as charged in the within indictment."[28] Mary Abernathy looked alarmed but said nothing. Captain Frank then escorted her back to the jail.

Two down. Back at his farm that evening Robert Allen pronounced benediction on the proceedings. "And one more of the Pollard murderers, Mary Abernathy, was tried today, and the jury composed of 8 white men and 4 negroes, (she being a negro herself) . . . by their verdict, say she must be hung. And *All the people say, Amen.*"[29]

CHAPTER

7

THE PRINCE OF LIARS

B y the time Mary Abernathy's trial concluded, that of Pokey Barnes was well begun. The soldiers had come for Pokey at sunset on Tuesday, as soon as Mary Abernathy's case was sent to the jury.

Legally Pokey's case began much like the other two, but the night atmosphere was different, cooler and a little eerie. By day Judge Orgain looked serious. By night the lamplight chiseled his features into a portrait of perfect austerity. For Pokey the presence of authority was normally a temptation to irreverence. In this contest, however, Pokey was playing for her life, and she was to play it brilliantly and straight.

Like Solomon Marable and Mary Abernathy, she could neither read nor write, and she had no counsel. She pleaded not guilty and went on to scratch four potential jurors. Judge Orgain impaneled the remaining twelve: two black, ten white.[1]

Edward Pollard was again the prosecution's first witness, and as before, he rendered a methodical account of his movements on the afternoon of the murder. He did not mention Pokey Barnes until the very end, for he had not seen her that day until after the murder. After he sounded the alarm, Pokey had come running from the direction of her house, right behind a group of farmhands who had been working in a cornfield nearby. Edward's testimony here did not trouble Pokey; she planned to tell the jury the same thing herself.

Edward told one new story, however, about a confrontation that had taken place the previous year. One hot August afternoon, his wife, Lucy, had encountered Pokey Barnes and two companions. Their conversation quickly turned into a "difficulty" between Lucy and Pokey. Pokey used some rough language and even threatened to shoot Lucy. Or so Lucy had told Edward; he had not witnessed the episode himself.

It was late when Edward stood down, and Judge Orgain adjourned court for the night. The story of Pokey's altercation with Lucy Pollard was clearly hearsay and of dubious value as evidence. But the jurors had heard it. As they crossed the road to their hotel, vivid new impressions filled their heads: Pokey Barnes had a temper, a sharp tongue, and possibly a grudge against Lucy Pollard.

*   *   *

ASK ALMOST ANYONE in Finneywood, and they would tell you that the Barnes sisters had a reputation as wild women.

It is not clear what Mary Barnes and her husband, Joseph, did to produce such rowdy offspring. Mary had started life in North Carolina as Mary Burwell, born to enslaved parents in about 1848. At Christmastime in 1853 the white Burwells moved their entire farming operation, with twenty slaves, to Finneywood in Virginia. The trek to Virginia must have been one of Mary's sharpest childhood memories, not least because as a five- or six-year-old she would have begun working at about the same time.[2]

For a hundred reasons, enslaved children grew up fast, and during the war they grew up faster. In 1864, at about sixteen, Mary gave birth to her first child, a very light-skinned child, suggesting the possibility of a white father. When the census taker came around in 1870, he found Mary living with her six-year-old daughter Lizzie and with Joseph Barnes, who had grown up on a larger plantation a few miles away. Joe worked as a farmhand for Mary's former owners. Mary was their cook. The next year the two stood in front of the Presbyterian preacher and were married, Joe at five feet nine standing a head taller than Mary. Both were twenty-three years old.

Like most freedpeople, they started out with no economic assets other than their labor. Over time most black families acquired at least a modest sum of taxable property—typically a couple of hogs, a cow, and eight or ten dollars' worth of cookware and tools. But year after year Joe Barnes turned up in the tax books unburdened by any worldly goods whatever.

They had many children, fifteen altogether, nine living after the youngest was born in 1888. By this time the older ones were gaining a certain notoriety, while Joseph became known as an affable soul with no control over his unruly daughters. Lizzie, the eldest, was the leader in mischief, arrested first for assault and battery, next for petty larceny, and then on a felony charge of breaking and entering. Rosa, at twenty, was originally charged in the same breaking-and-entering episode but was let go after she gave evidence against her sister. Rosa was not married but was eight months pregnant; the sheriff may have thought he had enough on his hands without turning the jail into a maternity ward. Rena meanwhile had racked up her first petty larceny charge at age fifteen. All the Barnes sisters, including Pokey, were good with their fists.[3]

Unlike the others, however, Pokey as often as not had taken the respectable path. At eighteen she had married George Bacon in a legal ceremony performed by a minister. After her young husband died in a railroad accident, Pokey took back the Barnes name, a practice fairly common among nineteenth-century women.[4] An able worker, especially with an iron, Pokey never lacked for employment. She was bright, too, and could have soared right out of that neighborhood had there been anywhere to go.

Her living arrangements would not pass muster with the church people, though. Before she was arrested for Lucy Pollard's murder, she had been living in the house on the line fence with Ben Knight, a widower and father of a twelve-year-old with the poetic name of Grace Christmas Knight. They made a neat little family: thirty-eight-year-old Ben, Pokey at twenty-three, Grace, and Pokey's five-year-old, Martha Ann. But Pokey and Ben were not married.

Pokey's quarrel with Lucy Pollard was already on the table. She could only wonder what else the prosecution might dredge up about her.

*   *   *

WEDNESDAY MORNING WAS bright and warm. The prosecution opened by calling Solomon Marable, who repeated the story that had already convicted Mary Abernathy. When Solomon finished, the judge turned to Pokey: her turn to question the witness.

Few in the courtroom expected much of a show. Since her arrest Pokey had kept to herself, saying little to reporters in Petersburg and less to the press in Richmond; one Richmond reporter implied that she was feebleminded.[5] The Fort Mitchell people, however, knew a different Pokey Barnes and were not surprised when she approached the witness stand like a veteran trial attorney.

"Solomon," she said, "did you see me at Mr. Pollard's that Friday?"[6]

"Yes," he answered softly.

Pokey asked again, louder this time, "Did you see me at Mr. Pollard's that day?"

"Yes, I saw you there."

"Where was I when you saw me?"

"Up at the house."

Pokey, the attorney, then asked the key question: "Then, Solomon, why did you tell the grand jury and the jailer that you never saw me until I came running down to the spring?"

Solomon tried to evade the question. Pokey persisted. "Did you or did you not tell the jailer at Petersburg that you saw me on Friday on the road near Fort Mitchell?"

"I don't recollect," said Solomon.

Pokey brought out the heavy artillery. "Then you tell this jury whether you, when you kissed that Bible to tell the truth, told the grand jury and jailer a lie, or are you telling the lie now?"

"What I said the first time was false," Solomon confessed. "I'm telling the truth now."

Pokey had made Solomon confess himself a perjurer. She was dazzling. She had no further questions.

With that, Captain Frank and twelve of his men escorted Solomon back to the jail.[7] The women usually got a six-man guard. Solomon got double that, partly in deference to his terror of lynching, partly in recognition of the belief that as the one confessed killer he was the most vulnerable to attack. As Captain Frank walked at Solomon's elbow, they chatted about the progress of the trials. Frank Cunningham, master of morale, chieftain of charm, was worming his way into Solomon's confidence.

*   *   *

POKEY CALLED HER first witness, Ellen Gayle, a stumpy woman of thirty-five or so. Like most other local blacks, Ellen Gayle worked for white people, sometimes in the field, other times in the house. She lived near Fort Mitchell with her six children, raising hogs and chickens. It was on account of the chickens that Pokey had walked to Ellen's on the morning of the murder.[8] The two had then spent much of the day together, but exactly how much of the day?

> Pokey come to our house about eleven o'clock. [Ellen Gayle lived about a mile west of Fort Mitchell, two miles altogether from Pokey's.] Pokey asked me to let her have a chicken. I told her I couldn't do it. She said she was bound to have a chicken, saying if I would let her have one she would let me have some meal to make bread for my children. I let her have the chicken. If one of my elder children was at home I would send him for the meal, but there wasn't anybody but the little ones at home so I went myself.[9]
>
> Then we went on by Mr. Fore's and got some clothes [for Pokey to take home and wash]. We went on to Mr. Weatherford's house, and the one o'clock train passed while we were there. Davey Williams and Charlie Bailey

met us at Mr. Fore's and come home with us, and we went on up the road. At the red gate Ben Knight told Pokey he wanted to see where the men were going to work [Williams, Bailey, and Knight, all black farmhands on the Fore place, were about to start work near Pokey's house].

We kept on up to Pokey's house, and she cooked for us and asked me to eat, but I said I was not hungry. I had the headache mighty bad. She told me to eat a few mouthfuls, and maybe 'twould do me good, and so I did. The men had gone to work.

We ate and then lay down on the floor. While we were laying down Aunt Betsy Ellis, Mary Craghead, and Rosa Barnes came in and sat down awhile [Betsy Ellis had helped shroud Lucy Pollard's body. Mary Craghead was her married daughter, and Rosa Barnes was Pokey's younger sister. All of them lived in Finneywood, three miles below Fort Mitchell].[10]

Aunt Betsy said to Pokey: "Come and take a walk; we are going to Thompson's after cherries." This was about four o'clock.

Rosa Barnes stayed behind, but the other women headed for the Thompson farm, which bordered Edward Pollard's on the north. "I only started out to walk a little way. Pokey and I walked some of the way, and then we turned back and came back home to Pokey's."

So far Ellen Gayle was supplying Pokey with an alibi. Lucy Pollard had been killed after 4:00 P.M. From 4:00 until at least 4:30 and perhaps later Pokey was with Ellen. But then Ellen checked out.

"As soon as we got there I lay down and went to sleep," Ellen said, "and don't know where Pokey was while I was asleep. When I woke it was about 6:30. Pokey was sitting in the window when I went to sleep and wide awake when I got up."

After that Betsy Ellis and Mary Craghead returned to Pokey's house with the cherries, and all the women walked to the field to take Mary Barnes a drink of water. They had started back toward Pokey's when suddenly they heard Edward Pollard hollering and ringing the farm bell. Pokey ran toward the bell. Ellen headed home.

Could Pokey have slipped away while Ellen was sleeping? Could she have walked swiftly to the Pollard house, robbed it and hit Lucy with a stick, and then come back home and composed herself before Ellen Gayle awoke?

Pokey had three more witnesses.

Betsy Ellis and Mary Craghead both confirmed a portion of what Ellen Gayle had said. Craghead estimated that they were about a half mile past the Pollards' house when Pokey and Ellen turned back. But neither witness was able to say exactly where Pokey went once she and Ellen were out of sight.[11]

Ben Knight had the same problem. Knight had been replanting corn in the field west of Pollards' when he saw Pokey and the other women walk out toward Thompsons'. He then saw Pokey and Ellen returning about three-quarters of an hour later and did not see Pokey leave the house after that. On cross-examination Knight had to admit that Pokey could have left the house without his seeing her. He insisted that this was improbable, but the prosecution made its point: Pokey had called four witnesses, and no firm alibi had come together.

After Ben Knight stepped down, the proceedings sputtered for lack of witnesses. An exasperated Judge Orgain sent deputies to haul the absent witnesses in and at 6:30 P.M. adjourned court for the day.[12]

Among the spectators there was a good deal of grousing about the judge's conduct. Because Pokey had no lawyer, it was Judge Orgain's duty to assist her. But some people thought the judge was gift-wrapping the case for the defense, not only informing Pokey of her rights but at times assisting her in questioning the witnesses.[13]

The complaints filled the ears of the soldiers, who responded with both entertainment and a show of strength. After supper they put on a full-dress parade, stepping as snappily as they could in a stubbly wheat field. Later a clown act got soldiers and citizens laughing together.[14]

That night the entire battalion slept around the jail.

*   *   *

"JULY 18—CLEAR and Extremely Hot, Smoky and dry, the mercury scored 96 today above zero, and everything wanting rain badly." On

Robert Allen's farm the hands were back at work, plowing, hilling, and worming tobacco. Except for the extreme heat, it was a good day to work in the crop, for very little was happening at the courthouse.[15]

Court was scheduled to begin at 10:00 A.M. but was again delayed for lack of critical witnesses. In the hottest part of the afternoon Constable Clements rode up from Fort Mitchell, escorting twelve-year-old Grace Christmas Knight, Pokey's best hope for a complete alibi. Court resumed immediately.

On the day of the murder, Grace said, she was at home all day, washing clothes; among other things, she washed two skirts for Mary Barnes. Pokey and Ellen Gayle left the house to go to Thompsons' for cherries but then came back. Ellen lay down. Pokey did not leave the house during the time that Ellen slept.

The commonwealth attorney subjected Grace Knight to a rigorous cross-examination, but she stuck to her story and insisted that no one had told her what to say.[16]

Pokey Barnes had her alibi—if you believed a twelve-year-old.

Pokey wanted to call one last witness, her sister Rosa. But Rosa had given birth only three weeks earlier and could not walk the twenty miles from Finneywood to the courthouse. Judge Orgain sent a buggy for her, but the trial could proceed no further this day.[17]

The murmuring grew more intense. Grace Knight's testimony was central to Pokey's case, but the reporters all but ignored it, featuring instead the likelihood of mob violence. Men now made open threats of a lynching should Pokey Barnes be acquitted. The *Dispatch* reporter interviewed a man from Fort Mitchell; if the court did not root out the murderers, the unnamed man said, then the people would. "This they have determined to do," said the *Dispatch*, "so that the men may go about their daily vocations with some surety that on their return home they will not find their wives and daughters hacked to pieces; and also to relieve the minds of the women of the apprehension that whenever the male members of the family are absent they are exposed to the fate that befell Mrs. Pollard."[18]

The soldiers prepared for another long night, their effectiveness as a fighting force jeopardized by illness. Dozens lined up at sick call each morning, some with headaches brought on by heat and fatigue, others with a mysterious affliction thought to have been caused by the well water.[19] None of this was reported at the time; both the *Times* and the *Dispatch* printed cheerful stories to reassure the folks back home.

On this sweltering night—it was Thursday now—Captain Cunningham once again lodged the prisoners in the courthouse. After they were squared away, all together in one room, Cunningham decided to make one last try with Solomon Marable.

"You are bound to hang," said Cunningham, "just as surely as you are living now. There is no earthly hope for you. God may forgive you for killing Mrs. Pollard, but if you go away from this life with the crime on your soul of having sworn falsely against innocent people, you will be doomed to the horrors of eternal damnation, and that in a greater degree than anyone can imagine." Captain Frank liked it up there on the high ground. "If you have told the truth in this matter, stick to it, but if not, then tell the truth, and I tell you that every man here will die before you shall be lynched."[20]

Solomon thought for a moment and then spoke. "I haven't told the truth—all of it," he said. "But I will tell it to you."

*   *   *

At NINE-THIRTY the next morning Cass Gregory, wearing his deputy sheriff's hat, drove into Lunenburg Courthouse. He had risen early, fetched Aunt Susan Thompson, and brought her to the courthouse to testify. It had been a dusty drive up from Fort Mitchell; the farmhands they passed along the way were working in soil as dry as ashes.[21]

They found the village in a state of acute confusion. All morning little groups of worried-looking men went to the jail, stayed awhile, and came out looking as worried as before. Rumors abounded: Something was up with Solomon. He was telling a new story. When the trial resumed at noon, the courtroom was packed.[22]

Everyone wondered when Solomon's bombshell was going to burst. Not yet. The prosecution instead called Susan Thompson.

A black woman of middle age, Susan Thompson had been standing right there with Pokey Barnes, at the edge of the Pollard property, on the day Pokey quarreled with Lucy Pollard. It had happened the previous August, and Mrs. Pollard had spoken first. "Pokey, I always like to live friendly with everybody, but Mr. Pollard says you and your children have a slick path to my garden."

Pokey denied that they had taken anything from the Pollards' garden. In fact Pokey claimed to have more vegetables than Mrs. Pollard did and offered to give her a mess.

One word led to another. Mrs. Pollard ordered Pokey off her land. Pokey said, "I walk where I please." Mrs. Pollard said something else, and then the last thing Pokey said was, "Damn you, if you was in the road, I would shoot you."

An idle threat? Earlier the prosecution had called Juby Duffer, who had arrested Pokey the second time. Pokey hadn't been carrying anything incriminating, Duffer said—no money or jewelry, and no suspicious clothing—but she was carrying a garment of her own, shaped into a bundle. Inside it was a pistol.[23] Pokey was suddenly looking like a rough customer.

Susan Thompson understood the damage her testimony might do and sought to soften it. "Pokey had a high temper," she said, "got mad quick, and got pleased mighty quick," but was "a very good sort of a woman, with the exception of her temper."[24]

Now Pokey Barnes took the stand in her own defense:

> I don't know anything about the murder of Mrs. Pollard. I went to Fort Mitchell in the morning and came back home in company with Ellen Gayle. About four o'clock, Ellen and I went with Betsy Ellis and Mary Craghead a part of the way to Mr. Thompson's, came back in fifteen or twenty minutes, remained home until near sundown, at which time Ellen and I went walking with Betsy Ellis and Mary Craghead, as they came back from Mr. Thompson's.
>
> While we were out walking near Mr. Pollard's field, about a quarter of a mile from my house, mamma hollered to me to bring her some water. I went to the spring and got her some water [this was not the spring behind the Pollard house, but another one closer to Pokey's]. Then Ellen and I came on back, and just before getting to my house I heard the bell ringing and a hollering over at Mr. Pollard's.

> I ran on ahead of Ellen and told them at home that some-
> thing serious must be the matter over at Mr. Pollard's. That
> is all I have to say.[25]

William Bernard, the assistant prosecutor, then rose and asked
Judge Orgain to send the jury out of the courtroom. This was it.

"If the court please," Bernard explained, "the office of prosecuting attorney is anything but a pleasant one, and I assure you when I
took this place as Assistant Commonwealth's Attorney, I took it only
to lend my humble aid to bring the murderers of Mrs. Pollard to justice. This morning, in company with the Commonwealth's Attorney, I
went to the jail, and heard Solomon Marable make a statement so
entirely different from what he has formerly made that I ask your
Honor to apprise the prisoner of her right to have Solomon Marable
brought into court.[26]

"If his statement this morning be true, Pokey Barnes is innocent."

Judge Orgain called the jury back into the courtroom and
ordered Captain Cunningham to go get Marable.

The first question put to Solomon was whether Pokey Barnes
was involved in the murder of Mrs. Pollard.

"No, sir," said Solomon. "She was not with me. 'Twas a white
man."[27]

Solomon's opening words rocked the courtroom. Then silence
fell as the spectators strained to hear what he would say next.

"This white man stopped me while I was on my way to the saw
mill near Fort Mitchell, and held a pistol in my face, threatening to
kill me if I didn't step and go with him."

Bernard asked Solomon why he went with the white man.

"He made me go. He pointed a pistol at me, so I followed him,
and when we got to the spring he made me go on with him to the
house. He said he was going to make a noise, and when Mrs. Pollard
come out, I must catch her. Mrs. Pollard would be coming out the
back door where I was hid."

Solomon's story unfolded in a halting way, with many hesitations
on Solomon's part and many questions from Bernard. The press
reported his story thus:

> The white man went on round the front of the house, and
> Mrs. Pollard came out kind of backwards, and I grabbed
> her, and the white man asked Mrs. Pollard if she knew
> him, and she told him he was a white man. The white man
> then hit her with the helve of the axe, and then she fell
> down, and he hit her with the axe blade. He then put his
> pistol against my head and carried me with him through
> the house and he took the money.
>
> He handed me two twenty-dollar bills, and told me to
> go far away and spend the money and before going to mail
> the money to myself, which I did. He asked me if I knew
> anybody around there. I told him Pokey Barnes, Mary
> Abernathy, and Mary Barnes. The white man then told me
> to tell you all the tale I done told you on Monday.

Neblett came out swinging. "Who told you to tell this tale, you
know it is a lie? On Monday night, with tears streaming down your
cheeks and your hands lifted to Heaven, you said, 'I know I got to
soon meet my God, and if de women want in it I could not put dem
in it; dis is de truth, and nothing but the truth.' Now, Solomon, was
that a lie?"

Solomon said nothing. A minute went by, and then two. It was
ninety-four degrees. Three minutes. Four. After eight full minutes
Solomon spoke.

"Yes, sir."

Neblett tried again. "Now, Solomon, tell the truth. I know you are
lying. Did not Mary Abernathy and Pokey help you kill Mrs. Pollard?"

Ten more minutes went by. Solomon was gazing around the
courtroom. Finally, in a voice barely audible, Solomon said, "Mary
Abernathy got possession of the money."

Just then a commotion erupted in the jury box. A juror was whispering something to Sheriff Cardozo, who approached the bench and
whispered to Judge Orgain: Someone among the spectators was
winking or blinking at Solomon Marable.

"Mr. Sheriff," the judge said for all to hear, "someone is tampering with the witness. You will clear the court of all but the witnesses,
jury, bar, and military." The reporters were also allowed to stay.[28]

The room emptied slowly through the one exit. As the crowd

spread across the courthouse green, Major Derbyshire thought fast. Acquitting Pokey Barnes would be dangerous enough, but Solomon's accusing a white man was an invitation to fury. Derbyshire ordered a drill on the courthouse lawn on the pretense that the men needed exercise.[29] That way every soldier was on his feet, rifle in hand.

Solomon was still on the stand when the trial resumed. Bernard pressed him. Had anyone put him up to telling the yarn about the white man? Yes, Solomon replied, some white folks had promised they would help him if he would put a white man in the case and vindicate the women. But in his maddening way he would not say who those white folks were.

In any case, Solomon Marable recanted his story about the white man. Pokey listened, thinking how ugly Solomon looked sitting up there.

Neblett rose for the closing argument. "Live or die," he said, "sink or swim, the prosecution rests its case here." Solomon Marable was technically a competent witness. "Gentlemen," Neblett continued, "if you do not believe Solomon's testimony, I must confess that the prosecution has no case. If you believe Solomon, she is guilty, and should hang as high as hemp could tie her."[30]

There was one other thing. "While you are sitting on this jury," Neblett concluded, "your wives at home are pressing your little infants closer to their bosoms as a result of this recent atrocious murder. Now, won't you protect them?"

It was a smart pitch for hard times. The day of military valor was over. If protecting meant merely providing, that was little help. The farms were worn out, and the depression went on and on, the farmers victim to global economic forces they could scarcely comprehend. Indebtedness was epidemic. You couldn't afford to keep your children in school, or to pay the doctor, or to settle your bill at the store. But you could hang Pokey Barnes.

Court recessed for supper. When everyone returned, Bernard made his closing statement, and the jury went off to deliberate. Pokey went back to the jail to wait.

The jury came back at 11:00 P.M., wanting to hear Marable once more. Solomon was brought into court and reiterated his original story, implicating Pokey and the two Marys. When he was finished,

Pokey was allowed a final statement. "You men of the jury," she said, "please believe my witnesses, who have not lied. And don't believe Solomon, who has lied to you all."[31]

The jurors deliberated that night and all the next morning. At one in the afternoon they sent word that they were ready. Pokey was brought up from the jail. The jury shuffled in. The foreman rose and pronounced Pokey Barnes guilty of murder in the first degree.

Then Pokey did something that astonished everybody.

Pokey laughed.

*   *   *

AFTER THE FIVE agonizing days it had taken to convict Pokey Barnes, the trial of her mother, Mary, on July 20, seemed an afterthought. "Like an old woman's dance," as the saying went, "it was soon over."[32]

The tiny woman who sat alone at the defendant's table did not look like a criminal mastermind, but that was how Solomon Marable and the prosecutors portrayed her. No one claimed that Mary Barnes had actually swung the ax. Edward Pollard had said a dozen times that she had been with him in the field at the time of the murder. She was charged therefore as an "accessory before the fact," as Judge Orgain defined it for the jury, "one who being absent at the time the felony is committed does yet procure, counsel, command, aid or abet another to commit a felony." The jury needed also to understand that the law held accomplices as guilty as perpetrators. For an accessory to first-degree murder, the penalty was death.[33]

It was Saturday, and all the officers of the court were eager to get a verdict that night. Outside, the soldiers were breaking camp—burning rubbish, striking tents, packing wagons. Inside, Mary Barnes conducted her defense as best she knew how.

Taking the stand for the last time, Solomon Marable said he had learned of the conspiracy on a Friday, one week before the murder, when Mary Barnes had approached him at Mr. Pettus's well. She had a plan to get money, she told him, and had Pokey and Mary Abernathy to help her; if Mrs. Pollard recognized them, they were going to kill her. As instructed, Solomon went to the Pollards' the next Thursday and saw Mary chopping bushes near the fence south of the house. She said then to come back the next day, when Mary Abernathy would get her the key.

Mary Barnes concentrated her defense on Solomon's first contention, hoping to demonstrate that she could not have spoken with him a week before the murder; she had gone to Chase City that day. Her witnesses, however, were disasters. She asked J. J. Watson, "Did I see Solomon on Friday 'fore Mrs. Pollard was killed?"[34]

"I don't know," Watson said. "Both of you were working at our house, and you could have seen him."

"Did not I go to Chase City on Friday 'fore the murder?" she asked Fannie Ellis.

"You went one day," Ellis replied. "But I don't think it was Friday; it was my wash day, and I always wash on Thursday."

So it went. Mary Barnes at length gave up on her useless witnesses and took the stand herself to give a straightforward account of her movements on the day of the murder. "If you hang me today," she said, "I'll die with the truth on my lips. I never had nothin' to do with the killin' of Mrs. Pollard nor never said anything about it to Solomon."

At 7:30 P.M. Judge Orgain gave the case to the jury. To his credit, the judge made sure that the jury understood that from the outset of the trials, Solomon's stories had been full of shifts and contradictions.[35]

The jury, eight white men and four black men, returned shortly before midnight. The foreman rose and read a surprising verdict: "We, the jury, find the prisoner, Mary Barnes, guilty of murder in the second degree, as charged in the within indictment, as accessory before the felony committed, and ascertain her term of confinement in the penitentiary ten years."

The prosecutors shook their heads. They thought they had made it clear that if Mary Barnes had in fact plotted the crime, she should hang. The common sense of the jury, however, was at odds with the law. Aiding and abetting, they thought, was simply not as serious as committing. Or perhaps they believed she had plotted only robbery, intending no bloodshed. In any case, Mary Barnes had no blood on her hands. Prison would do.

Reared in slavery, Mary Barnes had long since learned to mask her feelings in the presence of white people. She took the verdict without visible emotion. Judge Orgain immediately sent for the three other prisoners. When all had assembled in the courtroom, he proceeded to sentencing.

Solomon stood first, the judge addressing him in the third person. "It is considered by the Court that the said William Henry Marable, sometimes called Solomon Marable, be hanged by the neck until he be dead. And that the execution of this judgment upon him, the said William Henry Marable, sometimes called Solomon Marable, be made and done by the sheriff of this County, on Friday, the 20th day of September next, between the hours of ten o'clock in the forenoon, and two o'clock in the afternoon of the same day, at the usual place of execution."

Mary Abernathy was next,

"hanged by the neck until she be dead . . ."

and then Pokey Barnes

"at the usual place of execution."

Not until that moment did Pokey realize that they actually meant to hang her.[36]

*   *   *

At FIVE-THIRTY the next morning the First Regiment formed a long column and moved out of Lunenburg Courthouse. With them were three of the four prisoners—Solomon Marable, Mary Abernathy, and Pokey Barnes—all destined for the Richmond city jail, to be kept safe from lynching so that sixty days hence they could be hanged legally.

Left behind once again was Mary Barnes. The next day Sheriff Cardozo was to transport her to the state penitentiary in Richmond; he believed her in no danger. But who was in danger and who was not? Mary's husband, Joseph, no longer felt safe in the neighborhood where he had lived for decades. As the military convoy snaked its way to Meherrin, Joe Barnes followed, willing to eat some dust for a ticket out of the Southside. The convoy reached Meherrin in six tedious hours; the soldiers then waited, sweltering by the tracks, for three hours more. When the train at last chugged in, they exploded into activity, 120 men struggling to load tons of equipment in nothing flat. Amid the bustle Joe Barnes quietly boarded the train.[37]

CHAPTER

8

"MIRABILE MARABLE"

If in the summer of 1895 someone had thought to award a prize to
Richmond's ugliest building, the city jail would surely have been a
contender. It was actually an assemblage of several ugly buildings
that had been added at intervals, the final product resembling a clus-
ter of odd-size shoeboxes. It had hardly any windows. Abutting the
back wall on the south were the city stables, and next to them was a
city dump, where sanitation crews emptied wagonloads of ashes and
trash and horse manure. September to May the inmates of the jail
shared the noxious air with the long-suffering children and teachers
of Marshall Elementary, a school for black children across the
street.[1]

Only six blocks from Capitol Square, the jail stood on much

lower ground, in the creek bed known as Shockoe Bottom. On the heights to the east was the leafy, genteel neighborhood of Church Hill, home to Captain Frank Cunningham and his new handyman, Joseph Barnes. The heights to the west were dominated by the Capitol building and New City Hall, a stone's throw apart from each other but so different they seemed to belong in different cities. In fact they belonged to different centuries. The Virginia Capitol, designed by Thomas Jefferson in the 1780s, was classical and clean, a light Roman temple with a commanding view of the James River to the south. The city hall, completed in 1894, was heavy and heavily ornamented, a massive Victorian pile of gray stone, with arched windows and doorways, and a profusion of pilasters, balusters, steeples, gables, clocks, spires, and chimneys.[2] It was a paradise for pigeons and a wonder to behold.

On Monday, July 22, the day after the Lunenburg prisoners arrived in Richmond, John Mitchell, Jr., made the steep descent from the city hall to the city jail to meet them. As much as anyone in Richmond, thirty-two-year-old Mitchell moved easily between high ground and low. A member of the city council and a player in Republican politics, he rubbed elbows with the city's powerful white men. As editor of a weekly newspaper, the *Richmond Planet*, he ranked among the state's most influential black men. But he also sought out Virginia's poorest, most mistreated black people, venturing into dank local lockups to get the stories of those wronged by the justice system. A handsome bachelor, Mitchell was a good man to have on your side, for he would go anywhere and feared no one.[3]

Born to enslaved parents in 1863, Mitchell had grown up with

John Mitchell, Jr., a member of the Richmond city council, edited the weekly Richmond Planet *and launched a campaign to reopen the Pollard murder case. This portrait originally appeared in I. Garland Penn,* The Afro-American Press and Its Editors *(1891).*

PHOTO COURTESY OF THE RARE BOOK, MANUSCRIPT, & SPECIAL COLLECTIONS LIBRARY, DUKE UNIVERSITY.

Richmond as it recovered fitfully from the devastation of war. The city's development was unique, not because of its size (ninety-two thousand people, while the nation's biggest cities topped a million), or its racial makeup (40 percent black—par for the South as a whole), but because no other place could match it as a shrine to the Confederacy. For this Mitchell himself had no enthusiasm, but the 1890s had seen a groundswell of nostalgia for the Lost Cause among elite whites. These people took immense pride in Richmond's past as the Confederate capital, and with effort they could make their stamp on the landscape. Thus a dogged band of women had rescued the Confederate White House, transforming it into a museum for Civil War relics. A striking new statue of Robert E. Lee stood at the outer reaches of Monument Avenue, and plans were afoot for the biggest reunion of Confederate veterans ever, an extravaganza to be staged the following summer.[4]

As might be expected in a place so focused on the past, Richmond's entrepreneurs often displayed ambivalence about the technological innovations that drove American industry.[5] Tobacco manufacturers only reluctantly installed the swift new machines that rolled out cigarettes by the millions. After the war, as before, tobacco was the city's leading commodity. Flour and iron had also been big before the war; they were surpassed afterward by new products great and small, from locomotives to little bottles of meat juice, a tonic for the blood. The city had a significant commercial sector as well; rural storekeepers in Virginia and points south tended to buy their merchandise from Richmond wholesalers. Meantime, with each month electricity extended its reach. Telephones were still rare in 1895, but the first poles had been raised, and electric streetcars were fast replacing the old rigs drawn by horses and mules. In any part of the city technology's progress was easily measured by the density of wiry clutter overhead.

John Mitchell's part of the city was Jackson Ward, the heavily black district he represented on the city council. The brainchild of Conservatives, Jackson Ward had been created in 1871 shortly after black men had gotten the vote. The object was to confine the effective black vote to a single area; while that one ward would likely elect black city councilmen, all the others had white majorities and could be trusted to elect white men. The city council would thus remain firmly under white control.[6] A "shoestring ward," Jackson Ward stretched over the entire northern fringe of the city, then dropped into Shockoe Bottom, turning sharply southward and taking in the jail (and the stables and dump) along the way. The ward ended abruptly at Broad Street, the east-west thoroughfare that served increasingly as the symbolic border between black and white Richmond.

On this steamy Monday, Mitchell was more journalist than alderman, bound for the jail to get photographs and a story. He knew that people wanted to read about Lunenburg; when the prisoners arrived at the jail the night before, they had been greeted by a thousand gawking spectators. Now Mitchell entered the jail through its one door and found himself in a narrow courtyard that was crammed with supplies and open to the sky.

The cells lay to the left in two long parallel buildings, each with two tiers. Solomon Marable was locked up with the other black men in the back building. The nearer cellblock held white men, and above them lived all the women. Only two cells were allotted to white women, a result of the justice system's resolute efforts to keep white female offenders out of jail. Beyond a heavy iron grate were the five cells allocated to black women. These were relatively large, about twelve by sixteen, but crowded nevertheless. Pokey Barnes and Mary Abernathy shared their cell with four other inmates.[7]

When Pokey and Mary appeared, Mitchell posed them elbow to elbow on a catwalk above the courtyard where plenty of natural light shone in: Pokey the taller, Mary a shade lighter and much heavier. After the photographs had been taken, they sat down, and Mitchell asked Mary Abernathy to speak.

The first portion of her story jibed with the newspapers' reports of the trials. But then she came to the conversation on Edward Pollard's front porch.

" 'Well, Aunty,' " Pollard had said, " 'I have had one of the cadfoundest cursings put upon me I ever had.' He asked me did I know the Thompsons. I did not know those that live there close to him. He says, 'You needn't want to know them. He shook his fist in my face and said if I repeated the word I said before he would squash me in hell.' Mr. Thompson called Mr. Pollard a hog stealer and a land stealer and a thief in every degree. Mrs. Pollard went on to say something. I don't remember what she said, but Mr. Pollard said, 'You talk too much anyway.' "[8]

Mitchell could hardly believe what he was hearing. A man named Thompson had threatened to kill Edward Pollard on the very day his wife was murdered. And not a word of this had come out in court. By the time the interviews ended, Mitchell had made two decisions. First, he had a headline for Saturday's edition of the *Planet*. WOMEN INNOCENT, it would say. Second, he was going to see a lawyer.

*   *   *

HALF A DOZEN black men practiced law in Richmond. Mitchell could have hired one of them, but he knew that any black lawyer would have two strikes against him: He would be lampooned in the white press, regardless of his abilities, and he would have a hard time getting a fair hearing from white jurors. So Mitchell went downtown to the office of Congressman and Captain George Douglas Wise.[9]

Wise listened and looked Mitchell over with hooded eyes, set deep in a longish face, the brows permanently arched as if special effort were needed to hoist the heavy lids. In another man such eyes might have looked sleepy. In Wise's case they made him look superior and slightly bored, as though nothing could surprise him.

His appearance was otherwise standard-issue urban professional: hair clipped short and brushed to the side to emphasize a high forehead and a full mustache. His was the tidy, homogenized style of the New South, nothing like the flowing locks and riotous beards of the Confederate generation. Wise had fought for the Confederacy, though—hence "Captain" Wise—and he had been wounded, a durable asset in his political career. For ten years he had prosecuted criminals as Richmond's commonwealth attorney. Thereafter the city's voters sent him to Congress for seven consecutive terms— until 1894, when he met defeat in a bruising and allegedly crooked election. Back in Richmond, he was thought to be laying the groundwork for a campaign to recapture his congressional seat in '96. Meantime he kept his name before the public by taking on a series of high-profile criminal cases.

Former Congressman George Douglas Wise [left] led the legal team of Richmond attorneys who appealed the convictions of Mary Abernathy, Mary Barnes, and Pokey Barnes. Henry Wood Flournoy [center] and Alexander Barclay Guigon [right] assisted.

WISE AND FLOURNOY IMAGES FROM THE *RICHMOND DISPATCH*, 11 FEBRUARY 1896; GUIGON IMAGE FROM THE *RICHMOND TIMES*, 15 MARCH 1896. ALL COURTESY OF THE LIBRARY OF VIRGINIA.

Wise agreed to defend the three women. He wanted help, though, and in a matter of hours recruited another elite Richmonder, Henry Wood Flournoy. Like Wise, Flournoy was a Confederate veteran and an experienced operative in the Democratic party, having served as secretary of state under the previous governor. Also like Wise, he carried a title from the past, in his case Judge, dating from the 1870s, when Flournoy had served on the bench in Danville. Flournoy had a square build, bushy eyebrows, the beginnings of a double chin, and a flair for oratory. One more thing: His people were from the Southside. Flournoy was the man to sway a jury of tobacco belt farmers.[10]

Should they get so far. Their greatest obstacle arose from the law concerning appeals. At the close of a typical trial in the county court, the lawyer for the defense filed a bill of exceptions, a list of alleged mistakes made by the judge or other officers of the court. That list of mistakes became critical if the client appealed to a higher court; if the appellate judge found that the county court had made a crucial mistake, then he could order a new trial. But none of the women had had counsel the first time around. No counsel, no exceptions; no exceptions, hardly any basis for appeal.[11]

Wise and Flournoy decided to enlarge their team, engaging a junior colleague, "Captain" Alexander Barclay Guigon, a learned, pale,

and upright-looking man who varied the standard lawyer's look by waxing the tips of his mustache. Too young to have served in the war (he was thirty-six to Flournoy's forty-nine and Wise's sixty), he had acquired his title as a volunteer in the militia.[12] The three attorneys conferred with one another and then headed to the city jail to interview their new clients.

*   *   *

ACROSS TOWN "OLD" Mary Barnes was learning to live in Richmond's other teeming, noisome jail, the Virginia State Penitentiary. The women's department was almost all black and largely a juvenile detention center. Of eighty-five female inmates, only five were white; many of the inmates had been just sixteen or seventeen when they were committed. Fewer than ten in the whole place were as old as Mary Barnes.[13]

She was booked two days after the close of the trials in Lunenburg, her height recorded at five feet one inch, her color "black." She was inspected for identifying marks: "Scar on right fore arm. Scar on left Butt." She was given a prison-issue shirtwaist of heavy cotton, like pillow ticking only with broader stripes, and told she could have a bath and a clean dress on Sunday.

Supper was a mug of coffee and a hunk of bread about four inches square. At sundown Mary was locked into a six-by-ten cell by herself. Her furnishings: a bed, a bench, a box, and, in lieu of plumbing, a bucket.

In the morning she was introduced to the shoe factory, an awesome shop that employed all the women and seven hundred of the twelve hundred men. As a greenhorn Mary Barnes was set to clipping threads, ten hours a day, six days a week. When there was overtime, inmates could earn wages. They could bank the money or send it home, but many were hungry and bought food instead.

At noon they lined up with their tin mugs and pans to receive the day's big meal, usually some kind of mystery meat stewed with vegetables or rice. For breakfast they got coffee and bread or potatoes, plus salted fish on half the days and on the other half molasses, the one item of prison fare that came near satisfying Mary's sweet tooth.

The superintendent was famous for his insistence on absolute control; refractory prisoners, women included, were laid over a barrel and flogged.[14] Mary Barnes did her work, blended in as best she could with the youthful prisoners around her, and survived the first week. One week down, 519 to go.

* * *

FOR POKEY BARNES and Mary Abernathy too, the first week in Richmond required adjustments to the routines of a big-city jail. But they took heart as a formidable coalition of allies began to take shape. John Mitchell, Jr., had become their point man and had hired them a first-class legal team. They also got a timely boost from Captain Frank Cunningham. As commander of the courtroom guard in Lunenburg, Cunningham had heard almost all the trial testimony. Now he told a *Dispatch* reporter he believed the women were innocent.

The *Dispatch* featured Cunningham's opinion on its front page, reason for the Lunenburg women to hope that the white press would pay attention to their plight. Besides word of mouth, the only way to get news in the 1890s was from a newspaper, so newsprint was everywhere you looked. Richmond supported four English-language dailies: the *Times*, the *Dispatch*, the *State*, and the *Star*—all published by whites—along with Mitchell's weekly *Planet*.[15] The *State* and *Star* were relatively modest productions, pitched to a blue-collar readership, but the *Times* and the *Dispatch* aspired to dominate all the markets, and they battled daily for preeminence in the city and state. The Pollard murder offered them an abundance of sensational possibilities. Once the soldiers of the First Regiment were safely home, the reporters and editors started asking questions.

On Wednesday, July 24, three days after his incarceration in the city jail, Solomon Marable gave them their first big scoop. In the presence of white reporters, jail officials, and John Mitchell, Jr., he changed his story. Or rather, he changed back to the story about the white man, the one he had begun to tell during the trial of Pokey Barnes. This time he gave a fuller account. He also gave a name.

"I met a white man named Thompson that day by the side of a fence at Fort Mitchell." Solomon had cleaned himself up since arriving at the jail; he had a jaunty haircut and his first shave in weeks. "I told him I was going to the saw mill. He said, 'No you ain't, damn it, you've got to go with me,' and he drew his pistol on me and told me to come up beside him, that he had had some words with Mr. Pollard and he was going to kill him. He went down there at the old house at the spring branch, and kept his pistol drawn on me until after I and him parted."[16]

Marable skipped the part about the murder itself, instead explaining why he had implicated the three women:

> After he killed the woman, he asked me who was living around there. I told him Mary Barnes was working there and he asked me who else was there and I told him Pokey Barnes was living right there on the line of the fence. He asked me who else and I told him Mary Abernathy was living on Mr. Pollard's place and he said that was all he wanted. Then he said that if I told it in any different way than he told me to tell it, he was going to kill me on next sight.
>
> He told me to take that money he gave me and not to spend it around there—go to Chase City and spend it. Leave enough to send back in a registered letter to myself and to name myself something else and write it back to myself.

A reporter returned to the moment of the murder. Had Solomon witnessed the killing itself? Solomon replied:

> Yes, I saw Mr. Thompson strike her. He hit her with the axe-helve, the first time. He told her he couldn't get a chance at her husband, but he was going to kill her and he struck her before she said anything. He then hit her with the eye of the axe.
>
> When he went to strike her I jumped up and he said, "Damn it, where're you going?" Then he took me by my arms and carried me through the house with him and had his pistol drawn on me all the time. He reached on the side there and got something I don't know what it was and put it in his pocket. I was crying. I saw him with the paper money. I saw no gold or silver. He gave me two pieces of paper money, but I didn't know how much it was until I

got to Chase City and it was two twenty dollar notes. Mr.
Thompson was not at the courthouse during the trial and
not at the burial either. He is a drinking man and a mighty
rough fellow.

John Mitchell, Jr., was struck by Marable's new confession. The
white press, however, remained noncommittal. Solomon Marable—
"a great liar," "a colossal liar," "the Prince of Liars"—had changed his
story too many times.[17] But then a new character named John Dern
washed up from Lunenburg, and the white press reconsidered.

John Dern's disturbing story broke on the same day that
Solomon named Thompson as Lucy Pollard's killer. A German immigrant of about fifty, Dern had fled Lunenburg with his wife, his three-
year-old daughter, the clothes on his back, and a shocking story of
persecution. The *Richmond Times* promptly labeled his case "The
Lunenburg Outrage."[18]

Dern spoke little English, but Richmond had a large, well-
organized German community, and he quickly found benefactors and
a translator. The trouble, he said, was about moonshine. Three
months earlier Dern had purchased a forty-acre farm in Lunenburg
from an agent in New York. After settling in, he was approached by a
band of moonshiners who wanted him to join them in distilling ille-
gal whiskey. "I refused them, and told them that the moonshiner
business was against the law, and I would not have anything to do
with them. I told them they ought not to do that kind of business."

For that the moonshiners made Dern pay. On the last day of June
they came to his house, decked him with a blow to the abdomen,
and insulted and struck his wife. Dern had them arrested, but they
made bail and returned several times. They knocked the wheels off
his buggy, said Dern, smashed up his furniture, stoned his house,
stole his horse.

"You see I am in a bad fix," Dern said. "I can make a living on my
farm, but I don't dare return to Lunenburg. These men have threatened my life, and declared they would kill me."

In subsequent days, dissenters from Lunenburg complicated the
story, suggesting that John Dern had brought much of his misery
upon himself. But Dern's initial splash in Richmond was a godsend

for Pokey Barnes and the two Marys. By the end of the week every newspaper in the city was calling for new trials.[19]

*   *   *

FOR THE THREE accused women, this week had brought two huge and entirely unpredictable developments: They had acquired influential backers, white as well as black, and the newspapers had put forward alternate ideas about who might have killed Lucy Pollard. Could it really have been a white man? Solomon Marable now said so, and by the end of the week he had specified a first name; according to Solomon, *David* Thompson had swung the ax.

Capping the week's pivotal developments, the *Dispatch* sent a lawyer and a reporter to Fort Mitchell. Not to be outsleuthed by the *Dispatch*, the *Times* sent down its own man, both lawyer and reporter in one. Thus was a new wave of amateur detectives loosed upon Lunenburg, tramping over the Pollard farm, interviewing whoever was handy, poring over documents at the courthouse. They got back to Richmond in time to make their deadlines for the Sunday papers. And one of them came back with an entirely new white man story.

9

THE RISE OF
EDWARD POLLARD

There was no fort at Fort Mitchell. Once upon a time there dwelt in this settlement a certain Miss Mitchell, to whom men were drawn like the proverbial moths to a flame. She would choose one, install him as her favorite, then jilt him after a time and move another into his place. Local gossip naturally centered on the man of the hour: "So who's holding the fort now?" That, legend had it, was how Fort Mitchell got its name.[1]

Before the Pollard murder, little distinguished Fort Mitchell from any other whistle-stop in that region. Several houses were sprinkled along the wagon road, some on the Lunenburg side of the county line, the others on Charlotte County's side to the west. A plain clapboard train station had been built in 1883, when the railroad was completed between Chase City and Keysville. The station made an ideal spot for loitering; a wide porch surrounded the entire building, casting shade for idlers at all times of day. There were two general stores, a post office in one and a saloon in the other. The one church, Mount Mitchell Baptist, had been founded in 1866, when people recently emancipated from slavery withdrew from the church of their former masters to found their own congregation.[2] Like Fort Mitchell itself, Mount Mitchell was imaginatively named, there being no suggestion of a mountain anywhere nearby.

William M. ("Billy") Justis had his first look at Fort Mitchell a week after the trials ended in Lunenburg Courthouse. A Richmond attorney, Justis specialized in evidence, digging it up and then laying it out with a ruthless logic that led juries to acquit. Today he meant to apply his investigative skills to the mystery of Lucy Pollard's death, and when he had his facts, he would write them up for the *Richmond Times*.[3]

Justis went through Pollard's outer gate and headed for the house, losing sight of it briefly in the two places where the road dipped. When he came out of the second sink, he saw Wilson Abernathy plowing. Mary Abernathy would be relieved to hear her husband was all right. But how could Wilson abide his situation? Wilson had dug Lucy Pollard's grave the morning after the murder; at that very hour his wife had been held for questioning.[4] Then Edward Pollard had testified at Mary's trial, doing his considerable best to see her convicted. But Wilson was still here, bound by a contract and the fact that his own crops grew in Pollard's ground.

The scene of the crime looked homespun and tranquil. The yard was shady and level, enclosed by a picket fence about four feet high; the front gate was just wide enough for a wagon to pass through. Awaiting him on the front porch was a young white woman with a small child. Justis went in and introduced himself.[5]

The woman, Maggie Coley, was married to Edward's nephew; she and her husband were living at the farm for the time being, helping out. Edward, she said, had gone to his other farm in Charlotte, but she was happy to show the visitor around.

The outbuildings in Edward Pollard's yard formed a rough semicircle around the dwelling house.[6] Standing on the porch and facing the front gate, Justis could see two of the buildings off to the right and just inside the front fence: the cornhouse, where Edward Pollard had helped Austin Clements load the three barrels of corn, and behind it the stable. To see the cowshed, due west of the house, one had to step off the porch and walk clockwise around the corner of the house. Another right into the back yard, and there, directly behind the house, stood two old low buildings that must have once formed the farm's nucleus. One had been a house, and the other a kitchen, tandem structures put up in a time when fire-prone kitchens were built apart from houses. Lucy Pollard had cooked not in this old kitchen but instead in a lean-to attached to the back of the main house. In that one respect, the Pollards' was a modern dwelling.

Next to the abandoned kitchen a narrow gate opened onto a path leading down to the spring. Justis proceeded down the path,

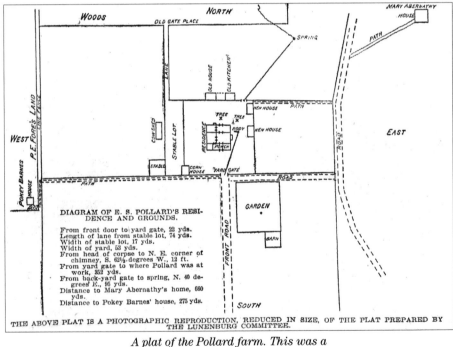

A plat of the Pollard farm. This was a newspaper reproduction (not to scale) of a hand drawn map used in the trials.

PHOTO FROM THE *RICHMOND TIMES*, 11 AUGUST 1895, COURTESY OF THE LIBRARY OF VIRGINIA.

braking as he stepped, surprised at the steep descent. Down at the spring he found himself in a different climate. Up above, the sun was glaring, and a high, hot wind blew from the southwest. By the spring it was mossy, shady, almost still, and much cooler. You could see why Edward Pollard had sited his house near this place. You could also see how Solomon might enjoy hiding out here, taking the day off from the noise and dust of the sawmill.

What you couldn't see was the house or the yard. Solomon had told the grand jury that he had waited by the spring, that he had looked up and seen Mary Abernathy beckoning to him from the yard above. Justis now saw that this was impossible; the slope was too steep.[7]

Justis climbed back up to complete his circuit of the yard, taking note of two good-size chicken houses. It was originally thought that Lucy had been on her way to set hens when she was attacked. Maggie Coley showed Justis the exact spot, pointing gingerly with her foot to a small, rusty hollow about twelve feet from the northeast corner of the house. In that hollow Lucy Pollard's battered head had come to rest, her feet pointing toward the house.

Justis dropped to the ground and looked southward across the front yard. From the place where Lucy Pollard fell, he had a clear view to the front gate. With that, Billy Justis had the core of his story.

*   *   *

FOUR DAYS LATER Justis returned to Fort Mitchell, this time finding Edward Pollard at home. Edward lay down obligingly on the ground, his head in the rusty hollow, his feet pointed to the house. His wife, he said, had been lying "just so." Justis walked to the front gate, about thirty-three paces, and wheeled around. "The body" was as big as life.[8]

Here was the puzzle. To date all parties thought the murder had taken place between four-fifteen and four-thirty. At four o'clock Edward, Lucy, and Mary Abernathy were gathered on the Pollards' porch. Mary Barnes was on her way up from the spring with fresh water, had just stepped into the yard with her bucket when the four o'clock train blew. After everyone drank, Edward hitched his gray mare to the plow, ordered Mary Barnes to bring in Lucy's stovewood, and walked out to the field. After she made several trips to the woodpile, Mary Barnes picked up her hoe and followed Edward to the field, about fifteen minutes behind him.

Solomon Marable had told many stories about what came next. Common to all of them, however, was the timing. Very shortly after Mary Barnes went out the front door to the field, Lucy Pollard walked out the back door into the yard, where she was throttled and then bludgeoned with the ax. Time of death: approximately four-thirty.

Edward Pollard took the story from there. Out in the field he showed Mary Barnes how he wanted his potatoes hoed, and then he went on plowing, one ear open for an approaching wagon. At about six o'clock Edward heard Austin Clements coming; Edward unhitched the plow and led his mare back to the house. He walked straight to the front gate, opened it, led his mare through, and then let her go.

Later he found his wife's body, only ninety feet from the gate. How could he *not* have seen his wife's body when he came in from the field? A few minutes behind Edward, Austin Clements and his son Willie drove a two-horse wagon through Pollard's front gate. How could *they* have failed to see the body?

Justis wanted to put the question directly to Clements, so he made a third journey to Fort Mitchell. Austin Clements was gone for the day, but twelve-year-old Willie was home and willing to talk.[9]

Mr. Pollard had seen them coming, Willie said, and had gone ahead of them. When they got to the yard gate, Pollard opened it. Willie then told Justis:

> Father and I drove through the gate, and turning to the left went over to the corn house, while Mr. Pollard walked over to the front porch and washed his hands. He then came over to the corn house, and said he called his wife twice, but I did not hear this. We then began to measure out the corn, Mr. Pollard standing in the door of the corn house.
>
> When we had finished measuring the corn, Father and Mr. Pollard went over to the house, and were there on the porch three or four minutes. I think they were fixing a paper. Then Father came out, and we started to go home. I

think Mr. Pollard went back into the house. I drove the wagon, and Father walked on about forty or fifty feet behind, to see that the corn did not spill.

Some time after we got home a messenger came for Father saying that Mrs. Pollard had been killed. Father then said that just as we got to the big gate he heard a bell ringing, but he thought it was Mr. Pollard calling to get up the cows. I did not hear the bell ring, nor did I hear anyone shouting. I reckon it took us ten minutes to get to the big gate.

Justis asked young Willie whether from his vantage point in the wagon he had a clear view of the area in which Lucy Pollard's body was found.

"Yes, sir," the boy answered, "when we went in the gate we could see all the left side of the yard, but we were not noticing that way."

We were not noticing that way. Or was there nothing to see?

Over the course of a week the *Richmond Times* printed three long investigative reports by William Justis. Edward Pollard, he argued, could not possibly have missed seeing Lucy's body, and even if that was possible, it was not possible that Austin and Willie Clements, seated four or five feet up on their wagon, could also have failed to see her. One conclusion remained: Lucy Pollard died much later than anyone had thought. When Edward came in from the field, Lucy was still alive.

Justis named no names. But as he pounded away on the location of the body and the gate, his implication was clear: Ten minutes passed between the departure of Austin and Willie Clements and the ringing of the alarm.

Just enough time for Edward Pollard to kill his wife.

*   *   *

WOULD EDWARD POLLARD kill his own wife? And just who was Lucy Pollard anyway?

After the trials the reporters intensified their coverage of the case, along the way breathing momentary life into many of the principals: the forlorn Mary Barnes, the earnest and talkative Mary Abernathy, the baffling Solomon Marable. They wrote of Mary Barnes's husband and Solomon Marable's wife. But they wrote next to nothing about the life that had been snuffed out.

Lucy's portrait helped not at all. Readers got only a vague idea of her looks from a portrait printed periodically in the *Times* and the *Dispatch*. Lacking the halftone technology needed to print photographs, the big dailies employed artists to make photographic images into engravings. The artists were sometimes brilliant, but in this instance almost everything was lost in translation. The newspaper Lucy had a boilerplate face, the kind that might appear in an advertisement for Hood's Sarsaparilla or Carter's Little Liver Pills.[10]

In the original photograph, by contrast, Lucy Pollard looked ferocious. She was well enough formed, with strong shoulders, a full bosom, and the slender waist that could be achieved with sufficient pain and whalebone. But what a face! Eyes slightly crossed, mouth turned down at both corners into a permanent scowl, she looked at once defensive and defiant. Surely that face held a story. The newspapers, alas, failed to go after it. Like most people from propertied families, however, Lucy Pollard left traces elsewhere, traces that deepen the mystery of her death.

She may have known Edward when she was a girl; both were raised in Nottoway County, which bordered Lunenburg on the north.

Although intrigued by the murder, the newspaper reporters exhibited no interest in the life of Lucy Pollard. Compare her photograph [left] with the engraving published in the Richmond Dispatch, *8 August 1895 [center], which flattened her appearance into an image resembling those used to market medicines to middle-aged women; this particular ad appeared in the* Dispatch, *5 September 1895 [right].*

IMAGES COURTESY OF REGINALD H. PETTUS AND THE LIBRARY OF VIRGINIA.

She would not, however, have thought of Edward as a marriage prospect. He was the son of a dirt farmer. Her people were planters, or at least they started out that way.

Her father, Liberty B. Fowlkes, had inherited land and slaves from both his parents and added to his fortune in 1825, when he married Harriet Bruce of Lunenburg. Lucy Jane, born in 1838, was the youngest of their five children. Sometime before Lucy turned ten, she lost her mother. Her father, widowed in his forties, was soon smitten by Sarah Ellington, daughter of a poor to middling farmer who lived nearby. At twenty-two, Sarah was only three years older than Liberty's eldest daughter. Sarah and Liberty married and proceeded to populate the country at a pace unusual even for the fertile Fowlkes clan. Beginning in 1849, Sarah had twelve babies in seventeen years.[11]

For a time they prospered. Liberty drove a phenomenally expensive carriage, and on the eve of the Civil War he owned a thousand acres and twenty-three slaves. But the war hit him hard, and for reasons that are not clear, he fell farther and faster than most men of his class. When he died in 1875, he left only a hundred acres to support Sarah and the eleven children who remained at home, the eldest of whom was Lucy, still single and by this time in her late thirties. Living in a crowded, impoverished farm family of a dozen people, including several young children and no live-in domestics, Lucy must have had many burdens. The census taker nevertheless listed her as having "No Ocupation."[12] Of the nineteenth century's hundred ways of hiding the work of women, at least a dozen were invented by the Census Bureau.

Lucy Fowlkes ultimately did leave home. The 1880 census taker found her in Finneywood, three miles south of Fort Mitchell, serving as "House Keeper" in another large family, this one headed by her cousin James L. Thompson. Edward Pollard lived nearby. The next time Lucy Jane Fowlkes appeared in the records it was June 18, 1882, her wedding day.[13]

*   *   *

THIS IS THE hardscrabble history of Virginia: Work hard. Marry up. Spend little. Sue the men who owe you. It worked for Edward Pollard, whose marriage to Lucy Jane Fowlkes moved him another rung or two up the ladder.

He was born in 1822. Nottoway County was the same sort of place as Lunenburg; tobacco flourished there, and slaves outnumbered whites three to two. Like most whites, however, the Pollards were plain farmers who owned no slaves. During most of Edward's childhood they owned no land either. Then, when Edward was sixteen, his father managed to make a down payment on a small farm. Edward was strong and a hard worker, the eldest child and only son; it may have been his increasingly valuable labor that lifted the Pollard family just over the edge into landownership.[14]

Even so, Edward's prospects looked bleak; his father had decreed that at his death the land would be divided equally among his children, leaving Edward only a few acres. In 1846, at age twenty-four, Edward became a peddler, working a circuit from farm to farm through the counties of the Virginia Southside.[15]

Hawking goods from a cart was not a prestigious occupation, but it was a marvelous way to meet women. In the southwestern corner of Lunenburg County, Edward met the widow Frances W. Thompson, and in 1848 they married.[16] It must have been one of the great scenes in the history of Lunenburg marriages when the jug-eared youth claimed his seasoned bride. Edward was twenty-six. Frances was fifty if she was a day.

When the census taker came around two years later, Edward (or perhaps Frances) reported her age as forty. Nineteenth-century people often adjusted their ages as it suited them, a practice facilitated by skimpy record keeping. In any case, Frances had adult children—three of them—plus two children still in their teens, one of whom grew up hating Edward Pollard.[17]

Frances Thompson had a farm, and by marrying her, Edward gained a foothold as an owner of land and slaves. He did not own these assets outright; they would one day pass to Frances's children. But he was empowered to manage and profit from them, a big jump from the peddler's cart. He now had 156 acres to cultivate without paying rent and four young slaves who had to work for him without wages.[18] Edward Pollard was on his way.

Before long he bought land of his own. Instead of investing in improvements on his wife's farm, Edward used its earnings to buy two other tracts that he fully controlled. The 1860 census valued his real estate at $1,640, his personal property, mostly in slaves, at nearly $4,000.[19]

The Pollards survived the war with comparatively little damage. Lunenburg's lack of railroads and industry for once proved a blessing; the county held no strategic value for the Yankees and therefore saw little fighting. Nearly forty years old in 1861, Edward enlisted as a private and served the Confederacy as a courier for exactly one week before an exemption came through. He was home for good by January 1862.[20]

The records do not tell how the Pollards and their former slaves weathered the transition to free labor when the war ended. Edward, who owned far more land than he could work himself, rented some out and patched together what labor he thought he could afford, hiring boys as young as eight and ten to help him. Women would work for half of what men were paid; when Edward hired Mary Barnes many years later, he was continuing a long tradition of employing the cheapest labor available.[21]

Edward's wife, Frances, died in the spring of 1873, of causes not recorded. Fifty-year-old Edward married again within eight weeks. His bride: Betsy Lewis, the never-before-married younger sister of the wife he had just buried. Just how much younger? The marriage register said Betsy was forty. She was in fact sixty-three.[22]

Betsy Lewis had a farm, a good thing for Edward, as the death of his first wife had terminated his rights in the land that had given him his start. He also bought land; when real estate prices plunged in the depression of the mid-1870s Edward got two hundred acres on very advantageous terms. Sixteen of those acres he gave to a carpenter, in exchange for building him a house—with a big room, a little room, a long front porch, and a steep roof. Edward and Betsy moved in just before Christmas 1878.[23]

There they lived until Betsy died in 1882, age seventy-two, of causes not recorded. Less than eight weeks later Edward married Lucy Jane Fowlkes. The marriage register said she was thirty-eight. She was really forty-four.

*   *   *

BY THE TIME he married Lucy, Edward Pollard had become a substantial farmer. But land and cash alone did not determine status;
inasmuch as Lucy had originally come from a planter family, she was
considered Edward's social superior. Moreover, unlike Edward's first
two wives, Lucy could read and write.

It looks as though she took on the project of sprucing up
Edward. They went all the way to Farmville to be photographed,
Lucy dressed to the nines. Edward's outfit suggested compromise:
He wore the sort of plain suit that farmers wore for church and jury
duty and hence managed to look respectable from the ankles up. His
boots, though, were scuffed and old. He sat as though he didn't know
quite where to put his feet.[24]

At about this same time Edward took to moneylending in a big
way. In the 1870s, pre-Lucy, Edward had now and again lent money
to neighbors, modest sums in the ten- to twenty-dollar range. After
he married Lucy, the amounts increased tenfold, up to three hundred
dollars at a time. He also lent the money in style. Edward, or possibly Lucy, had visited a job printer and come home with a stack of
forms as official as any bank's.[25]

FORT MITCHELL, VA., _____ 188__

_____ days after date _____ promise to pay to
the order of E. S. POLLARD _____ Dol-
lars, for value received, and _____ hereby waive the
benefit of _____ Homestead Exemption as to this
debt.

Given under _____ hand and seal this _____ day
of_____, 188__.

_____ [Seal]

_____ [Seal]

Was this Lucy's idea? Lucy's money? Like women everywhere,
rural women had a hard time making independent livelihoods. But
they worked nearly all their waking hours, and a physically strong

woman like Lucy could perform an immense amount of productive labor. Women had charge of dairy cattle and poultry (chickens, of course, but also turkeys, geese, and ducks) and hence of butter, cheese, eggs, and feathers. They stitched every kind of garment, grew vegetables, dried summer fruits for consumption in winter, gathered sumac for medicines. All these goods could be consumed at home or bartered to neighbors, but depending on access to markets, they could also be sold for cash.[26]

Wherever the money came from, Edward Pollard's moneylending did nothing for his popularity. Loving one's neighbor was a trial when the neighbor was your creditor, and it got worse with the depression of the mid-1890s. The Pollards had cash to spare when most families ranged from struggling to destitute. Of course, no one but the Pollards themselves knew how much they really had, so the impression went abroad that they were rich, that somewhere in the little house with the steep roof they had stashed thousands. Edward meanwhile always thought he was poorer than he was, and he could never own up to his own relative prosperity. "I have always been poor," he told the court, "and am poor now."[27]

For this reason, perhaps, he was easily drawn into disputes, always over property, and he stood up for his interests with impressive, sometimes extravagant resolve. With his next-door neighbor Paul Fore, the dispute concerned stray horses. Two of Edward's horses got loose one day and wandered across Fore's fields. Fore caught the horses, intending to return them when Edward paid for the damage they had done. But Edward refused to pay and instead sued Fore for unlawfully detaining his property, an outsize resolution to a problem best solved with an apology and a dollar.[28]

Apologies came hard to Edward, as did forgiveness. Edward stopped speaking to Lucius Pettus after a dispute over the possession of a steer. Not even the massive tragedy of Lucy's death could soften Edward on this. The morning after the murder Pettus was among the many people milling around the Pollard place. The sheriff asked Edward if he wasn't going to ask Lucius to sit down to breakfast. Edward said no, that he had made up his mind never to speak to Lucius anymore, and he was going to stand by it.[29]

Messiest of all was the great road imbroglio. Bill Thompson was

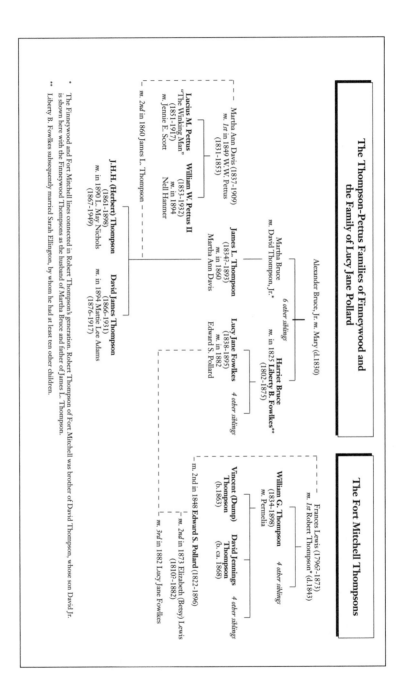

The Thompson-Pettus Families of Finneywood and the Family of Lucy Jane Pollard

The Fort Mitchell Thompsons

Alexander Bruce, Jr. *m.* Mary (d.1830)

Frances Lewis (1796?-1873)
m. 1st Robert Thompson* (d.1843)

Martha Bruce
m. David Thompson, Jr.*

6 other siblings

Harriet Bruce
m. in 1825 **Liberty B. Fowlkes***
(1802-1875)

Martha Ann Davis (1837-1909)
m. 1st in 1849 W.W. Pettus
(1831-1853)

James L. Thompson
(1834?-1893)
m. in 1860
Martha Ann Davis

Lucy Jane Fowlkes
(1838-1895)   4 other siblings
m. in 1882
Edward S. Pollard

William G. Thompson
(1834-1898)   4 other siblings
m. Permelia

Vincent (Dump)
Thompson
(b.1863)

David Jennings
Thompson
(b. ca. 1868)

Lucius M. Pettus
"The Winking Man"
(1851-1917)
m. Jennie E. Scott

William W. Pettus II
(1853-1932)
m. in 1894
Nell Hanner

m. 2nd in 1860 James L. Thompson

J.H.H. (Herbert) Thompson
(1861-1898)
m. in 1890 L. May Nichols
(1867-1949)

David James Thompson
(1866-1931)
m. in 1894 Mattie Lee Adams
(1876-1917)

m. 2nd in 1848 Edward S. Pollard (1822-1896)

m. 2nd in 1873 Elizabeth (Betsy) Lewis
(1810?-1882)

m. 3rd in 1882 Lucy Jane Fowlkes

* The Finneywood and Fort Mitchell lines connected in Robert Thompson's generation. Robert Thompson of Fort Mitchell was brother of David Thompson, whose son David Jr. is shown here with the Finneywood Thompsons as the husband of Martha Bruce and father of James L. Thompson.

** Liberty B. Fowlkes subsequently married Sarah Ellington, by whom he had at least ten other children.

DRAWN BY CONNIE SMITH FROM INFORMATION COLLECTED BY THE AUTHOR.

Edward's stepson, the youngest child of Edward's first wife, Frances, but Edward called him one of "*those* Thompsons." "You needn't want to know them," he had told Mary Abernathy. The bad blood probably went back decades, to the day when the young Edward Pollard had waltzed off with Bill's mother; Bill had only been fourteen at the time. The latest controversy had begun in March 1894, when Edward petitioned the county to open a road to shorten his drive from his house in Lunenburg to his farm in Charlotte. By this time Bill Thompson was about sixty and as stubborn as Edward. Thompson also had power: The county appointed him to a three-man committee to examine the proposed route of Edward's road and report back on the desirability of building it.[30]

If Edward had gotten his wish—a road to his very doorstep paid for by the county and maintained by his neighbors—it would have been a huge boon for him, a fact not lost on the committee of three. In April they reported that the road would mainly benefit Edward Pollard and should therefore not be built on the county's nickel. Edward persisted, however, somehow persuading the county court to appoint three different men to consider the project one more time.

The result was the same: no public road. But Edward fought on. First, he stiffed the men who had disappointed him. Because he had initiated the surveys, Edward bore responsibility for paying a dollar to each committee member. He refused to pay them, however, challenging all six to take him to court. Second, road or no road, Edward insisted on driving his buggy over the route, trespassing on land leased by Bill Thompson. Thompson retaliated the following spring, plowing up the land that Edward thought should be dedicated to his road. But Edward drove over it anyway, right through the ruts! Thompson was furious, and there things stood, down to the day of the murder. "I have not set horses with Bill Thompson in many years," Edward told a reporter.[31] That would qualify as an understatement.

Two weeks after the close of the trials a *Dispatch* man interviewed Bill Thompson, who now confessed to quarreling with Edward on the morning of the murder. "Vincent, my son, met him on that morning as he was riding across the field and told him that I said he was not to ride across my field. Mr. Pollard told Vincent that I had given him permission to do so. That was untrue, and when reported to me made me mad. I saw Mr. Pollard as he was riding back across the plowed land, and we had some hot words, in which both of us used considerable abuse."[32]

So this was the "cad-foundest cursing" Edward had told Mary Abernathy about. Bill Thompson claimed that it went no further. "I never dreamed of doing him any bodily harm," Thompson said of Edward, "and, as for his wife, I would not have hurt a hair of her head for a mint of money."[33] Indeed Bill Thompson was not a suspect; the five hands who worked for him that day all said he had been in his field until after sundown. But as the road controversy made clear, Edward Pollard had made plenty of other enemies.

We know only two things about Lucy Pollard in this period, both from the late summer of 1894. In August, as the trials had revealed, she had her showdown with Pokey Barnes, a fight in fact initiated by Edward, who had sent Lucy as his proxy to order Pokey off his land. Then, in early September, Lucy joined the Friendship Baptist Church. Although people attended services in droves, actually joining a church was a major life decision, on a par with marriage. Often it happened after a period of intense personal turmoil; ideally it happened when that turmoil lifted in a mysterious experience of rebirth. To join was also to unite with a human community of believers. It was perhaps no coincidence that Lucy made her public commitment to the people of Friendship Church just as Edward was shucking off neighbors left and right. As it happened, Edward's arch-enemy Bill Thompson was baptized by Friendship's pastor on September 1. Lucy joined the next day.[34]

*   *   *

"I HAVE BEEN represented to be the murderer of my wife," Edward told the *Dispatch*, "when, as a matter of fact, her death was the greatest blow I have ever sustained. I have never recovered from the shock, and I fear that I never will."[35]

Would Edward Pollard kill his own wife? His life story suggests not. True, his marriages were economically motivated. He was also a cantankerous neighbor. But his previous wives both had lived to a good old age; nothing suggested he would marry a woman for her property and then kill her. Nor did his recorded past indicate a tendency to violence. Instead he tended toward the cooler forms of aggression: grudges, lawsuits, refusing to speak. The Edward as killer theory, moreover, did not explain how Solomon Marable had landed in Chase City with those two twenties or why Marable would pin the murder on the still-shadowy David Thompson.

But the Edward theory was a blessing for Pokey and the two Marys. Of course! readers would think, of course the husband did it! Or did he? Either way, they would pay attention. When the *Richmond Times* fingered Edward Pollard, the Lunenburg case suddenly took on the elements of the classic crime sensation: a white woman horribly murdered; her husband a prime suspect; a deepening sense of mystery that fascinated readers and kept reporters guessing for months.[36] Ax murders sold papers, especially when the alleged killer was intimate with his victim. The longer the white dailies birddogged this particular ax murder, the better the accused women's chances of establishing their innocence.

In the meantime Edward's quarrelsome past suggested another line of inquiry. Pollard had numerous enemies; he was inordinately fond of money. What better vengeance than to take the money right out from under his nose?

Together, all the new theories did what the trials had failed to do: They opened the public mind to the possibility that the three women might indeed be innocent. Surely there must be a better explanation, a story more plausible than the rambling, contradictory tale originally told by Solomon Marable.

So went the talk in Richmond. Not in Lunenburg, however. The question in Lunenburg was how to make the convictions stick.

CHAPTER

10

THE THIRTEENTH
JUROR

The day after the trials ended in Lunenburg Courthouse, the
Board of Supervisors ordered the filthy courtroom carpet taken
up and thrown away. All the bedding in the jail—nineteen blan-
kets and one sheet and pillowcase—went out to be washed, heavy
work that took two whole pounds of soap. The jail itself was
scrubbed down too, and its interior walls were sanitized and bright-
ened with fresh whitewash.

Some of this work was required by law; the jail had to be white-
washed twice a year, as the old joke goes, whether it needed it or
not.[1] But the scrubbing had a ritual dimension as well, as the villagers reclaimed the space from outsiders and tried to close the
book on a horrific crime.

Trouble was, the book would not close. Almost every Richmond newspaper that made its way to the Southside expressed doubt about Lunenburg's brand of justice. According to the *Times*, a group of white men had asked Frank Cunningham to give up Solomon Marable so they could extort from him the location of the money. Worse, said the *Dispatch*, two local officials, one a deputy sheriff, had approached Mary Abernathy and threatened to kill her husband if she didn't tell where the money was. Safe now in Richmond, Mary still feared for Wilson's life.[2]

The Richmond press also raised the crucial question about the quality of the evidence presented in the courtroom. Had the women been convicted on Solomon Marable's testimony alone? If so—the papers were unanimous on this—the women had new trials coming; no one should be hanged on the word of a perjurer like Marable. But perhaps there had been corroborating evidence. If so, said the press, Lunenburg would do well to produce it.

Ten days after the trials closed, "the people" of Lunenburg— actually several dozen white men—gathered at the courthouse to formulate a response. Their county had been grossly misrepresented, they thought, and they were angry. They kept their meeting tidy and dispassionate, however; no point in giving more ammunition to the Richmond reporters, who already thought that white Lunenburg was bloodthirsty and vengeful.[3] The assembled citizens appointed a Committee on Facts to make a systematic presentation of all the evidence against the women.

Although six men were named, it soon emerged as a committee of one, Cass Gregory, the self-possessed tobacco broker who had taken a leading part in the investigation from its first hours. Now he would spearhead an aggressive campaign to persuade the public that Lunenburg had tried and convicted the right people. As the citizens and the press requested, he planned to present all the incriminating testimony from the trials. But he intended to do more: He intended to produce new evidence as well. That evidence lay in Fort Mitchell, and Gregory turned toward home to get it.

* * *

IN ANY OTHER year August would have brought dog days, with the upper class on vacation, everyone else in slow motion, and the newspapers reporting next to nothing. This August, however, the press clattered out new revelations in almost every edition. Whatever might happen in the courts—the women's appeal in circuit court was still six weeks off—Pokey Barnes and the two Marys were going to be retried first in the Richmond papers.

Ominously for the women, much of the new copy was generated by Lunenburg's newly organized white citizens, who hoped to influence the public in general and the governor in particular. Should the women's appeal fail in the courts, they would undoubtedly turn to Governor O'Ferrall, who had the power to spare their lives or even pardon them altogether and set them free. But not if the white Lunenburg citizens could help it. They had already chosen a delegation to meet the governor in person to present the report of their Committee on Facts. Meantime, as everyone knew, the governor read the papers.

First to be subjected to the new scrutiny was Pokey Barnes, the formidable and intriguing Pokey, who had cross-examined Solomon with the skill of a lawyer, who had laughed when the jury pronounced her guilty. Pokey had made a strong impression during her trial, but the newspapers' reports of her actual testimony had been garbled and thin. Now the papers started over, and Pokey herself had the first word, thanks to John Mitchell, Jr., and his weekly *Planet*.

"I was washing for Mrs. Fore," Pokey told Mitchell. "I got through ironing on Thursday night." The next morning, the day of the murder, she walked the mile to Fort Mitchell to deliver the clean clothes. "That morning as I was going on I saw Solomon Marable sitting on Mrs. Spencer's store-porch. I passed on and did not speak to him."[4]

Then she walked to Ellen Gayle's house, a mile west of Fort Mitchell. Ellen reluctantly agreed to trade a chicken for some cornmeal and a child's dress. Pokey and Ellen then headed to Pokey's to fetch the meal. "Just before I got to my house I hollered to Ben Knight's daughter Gracie to make up the fire so I might cook me some bread when I got there, and I cooked it and me and Ellen ate and laid down in the floor." Before long, Betsy Ellis, Mary Craghead, and Rosa Barnes came by; Pokey got up and put on her dress, and everyone but Rosa headed for Thompsons', hoping to get cherries.

After walking with their friends about halfway to the Thompson farm, Pokey and Ellen returned to Pokey's house. "Then I got me a chair and sat down at the window and took my little girl, five years old in my lap. We sat there and talked until Aunt Betsy and Mary came back from after the cherries." Then they all walked out again.

Pokey continued her story:

Aunt Betsy said she guess she would work for Mr. Fore the next week. She asked me could she stay at our house at night. I told her yes'm. We looked across Mr. Pollard's field and we saw Mamma at work on the hill. And she hollered to me to bring her some water and I told her we didn't have anything to bring it in. She said, "Oh, bring me the water," and Aunt Betsy and her daughter Mary poured the cherries together and we took one bucket, went to the spring and carried her the water. She drank and set the bucket down. I said it's Mary's bucket. She's waiting for it. She took it up and drank and handed the bucket back. Then Aunt Betsy and Mary took the bucket and walked off to their home.

We started to walk off and Mamma said, "Don't go, I want to get two chickens," and asked Ellen what she asked for them. Ellen said they were thirty cents a pound in Richmond. Mamma told her she wouldn't give her thirty cents a pound. [Ellen settled for less, twenty-five cents for two chickens, then thought for a moment and decided she would rather be paid in meat than money.] She told Mamma to get her a quarter's worth of beef from Mrs. Lucy Pollard, and Mamma told her she would do it.

Then me and Ellen started back to my house. Before we got to my house I heard Mr. Pollard's bell ring three times. I said to Ellen, "Hump! Mamma won't have to work now." He was hollering at the top of his voice. I told her that someone must be sick. Mamma ran. I went towards my house and found Mr. Fore's hands running towards Mr. Pollard's house. I told my sister to holler to them to run and we all went running up to the house, and left Ellen at the Gap. She didn't go to Mr. Pollard's. That's all I know about it.

Like most days, the day of the murder was one of bargaining. Pokey's story finally made sense, because almost every move on that sticky Friday involved an economic transaction. Food, clothing, even shelter: All were bargained for in a single day. This was the hidden economy of the poor, a ceaseless exchange among women who struck deals in person and moved goods, one house to another, on bare feet.

*   *   *

IT DIDN'T TAKE Cass Gregory long to come up with a different story.

At the trials Ellen Gayle had provided an essential portion of Pokey's alibi, swearing that she and Pokey had been together at the time of the murder, first walking toward the Thompsons' farm and then returning to Pokey's house. Now, in the first week of August, Gregory took a *Dispatch* man to see Ellen Gayle. The reporter listened while Gregory subjected her to a "severe cross-examination."[5]

At about four in the afternoon, Ellen now said, she had walked north from Pokey's house with Pokey, Betsy Ellis, and Mary Craghead, all headed for the Thompsons'. When they got into Thompsons' woods, about 300 yards north of the Pollard house, Ellen and Pokey turned back. However, they did not go straight to Pokey's. Instead they walked onto Edward Pollard's land at an old gate, about 150 yards behind the house. Ellen stopped there, but Pokey continued down the lane toward the house. Ellen suspected Pokey was going there to steal, and in the reporter's words, "she didn't propose to be mixed up in any such doings." Ellen walked over to Mr. Fore's fence line and sat down to wait. She had lost sight of Pokey, who was gone for half an hour, perhaps more. Pokey then caught up with Ellen, "out of breath and very hot, with the sleeve of her dress torn to the elbow." Ellen asked what had taken her so long. Pokey said she had stayed longer than she'd meant to, "but she wan't doing nothing, just walking about."

Pokey's alibi was up in smoke.

*   *   *

THE INK WAS hardly dry on Ellen's new story when a *Times* reporter appeared at the Richmond jail to tell Pokey about it and to solicit a reaction. Pokey was looking sharp, dressed in a lacy new shirtwaist.

Ellen lied, Pokey said, and she knew why. "It was well known among the negroes of Lunenburg," the reporter explained, "that Ellen Gayle was angry with her [Pokey] for having won the affections of Ben Knight, a negro farm hand, who was devoted to Ellen before her own superior attractions won his heart." In Petersburg the *Index-Appeal* picked up the story and put it more bluntly. Ellen "wanted to keep Pokey Barnes in jail so she could have her lover."[6] It was doubtful, however, that this revelation would aid Pokey's case, for it was followed almost instantly by two others, one that exposed Pokey's temper, the other clarifying her relationship with Ben Knight.

Why had Ellen Gayle initially given Pokey Barnes an alibi, testifying that she had been in Pokey's company all afternoon? Cass Gregory again had an answer. Ellen, he explained, was mortally afraid of Pokey, and with good reason. One time Pokey had gotten in a fight with a neighbor named Cora Knight and had beaten her so badly that not long afterward she died.[7]

The cause of death was soon disputed, Pokey's supporters claiming that Cora Knight had died of natural causes. But no one denied that the assault had taken place. Clearly Pokey Barnes was capable of throwing a punch, not a virtue as far as her white neighbors were concerned. A Chase City correspondent interviewed the local constable, who stated that "time and again" he had been called to arrest the Barnes sisters for fighting. A white farmer from Finneywood added that the Barnes women were "terrible people." Such judgments were confirmed when Pokey's sister Lizzie came up for trial at the August term of Lunenburg court, accused of stealing two bushels of sweet potatoes. They were worth only $1.50, but she had allegedly broken into the barn where they were stored and was thus charged with a felony. Promptly convicted, she was sentenced to two years in the penitentiary.[8]

Meanwhile Cass Gregory wanted the Richmond press to understand that Pokey lived with a man to whom she was not married. Ben Knight, he wrote, was Pokey's "husband (pro. tem.)."[9] That was not all. Two days after Ellen Gayle blew away Pokey's alibi, Gregory topped off his campaign to expose the sins of the Barnes women by slipping the *State* a purloined letter.

*　　*　　*

THE *RICHMOND STATE* was a plain two-cent paper, with no illustrations, no Sunday edition, and no funds to send reporters sleuthing about Lunenburg. But every so often the *State* played David to the big papers' Goliath and scooped them both. Thus it was with a letter allegedly composed by Joseph Barnes and sent to his wife, Mary, back in July. At that time she was in the Lunenburg jail awaiting trial.[10]

Finneywood, Va., July 5, 1895

Mrs. Mary Barnes:

I received your postal from Lunenburg jail and was utterly astonished when I received it to think that you would ask me to send you clothes. You know you carried all of your clothes down to Mr. Pollard's Monday before the murder was committed, and six months before that you carried all of them from my house to Scott Abernathy's, Wilson Abernathy's brother. Why don't you go to Wilson? You have been going to him for the last three years, and have not paid any attention to me or my little children, not even washed for us, cooked or patched our clothes. . . . I have long since laid you aside as my wife, since you had taken Wilson for your husband. Didn't his own daughter tell me that you had taken up with her father, and that she knew that it was so, for she had caught you? I told you then that you would come to some bad end, and your reply was: "What in the hell have you got to do with it? I will do as I please." . . . You told me I had nothing to do with you, and I will not. Go to Wilson for help if you want any. Don't ask me, for I have had nothing to do with this scrape. . . . They say, Mary, that you planned the way to kill Miss Lucy, and I say if you did hanging is too good for you. Solomon said you told them where everything was, and was the first one to think of this awful butchery. Besides getting all the money you took all her clothes, so that the poor woman did not have decent clothes to bury her in. You told me the week before, when we were quarrelling, that you did not care anything for me, and that you and Wilson were going to Baltimore this fall; and you said as soon as you could get the money you were going to leave here. . . . Little did the people think when you negroes were holding prayer meeting, first at Charles Knight's and then at Wilson's, and you at them every night, instead of being at home with me and the children, that you were planning this terrible thing. Now you had better be on your knees praying for your soul. I want you to remember what I so often said, that the old pitcher never went to the well but so many times but what it got the bottom knocked out of it. Now, if I was in your place I would tell everything I know about this thing, for I have heard the white folks say that it will do you more good than anything else, and it can't make them think any less of you than they do now; for everyone, black and white, believes you guilty, and even your old associates that you used to run with say so; and why? Because we could not keep you from down at Mr. Pollard's. Sol. has told all; now you make a clean breast of all you know, and that may clear you; if that don't nothing will. Mr. Lucius Pettus says it will, and all that will do any good now is to tell every one that is in it. I firmly do believe that you and Wilson are at the very bottom of this, and if you are, just tell it, for the white folks say you will be hung for what Sol. has said about you.

JOE BARNES
per Nell H. Pettus

Barnes could read just a little but could not write. According to the *State*, he had dictated the letter to Nell Pettus, the wife of his boss, W. W. Pettus. She then read it back to Joseph three times in the hearing of J. J. Watson, Mrs. Martha A. Thompson, and her husband—all of them white people from Finneywood who signed a statement saying Joe Barnes had declared the letter "true and just as he wished it written."

Was the letter authentic? Think back to July 5. That day, with the trials beginning in a week, Sheriff Cardozo rode house to house in Fort Mitchell summoning witnesses, among them three of Joseph Barnes's daughters. For days it had been rumored that there would

Joseph Barnes, husband of one of the suspects and father of another, fled Lunenburg when his wife and daughter were taken to Richmond, Virginia's capital.

PHOTO FROM THE *RICHMOND PLANET*, 19 OCTOBER 1895, COURTESY OF THE LIBRARY OF VIRGINIA.

be further arrests, and indeed on July 4 Fort Mitchell's justice of the peace had ordered the arrest of Fannie Marable.[11] Joseph Barnes must have feared he would be next. He had powerful incentive to produce evidence that he had not conspired in Lucy Pollard's death.

The text printed by the *State* a month later, however, appears to have been doctored for a nonlocal readership. Consider the sentence on Mary's taking her clothes "to Scott Abernathy's, Wilson Abernathy's brother." Mary would hardly need to be told that Scott Abernathy was Wilson's brother. Comparable oddities appeared in the mention of prayer meetings: ". . . you negroes were holding prayer meeting, first at Charles Knight's and then at Wilson's." You negroes? And why would Mary need to be instructed on the locations of the meetings?

Equally strange was the letter's sudden disappearance from public view. The *Dispatch* printed an excerpt the day after its publication in the *State*, but after that the "tell-tale letter" dropped out of sight.[12] Had the letter been authentic, it would surely have lived to see another day, especially given the extreme weakness of other evidence against Mary Barnes.

And what of the Finneywood people who claimed to have witnessed the letter's original composition? No one said so at the time, but all of them had intimate connections to one David Thompson.

*   *   *

CREDIT THE BARNES karma; the day after the letter was published, the zigzagging fortunes of Pokey Barnes shifted again. The *Dispatch* broke the story: At least three jurors in Pokey's case doubted the justice of their verdict. They had even looked into reopening the trial.

The key individual was a farmer named James Hazlewood. On the last night of the trials Hazlewood had headed home, alone with his conscience after five intense days of jury service. Twelve miles south of the courthouse, he saw a light in the window of I. B. Bell's law office. Hazlewood knocked, and Bell asked him in. A troubled Hazlewood said he was afraid he had done wrong. He wanted to know if there was any way to change his vote.

He also had company. Hazlewood returned to Bell's three days later with fellow juror Chriss Edwards. "They said that they had been coerced into agreeing to the verdict," said the *Dispatch*, "and only agreed after having been abused for some time by their fellow-jurymen."[13] Hazlewood and Edwards were white; they believed that one of the black jurors, Henry Governor, shared their doubts.

Bell advised the conscience-stricken jurors that it was too late for them to act. The *Dispatch*, however, was happy to act for them. THEY WERE COERCED, shouted the headline.

On the defensive once again, Judge Orgain convened a special grand jury in Lunenburg Courthouse to investigate the charges of coercion. James Hazlewood should have been the star witness, but he did not appear; he was out of the county, or so it was said. Two other jurors, Governor and C. W. Walker, testified "that their verdict was in accordance with their oath and honest convictions." Chriss Edwards was a bit more interesting. After the trial ended, as "a conscientious man, he was afraid that he might have made a mistake." But now Edwards declared himself "fully satisfied of the righteousness of said verdict."[14] Case closed. To a man, the witnesses claimed that no one had been coerced or intimidated.

But what about a different sort of pressure? What about exuberance? Two days after the sitting of the special grand jury, James Hazlewood wrote to the *Times*, for the first time speaking publicly for himself. Pokey's, he said, was "one of the wildest juries I was ever on." Yes, he had told attorney Bell that he had been abused by other jurors. But what he had meant was that "they were very pointed in their criticisms of anything that looked to the turning of the prisoner loose." Hazlewood had been the last to cave in. In the end, he insisted, he was "induced" to condemn Pokey, not "forced."[15]

Although Hazlewood defended the essential legality of what the jury had done, the episode was a gift to Pokey Barnes. Hazlewood still thought the jury had convicted on insufficient evidence. He risked the lasting contempt of his neighbors in saying so and opened the first crack in the facade of unity among the white people of Lunenburg.

Doubts about the jury also fed debates among newspaper editors and the people who wrote them letters. Was a fair trial *ever* possible when public opinion was so bitter that it was necessary to call out the militia? Even in the Southside, where the press generally sympathized with the Lunenburg establishment, some editors were skeptical. "Guard it as best you may," said the *Brunswick Gazette*, ". . . the thirteenth juror will enter the jury-room and will dictate the verdict."[16]

CHAPTER

11

TAKING SIDES

John Mitchell, Jr., had just put the finishing touches on the August 3 *Planet* when he bumped into Rosa Dixon Bowser on the street. On Sunday Bowser had heard Mitchell speak in church on the plight of the Lunenburg women. Now she pumped him for the latest on the case. She had news for Mitchell as well, wonderful news about women organizing.

Rosa Bowser seemed lit up from the inside; she had a luminous complexion and as much energy as any three ordinary people combined. At forty she was older than Mitchell, but they had much in common, including their alma mater, the Richmond Normal and High School. In slavery Virginia had made it a crime to keep a school for black people. It was thus an event of enormous importance when

"Colored Normal" was founded after emancipation. Rigorous and selective, the school each year graduated some twenty men and women for the teaching profession, an elite cadre of educators who were meant to lead the race to the full exercise of its new freedom.[1]

The precocious Rosa Bowser provided one of Normal's first and best success stories; in 1872, at only seventeen, she was the first black woman appointed to teach in the Richmond public schools. When she married in her mid-twenties, she felt compelled to resign her public school post, but after her husband's untimely death less than two years after their wedding, she returned to the Richmond schools and thereafter taught virtually nonstop. She taught public school children by day and workers by night; Sundays she taught in church; summers she taught teachers. She belonged to a host of organizations geared to self-improvement and race progress, and as the founder and guiding spirit of Virginia's black teachers' association she was known statewide.

Bowser corresponded with like-minded women in the North as well, hence her news for Mitchell: For the first time African American women had begun to form a national organization; representa-

Rosa Dixon Bowser, educator and activist, founded the Richmond Women's League to raise money for the legal defense of the Lunenburg women. This was the city's first federation of African American women's organizations.

PHOTO FROM THE *RICHMOND PLANET*, 12 JANUARY 1895, COURTESY OF THE LIBRARY OF VIRGINIA.

tives from ten states had met in Boston just two days before. Mitchell did not need to be told what drew them together. Since the late 1880s the forces of white supremacy had achieved some ominous victories, with deadly consequences for black southerners and revolutionary implications for the southern social order. In their social standing these white supremacists bore scant resemblance to the fringe groups who bore their banner a century later. The white supremacists of the 1890s were influential and comparatively prosperous pillars of their communities. They smarted from the Confederacy's defeat, they chafed at sharing power with blacks, and they believed the South should be theirs to rule.[2]

Control of government was critical to their self-image and their purposes, and they moved early to try to nullify the black vote. Achieving only uneven mastery through fraud and intimidation, they turned in the 1890s to the law. Mississippi led the way in 1890, writing a new constitution that disfranchised most of the state's black voters. In the summer of 1895 South Carolina was preparing to follow suit, and every other southern state was watching.

Looming almost as large was segregation, the legally mandated separation of blacks from whites. By law or custom, much was already segregated. Public schools had been segregated from the start, the shabby facilities allotted black students (when any facilities were allotted black students) exposing what was also intended: to discourage and debase black southerners in the process of isolating them. In the late 1880s segregationists targeted the railroads, and by 1895 every southern state except Virginia and the Carolinas had required the railroads to segregate passenger cars. Debates in the press suggested that those three states would not hold out much longer.

All the while, African Americans were stunned by the surge in lynching and by the willingness of some white editors and politicians to excuse it, condone it, even help set specific lynchings in motion. The white press almost always blamed black men, claiming they brought lynching upon themselves by making sexual assaults on white women; who could blame a chivalrous people for rising in righteous anger?

Ida B. Wells could. The young black editor of a Memphis, Tennessee, newspaper, Wells experienced a horrific epiphany in 1892, when her friend Thomas Moss was murdered in cold blood with two other black men. Their offense: They had opened a store that took business from the white grocer across the street. A shaken Wells investigated and learned that most lynchings involved no rape charges at all. She also hinted that some instances of alleged sexual assault were actually consensual affairs, the white woman crying rape to save her own reputation. Run out of Memphis, and her press destroyed, Wells stepped forward to lead an international campaign to expose lynching as terrorism.

The move to organize black women nationally had been galvanized by her campaign. Taking her cause to England, Wells had found especially devoted backers, who in 1895 called on the American press to denounce lynching. In response, one John Jacks, president of the Missouri Press Association, published an open letter dismissing black women as nothing but thieves and prostitutes. Insulted one too many times and determined to speak for themselves, black clubwomen in Boston called a national meeting.[3]

Rosa Bowser had been unable to go to Boston herself but planned to do all she could to support the effort. The women's organizations of Richmond, she told Mitchell, were ready to federate with the national group and with one another. Their first project: to raise money for the defense of the Lunenburg women. "No better time than now," Mitchell replied.[4] He'd hired three pricey lawyers and had almost no money to pay them.

Marietta Chiles, another teacher and activist, was the first person they brought into the loop—no surprise, as Chiles and John Mitchell were "an item." Whenever local gossips ran out of new stories, they could always return to a staple: When were those two going to get married?

The Richmond Women's League came into being on August 9, when more than two hundred women gathered at the First African Baptist Church. They elected Bowser their president and Chiles secretary, and they vowed to raise five hundred dollars, at the time an enormous sum.

They got off to a fast start. Black Richmond was home to more organizations than anyone could count, a high proportion of them

Marietta L. Chiles, a schoolteacher and co-founder of the Richmond Women's League. In addition to fundraising, members of the Women's League supported the Lunenburg women with prayer, visits, and gifts, including clothing and sewing materials.

PHOTO COURTESY OF FANNIE SIMS GODLEY AND LILLIAN W. LOVETT.

female. Some were sisters to men's fraternal associations, Rebekahs matching up with Odd Fellows, the Courts of Calanthe with their Knights of Pythias. Baptist and Methodist women formed circles to support their churches. Mutual benefit societies meanwhile numbered in the hundreds, some small and autonomous, others gathered under the umbrellas of large outfits like the Tents or the Independent Order of St. Luke. The mutual benefits were the economic salvation of Richmond's domestics, laundresses, and tobacco factory hands, who in the best of times lived precariously. In return for modest weekly dues, members got help in sickness or unemployment. The mutual benefits also assured their members decent burials when the time came.[5]

Vulnerable themselves, and many of them born in rural places like Lunenburg, Richmond's everyday working women identified profoundly with Pokey and the two Marys. They had learned long since that their strength lay in numbers. The Women's League collected more than one hundred dollars in its first week. John Mitchell, Jr., rejoiced in the group's success, printed news of every dime collected, and began to think he might be able to pay the lawyers after all.

The Richmond Planet *published the first photographs of the Lunenburg prisoners on August 3, 1895. The* Planet *was several years ahead of the white press in acquiring the technology to publish halftones on newsprint. [clockwise from bottom: Solomon Marable, Pokey Barnes and Mary Abernathy, Mary Barnes]*

PHOTOS COURTESY OF THE LIBRARY OF VIRGINIA.

*   *   *

THE AUGUST 3 *Planet* meanwhile was a triumph. Arrayed across the front page were halftone photographs of the Lunenburg prisoners, the first published anywhere. None of Richmond's white newspapers could come near it; not for another five years would they adopt the technology needed to mass-produce photographs on newsprint.[6]

Mitchell had good reason for jumping so far ahead of them. White supremacists used visual weapons as well as political and economic ones: American print culture—sheet music, political cartoons, cereal boxes—abounded with nasty caricatures of black people. When halftone technology became commercially feasible in the early 1890s, it was seized by publishers like Mitchell, empowered for the first time to put lifelike African American portraits before the public.

Thus Solomon Marable, wearing a plain shirt buttoned at the throat, gazed straight at the camera. Off by herself stood a barefoot Mary Barnes, thin forearms hanging from the sleeves of a slack prison-issue dress. Mitchell wrote her a particularly pitiful caption: " 'Poor Pokey! Poor Pokey! Poor Pokey! And I here in the Penitentiary.' " In the third photograph Mary Abernathy stood next to Pokey Barnes on the jail catwalk, Mary's arms clasped high across her middle in the way of pregnant women. Her fifteenth child, Mitchell now announced, was due at Christmas.

*　　*　　*

ON AUGUST 8, not quite three weeks after the close of the trials, Cass Gregory brought to Richmond the report of the Committee on Facts, the document meant to show that the women had been convicted on solid evidence, not on Solomon's word alone. Its very first "fact," however—the date of the murder—was wrong, off by one day.[7] And even the friendliest readers would be hard pressed to find the chain of evidence they were looking for.

The metaphor of the chain was important. Except for Solomon Marable's various confessions, all the evidence against the women was circumstantial. In itself this did not mean that Lunenburg had a weak case. Nineteenth-century courts gave as much weight to circumstantial evidence as to any other kind. To get a conviction, however, the prosecution had to show that the circumstances formed a chain, one linked tightly enough to lead each juror to a moral certainty of the suspect's guilt.

Gregory's report, published in full in both the *Times* and the *Dispatch*, produced no such chain and actually presented precious few new links. With respect to Mary Barnes, for example, the report gave just one new clue, this one about keys. The robbery had been uncommonly tidy; instead of ransacking the house, the thief had apparently used the Pollards' keys to open cabinets and trunks, then carefully closed them again to preserve the impression that nothing had been disturbed.

How had the thief acquired the keys? In Mary Barnes's trial Edward had claimed that only he and Lucy knew where the keys were. But now the committee report claimed that Mary Barnes knew too; she had admitted as much during her trial. On the afternoon of the murder, just before she went out to the field to join Edward, Mary had asked Lucy Pollard for medicine. Lucy had then unlocked the medicine cabinet and produced a dose of spirits of turpentine and camphor. According to Gregory, this was "a very strong circumstance against Mary Barnes."

On Pokey, Gregory's report revealed nothing beyond the stories he had already leaked about Ellen Gayle's change of tune and Pokey's brawl with the late Cora Knight. Since this information had not emerged until after the trials, however, it remained impossible to see why the jury had convicted her.

Gregory had more on Mary Abernathy, four new and potentially incriminating particulars. Most serious was an inconsistency in Mary's statements about whether she had seen anyone suspicious on the day of the murder. When questioned the very first time, on the night of the murder, Mary Abernathy claimed she had seen no one suspicious near the Pollard house. She had said it twice, clapping her hands for emphasis as she said she'd seen nobody, "good, bad, or indifferent." But Lula Knight said otherwise. According to Lula Knight, when Mary Abernathy returned home, she had told her husband, Wilson, she had seen "that man going down the fence."

"What man?" Wilson had asked.

"That tall man."

Said Wilson, "That was Solomon."

Both Mary and Wilson initially denied that this conversation had taken place. Later, when they were questioned separately, each admitted having spoken to the other of Solomon.[8] Remember, said Gregory, that Solomon was not a suspect in the first hours after Lucy Pollard's death. Why, then, would they deny that Mary had spoken of him—unless she shared Solomon's guilt?

There was a problem with one of Wilson's other statements as well. During Mary Abernathy's trial Wilson testified that after Mary had come home from the Pollards', she mentioned Mr. Clements's coming for corn. Mary challenged her husband's recollection then and there. "I didn't tell you nothing about corn," she said.[9] Wilson later recanted, saying that he had learned about the corn later and that in the excitement of the trial he had become confused. But to Cass Gregory the conclusion was obvious: Mary Abernathy had helped commit murder, had helped herself to the Pollards' worldly goods, and had yet to make her exit when Austin Clements came for the corn.

What did she do with the money? "I am the head of this money," she had told Solomon, and when she could get away, she planned to hide it in another Lunenburg neighborhood. (So Solomon had testified at his own trial.) Recall, said Gregory, that Mary Abernathy was arrested the day after the murder but subsequently set free. At the first opportunity she fled the neighborhood, just as Solomon had said, heading to her sister-in-law's at Rehoboth.

Finally, Mary Abernathy had clearly been acquainted with Solomon Marable; she had admitted he had come to her house on the Wednesday before the murder. Mary had made a bucket of lunch for her son Willie; Solomon had come by and then walked with Willie to the place they were working that day on the railroad.

Thus did Cass Gregory construct his indictment of Mary Abernathy, a gossamer case, thin and airy. Of physical evidence, there was none: still no blood, no money, no bedding or dresses, and no eyewitnesses except for Solomon Marable.

*   *   *

WORKING TO MARY Abernathy's advantage meantime was the matter of character. Had Gregory been able to dig up any dirt on the Abernathys, it would have found its way to the Richmond papers. But none was to be found, and as August wore on, Mary Abernathy stood firm. "I never believed God would let me hang for a crime I never committed," she told Mitchell.[10] Mary Abernathy, mother of nine living children, a professed Christian, and a woman of generous size, looked a lot more like a mammy than a murderer.

In 1895 that might count for something. In the 1890s multitudes of mammies populated the pages of southern literature. While the mammy figure was mostly the invention of a gang of sentimental white writers, her existence on the old plantation was rapidly transformed from fantasy to legend to indisputable "fact." The mammy of legend ruled the Big House (ordinarily a fantasy itself). She made the white children mind, told them stories, brought them up to be self-respecting, and held them close. They were devoted to her, and she to them.[11]

That was the point, of course. Mammy lived in literature to bestow the love and admiration of black people upon their one-time owners. The more the white supremacists achieved, the more was mammy needed to assure her now-grown white children that they still merited her devotion.

Other than mammy, the white press produced precious few black characters that could be construed as positive. So some black writers used the tools they were handed, betting that white people's declared love for mammy could be strategically deployed on behalf of living black Americans. Thus did John Mitchell, Jr., work the case of Mary Abernathy. If Lunenburg executed her, he wrote, "No more will the white people in the neighborhood have the benefit of her friendly advice, nor feel the softness of her motherly hand."[12] The trick was to get white readers to look at Mary and see mammy.

Mitchell could write as sentimentally as any of mammy's white inventors. But unlike them, he did not ignore the possibility that mammies had children of their own. He evoked Mary Barnes's grief at Pokey's fate; he wrote of Pokey's "little chap" and of Mary Abernathy's children left in Lunenburg while their mothers languished in jail. His editorials bordered on the sappy at times, but consider: In 1895 black southerners still placed want ads in newspapers in hopes of locating family members sold away from them during slavery.

*   *   *

ON MONDAY, AUGUST 12, scores of parched farmers converged on Lunenburg Courthouse. The stalls lining the roads into the village were loaded with watermelons and jugs of sweet cider, the market women doing a terrific business as the temperature headed for the high nineties. The crowd headed for an "Indignation Meeting."

The previous week about fifty of them had given a rousing send-off to Cass Gregory, who then journeyed to Richmond to present the report of the Committee on Facts. But nobody in Richmond bought Gregory's report. The *Dispatch* responded in soothing tones but was noncommittal on the evidence, the *Star* was inclined to believe that in Lunenburg the spirit of mob violence still prevailed, and the *Times* argued with the report in dizzying detail, though it did not offer an explanation for Mary's "good, bad, or indifferent" statement.[13] The *Times* also had the nerve to lecture the benighted citizens of Lunenburg on the ABCs of criminal justice, to wit: "the case should be patiently and intelligently investigated in all its ramifications, that the guilty parties may be punished for the murder, and that we should run no risks of punishing persons who are innocent."[14]

Now 250 livid men stood up for old Lunenburg. They passed passionate, unanimous resolutions, defending the integrity of their judicial process and promising to boycott the *Richmond Times* until it issued a full apology.

"Resolved further," read their statement, "that the officious and unwarranted attack on the people of our county by The Times created a great deal more excitement among our people and the people of the adjoining counties than the Pollard murder, and justly so."[15]

And justly so? Here made manifest was the strange and powerful entity that white men called honor. Honor was about reputation, public standing, the worth of men in the eyes of their equals. It was also about sticking up for oneself in the face of insult.[16] To the assembled white citizens of Lunenburg, Lucy Pollard's murder, though a horror and a tragedy, was less disturbing than honor impugned.

Their resentment burned the hotter because the insults came from the city, the capital no less. "Now it seems . . . that the people of Lunenburg are incapable of self-government," came a sardonic voice from Lunenburg, "and will have to be looked after and supervised by big Richmond."[17] City against country, central power versus local: The tensions were as old as cities themselves and never far below the surface. It took very little—a few condescending editorials would do—to set them on a career of their own.

By the middle of August the Pollard murder was carrying a monumental load of freight. The story had begun with the death of a woman. Now, increasingly, it was about honor among men. As if to underscore the point, the First Regiment, Virginia Volunteers gathered on Saturday night at the Richmond armory, where they collected their pay for duty at the trials and joined in the singing of their new anthem, "The Battle of Lunenburg."[18]

*　　*　　*

Shortly after Lunenburg's white citizens held their "Indignation Meeting," the *Richmond Dispatch* threw its editorial support to their side. This move surprised no one; the *Dispatch* had a hefty circulation in the white Southside, and its hostility to the aspirations of black people was legend. But it promised trouble for the women, as it was the state's largest and most powerful newspaper. The reform-minded *Times* meanwhile dug in on the women's behalf. In the heat of late summer the two papers disputed almost every detail of the case, the discourse often proceeding at the approximate level of eight-year-olds arguing a play at second base: Safe! Out!

For example, the Winking Man. The trial of Pokey Barnes had been interrupted when a front-row spectator had been spotted winking or blinking at Solomon Marable, who was on the stand then and had just made his sensational switch to the white man story. Why would the spectator signal Solomon at that moment, asked the *Times*, unless he was protecting the perpetrator?

From Finneywood, courtesy of the *Dispatch*, came an answer from the Winking Man himself, a farmer named Lucius Pettus. "I was in the courtroom," Pettus said, "and if I winked I was entirely unconscious of it." He went on to explain. "Occasionally while at rest, there is something that seems to strike me in the side of my tongue, and makes my face draw up or twitch, and sometimes people have asked me if I was winking at them."[19]

Solomon Marable, however, was certain Pettus had tried to intimidate him, a claim that took on greater plausibility when one of the soldiers came forward. Private Tony Miller recalled observing Pettus outside the hotel on the evening of the winking incident. Pettus had at first denied that he had signaled Solomon but then had changed his tune: "He did wink at the witness, but it was to make him tell the truth, and not a d___ parcel of lies."[20]

The "Winking Man." During the trial of Pokey Barnes, Solomon Marable fleetingly implicated a white man in the murder, but quickly switched back to accusing the women—the latter move allegedly in response to a spectator who winked or blinked at him in a threatening way. Two weeks after the trials closed, the press identified the Winking Man as Lucius Pettus, a farmer from Finneywood.

IMAGE FROM THE *RICHMOND DISPATCH*, 15 SEPTEMBER 1895, COURTESY OF THE LIBRARY OF VIRGINIA.

From Lunenburg via the *Dispatch*, however, came yet more contrary testimony. According to Finneywood's preacher, Pettus often winked his eyes when excited, even in church. Cass Gregory weighed in as well: When Pettus strongly agreed with a statement or was deeply interested in a question, he would give a quick nod. Lucius Pettus, in short, was a "habitual winker."[21]

Safe.

Out.

While the *Times* and *Dispatch* debated the qualities of Pettus's interesting face, John Mitchell, Jr., got a fix on his relationship to David Thompson—and indeed on Thompson himself. On August 10, two days after the publication of Cass Gregory's report, the *Planet* revealed some eye-popping news: There were *two* David Thompsons. One, the twenty-five-year-old son of Edward Pollard's nemesis Bill Thompson, farmed near Fort Mitchell. Despite the fact that both his father and brother had quarreled with Edward on the day of the murder, this was not the Thompson accused by Solomon Marable.

Solomon's white man was David James Thompson, who lived in Finneywood. Lucius Pettus, said the *Planet*, was his older half brother. Lucius was not on speaking terms with Edward Pollard.

Lucius had also been mentioned in the "tell-tale letter" attributed to Joseph Barnes. Had the letter lived a longer public life, someone might have connected the rest of the dots: The white people identified as present when Joseph dictated the letter all were close to David James Thompson: Martha A. Thompson was his mother; Lucius and W. W. Pettus were his half brothers, Martha's sons by her first marriage. To add one more layer, this was the Thompson family with whom Lucy Pollard had lived fifteen years earlier, before her marriage to Edward Pollard.

By mid-August untold numbers of Virginians had sorted themselves into opposing camps. Around the women gathered an interracial constellation of people and papers, chief among them John Mitchell, Jr., and his weekly *Planet*, Rosa Dixon Bowser and the new Richmond Women's League, Captain Frank Cunningham, the three white lawyers, the city's black clergy, and the daily *Times*. Against the accused women stood Lunenburg's elected officials and vocal white citizens, their counterparts in surrounding counties, the Southside's small-town newspapers, and the *Richmond Dispatch*.

About Solomon Marable meanwhile there was no controversy. He would and should hang, or so most people thought—until a Catholic priest took his part, giving added weight to the white man story and offering everyone a lesson in the qualities of mercy.

CHAPTER

12

BAPTISMS

"*Exi, immunde spiritus, et da honorem Deo vivo et vero.*" It was language seldom heard in the Richmond city jail. "*Fuge, immunde spiritus, et da locum Iesu Christo Filio eius.*" ("Go forth, unclean spirit, and pay homage to the living and true God. Depart, unclean spirit, and give place to Jesus Christ, his son.") Solomon knelt before the priest, who had heard his confession and now held a pitcher of water above his head. "Solomon Peter Claver Marable, I baptize you in the name of the Father, and of the Son, and of the Holy Spirit."[1] The ever-changeable Solomon Marable was changing into a Roman Catholic.

For seven weeks he had languished in the city jail, and while it seemed that all Richmond lined up to defend the women, not one

soul stood up for Solomon—except for Lambert Welbers. Father
Welbers, German by birth, had been sent to Richmond two years earlier to head the city's one black Catholic church. His congregation
had been founded only ten years earlier, and despite the priest's best
efforts, converts were hard to find. Although several dozen black
children attended his school, their parents took them to Baptist
churches on Sundays to inoculate them from the catechism they
learned during the week. Few of the schoolchildren became
Catholics.[2]

"Inasmuch as ye have done it unto one of the least of these my
brethren," Jesus said, "ye have done it unto me." For Father Welbers
this verse from the Book of Matthew was both an article of faith and
a strategy for increasing his flock. Shortly after Welbers had arrived
in Richmond, he set up a foundling hospital and orphanage; the
infants left on his doorstep would grow up Catholic. In the meantime
the priest's definition of the "least of these" extended to felons.
Accompanied by a small band of Franciscan nuns, Welbers visited
the penitentiary and the city jail, seeking potential converts among
the inmates.[3]

It was a stifling day in the hottest September anyone could
remember, and the priest's words floated on the jail's thick air. "*Vade
in pace, et Dominus sit tecum.*" ("Go in peace, and the Lord be with
you.") When Solomon got to his feet, he towered over his new spiritual adviser. Welbers was a small, exacting man, with a high forehead, pallid complexion, and youthful curve to his mouth. Like
everyone in his order, he was clean-shaven. Though only thirty-three,
Welbers spoke in the sage tones of a much older man. A person who
knew him only through his published sermons would peg him at
fifty, at least.

Solomon's execution was eleven days away.

Welbers had done his best, had gone to see Governor O'Ferrall to
plead for a reprieve. But the governor hadn't budged. When Welbers
informed Solomon of the governor's decision, Solomon dropped his
chin to his chest, for a long while saying nothing. At length he lifted
his head. "The Lord's will be done"—Solomon sighed—"but it's
unjust." Then he asked to be baptized a Catholic. Welbers suggested
September 9, the saint's day of Peter Claver. In the eighteenth century

Peter Claver had migrated from Spain to Colombia, where he minis-
tered to slaves as they staggered off the ships from Africa. For
decades he worked in the slave pens, on plantations, among seamen,
convicts, and even lepers, "the least of these," to be sure.[4]

John Mitchell, Jr., was struck by the change in Solomon Marable.
Mitchell had once editorialized that Marable was "unfit to breathe
God's free air." But now Solomon seemed wistful and penitent, and
as the execution drew nearer, the *Planet* presented him in a new
way. This Marable came across as a human being, a strange human
being, to be sure, and a criminal. But he had human attachments and
very human anxieties; as he prepared for death, he began to worry
about what would happen to his body. He sent a letter to his wife,
Fannie, asking her to have him buried in North Carolina. Mitchell
printed her reply in the *Planet*.[5]

> Dear husband:
> I received your kind letter, the 22nd ult. You may be sure
> that I was glad to hear from you because I thought you
> had come to a point that you couldn't write to me any
> more. Oh, what joy it was to me to get your letter! I hap-
> pened to be at Stovall when the mail came right to the P.O.
> I went feeling sad for fear there wasn't any letter for me.
>
> You don't know how my heart did leap with joy when
> the letter was handed to me; but I was much disappointed
> when I opened the letter and found that you didn't send
> your photograph like you told me in your last letter before
> this. Please don't disappoint me any more, but send it the
> next time, because my mother wants to see it as well as I
> do. Hope that you will not think hard of me for not send-
> ing the box as I told you in my letter. I would have sent it,
> but work went down, so that I couldn't get anything hardly
> for my children to eat.
>
> I had to give one week to the protracted meeting to see
> if I couldn't find rest for my soul, and I have found rest in
> Jesus for my weary soul, and I hope that you will soon find
> rest for your soul, like I have for mine,—a rest in Jesus.
> We did have a good meeting. There were eight converts
> that week. There will be baptizing at Davis' Chapel, Sun-
> day. Everybody say you must pray that the good Lord may

save your soul at the last day.

So I must tell you something about the children. Henry is just as fat as he can be, but poor little Johnny has been very sick indeed. He is not walking yet, but I hope he will walk before winter comes. So I will close on them.

You say you would let me know as soon as you found out about getting your body. See what it would cost me to have it brought here. If it would cost me anything I couldn't have it brought here, because I am not able to pay for it being brought here. But if it won't cost me anything, I will meet it. As that is the last thing that you ask me to do for you, I will try and do that if I can.

Your mother says that she could not help me any at all, if it costs anything. She says she is not able, and so I will bring my letter to a close by asking you to write again soon.

All are well at home. Much love to yourself. Pray that I may meet you in glory by and by, where we will part no more, but live with God forever in that bright and happy land.

Your darling wife,
FANNIE MARABLE

For the time being, Solomon would have to suffer uncertainty about what would happen to his mortal body. He worried for his soul too. Although Father Welbers had heard his confession, he insisted that Solomon do more. "When a Catholic has sinned, it is not so easy to obtain pardon," the priest explained. "If he has wronged another in his goods or reputation he will have to restore the ill-gotten goods and repair the injured reputation as a condition for absolution."[6] Solomon realized he must try to make up with the women he once had blamed for Lucy Pollard's murder. Mary Barnes, across town in the state penitentiary, was out of reach, but Pokey and Mary Abernathy were just across the way. He asked permission to see them.

Unlike Solomon, the women had cause for optimism. In twenty-four hours their attorneys would take their case to the circuit court. It had been a long wait, but Mary and Pokey had been sustained daily by the Women's League, whose support was direct and personal as well as financial. League members had visited in a steady stream, joining Mary and Pokey in prayer and song and often bearing gifts. This one brought food, that one a dress, someone else offered fabric or yarn to provide work for their hands—so many things altogether that John Mitchell, Jr., put out an appeal for a trunk to store them all.[7]

Pokey and Mary crossed the courtyard and were shown into the office. Several men awaited them: City Sergeant Charles Epps, who ran the jail, John Mitchell, Jr., attorneys Flournoy and Guigon, and of course, Solomon Marable, who gazed down at the women, for an uncomfortable minute not speaking. He had not seen the women since the day they had all been brought to Richmond. Flournoy prompted him. "Solomon, you want to say something to these women, I believe."

"Yes, sir," Solomon replied. Mitchell recorded the exchange that followed.[8]

"I ask pardon, Aunt Mary, for what I have done. I told stories on you, but God has forgiven me and I hope you will."

Abernathy looked him in the eye. "Solomon, does you know that God has forgiven you or does you think it?"

"I know he has forgiven me."

"Well, Solomon," said Mary, "if you know that God has forgiven you, I'll forgive you, too."

Solomon turned to Pokey. "Pokey, God has forgiven me and I hope you will forgive me."

Pokey looked at him for a long time. Solomon shifted his gaze to the floor. "Solomon," she finally said, "I forgive you, but I can never forget you."

* * *

THE NEWSPAPER BUSINESS could take a man to some strange places. At five the next morning John Mitchell, Jr., and his photographer J. C. Farley wandered along a dark country lane in the middle of Amelia County. A few hours earlier Mitchell had heard Solomon Marable beg the women's forgiveness. A few hours more and the circuit court would at last hear the three women's cases. The situation of Pokey Barnes and Mary Abernathy was urgent, their appointment with the executioner only eight days away.

Mitchell and Farley had taken the night train from Richmond, traveling thirty-odd miles and arriving at 4:30 A.M. Because the trains stopped there, Amelia Courthouse was a bit bigger than its Lunenburg counterpart, but to a lifelong city dweller like Mitchell, it was pure boondocks. At daybreak Mitchell and Farley walked by "the place called a hotel, for the want of a better name," and saw what happened in case of overflow: Three very uncomfortable-looking men had stretched out on a blanket on the front porch. Mitchell had not planned to stay in the hotel anyway; he knew better than to expect such a place to serve black customers and thus had arranged to stay in a private home. Not wanting to disturb their hosts so early in the day, however, Mitchell and Farley took a moonlight stroll into the countryside.[9]

When court opened at ten, Mitchell and Farley found seats in the jury box. Neither jurors nor witnesses would attend this proceeding, nor would Pokey or the two Marys, their guilt or innocence not presently at issue. On trial instead was the Lunenburg court, and only one question mattered: Had the original trials been conducted according to law? If the judge found that the Lunenburg court had made some essential mistake, he would issue writs of error and supersedeas, temporarily saving Pokey and Mary Abernathy from the gallows. Later a second proceeding would determine whether the women, Mary Barnes included, would get new trials.

"Well, gentlemen, we are ready to proceed."[10] Fifty-three-year-old Samuel F. Coleman ascended the bench, chewing an unlit cigar. Scarcely visible behind the stacks of lawbooks they had brought with them sat the three attorneys for the women. As expected, William E. Neblett appeared for Lunenburg. Not expected was the additional lawyer at Neblett's side.

Lunenburg County had hired a big gun to match the firepower of the legal team from Richmond. Fifty-two, with hair and goatee going to silver, William Hodges Mann looked as if he belonged in the governor's mansion (he got there in 1910); by any reckoning he was a worthy adversary. He was only twenty-seven years old when he was named judge of the Nottoway County court in 1870, and despite the turbulence of Virginia politics in the 1870s and 1880s, he had been appointed to one term after another. The money, however, lay in working for the railroads. Though he had married profitably, he had also undertaken the support of nine orphaned nieces and nephews. In 1891 Mann left the bench and became counsel for the Norfolk & Western, taking the title of Judge with him, of course. Now he sat at the front of the courtroom, looking like some people's idea of God.[11]

Alec Guigon stood up, a sheaf of papers in hand. The problem, as the press had explained early on, stemmed from the absence of counsel during the trials. Normally, at trial's end the defense filed a bill of exceptions. Inserted into the trial record, the exceptions provided the basis for an appeal. But what if no exceptions had been filed?

The women's legal team came in with two strategies. One was to grab a big bat and go for the home run. This case was so extraordinary, the lawyers would argue, and the verdicts so grossly contrary to the spirit of justice, that the judge must act on innate principles of fairness, call off the hangings, and award a new trial.

It was a rare judge who would stray this far from established procedure, however; precedent stuck to Virginia judges like white on rice. Hence the second, more conventional strategy. Sometimes, apart from the bill of exceptions, the trial record itself gave evidence that the court had made at least one fatal mistake, and if so, the suspect was entitled to a new trial. But this approach too could be

William Hodges Mann, retained by Lunenburg's county government to make the convictions stick, became governor of Virginia in 1910.

PHOTO COURTESY OF THE LIBRARY OF VIRGINIA.

treacherous. A trial record was a slender thing, a skeleton of indictments, pleadings, motions, and judge's orders. It did not go to the
heart of the case. It contained neither attorneys' questions nor witnesses' answers. The record of Pokey's trial, the longest of the three
in question, occupied less than four handwritten pages. None of the
trial records in the Lunenburg case even hinted at the danger of
lynching, the presence of the military, or the contradictions in
Solomon's stories.

To Alec Guigon fell the task of fattening up the record. He had
in hand several papers that documented the atmosphere of terror in
Lunenburg Courthouse. If Judge Coleman agreed to consider even
one of them, the women's chances might dramatically improve.
Guigon took his listeners back to the anxious days before the trials,
when Sheriff Cardozo had first called for troops. William Neblett, no
less, had backed the sheriff with a letter to the governor, a letter
Guigon now read to the court. "The feeling against the prisoners is
so strong . . ." Neblett had written, "I fear the parties charged with
said offence, will not be tried by the civil authority."

Guigon then moved to a statement from the commanding officer
at Lunenburg Courthouse. "I was and am under the impression that
the prisoners were in great danger of lynching during the entire time,
in spite of the presence of the military, and that without their presence, the lynching of all of them would have been a foregone conclusion. And further, that threats were openly made that in the event of
the acquittal of any of them, . . . they would certainly be lynched, had
they been without the protection of the troops."[12]

Objection! Lunenburg's lawyers thought the judge had heard
enough, and to Guigon's frustration, Judge Coleman agreed. He would
consider no additional documents after all, a significant victory for
Lunenburg. His job done, Guigon made a show of putting his papers
away.

Flournoy rose next, his central task to pick apart the record as it
stood, pointing out flaws potentially serious enough to warrant new
trials. His team had identified four such flaws. First, the record left
out language that showed the jurors to be qualified for jury service.
Second, Pokey Barnes and Mary Abernathy had been indicted jointly,
in a single act of the grand jury, but then were tried separately,

although neither had elected a separate trial. Third, Judge Orgain erred in his instructions to all three juries, suggesting that the burden was on the women to establish alibis. Not so, said Flournoy. The burden of proof was at all times on the prosecution. Fourth, in none of the trials had the juries been properly kept. In capital cases, jurors were to be kept together at all times; when court recessed, the jurors must be in custody of a sworn officer of the court and not able to communicate with outsiders. Furthermore, the record must *state* that the jury was kept properly. But on this issue, Flournoy pointed out, the trial records said nothing.

As Flournoy elaborated each point, it became clearer than ever that this proceeding was about the law itself, the integrity of the process by which the courts decided to take a life or spare it. For every possible error he cited a long string of authorities—judicial opinions and legal treatises, most of them stacked on the attorneys' table. The books were meant to impress the judge and also to serve as his reference library; Judge Coleman was expected to study the case overnight.

When Flournoy cranked up the oratory, he could be heard all the way out to the courthouse green. At the end of his long, technical address, he raised his voice and the stakes, finally broaching the subject of race. "We know that there is a growing and perplexing question in this country. It is the Negro question." Still seated in the jury box, John Mitchell, Jr., snapped to attention. "One way to settle it," Flournoy went on, "the best and the right way to settle it, is for the white people to do justice to them. Standing in the temple of justice, I do not fear to say that I am in favor of the same rights and privileges before the law as is accorded the white man. There is not a white man in this county who would have convicted the women on the testimony adduced. Let justice be done, though the heavens fall."[13]

Flournoy resumed his seat behind the piles of books, and William Hodges Mann rose to answer briefly for Lunenburg. Hired only a few hours before, Mann had to improvise, but he knew enough law to offer plausible rebuttals to Flournoy's claims of flaws in the trial records. Mann also understood the uses of grace, expressing nothing but sympathy for the women's plight. But alas, the law simply did not empower the courts to help them. Let the women go to the governor, Mann said. Surely, if they had been wronged, the governor would use the pardon power to set things right.

George Wise rose to make the day's final speech. "Every man," he began, "is entitled to a fair and impartial trial." Of course he would go to the governor if it came to that, but the women had been failed by the courts, and if the courts offered them no remedy, then the rights of all Virginians were in jeopardy. "Have my clients had a fair and impartial trial? Have they had a fair and impartial trial when the courthouse in which they were tried was surrounded by armed men? Was it *ever* the case in the history of any civilized state that women were sent to death under the verdict of a jury when armed men in the court room gave orders along with the judge on the bench?" Once a prosecutor himself, Wise turned and glared at William Neblett, then continued.

> So help me God, I will never prosecute a case in which bayonets play a conspicuous part, and the prisoners have to be surrounded by armed men. Where arms prevail, the law is silent.[14]
>
> And the law was silent when these women were condemned to death. There was not one particle of testimony to convict these women but that of Solomon Marable, who stood up before the jury and told them that every word that fell from his perjured lips was a lie. Never was I willing that a person should be convicted upon the testimony of a confessed murderer.
>
> I believe that the vengeance of almighty God will visit itself upon those who take life without due process of law. God grant that the day may never come again, when the verdict of a jury will depend upon the clamor of a mob. Crucify him! Crucify him! And he died upon the cross.

Wise lowered his voice and turned matter-of-fact. "I want to call your honor's attention to Bishop and Wharton on Criminal Proceedings." Looping back to the trial record, Wise conducted a long, exhaustive review of each possible error. Then he made a last plea: "I beg your honor, I ask you in the name of that God before whom we are to appear. I beg you to search that record and render a decision in keeping with justice and humanity."

From the jury box John Mitchell, Jr., had watched every gesture, absorbed every word. His team had been masterful: "pale, thoughtful, painstaking" Guigon; "impulsive, fiery" Flournoy; and the incomparable Wise, who now took his seat after delivering as fine a summation as Mitchell had ever heard.[15]

Everyone was drained. It had been a long day, and hot. The attorneys listened for the standard words of adjournment, wanting especially to know what time they would convene in the morning to hear Judge Coleman's decision.

But the judge was ready to rule. "I have given the case a great deal of thought," he said, "and have endeavored to find some ground on which I can grant the writ. I am sure were I to grant it, I would satisfy the greater majority of the people, but I can't do so without uprooting the whole system of criminal proceedings in the State. Therefore, the writ is refused." Without a word of further explanation, court was adjourned.[16]

CHAPTER

13

WHITE MAN STORIES

T he next afternoon John Mitchell, Jr., went to the jail to break the news of Judge Coleman's decision. A *Times* reporter, however, had gotten there first. Mary Abernathy, who normally sat sewing behind the iron grate that fronted the women's cellblock, was frantic and pacing. "I don't know which way to walk," she said, "nor what to do."[1]

Pokey Barnes kept silent but had clearly been crying. As Mitchell approached, she pushed through the bars a note she had dictated. "I am saved," it said, and went on:[2]

> I believe in the Lord Jesus Christ. Behold I stand at the
> door and knock, if any man hear my voice and open the

door, I will come in to him and sup with him and he with me. I have given up this world—my mother, father, and sisters and my brother and child. Am ready to meet my God. There is nothing in this whole world to care for. All I want now is to reach my heavenly home above. I am ready to meet God with no guilt or sin in my heart. I want to meet them all in heaven.

This was written by Pokey Barnes: born in the year of 1872, age 25 on the 15th of March in the year of 1896. Married in the year of 1890.

The hour appointed for their hanging was one week away. The *Times* reporter had told them that the writs had been denied, but he had not explained the remaining options. So here was Mary near panic and Pokey composing her own obituary.

Mitchell got Mary Abernathy to sit. He could not explain the judge's reasoning, but he could offer reassurance: At that moment their legal team was preparing papers for the Supreme Court of Appeals, Virginia's highest tribunal. Should the high court let the hangings go forward, they would appeal to Governor O'Ferrall, who could give them a reprieve or even a pardon. Mitchell gave the women all the encouragement he dared. When he left, they were almost calm.[3]

Still, they would have a painful wait. It was now Friday. Not until Monday could the high court hear their appeal. With luck they would get a decision on Tuesday.

*   *   *

SHORTLY AFTER SEVEN on Tuesday morning, Cass Gregory appeared at the door of the Richmond jail. He had been quiet in recent weeks, having moved to South Carolina to launch a tobacco brokerage. But he had not lost interest in the Pollard murder. He had traveled all night, four hundred miles by train, in hopes of interviewing Mary Abernathy and Pokey Barnes in their most desperate hour.[4]

Gregory asked permission to speak with the condemned women, one at a time. The deputy fetched Pokey from the women's cellblock and brought her out to the balcony over the courtyard. "Pokey," said Gregory, "I came to see if you will tell me who killed Mrs. Pollard, and where the stolen goods are."[5]

Pokey was stunned. "I done told you a thousand times that I don't know nothing about the killing of Mrs. Pollard, nothing about money and nothing else."

Gregory persisted. "Judge Coleman has refused to grant you a new trial and I am pretty sure that the Supreme Court isn't going to interfere. If you will make a clean breast of it, I will go to the governor and get you off."

"I can't tell you that I had killed Mrs. Pollard when I didn't kill her," Pokey insisted, "and I can't tell you that I saw anybody else kill her when I didn't see them kill her."

Seeing his best hope slip away, Gregory reminded Pokey that if the Supreme Court did not intervene, she would hang.

"They'll have to go 'long and hang me, then. I can't help it." Pokey turned and marched back to her cellblock.

A short time later the deputy came back with Mary Abernathy. "Mary," said Gregory, "I have come all the way from Sumter, South Carolina, to meet Captain Cunningham to save the necks of Pokey Barnes and yourself. Mary, if you will confess the part you took in the murder, and surrender all the stolen money and property, I will draw up a petition and take it to the judge, and the commonwealth's attorney, and the jury, and will go to the governor myself and get you out of this."[6]

Mary Abernathy walked along the railing of the balcony. "If you were to put a whole regiment of soldiers in front of me I could not tell you anything about that money to save my life. I know nothing about it."

Gregory repeated his offer, but Mary would have none of it. Half an hour after he had come, Gregory left the jail.

*   *   *

JOHN MITCHELL, JR., spent Tuesday morning at the *Planet* office, sweating out the decision of the Supreme Court of Appeals. Required by law to hold some of their sessions outside the capital city, Virginia's five high court justices were meeting this week in the Shenandoah Valley town of Staunton. Alec Guigon, the junior member of the women's legal team, had gone to Staunton and stationed himself outside the judges' chambers, ready to sprint for the telegraph office as soon as they emerged with a decision.[7]

At last, at 11:40 A.M., a messenger arrived at the *Planet* building, bearing five of the loveliest words Mitchell had ever read: WRITS GRANTED ALL THREE CASES. Mitchell slapped the telegram up on a bulletin board and raced to the jail with the news. "Thank God! Thank God! Thank God! Thank God!" Mary Abernathy shouted. "The devil is about to be whipped at last!"[8]

Reporters came and went the rest of the afternoon. Mary and Pokey were full of cheerful chatter, regaling the newsmen with the story of Cass Gregory's peculiar offer to "save their necks." Attorney George Wise too was talkative on this glad day, happy to explain what he could about the law. The writs of error provided only a stopgap, postponing the hangings until the justices could hold a second hearing to decide whether to grant new trials. Not until this second hearing, which might be several weeks away, would the judges reveal why they had decided in favor of the women.[9]

As for Cass Gregory, Wise condemned his visit to the jail in the strongest terms. But Wise knew a gift when he saw one: In spite of himself, Gregory had generated powerful evidence of the women's innocence.

* * *

JOHN MITCHELL, JR., awoke early the next morning and lay in bed for a few delicious minutes, thinking with satisfaction about the events of the previous day. Then it dawned on him fully for the first time: Solomon Marable was really going to die. In two days.

Mitchell jumped up, dressed in a hurry, and rushed to his office. When his typist arrived, he began dictating a petition, a plea to Governor O'Ferrall to give Solomon Marable thirty more days to live. Mitchell looked up in mid-sentence and saw Father Welbers in his doorway. This was one of the priest's virtues: He would enter black businesses and homes, instead of expecting black people to come to him.

When the petition was finished, Welbers took it to the governor. Afterward Mitchell called on O'Ferrall as well. The governor received each of them politely and heard them out, but they came away believing Solomon would hang in forty-eight hours.[10]

*   *   *

IN 1879 THE Virginia legislature had abolished public hangings, falling in line with reformers who for decades had argued that only barbarians made a spectacle of execution. Hence the arrangements in Lunenburg Courthouse: A crude scaffold had been erected behind the county jail. Around it stood a high temporary fence intended to prevent the populace from watching Solomon Marable drop to his death.[11]

A plain coffin had been nailed together, the grave dug. The rope had arrived too, a special rope that belonged to the sheriff in Danville. For twelve years he had lent it out for executions all over Virginia. Sheriffs helped one another when called upon to hang someone. They also engaged in an informal contest to see who could hang a person at the least expense. The equipment intended for Solomon fell in the middle range: $12.63, including labor and shipping charges on the rope.

Early on Wednesday morning, September 18, Lunenburg's Sheriff Cardozo and three deputies set out for the train station in Blackstone and thence to Richmond to take custody of Solomon Marable. About Pokey Barnes and Mary Abernathy, they were not sure. They knew the women's petitions had gone to the Supreme Court of Appeals, but with no telegraph in Lunenburg Courthouse, they had no way to learn of the outcome. Their wagon had room for the women, just in case.[12]

The four men reached the Richmond city jail at 4:00 P.M. and were immediately served with a restraining order respecting Mary Abernathy and Pokey Barnes. Solomon, however, was told to be ready to travel the next morning. He said he would go without a struggle. He also stuck by his white man story. "The women are innocent," he declared. "I'll look Dave Thompson in the face on the gallows and tell him he killed Mrs. Pollard."[13]

At 9:00 P.M. a message came from Governor O'Ferrall: Sheriff Cardozo and his deputies must come at once to the Executive Mansion. Cardozo, the governor thought, should be the first to know: He had decided to respite Solomon Marable for thirty days.

He believed he was taking a terrible chance. Those who claimed to understand lynching saw it as a natural human response to a faulty justice system; people took criminals into their own hands in part because the courts were slow and entirely too lenient. Almost everyone thought Solomon guilty of an atrocious crime. What better way to incite the mob than to grant him a reprieve? On the other hand, as a former judge O'Ferrall knew Marable might have a second trial coming. The Supreme Court had found flaws in the women's trials; perhaps Solomon's had been flawed in the same way. In any case, an illiterate man had been tried for his life in the presence of soldiers and without counsel—altogether a sad reflection on Virginia justice, O'Ferrall thought.[14]

News traveled erratically in 1895. Solomon Marable was told of the respite right away and slept soundly for the first time in many nights. No one thought to tell Father Welbers, who came to the jail at six the next morning, thinking he would say mass and administer communion before Solomon was carted off to his death.[15]

That same day word reached Fort Mitchell via a reporter in Keysville, who took the story from the Associated Press wires and rode nine miles to the Pollard farm. Outside the Abernathy cabin he found Wilson loading a wagon. Unaware of his wife's new lease on life, Wilson had planned to rise early and take the children to see their mother for the last time.[16]

In Lunenburg Courthouse the villagers learned the execution was off when Cardozo returned empty-handed from Richmond. The news did not travel far into the countryside, however. The next day hundreds poured in from outlying districts—people attended executions in droves, even if they could not witness the actual hangings—only to discover that no one would die after all.[17]

*   *   *

NEXT TO SOLOMON Marable, John Mitchell, Jr., and Father Welbers, the happiest man in Richmond was William L. Royall, editorial writer for the *Richmond Times*. For days he had been calling for a new trial for Solomon as well as the women. "Let us have this whole business grubbed up," he wrote, "and a new start taken."[18]

Royall's essential backer in grubbing up the case was his friend, patron, and boss, the publisher of the *Times*, Joseph Bryan. They made an interesting team. Royall (Buck to his friends) was brilliant, mercurial, and often broke. Joseph Bryan, by contrast, was a man of steady habits, a masterful businessman who owned not only the *Times* but also significant interests in timber, mines, railroads, and real estate. He followed the same routine each day and at night fell asleep the moment he closed his eyes.[19]

Royall and Bryan shared two political passions: Their editorial page emphatically preached the gospels of sound money and honest elections, neither calculated to win friends in places like Lunenburg. Like farmers almost everywhere, Southsiders were fast embracing the cause of free silver, believing their deliverance from debt and depression depended on abolishing the gold standard and putting more money—lots of silver—into circulation. Royall and Bryan thought this was insanity. They were "goldbugs," men to whom the gold standard was sacred.

The issue of election fraud had a less apocalyptic feel; everyone agreed that elections should be honest. In practice, however, fraud ran rampant, especially in the Southside. After the war, when black men got the vote, the outmanned whites had done whatever seemed necessary to stay alive in politics. Some white office seekers, by habit or conviction Democrats, had courted the black vote by declaring themselves Republicans; Judge Orgain, among others, had initially run on the Republican ticket.[20] But in Lunenburg, as elsewhere, corruption ultimately carried the day.

The great wire pullers were railroad executives, who transferred funds to friendly politicians; the politicians in turn bought votes and once in office looked out for the railroads' interests. Where cash failed, polling place mayhem often succeeded: The victors stuffed ballot boxes, tossed out their opponents' ballots, or simply falsified the count, options that worked better after 1884, when a Democratic legislature arrogated to itself the power to appoint local election boards. An even uglier set of tactics included violence, threats of violence, race baiting, and arresting black men on bogus charges; any man convicted of a felony or even petty larceny lost his right to vote.[21]

By the 1890s the system was utterly corrupt. In some counties white Democrats routinely stole elections, not only from Republicans and Populists, but from each other as well. Corruption touched state-level offices too. Governor O'Ferrall was widely regarded as a man of principle, but fraud accounted for his large majority in 1893. Robert Allen, the Lunenburg diarist and farmer, made the point with a strategically placed dollar sign: O'Ferrall had been "Elected or rather counted in by a Majority of $45,000."[22]

Publisher Joseph Bryan made it his business to expose the full extent of crooked elections in Virginia. To this mission editorial writer Buck Royall contributed his customary rousing prose, happily lecturing the Southside on the fundamentals of democracy and injecting the entire subject with moral outrage.

The conduct of the Pollard murder trials gave him yet more opportunities to ride his high horse. And in Solomon Marable's case Royall meant to do more than editorialize. An attorney as well as a writer, Royall set out to get Solomon a new trial. If he had to, Royall promised, he would take the case all the way to the United States Supreme Court.[23]

*　　*　　*

WITH THE COLUMNS of both the *Planet* and the *Times* at their disposal, advocates for Solomon and the women gave new life to old questions about what had happened on June 14. Suddenly the white man story was back in the headlines, its plausibility enhanced by a finally consistent Solomon Marable.

"He made a noise at the door." Forty-eight hours before he was scheduled to hang, Solomon had made what he thought was his dying statement. With David Thompson pointing a gun at his head, Solomon said, the two of them had crept to the back of the Pollard house, Thompson standing on one side of the door, Solomon on the other. Just as Lucy Pollard came out, Thompson cut around the corner of the house.

> She saw his shadow [Solomon said]. She looked at it and commenced walking backwards. She backed upon me and I caught her by the hands. No sooner than I caught her by the hands and by the throat, he came back around there and he asked her, "Do you know me?" She said, "You are a white

man." Then he asked her how long Mr. Pollard had been back. I do not remember whether she said he had come back about 12 or before 12 o'clock. He says, "I come to kill Mr. Pollard, but I can't get a chance at him, so I'll kill you."[24]

Then he took up the axe and struck her three licks with the helve. As the first blow was descending, I turned her loose and he struck her two more blows with the helve after that. I jumped up. And he said, "Where in the hell are you going?" I told him I want going nowhere. Then he commenced hitting her with the axe part. Then after he got done hitting her with the axe, he said, "Where are you going?" I said, "I am going home." And he said, "No, you ain't, you've got to go with me."

Emboldened by the fine grain of Solomon's latest confession, the *Times* and *Planet* struck up a duet of accusations against David James Thompson. "A short time ago," said the *Times*, "he had some trouble with a negro man in Lunenburg, and stabbed the negro with a knife quite seriously, according to reliable information from a well-known citizen of Lunenburg. Thompson, realizing that the serious condition of the man's wounds would likely get him into trouble, paid the injured man a considerable sum of money to leave the county and go over into the state of North Carolina." The *Planet* chimed in with an even graver charge: that Thompson had killed a black man in Halifax County, forcing him to drink whiskey until he passed out and died.[25]

Anyone looking to clear Pokey and the two Marys would find encouragement in the revival of the white man story, especially in its consistency. At the very beginning, when Solomon had pinned Lucy Pollard's murder on the women, his story had changed every time he told it. The David Thompson story was different: Over time Solomon added detail, but his account was essentially the same from one rendition to the next. Either Solomon had learned to tell the same lie six consecutive times or he was telling the truth.

*　　*　　*

NEWSPAPERS IN THE 1890s sometimes made things up, but they did not invent David James Thompson. At twenty-nine, Thompson stood at middling height, with a wiry build and sharp facial features. He had long, sandy sideburns, longish, curly hair, and a mustache. He also had advantages. The white Thompsons were the biggest fish in the small pond of Finneywood, Virginia, about three miles south of Fort Mitchell, and David was heir to his deceased father's several enterprises. His subordinates called him the Boss.[26]

When the *Times* accused him of murder, Thompson quickly rose to defend his name. "Your paper makes me out a regular desperado," he wrote. "I was born October 16, 1866, on a farm known as Moore's Hill, not a half-mile from Finneywood, Va.; worked on same farm until June 11, '83, when I came to Finneywood, Va. . . . and commenced the mercantile business for my father." His father, James L. ("Jimmie") Thompson, had been a storekeeper, the Finneywood postmaster, and the local agent for the railroad, and David had served as his deputy in all three capacities. In 1893 his father died, or as David put it, "God, with His all-infinite mercy, saw cause to call him home." David James Thompson at age twenty-seven was named postmaster, railroad agent, and merchant in his father's place. "I have in my care both women and little children to look after, and give satisfaction to both white and colored."[27]

This might be called the respectability defense; postmasters evidently were not supposed to be capable of murder. But Thompson claimed to have an alibi as well. "As to my whereabouts on the 14th day of June, I never left my place of business during the whole day, which I can prove by more than a dozen men, of both white and colored, and if necessary I can have them sworn, and publish to the whole world."

No idle threat: On the first day of October a justice of the peace took affidavits from four witnesses. The statements were short and to the point. F. T. Thackston, a railroad employee, worked nearly all day on a section of track about two hundred yards from the depot. He saw David James Thompson at all hours on that day; he did not leave the place from one to seven. Joseph B. Davis farmed about a mile and a half from Finneywood. "On Friday, the 14th of June, he went to Finneywood about 4 o'clock in the afternoon, and there met Mr. David James Thompson, and was with him there until about 7 o'clock, when they walked out to a field to look for some sheep, and they separated about sundown, which was about 7:30 o'clock."[28]

Daniel Ellis was working in the garden next to Thompson's house, about a hundred yards from the depot; he too had seen Thompson at all hours and had gone with him to hunt sheep when the sun was about half an hour high. J. J. Watson, Thompson's clerk and deputy postmaster, added that Thompson was working within a few hundred yards of the store all day. Watson saw him every twenty minutes or so from 9:00 A.M. until 7:00 P.M.

Were David Thompson's witnesses telling the truth or circling the wagons? Their statements were taken more than a hundred days after the murder, ample time to cook up an alibi.

*   *   *

ON OCTOBER 7 the high court of Virginia spoke in the case of *Marable* v. *Commonwealth*. Still sitting in Staunton, the Supreme Court of Appeals granted Solomon Marable his writ of error and supersedeas. Now his case was "on all-fours" with those of the women; he too would have a chance for a new trial.[29]

When reporters told Solomon the news, he smiled but seemed subdued and more interested in other things. To the *Times* reporter he spoke mainly of his wife. John Mitchell, Jr., had sent Fannie a train ticket so that she might have a final visit with her husband, and Solomon had every day been hoping that she would appear. She had not come, however. A terse, depressing letter explained why.

"Sol:—" she wrote, "My mind is so troubled, I hardly know what to write, but I try to write something to let you hear from us. We all have been sick, but poor mother. She has been down with the fever and don't get no better. She has but little appetite at all. If you were to see her, you would hardly know her."

Fannie and her mother had been robbed too, possibly by someone looking for the Pollard money. The thief had cleaned them out, "didn't leave me with a piece of anything as big as my hand, and you talk about me coming to Richmond. I would look like a fool coming stark bare-footed, and beside I can't leave my little children and mother on her sick bed. Don't know how I can do any more. Fannie Marable."[30]

Mitchell made a note to send Fannie five dollars and headed for the jail to congratulate Solomon on the court's action. Mitchell also brought a gift, the photograph of Solomon he'd taken on a previous visit. The other inmates gathered around Solomon, searching the photo for glimpses of themselves and joking about one another's looks. Solomon expressed no interest in the court's decision. Instead he stood smiling at his likeness.[31]

CHAPTER

14

NUNC PRO TUNC

Chesapeake, Va., Sept. 10, 1895

Hon. John Mitchell, Jr.,

Dear Sir:—I heartily sympathize with the innocent women, so much so that I have made myself busy in trying to solicit aid. I have succeeded in collecting the following from the Mount Maria Tent, No. 35, $5.00; African Baptist Sunday School $5.00; A.M.E. Church, Capersville, Va., $1.65. Total amount collected by me, $11.65.

From one whose heart is bowed in grief and prayer for the innocent.

Hattie Spady.

Winifrede, W. Va., September 10, '95

Editor Mitchell:

My Dear Son—You will find by my dictate I am one of the old time slaves. Way back in the dark days we called a smart young man our son. The day the Almighty winked at ignorance, the day we only had buttermilk and claber and punkin out of a gourd. Now I am an old man past work. I can chop a little in peoples' gardens occasionally. I can hardly make my bread. I left Richmond about 13 years ago on the account of the small pox and I have never been able to get back. My wife is much younger than I am and she can work for us both. She weighs 200 pounds; she worked for A. E. Dickerson for 13 years and made many friends.

I had a few cents laid away for a rainy day, but reading your paper I thought it advisible to take a little and send it to you for those poor women, please find inclosed money order $2.00. I hope in a few days to be able to send you more.

Yours truly,

Rev. John Anderson.

Glendora, Cal., 1895

Mr. John Mitchell, Jr.,
Dear Sir:

Please find enclosed two dollars to aid in saving the three innocent women, Mary Barnes, Pokey Barnes and Mary Abernathy. The amount was sent by Mr. John Woolfolk and Susie Eva, my 12 year old daughter. Words cannot convey our appreciation of your noble service to the race. I am yours with best wishes,

J. L. Edmonds.

P.S. Each sends one dollar.

It felt like Christmas every time the postman came. Although the *Planet* circulated mainly in Virginia, John Mitchell, Jr., traded news with other black editors, and as a result, the mail brought money from all over the nation—even from Montana, where four troopers at a remote cavalry post had collected $3.25.[1]

The Women's League too worked connections beyond Richmond. One member visited Philadelphia and returned with fifty dollars. Marietta Chiles had headed toward the ocean, organizing a Women's League in the college town of Hampton and inspiring the staff of an immense resort hotel to launch a club of its own. Despite layoffs at the end of August, the hotel employees raised sixty-eight dollars.[2]

In Richmond itself the Women's League in its first six weeks raised more than three hundred dollars from its member organizations. John Mitchell, Jr., had meanwhile mobilized the city's black business and professional men, and the ministers among them took up numerous collections for the women's defense. Fraternal orders contributed as well: Galilean Fishermen and Good Samaritans as well as Odd Fellows and Mitchell's own order, the Knights of Pythias.[3]

None of these organizations was recognized in the white press. Black churches, mutual benefit societies, and fraternal orders encouraged thrift, mutual charity, and wholesome living, and as the Lunenburg case made plain, they could be mobilized in a larger cause. They were entirely incompatible with theories of white supremacy, and the white newspapers, even the comparatively friendly *Richmond Times*, ignored them.

Fortunately the capacity of Afro-Virginians to raise money did not depend on the notice or approval of white people. The Hampton Women's League sent in $175—Christmas again!—and with each issue of the *Planet*, the list of contributors grew.

* * *

IN EARLY OCTOBER Lunenburg once again struck back. The Board of Supervisors voted to hire a lawyer, one who could persuade the Supreme Court of Appeals that the original convictions must stand. They turned once again to the sagacious and senatorial William Hodges Mann.[4]

Mann went right to work. George Wise and his colleagues, he thought, had good instincts, but on the Pollard cases they were mostly blowing smoke, a hunch that Mann confirmed once he had time to study the authorities. On almost every point made by counsel for the women, Mann believed he could launch an effective counter-attack. Just one thing stood in his way.

The women's lawyers had probably been right about the keeping of juries. When a court adjourned at mid-trial, the judge did have to charge a sworn officer to keep the jury together, in the officer's custody, and apart from outsiders. Moreover, the judge's charge was to be written in the trial record.

In none of the Pollard murder trials did the record contain the necessary language, a critical omission, Mann feared, possibly enough to win new trials for the women and even for Solomon Marable.

Unless . . . Unless at this late date the necessary language could still be inserted into the record. Mann knew of only one way to get this done, a nunc pro tunc order from Judge Orgain. *Nunc pro tunc* is Latin for "now for then." In this instance it meant adding language to the record that should have been there all along. If Judge Orgain *remembered saying* the necessary words, he could still add them to the record. Or so Mann would contend. It was a rare move, and it would surprise the other side. They would fight it, of course, but if Mann won on the nunc pro tunc issue, he thought he could win the whole thing.[5]

*　　*　　*

MARY ABERNATHY AND Pokey Barnes had thus far had an autumn of comparative tranquillity. Since September 17, when the Supreme Court granted their writs of error, the terrible anxiety had given way to something more like impatience. Pokey crocheted and paced; Mary sat by the grate, sewing for her unborn baby and longing to be at work in her garden. Breaks in the routine helped. On two special days Mary got letters from her firstborn, twenty-four-year-old Samuel, who worked in the shipyards in Newport News. His letters, though short, brimmed with consideration for his mother. He had managed to collect five dollars for her defense, and to Lunenburg he sent clothing for the younger children. He promised to come to her next trial and invited her to come live with him when it was all over. "If you get clear of this I want you to come straight to me and never go back to that county any more."[6]

Also, Joseph Barnes visited one day. Shy and near speechless, he handed Pokey a little gift wrapped in paper—a banana, as it turned out. Bananas were luxury food, exotic, wildly popular, and not easy to get in places like Lunenburg. Pokey was touched.[7]

It was too good to last. On October 21 the women learned that Judge Orgain wanted them back in Lunenburg. He wanted Solomon too.

The motor behind this gut-wrenching news was William Hodges Mann's request for a nunc pro tunc order. After giving due notice, Mann had gone to Lunenburg and asked Judge Orgain to amend the records in the Pollard murder trials. The judge professed himself willing to do so but feared his order would have no legal force unless he acted with the prisoners present in his courtroom. Orgain therefore ordered Sheriff Cardozo to "produce the bodies" of Solomon Marable, Mary Abernathy, and Pokey Barnes when the next session of the county court opened on November 11.[8]

Sheriff Cardozo happened to be in Richmond when the news broke and swiftly let it be known that this time he would not call for a military guard. His county already smarted from the attacks by the Richmond press; he was not about to insult the citizenry further by calling in troops to do a job they could very well do themselves. If the governor wanted soldiers, let the governor himself order them out—and let the governor take the inevitable heat.[9]

Governor O'Ferrall was on a train to Atlanta. When he got there, he sent a one-sentence telegram to the *Dispatch*: "I have given directions that the prisoners shall not go without military escort."[10] Legally speaking, he had no authority to issue such an order. Jurisdiction over the prisoners belonged entirely to Judge Orgain, who had every right to call them back to Lunenburg. In addition, the governor had no right to order out troops unless the sheriff formally requested them. What had begun as a stroke of creative litigation on the part of William Hodges Mann was fast escalating into a crisis.

*   *   *

How dangerous was Lunenburg? Mary Abernathy and Pokey Barnes told reporters that they expected to die at the hands of a mob. Once upon a time, perhaps, their sex would have afforded them some protection. But epidemics tended to claim new kinds of victims as they spread. Six months earlier three women and two men, all black, had been lynched in Alabama after a white farmer was found murdered. "Lynching women!" John Mitchell had written. "High heaven is there to be no rest for the weary, or protection for the guiltless?"[11] Significantly, none of the Richmond papers ever suggested that Pokey Barnes and Mary Abernathy were unlikely to be lynched because they were female.

Lunenburg's defenders meantime argued that there would be no lynching simply because Lunenburg did not operate that way. In this claim the past was on the county's side; no one had died at the hands of a mob in living memory. Yet only a month earlier two unnerving incidents had been reported in the Richmond press.

One story originated in a contention over rent between a black man named Allen Watts and a white man named Ashworth; Ashworth, his brother, and a third white man got to drinking, and the three decided to teach Allen Watts a lesson. They called him out of his house and beat him half to death, then broke into his house, intending to assault his wife also. The wife, Jennie Watts, managed to escape and called the law down on her husband's assailants. MORE LUNENBURG LAWLESSNESS, read the headline.[12]

Another September story concerned an alleged sexual assault in a farmhouse just a few miles from the Pollard place. One evening a white family, all except for the nine-year-old daughter, had been at work in their curing barn about 150 yards from the house. Their black employee, fifteen-year-old Wesley Winfield, went up to the house for supper and found the nine-year-old in bed asleep. She got up to serve his meal and then went back to bed. After he ate, the charges went, Wesley Winfield attempted an assault on the girl but was interrupted by the mother, who had just come in from the barn. The boy ran out the back door, but the girl's father soon caught him. The father wanted to kill him. The mother begged the father to desist.[13]

Wesley Winfield was turned over to a justice of the peace, given a hearing, and put in charge of a deputy to be delivered to the county jail. About two miles short of Lunenburg Courthouse, the deputy and his charge were intercepted by two men on horseback. The men were not masked; the deputy later claimed he did not know them. The men brandished pistols at the deputy and took young Winfield into the woods. The first reports out of Lunenburg speculated that Wesley Winfield was dead. Later reports said he was alive, that he had been thrashed and then let go.

Was this due process? No. Was Wesley Winfield proved guilty? No. Would most white people think it served justice? Yes, especially because it spared a child and her respectable mother a courtroom experience nearly as humiliating as the crime itself. So what would happen to Pokey Barnes? Or Mary Abernathy? Or Solomon Marable, who had, after all, confessed to murder?

*　　*　　*

THE NIGHT OF Friday, November 8, was gloomy and strangely warm in Richmond. Sheriff Cardozo and two deputies arrived well after dark and went straight to their hotel. Cardozo's orders were clear. On Monday, three days hence, he must produce Mary Abernathy, Pokey Barnes, and Solomon Marable in Judge Orgain's courtroom.

All eyes turned to Governor O'Ferrall. On Saturday morning he rose early and ordered militia units in Petersburg and Danville to fall in for a mission to Lunenburg. Richmond soldiers would not do. People in Lunenburg were still embittered against the Richmond militia, especially against Frank Cunningham, who was widely believed to have planted the white man story in Solomon Marable's impressionable brain, and some thought the soldiers had gotten away with the stolen money. From the city of Richmond, Governor O'Ferrall mobilized only the hospital corps, whose free clinic had won the gratitude of Lunenburgers during the trials in July.[14]

All day long the governor stayed shut up in his office in intense deliberations with his advisers. Whatever his course, he anticipated trouble. If he sent the military to Lunenburg, the whole state would yowl about the expense. If he sent the military without a formal request from Sheriff Cardozo, it would be worse. O'Ferrall would clearly be exceeding his statutory authority. He would be accused of tyranny—and rightly so. He also had to consider Sheriff Cardozo's opinion: The surest way to incite the mob was to send troops where they were not wanted.[15]

By nightfall the chamber just outside the governor's office looked like a war room. Hats in hand, all the high-ranking officers in the Virginia militia awaited the governor's orders. O'Ferrall was still inside, cooped up with his attorney general and churning over the options, all of them dangerous.

The governor finally emerged at 10:30 P.M. "The prisoners will not be taken back to Lunenburg," he said to the assembled officers. "Issue orders to the troops who are awaiting orders to disband." Then the governor dispatched a message to the jail. "Do not deliver the Lunenburg convicts to M. C. Cardozo, sheriff, as heretofore instructed, but retain them until I communicate with and hear from Judge Orgain."[16]

O'Ferrall would try to get the judge on board, to persuade him that the nunc pro tunc proceeding could go forward in Lunenburg without the prisoners present. The women's lawyers had already tried this, availing nothing. But O'Ferrall believed that a personal plea, hand-delivered by courier, would bring the judge around.[17]

In the meantime the governor spoke to the press, explaining the extraordinary thing he had just done. The constitution, he said, made it his duty to execute the laws of Virginia. Mob violence was against the law. By acting to prevent an outbreak of mob violence, he was merely doing his constitutional duty.[18]

Legally, this was weak. But Mary Abernathy, Pokey Barnes, and Solomon Marable would live to see at least one more day.

*   *   *

ON SUNDAY MORNING a northeaster pressed down on the city. Sheriff Cardozo and his deputies made their way to the jail through diagonal rain, proceeding immediately to the office of the man in charge, City Sergeant Charles Epps. John Mitchell, Jr., was already there, along with Mary Abernathy and Pokey Barnes, who stood by in their Sunday clothes, gazing upon their enemy.[19]

The sheriff fished his orders out of his pocket and handed them over. Adjusting his spectacles, Sergeant Epps read them, then spoke. "I have an order from the governor directing me to hold these prisoners. I am sorry, I would like to oblige you, Mr. Cardozo."

Cardozo inspected the governor's order, written in a bold, square hand by O'Ferrall himself. "Then you refuse to deliver these prisoners to me?"

"I do."

With nothing further to say, sheriff and deputies went back out into the rain and caught the noon train to Burkeville.

Cardozo had been too clever by half. He had counted on the governor's sending troops, calculating that as sheriff he would benefit from the military escort without suffering the political consequences of calling for it himself. So sure had he been of the governor that Cardozo had arranged transportation to carry the troops from the Burkeville station to Lunenburg Courthouse.

In the village of Burkeville twelve two-horse wagons and their dripping teams stood in line at the station. It had been raining all day. The train carrying Cardozo and the two deputies—and no prisoners and no troops—arrived in midafternoon. Cardozo retrieved his buggy and headed home, his humiliation accented by the squeaks and rattles of wagons returning empty to the farms from which they had come.[20]

*   *   *

GOVERNOR O'FERRALL SHOULD perhaps have known better than to mess with Lunenburg. The county had a reputation for going its own way and a nickname, the Old Free State, to match—both products of the secession crisis. Virginia did not leave the Union until April 1861, after President Lincoln had called on the state for troops to quell the rebellion in the deeper South. But influential citizens of Lunenburg were hot for secession from the beginning. In January 1861, with South Carolina, Mississippi, and Alabama already out of the Union, a mass meeting in Lunenburg urged Virginia to go out with them. Young Cornelius Tacitus Allen—Robert Allen's son and a chip off the old block—roused the crowd with a fire-eating ultimatum: If Virginia refused to secede from the Union, then Lunenburg should secede from Virginia. "Yes," someone shouted, "and set up a Free State of our own!" With varying touches of sarcasm and affection, the press had referred to Lunenburg as the Old Free State ever since.[21]

In 1895 the Old Free State was not about to surrender to a pack of arrogant busybodies in the capital. Ignoring the governor's personal plea, Judge Orgain upheld the dignity of his court, insisting on the prisoners' immediate return to Lunenburg. Once again Orgain sent Sheriff Cardozo to retrieve them. Once again Governor O'Ferrall put the military on alert.[22]

The deadlock between governor and judge touched off a frenzy of litigation, first in Lunenburg and then in Richmond, where the lawyers ricocheted between the circuit court and the Supreme Court of Appeals. Would the prisoners stay or go? The lawyers put on one show after another, seven proceedings in thirteen days, unfolding daily in the press like installments of a serial novel.[23]

At length, on November 22, the Supreme Court of Appeals swept the entire issue off the table, the high court itself taking custody of the prisoners. Solomon, Pokey, and the two Marys, said the court, all would stay put until the court decided the two central questions. First, could the court of Lunenburg lawfully amend the record to show that the juries had been properly kept? Second, would Pokey Barnes, the two Marys, and Solomon Marable, any or all, be granted new trials?[24]

The following week, just before Thanksgiving, the lawyers returned to the Supreme Court's elegant new courtroom to argue those two fundamental issues. They talked for two days, from beginning to end playing to a packed house. When the five justices had heard enough, they retired to their consulting room, where they worked together around an oak table, a fireplace giving them extra warmth and soft light. No one expected a decision for at least a week.[25]

*　　*　　*

JOHN MITCHELL, JR., had not visited Mary Barnes in ages. In the first week of December he made his way to the penitentiary to see her, his unpleasant mission to ask her to drop her quest for a new trial.

Although Mary Barnes was surviving, she was lonely and often depressed. She had long since become the stepchild among the Lunenburg prisoners, partly because her situation lacked urgency; ten years in the penitentiary was hard duty, but she was not facing execution. She also lacked the personal appeal that drew reporters to Pokey and Mary Abernathy. She had nothing to match Pokey's spunk or Mary Abernathy's way with words. None of the newspapers had reported any fresh news on Mary Barnes in months.

Mary Barnes had been abandoned by the press, and now Mitchell was asking her to give up her place before the bar of justice. With his three attorneys he had worked it through: Bad as prison was, Mary was safe there from mob violence. If she returned to Lunenburg for retrial, she might be lynched. If she were tried again and found guilty, the jury might give her a prison sentence even longer than the one she was already serving, and if it found her guilty of first-degree murder, her sentence would be death. If, on the other hand, she sat tight, and the attorneys won acquittals for Pokey and Mary Abernathy, she would have an excellent case for pardon by the governor.[26]

In the end it took little persuading. Mary Barnes told Mitchell that she never wanted to see Lunenburg again. She made her X on the petition and urged him to come see her more often.

*   *   *

THE SUPREME COURT of Appeals ruled on December 12, six months after Lucy Pollard's murder. After the court had disposed of several other cases, Judge Buchanan spoke in *Barnes* v. *Commonwealth*, the appeal brought in Pokey's name but understood to apply to Solomon and Mary Abernathy as well.[27]

First, in regard to Lunenburg's desire to amend the record, this could not be done. The judge was a "living record" of the proceedings in his courtroom during the term of his court; during the term, therefore, he could alter the record according to his memory. But memory would inevitably fade. The critical moment came at term's end, when the judge's mind would naturally close on the matters he had recently concluded.

The trial records would stand as they were, absent the new language Lunenburg wanted concerning the keeping of the juries. This, as William Hodges Mann had been shrewd enough to foresee, was the key issue. Judge Buchanan turned to the errors alleged by counsel for the women and dismissed them one by one—until he came to the question of the keeping of the jury during adjournments.

Did the record have to *say* how the jury was kept? This question had never before been decided in the Supreme Court of Appeals. The court had therefore examined trial records of recent capital cases to see what standard procedure in fact was. "They show," said Buchanan, "that the jury at each adjournment of the court was placed in the custody of the sheriff or other proper officer, with instructions not to speak to them himself, nor to allow any one else to speak to them, touching the trial. We think this may therefore be regarded as the settled practice in this State. . . . We think it may be safely said that any practice so salutary and wise . . . and which has been uniformly pursued for a great length of time, ought to be regarded as showing what the law is on the subject."[28]

Inasmuch as the record from Lunenburg failed to show proper custody of the jury, "the judgment of the trial court must be reversed, the verdict set aside, and a new trial awarded."

Mary Barnes, having withdrawn her appeal, would stay in the penitentiary. Pokey Barnes, Mary Abernathy, and Solomon Marable would remain in custody—in Lunenburg if Judge Orgain called for them—but they would get new trials.

The deputy jailer broke the glad news to his three Lunenburg prisoners, and John Mitchell, Jr., came by later to add his congratulations. Solomon had taken to wearing his rosary around his neck; Mitchell found him "as stoical as usual." The women, however, were wide awake, all smiles, reiterating their innocence, chafing to be set free. Mary Abernathy, more than eight months pregnant, delighted in the photographs Mitchell brought of her eldest son, Samuel. "Lor' there's my child!" she said. And she retreated into the cellblock to show her friends.[29]

CHAPTER

15

NEW LIFE

B essie Mitchell Abernathy came into the world on New Year's Day, her unusual birthplace the Richmond city jail. The guards were tickled and set up mother and child as comfortably as they could. Pokey, separated from her own small daughter for six months, installed herself as nanny. The jail physician wrote immediately to Judge Orgain: Mary Abernathy and her newborn had come through well, but Mary would not be fit to travel for several weeks.[1]

The next day John Mitchell, Jr., came to see Lunenburg's littlest prisoner, rejoicing with Mary and Pokey over the child's safe advent, sharing their relief that their return to Lunenburg would be delayed. Judge Orgain could order Pokey and Solomon back as soon as he received papers certifying the award of new trials, papers expected within the week. The lawyers, however, believed the judge would take the most economical course, waiting until Mary could travel— five weeks at least—and then send for Solomon and both women at the same time.[2] After that the lawyers would do their utmost to get Judge Orgain to order a change of venue. If they succeeded, their clients would be tried in some other county by some other judge. If they failed, the trials would again be held in Judge Orgain's court.

The baby would go to Lunenburg too. In the meantime she was the jail's infant princess, passed the day long from one set of eager arms to the next. She was cuddled, sung to, walked, rocked, and fussed over almost nonstop by thirty women inmates, several of them mothers themselves. They would miss her terribly when she was taken away.

* * *

THREE WEEKS PASSED. In deep winter the sun set by five o'clock, and the inmates went to bed early. Pokey Barnes was therefore sound asleep at 10:00 P.M. when a key turned the lock of her cell door. As she struggled up from sleep, she heard the jailer telling her she had ten minutes.

Mary Abernathy woke up too. Pokey asked her, Did Mr. Mitchell know about this? Mary Abernathy said she thought not. As soon as Pokey was dressed, the jailer came back for her. No time to pack anything. Pokey asked Mary to look after her things and to tell her father where she had gone.

Then Pokey made a regal departure, walking along the women's cellblock, shaking hands through the bars with all who were awake, asking them to pray for her. In the jailer's office Sheriff Cardozo waited with Solomon and a deputy from Lunenburg. A reporter asked her how she felt about going back. "If I must go," she said, "I must, and there ain't no use grieving about it."[3] Pokey's self-possession was perfect, even in the moment of gross indignity when she was handcuffed to Solomon. As the carriage rolled toward the train station, however, she broke down, shaking all over and crying bitterly. Cardozo tried to comfort her, an awkward gesture from a man doing his best to see her hanged.

Their train arrived in Blackstone at two in the morning, the rain falling in sheets. Cardozo decided to wait for daylight to start across the country. He took Pokey and Solomon to a hotel, where Pokey spent the night sitting up in a chair.

In the morning she could not eat her breakfast. Cardozo had it wrapped for her and, having decided not to wait out the rain, set out at nine. Solomon and the deputy went ahead in a buggy. Pokey rode with the sheriff. Although their buggy had a roof, rain blew in the front and side, soaking Pokey's arm and the front of her skirt.

They churned along for hours, wheels at times miring down to their hubs. When they came to the last creek, with the worst ford, the deputy and Solomon decided to swim their team across. Cardozo did not trust his young horse. He turned upriver to seek a safer crossing, adding several miles to their journey.

In midafternoon they pulled up at Fowlkes Brothers' store in Lunenburg Courthouse, where indifference—a studied indifference perhaps—seemed the order of the day. Cardozo took Pokey and Solomon into the store, where they sat slumped and exhausted, drying out by the big stove while the sheriff's men installed new wood stoves in their jail cells. As Pokey and Solomon were escorted to the jail, they could not help noticing that the scaffold built for Solomon in September was still standing. A few yards off was a rectangular hole in the ground, filling with muddy water. Solomon's grave had stood open for four months.

Cardozo had outfoxed everyone. John Mitchell, Jr., and the women's attorneys were caught completely off guard, unaware that Pokey and Solomon had been taken away until they read about it in the papers the next day. From the press also came word that Pokey and Solomon remained unharmed; on the jail's first floor seven men armed with double-barreled shotguns guarded them around the clock. Pokey had sent a message through a reporter: "I want Aunt Mary to know I got here all right."[4]

But Pokey was not all right. She was frightened all the time, and within a day or two of her soggy journey she came down with pneumonia.

* * *

It rained again two weeks later, when Sheriff Cardozo returned to Richmond for Mary Abernathy. He had given her a day's notice, a

Pregnant at the time of the murder, Mary Abernathy gave birth in the Richmond city jail on New Year's Day, 1896. In this photograph Bessie Mitchell Abernathy was five weeks old.

PHOTO FROM THE *RICHMOND PLANET,* 18 APRIL 1896, COURTESY OF THE LIBRARY OF VIRGINIA.

courtesy that allowed her time to prepare for her journey. Several of her supporters came to pray and wish her well. John Mitchell, Jr., brought his camera and, despite the poor light, took a portrait of mother and child. On the morning of February 6 Cardozo arrived at the jail to take Mary away.[5]

At the train station they made a short procession. Mary walked in front holding the baby, who was awake and wriggling. Cardozo came next; behind him a black porter carried the sheriff's suitcase and packages accumulated in a day of shopping. On the platform a reporter remarked upon the absence of any guards, just the opening Cardozo wanted. "No guards needed for this prisoner or any other," the sheriff replied. "All the talk about Lunenburg was a pack of lies."[6]

Their train arrived in Burkeville just after noon. Waiting for them in the rain stood a plain two-horse wagon with no cover at all. For a seat it had only a wooden plank. Mary took out some money her Richmond friends had given her and asked the sheriff to buy her an umbrella to cover her little daughter.

A single deputy drove the wagon, Cardozo following behind. In all the low spots, the earth was sheeted with water. The wagon rumbled and bounced over tree stumps that felt as if they were a foot high. One ferocious jolt broke Mary's seat. She rode the rest of the way in the wagon bed, still holding the umbrella over her five-week-old child. How they made it to Lunenburg Courthouse she could scarcely tell.

The point, Cardozo would have said, was that they *did* make it, the only dangers those posed by ugly weather and miry roads. Lunenburg was vindicated again.

*   *   *

ON A FROSTY February morning, four days after Mary Abernathy's return to Lunenburg, nearly two thousand people streamed into the courthouse, their mood lifted by the sunshine and bracing cold that had suddenly displaced the rain and fog. The village looked its best on this dazzling day. Conscious that reporters would descend on their county, the normally tightfisted Board of Supervisors had fixed up the courthouse, replacing cracked windowpanes and crumbling chimney bricks and painting all the woodwork, including the trademark exterior staircase. The courtroom had been painted too and sported a dozen brand-new spittoons.[7]

The brisk day contrasted with the plodding proceedings. Court did not open until after the noon meal. Judge Orgain then ordered Solomon Marable, Mary Abernathy, and Pokey Barnes into the courtroom. The guards took their time, clanking up the stairs with their three prisoners. Pokey, whose health had been closely monitored by a local doctor, looked nearly recovered from her pneumonia.

Wide-bodied Henry Flournoy, of all the lawyers in the room the most famous orator, stood up. He was not supposed to make a speech, but he started to make one anyway, and the judge let him proceed, as the defense attorney clearly meant to spread oil on the waters. Contrary to rumor, Flournoy said, his team did not represent the self-confessed murderer Solomon Marable (who had no attorney at this proceeding). They did not intend to implicate anyone new in the murder. Moreover, if at any time they became persuaded of the women's guilt, they would resign. As for the good people of Lunenburg, Flournoy had no ill feeling toward them, but he did believe they had prejudged the case, and thus his clients were entitled to a change of venue.

When Flournoy finally sat, George Wise questioned a string of witnesses, all men, all white. Do you think an impartial jury can be impaneled in this county? How many men have you heard express an opinion on the guilt or innocence of my clients? How many believe them guilty? Does anyone think them innocent?

He got muddy answers. Most testified that sentiment in the county ran against the women, but they still believed it possible to impanel an impartial jury. At one point Judge Orgain tossed out a rowdy drunk. Otherwise the afternoon was exceedingly quiet.

The next morning attendance at court was radically smaller. Of the 2,000 people who had packed the village the previous day, approximately 1,960 had returned to their kitchens and fields. That, it turned out, was the point. The attorneys had been stalling, probably in collusion with Judge Orgain, playing for time until all the spectators left town. Now Wise and Flournoy bore down, posing very pointed questions. Colin Bagley, who often served as deputy sheriff, took the stand first.[8]

"If these women are tried in Lunenburg by a jury from this or any other county," Wise asked, "and with the same evidence as at the former trial, and are acquitted, will they be safe?"

Bagley squirmed and managed a double negative. "I would not say they would not be harmed."

Wise pressed. "If you yourself were in the same position as my clients, would you worry about what would happen to you after you were acquitted and released?"

"I would be worried," Bagley said. "In fact, I would not like to be tried in this county at all."

Several witnesses had already rendered risky service as guards and drivers, and if the new trials were held in Lunenburg, they would likely do so again.[9] To a man, they expressed doubts about the women's safety. Judge Orgain listened as his police force, such as it was, folded. Then, in the fading light of a winter afternoon, Sheriff Cardozo himself took the stand. This time Flournoy asked the questions. If Mary Abernathy and Pokey Barnes were acquitted, would they be safe?

"I am very doubtful on this subject," Cardozo replied. "This point has worried me greatly."

Could the sheriff guarantee the women's safe conduct out of the county?

"I don't know about that. I would do my duty. On the whole I think it would be difficult to get them out."

When the last witness stood down, Judge Orgain turned to Solomon Marable, informing him that he too could move for a change of venue. Solomon nodded his assent. It was dark by this time, and the judge sent everyone off to supper, promising to announce his decision in the morning.

Two hours later the lawyers were quietly summoned from their hotel, called back into court with Mary, Pokey, and Solomon. Solomon had new shoes on. Hardly anyone else was there, just guards and a lone reporter.[10]

Holding his paper to catch the lamplight, Judge Orgain read his order, phrased in the traditional language of the law. "This day came again the prisoners, Pokey Barnes and Mary Abernathy, in the custody of the sheriff of this county, and the court, having fully heard the evidence and argument of counsel . . . doth sustain the motion made by the prisoners to change the venue, and doth order that the venue be changed in these cases to the County Court of Prince Edward." The judge then entered a separate order for Solomon, who would also be sent to Prince Edward for trial.

Before they knew it, Solomon, Pokey, and Mary with her baby found themselves moving through the woods, the sheriff and seven other armed men riding ahead and behind. The night was frigid and clear, with only a sliver of a moon. Pokey and Mary feared they might be lynched. But after several hours' travel they emerged at Burkeville. When the westbound train arrived, the sheriff took them aboard, with all the guards and weapons. At 2:45 A.M. they debarked in Farmville, the county seat of Prince Edward.

Compared with Lunenburg Courthouse, Farmville looked like a metropolis; in the darkness they could just make out several dozen stores along Main Street. They had to wake the man in charge of the jail. As he took out his keys to lock up the famous Lunenburg prisoners, they wondered what sort of place this might be, with a colored man for a jailer.[11]

*　　*　　*

IN AN IDEAL world the new trials would have been held far from the scene of the crime, in a county well out of the Southside. But in 1896 transporting the witnesses was simply too daunting. At the first trials it had been a hardship for some witnesses to travel halfway across the county. There was no thought of trying to get them halfway across Virginia.

So Solomon first, then Mary Abernathy and Pokey Barnes would take their chances in Prince Edward, a Southside county bordering Lunenburg on the northwest. The two counties had much in common, perhaps too much to suit the defense. Both depended on tobacco and upon a largely black labor force to grow it. In both, the conduct of politics was raucous and often crooked, as their white minorities had scratched and clawed their way to dominance, perpetrating sufficient fraud to neutralize the black vote and dislodge most black officeholders. Not surprisingly, newspaper coverage of the Pollard murder suggested that the powerful whites in Prince Edward identified strongly with their fellows in Lunenburg.[12]

The wild card, though, was Farmville, home to twenty-five hundred people—significantly, the minimum needed for the Census Bureau to rate a place as "urban." Farmville offered prospects not available in thoroughly rural Lunenburg. To blacks, the town offered a measure of economic opportunity and a chance to pull together in common cause. To whites, Farmville offered higher learning, with a men's college (Hampden-Sydney) close by, and in the town itself "the Normal," where women earned their teaching credentials. Farmville had two bookstores, an opera house, and a newspaper. "Cosmopolitan" would be taking it too far, but Farmville could occasionally sprout a new idea.[13]

On the outskirts of town stood the tobacco businesses that made it go—warehouses where farmers sold their harvests, and factories, wooden buildings three and four stories high, where black women and boys stripped leaves from stems. For Mary Abernathy and Pokey Barnes, however, the essential Farmville would be found in three buildings at the town's center: the blocky old jail, the First Baptist

Church, and the compact county courthouse. Built in 1872, after the heyday of the Roman revival had passed, the Prince Edward courthouse made the most of the curve. The base of the bell tower was shaped like a hoopskirt, the bell itself could be seen through an open archway, and sheltering the bell was a quaint little roof, itself bell-shaped.[14] The effect of the whole was charming. The trials of Solomon, Mary, and Pokey were to be held in a building that suggested, incongruously, a doll's house.

Next door stood the First Baptist Church, the indisputable center of black Farmville's political and social life. From Mary and Pokey's first day in Farmville, the church's women got busy, offering company, clothing, and gifts. Jailer Edward Matthews also belonged to First Baptist. Besides running the jail, he farmed, sold wood, and made buggy whips, enterprises that had helped him educate his children and buy a comfortable house on Main Street. Matthews was exceptional but not unique; other black proprietors ran a brickworks, a steam laundry, several grocery stores, the town's biggest meat market, three restaurants, and a small hotel, examples of what ambition and grit could achieve only a generation after slavery.[15]

For their part, Mary Abernathy and Pokey Barnes were delighted to have landed in Farmville. The jail was close to crumbling—a "regular shackledown," as the local paper put it—but the two women enjoyed light and air in their roomy second-floor cell. They had new bedsteads and mattresses, three chairs, a stove, and windows on three sides; the sun shone in most of the day.[16]

They felt unspeakable relief to be out of Lunenburg, where they had slept fitfully and started at every odd noise. Credit for their deliverance was due to many—not least, Judge Orgain, Sheriff Cardozo, and the sheriff's men. Governor O'Ferrall played a key part as well. Back in December, when the General Assembly convened in Richmond for its biannual session, the governor had pushed for tough new legislation to combat lynching.[17] Two weeks later, after the Supreme Court granted the Lunenburg prisoners new trials, O'Ferrall approached the legislature again. Fearful that the court's decision placed the prisoners in greater danger than ever, the governor asked for authority to send out the militia on his own, whether local sheriffs asked for it or not. He pressed for speedy action, hoping his bill would pass in time for him to send the militia back to Lunenburg Courthouse.[18]

The General Assembly balked at both proposals, but the governor had made his point nevertheless. Placed on the defensive, the delegates from Lunenburg pledged that local citizens would guarantee the prisoners' safety. The citizens in turn backed their representatives in a mass meeting at the courthouse, where they passed a series of resolutions composed by Cass Gregory. "We hereby pledge ourselves . . . we pledge ourselves . . . we further pledge ourselves." With each promise, the citizens staked more of their collective reputation on keeping the peace.[19]

The governor had done something remarkable. He had gone a long way toward modernizing the concept of honor, separating it from vengeance and hot blood, and reattaching it to self-restraint and the rule of law. It was a neat operation, one that could have been performed only by a soldier.

*   *   *

ONE WEEK AFTER Solomon, Pokey, Mary, and baby Bessie were delivered to the Prince Edward jail, a windstorm ripped through Farmville in the morning and Lunenburg at midday, flattening fences and trees, sucking embers right out of fireplaces, and touching off wildfires in pastures and fields.[20]

Behind the winds came a rumor: A lynching was planned for this very night. When the storm abated, Farmville's black clergymen called on their county judge and asked him to strengthen security around the jail. Although the judge promised them that he would take all necessary precautions, they feared he would not do enough. By sundown fifty black men had assembled at First Baptist, some to guard the jail, others posted on the roads. They watched until dawn.[21]

True to form, the *Dispatch* dismissed their fears as "a foolish apprehension on the part of the colored population of the town." The people, however, kept their own counsel. The next night and on all the winter nights that followed, Pokey, Mary, and Solomon could lie down to sleep, knowing that the men of the church stayed awake, patrolling the streets and roads of Farmville to keep them safe.[22]

CHAPTER

16

"A GONE CASE"

T he second trial of Solomon Marable for the murder of Lucy Jane Pollard commenced on March 16, 1896. After two days of testimony and eighteen minutes' deliberation, the jury found Solomon guilty of murder in the first degree.

The trial was less one-sided this time; Solomon had lawyers, two white Republicans from neighboring counties (whom no one claimed responsibility for hiring). They mounted an impressive defense, portraying Solomon not as innocent but rather as a weak man controlled by a mind or minds stronger than his own. They also kept picking at the nagging, scabby questions. Why had Edward Pollard and Austin Clements not seen Lucy Pollard's body when they came through the front gate? A white man had been implicated. Why had he not been investigated? Above all, where was the money? "There is mystery upon mystery," the lawyers said. Nothing would be cleared up by hanging Solomon Marable.[1]

The jury nevertheless bought the prosecution's case, one very like that made in Solomon's first trial. Witnesses laid out Solomon's movements in the days after Lucy Pollard's death: his possession of the suspicious twenty-dollar bills, the letter and cash he sent to himself from Chase City, his flight and capture. Most damaging, the jury heard his confession, though not from Solomon himself, who sat mute throughout his trial. Instead Cass Gregory did the honors, quoting from memory the substance of Solomon's words at his first trial. "I caught Mrs. Pollard by the wrist and put my hand up toward her throat. I then caught her by the throat and Pokey Barnes struck her three times with a stick. Mary Abernathy struck her with an axe."[2]

Nothing Solomon's lawyers said could overcome the power of Solomon's own confession. So, as the prosecution had predicted, "Marable is a gone case."[3] At the request of Solomon's attorneys, the judge postponed sentencing until after the women's trials. But everyone knew there was only one punishment for first-degree murder.

After his conviction Solomon was taken back to his ground-floor cell, a high-security cage barely wide enough for a bed. The close quarters did not seem to matter to Solomon, who turned to music and communing with his creator. He prayed a great deal. Occasionally he tried to study a simplified Bible that Father Welbers had brought him. Much of the time he lay on his cot, twanging on a mouth harp he had asked the jailer to buy for him. Other times he sang the spirituals of his youth, especially those about the afterlife. "I'll Soon Be Home over There," he sang, and "We Will Be at Rest on Judgment Day." Eventually he let it be known that he no longer wished to see Father Welbers but longed instead to see his old preacher from back home in North Carolina.

Solomon Marable was changing back into a Baptist.[4]

*   *   *

SNOW FELL ON April 9. Thus far it had been a "backward spring," as the farmers lamented: windy, wet, and cold. As if in perverse answer to their complaints, the weather suddenly turned, walloping the

Southside with record heat. A week after the season's last snow, the temperature spiked to ninety-four degrees. "It will surely form an Epoch in the weather history of this country," wrote farmer Robert Allen in his diary. "Oh it is oppressive, on laboring men and teams!"[5]

And, he might have added, on officers of the law and their quarry. On April 16 and 17 Thomas Dickinson scoured the baking landscape between Fort Mitchell and Chase City in search of witnesses for the trials of Mary Abernathy and Pokey Barnes. The trials should have gone forward a month earlier, right after Solomon's, but two dozen witnesses had failed to appear.

Dickinson, Prince Edward's forty-five-year-old county sheriff, did not look like a tough guy; the big mustache that slanted down to his jawline failed to disguise a weak chin and prominent Adam's apple. He carried a gun, however, as did his two deputies. Together they meant to collar the essential witnesses and haul them bodily to Farmville.[6]

Locating them proved a challenge in itself. Pokey's younger sisters, Rena and Rosa Barnes, did not even live in a house. They had been sent to the county poorhouse but refused to stay there and had become outlaws, camped in the woods near Chase City. Rena at seventeen was eight months pregnant with no husband in sight. And both had gotten in more trouble with the law, convicted in tandem for assaulting another woman. Rena had also been convicted of petty larceny.[7]

In the end Dickinson rounded up the Barnes sisters, seven other blacks, and two whites, none of whom wanted to testify, plus a black preacher who hitched a ride in hopes of reclaiming Solomon for the Baptist faith. Forty-eight hours before Mary Abernathy's trial was to

Thomas Dickinson, Sheriff of
Prince Edward County, Virginia.
IMAGE FROM THE *RICHMOND DISPATCH*, 17 MARCH 1896, COURTESY OF THE LIBRARY OF VIRGINIA.

begin, a pair of wagons bearing the witnesses creaked into the courthouse square in Farmville. The jail was already crowded. Not knowing where else to put them, Sheriff Dickinson stashed the witnesses
in the courthouse itself.

*　　*　　*

EARLY MONDAY MORNING, long before the first rap of the gavel, the
Prince Edward courtroom already told a story. Lengthwise down the
room's center, two parallel railings, which had gone up for Solomon
Marable's trial, created a passageway; blacks must stay on one side,
whites on the other—this, said the *Times*, to "avoid confusion and
anything like bad feeling." The judge had also ordered the benches
taken out, to discourage chronic loungers and make more room for
spectators. With benches gone and all standing room filled, the
courtroom held about three hundred people.[8]

The section reserved for black spectators was packed, the white
side less so, when Mary Abernathy's trial opened at two-thirty on
Monday, April 20. Mary sat at the defendant's table holding baby
Bessie, now nearly four months old. Jail life was not agreeing with
the child; "the small black mite," said the *Times*, "seems to have
grown smaller instead of larger during the past month."[9] Mary herself seemed composed. By her side sat her trusted attorneys, George
Wise and Henry Flournoy. Alec Guigon, the team's junior member,
laid low by migraine, had stayed in Richmond.

Looming above them all was Joseph Marshall Crute, now in his
twelfth year as judge of the Prince Edward County court. Judge
Crute's court started on time; attorneys and witnesses appeared on
schedule or paid the price. At forty-three, Crute had all his salt-and-
pepper hair and a full mustache, but his health had been uneven for
years, and he looked older than he was. He had dark, intense eyes
and a tightly set jaw. His lower lip protruded a bit, as though he were
always biting it.[10]

The change of venue dictated not only a new judge but a new
prosecutor as well, Prince Edward's commonwealth attorney, Asa D.
Watkins. A handsome, youthful forty, Watkins had been prosecuting
criminals for five years.[11] Technically Watkins was in charge of this
prosecution as well, but he might choose to sit back, acting only as a

figurehead. Certainly Lunenburg had plenty of other legal talent. Back as senior attorney was the crafty and courtly William Hodges Mann. Mann would have an able associate in Robert G. Southall, a rising star among Southside litigators. Finally, as Lunenburg's commonwealth attorney, William Neblett would take part; Mann and Southall would try to keep Neblett from embarrassing himself.

Time to select a jury. The sheriff had gone out of his way to summon what passed in Prince Edward for an impartial panel. All sixteen men, "substantial farmers," lived in the western end of the county, as far from Farmville and Fort Mitchell as one could get within the borders of Prince Edward. But every last one was white. The jury that had recently convicted Solomon Marable had been lily white as well, possibly a sign that in Prince Edward, white Democrats had attained a dominance that their Lunenburg counterparts still dreamed of. After lengthy questioning from Mary Abernathy's attorneys, twelve white men took their places in the jury box: two rows of tanned faces, pale foreheads, and an abundance of whiskers.[12]

The prosecution called Edward Pollard.

In the month since Solomon Marable's trial, Edward had taken ill. For a time he had barely been able to raise himself up in bed, and when he started coughing up blood, the doctors pronounced his condition critical. But he had recovered to a remarkable degree, enough

When Solomon Marable, Mary Abernathy, and Pokey Barnes were tried a second time, a change of venue took them to Farmville in Prince Edward County, where Judge Joseph Marshall Crute [left] presided and Asa D. Watkins [right] served as prosecutor.

IMAGES FROM THE *RICHMOND DISPATCH*, 18 FEBRUARY 1896, COURTESY OF THE LIBRARY OF VIRGINIA.

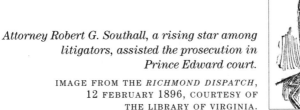

Attorney Robert G. Southall, a rising star among litigators, assisted the prosecution in Prince Edward court.

IMAGE FROM THE *RICHMOND DISPATCH*,
12 FEBRUARY 1896, COURTESY OF
THE LIBRARY OF VIRGINIA.

to take the train up from Fort Mitchell. Though he moved briskly to the stand, he looked emaciated and wan, his gray eyes more piercing than ever above hollow cheeks.[13]

Robert Southall rose for the prosecution. Southall was forty-two, tall, big-boned, and full-throated, the only clean-shaven officer of the court. He had a quick mind and a gift for reducing complex legal problems to commonsense principles. Southall asked Edward to recount everything that happened on the day of the murder.[14]

"I left home about 8 o'clock," Edward replied. In a thin voice he explained that he had made appointments with two tenants, intending that they should either pay him the rent they owed or else sign bonds promising to pay. The first tenant he encountered was Dump Thompson.

George Wise broke in. "Was that David Jennings Thompson?"[15]

"No, sir," Edward answered, "it was his brother I think."

For outsiders, sorting out Thompsons was not easy. Vincent ("Dump") Thompson was the son of the Bill Thompson with whom Edward had been feuding for decades. Although Dump was the grandson of Edward's first wife, Frances, Edward bore the young man no grandfatherly feelings. "I asked him for the $40 he owed me, and he told me he didn't have it. I said, 'You must give me your bond.' He said, 'I haven't time.' I said, 'You had better *take* time; I have plenty of blanks.' I said, 'If you don't give me a bond, I will sue you at once.' "

This chilly conversation over, the two went their separate ways. Before long Edward saw his enemy Bill Thompson coming. Edward was trespassing on Thompson's land, as he habitually did on the way to his Charlotte farm, and Thompson was incensed. " 'Why do you keep coming through here; why didn't you keep the straight path?' " Thompson had asked. Edward continued, "He cursed me and said if I came through there again what he would do. He doubled his fist and came towards me. I raised my stick up, and told him not to strike. He said I was a rogue and had tried to steal land from him and hogs from Mr. Knight, and he could prove it. He then turned from me and walked off, telling me what he would do if I came through there again."

From there Edward had gone about his business. By noon he had seen Constable Austin Clements, who at Edward's request served a warrant on Dump Thompson, demanding that Thompson appear before the justice of the peace to settle his debt to Edward.[16]

On the very day of the murder, Edward had set the law on one man and exchanged hot words with another. None of this had come out in the Lunenburg trials. Score one for Mary Abernathy.

Much of the rest of Edward's story was already familiar, but of course it had to be told afresh to the jury. Was Lucy Pollard murdered shortly after four-thirty, as the prosecution had it? Or significantly later, as the defense would insist? Timing mattered; just how much remained to be seen.

After Edward recounted the events of the afternoon, the prosecution pressed him for greater precision. "Mr. Pollard," asked Robert Southall, "what time did the sun set on that day?"

"You get an almanac," Edward shot back, "and *you* can find out." The spectators found this hilarious. Judge Crute rapped for order.[17]

Further questions from Southall elicited specific times. Edward had gone to the field at four-thirty. Mary Barnes joined him fifteen minutes later. Clements and his boy arrived at about six. Edward had found Lucy's body at about seven. When he put his hand on her, he could feel barely any warmth.

Did Edward know what his wife had done after he had gone to the field at four-thirty?

From what they found later, yes. "She had sewed on five buttons on a pair of my pants in front, and had marked thirty eggs." On each egg Lucy had written "15th," planning to count from the following day, June 15.

Thirty marked eggs, five buttons on the fly of Edward's pants: This was news, further evidence not brought out in the first set of trials. Wise and Flournoy took note. They could use this.

Southall's questions clarified the prosecutors' strategy. They would try to sell the jury the original gospel according to Solomon: Mary Barnes had scouted the house and procured the keys. Mary Abernathy had chatted with Lucy, while Marable skulked at the edge of the yard. After Edward Pollard and then Mary Barnes had left for the field, Mary Abernathy and Pokey Barnes murdered Lucy with Solomon's assistance and made off with the money.

George Wise rose to begin the cross-examination. Although Edward sat above him on the witness stand, Wise with his hooded eyes and raised chin appeared to be looking down at him. Outside, the temperature was well over ninety; in the courtroom it was at least a hundred.

Wise looped back and around almost everything Edward had already said, revisiting, amplifying, picking apart his every statement about objects, locations, times, persons, words. He wanted to know, for example, exactly what Bill Thompson had called Edward when he confronted him on the morning of the murder.

"He called me a damn rogue."

And what precisely had Thompson threatened to do if Edward cut through his property again?

"He told me he would kill me."

Wise moved to the question of what had been stolen from the Pollard house. To that moment Edward had testified only about the gold, the twenty-dollar bills, a bond, and a pair of bracelets. The prosecution had not wanted to muddy the waters with talk of stolen dresses and bedding. Wise asked if anything else had been stolen. Edward hesitated.

"I wish you would be particular and tell the jury everything as nearly as you can," said Wise.[18]

"I will," said Edward, "for I see you are mighty inquisitive."

"I am the most inquisitive man you ever met in your life." And so it proved. Wise pushed hard, so hard that some of the spectators began to feel sorry for Edward. Among the stolen goods, he thought, were a considerable number of pillowcases. After the murder he counted eleven pillows but only two cases. "Most ladies," he explained, "have about two slips to a pillow." As for dresses, he thought Lucy must have had more than the seven he found after the murder.

More reasonable doubt: Dresses and bedding would initially have been easy to identify and difficult to conceal, and none had ever been found.

As dark came on, a cloud of doubts filled the courtroom. Wise had elicited doubts about what had been stolen, about the old issue of the visibility of the body from the front gate, about the timing of almost everything. He got Edward to testify that Mary Abernathy had sat up all night watching over the body—hardly the behavior one would expect of a murderess.

Wise had one last set of questions. "Did you put up an advertisement on your gate after the murder, Mr. Pollard?"[19]

"Yes, sir, I did."

"What was it?"

"I put up an advertisement on my gate offering twenty cents on the dollar for the perpetrators of the crime, and the recovery of the money."

"Did not someone come to you," asked Wise, "and ask for fifty per cent for the recovery of the money?"

"A gentleman did ask me if I would not give half," Edward said.

"And you said you would not give over twenty per cent?"

This line of questioning unnerved the prosecution. Before Edward could answer, Southall was on his feet moving to adjourn. As it was 7:00 P.M., the hour all had agreed upon for wrapping up, Judge Crute committed the jury to the sheriff and called it a day.

*   *   *

THE CROSS-EXAMINATION of Edward Pollard resumed at nine-thirty on a sweltering morning. Wise started: "When we closed last evening, Mr. Pollard, I was asking you about an advertisement which you had put upon your front gate."[20]

Wise had not even posed his first question when Watkins waded in for the prosecution, contending that the entire line of questioning was irrelevant. Wise and Flournoy really needed this one. Cass Gregory had helped hang Solomon Marable and might soon do the same to Mary Abernathy—unless Wise and Flournoy could discredit him first. After long debate Judge Crute came down on their side.

"Mr. Pollard," asked a relieved George Wise, "who was the man who wanted you to raise the reward from twenty to fifty per cent?"

"Gregory," said Edward.

"Which Gregory?"

"Cass Gregory," Edward said, "H. C. Gregory."

A strange look came over Edward, who suddenly felt faint. He was helped from the witness stand and laid down carefully on a bench. Wise had promised to keep Edward on the stand for hours but had nothing to gain from torturing a sick witness. Even apart from his illness, meanwhile, Edward Pollard had become an increasingly sympathetic figure. He told stories on himself: He trespassed; he feuded with his stepson; he was stingy. He seemed, in short, to be a thoroughly honest man. It had been months since anyone had suggested that he might have killed his wife.

When Edward felt ready to return to the stand, Wise confined himself to one last line of questioning about the timing of the day's events: "Mr. Pollard, you have said that the railroad cars passed your place at four o'clock. All your other statements as to time have been guesses, have they not?"

"I measured the sun in the field when I started back to the house and it was an hour and a half high."

"Measured it how?" Wise was beginning to enjoy this exchange. "Explain to the jury what you mean by measuring the sun."

Edward stuck out his arms and held six fingers before his eyes. "Six fingers are an hour and a half; eight fingers two hours." The spectators, on this day mostly townsfolk, found this highly amusing. "You may try it any time you want to," Edward insisted, "and you will find it so."[21]

The one "timepiece" consulted by any party on the day of the murder, as the defense took pains to point out, was the four o'clock train. Everything else was guesswork. The defense had nothing further for Edward Pollard. The prosecution called Cass Gregory.

Gregory began with an account of his own movements on the day of the murder. He had been living in North Carolina then—in Roxboro, eighty miles south of Fort Mitchell—but was on a visit to his son about two miles east of the Pollard place. He went to Fort Mitchell to mail some letters, heard about the murder, stopped back at the farm to tell his son, and then the two of them hurried to the scene. He found Old Man Pollard lying on the ground beside his wife's body, weeping and moaning.

After a time, Gregory continued, he and Austin Clements had begun to look for clues. Gregory had asked Mary Abernathy if she had seen anyone lurking around the place that day. Said Mary, "I haven't seen no one today, good, bad, nor indifferent." She said it more than once and clapped her hands.

"Mr. Gregory," said Southall, "did you hear Mary Abernathy's testimony in her own case when it was tried in Lunenburg?"

"Yes."

"Did Mary say anything during the trial about having seen anyone that day?"

"She did," Gregory said. "She said that she saw a man—she could not tell whether he was a white or a colored man—down behind the high fence about 200 yards from the Pollard house."

"Then as I understand you," Southall said, "when you questioned Mary on the day of the murder, she said she had seen no one there that day, good, bad, nor indifferent, and yet when on trial she stated that she saw a man down by the fence, near the Pollard house. Is that right?"

"It is, sir."

Gregory stayed on the stand a good while, testifying, as before, about the layout of the Pollard farm, the condition of Lucy Pollard's body, and the evidence given in the first set of trials. George Wise lay in wait.

Wise began the cross-examination quietly. He took Gregory back to the Pollards' yard, where the neighbors gathered in the hours after the murder.

"Did you see Pokey Barnes there?"

"I did not," said Gregory. "I had never met Pokey up to that time."

"Did you see Old Mary Barnes there?"

"I did not. I did not know her either at that time."

Had he seen William Robertson? James Eubank? Gregory had not. But Wise could easily show that all those people had been there when Gregory arrived. Surely the jury would get the point: Cass Gregory, the leading authority on the murder of Lucy Pollard, had a very poor memory.

Wise pushed. "Did you take any notes of Mary Abernathy's evidence at the first trial?"

"I did not," Gregory said.

"Where were you and Pollard when that proposition about fifty per cent of the stolen money was made?"

"I could not tell."

"Pollard says you called him into his back yard," Wise went on. "Is that so?"

"If he says so, I guess it is true."

"Who were there when you made that proposition?"

"I don't remember."

"Mr. Pollard states that there were forty or fifty people at his house when you went there. Your memory doesn't seem to serve you as to some very important facts."

"No, sir."

"Mr. Gregory." It was time to lay before the jury the story of Gregory's strange mission the previous September. "Did you pay a visit to the prisoners after they had been taken to the Richmond city jail?"

"I did, sir."

"Where did you come from?"

"Sumter, South Carolina."

"And you came all the way to Richmond to see these prisoners?"

"That was part of my business."

"Now, Mr. Gregory, was not this visit preceded by a telegram?"

"Yes, sir, it was. I had seen in the papers that Judge Coleman had refused to grant a writ of error, and I dropped into the telegraph office." Gregory recited the text of the telegram he had sent to Frank Cunningham: " 'Try plan suggested. Can yet save necks.' I think these were the words I used. Captain Cunningham had been very eager to shield the Negro women. I knew if he tried that plan, he would have to do it right then."

"Did you get any reply to your telegram?"

"Yes."

"What was the answer?"

" 'Better come yourself. Have no recollection of plan.' "

"What did you do when you got Captain Cunningham's telegram?"

"I took the first train for Richmond."

"What did you ask for when you reached the jail?"

"I asked to see the youngest woman."

"Did you tell the officer that you wanted to see the women separately?"

"I wanted them apart so that one could not support the other."

Wise asked Gregory to repeat what he had said to Mary Abernathy.

" 'Mary,' " Gregory recalled saying, " 'if you will confess the part you took in the murder, and surrender all the stolen property, I will take a petition to the judge, jury, and commonwealth's attorney of Lunenburg for their signatures, and then to the governor for a commutation of your sentence from death to imprisonment.' "

"Well," said Wise, "what did Mary Abernathy say to your proposition?"

"She said that she knew absolutely nothing about the money or stolen property, and also knew nothing regarding the killing."

"How long was this before the day set for the execution?"

"Three or four days as well as I remember."

"And so, the plan was to hold out to a condemned prisoner life as bait for a confession?"

Wise had turned sarcastic, but Gregory did not respond in kind. "I was holding out a possibility of life, and I am of the opinion that the plan would have been successful had it not been for this new trial business."

"Mr. Gregory, you had no other business in Richmond than seeing the prisoners, did you?"

"If you want my whole purpose, I will give it to you flat-footed."

Wise said softly, "I know what your purpose was."

By the time Wise finished with him, it looked as though Gregory would do Mary Abernathy little damage. Some of his testimony was in fact helpful. He had recalled Mary's proclamation of innocence in the Richmond jail. He had said too that she had acted as though she had nothing to hide; when he searched her house on the day after the murder, Mary herself had opened up trunks and boxes and told him to look all he wanted.

Meantime Wise had begun to expose the obsessive side of Gregory's detective work. Wise got Gregory to state that in February, when Lunenburg was gearing up for the new trials, he had gone house to house in Fort Mitchell, interrogating nearly a dozen potential witnesses. Wise suspected worse—that Cass Gregory had attempted to induce those witnesses to manufacture testimony damaging to Mary Abernathy and Pokey Barnes—but this the jurors must come to suspect for themselves. For now Wise was content to expose Gregory's passion for the stolen money and his fixation on getting the women convicted.

These alone should have ruined Gregory as a witness against Mary Abernathy. But on the stand Gregory appeared to be anything but a man obsessed. No matter how much heat Wise put on him, he did not get flustered or lose his temper, and he showed not the least doubt about the wisdom of any of his actions. At one point William Hodges Mann asked Gregory why he had wanted Edward Pollard to raise the reward money to 50 percent. "As the murderer had not been caught," Gregory answered, "I thought that the larger reward would put people living at a distance on the look-out, and I was actuated solely by a desire to have the murderer captured."[22] Cass Gregory: Public Servant of the Year.

*   *   *

FOR WEEKS IT had been rumored that the prosecution had sensational new evidence against Mary Abernathy; before the trial began, Sheriff Cardozo had predicted that like Solomon's, Mary's was "a gone case, sure."[23] On the trial's second afternoon the prosecutors revealed more of what they really had. What they had was fragmentary and ambiguous, bits and pieces of conversations that had allegedly taken place in the days immediately following the murder.

Pattie Clements had testified under duress in Mary Abernathy's first trial. Now she was back, called by the prosecution to relate what Mary Abernathy had said to her on the Sunday after the murder, when Solomon was still at large and the women were held at the Clements house.

"She asked me if I thought that if the one who had Mr. Pollard's things would return them and put them where he could get them the matter would be dropped, so they could be turned loose. She also said that she hoped Solomon Marable would be shot if he was caught before he was brought back across the river."[24]

George Wise: "That was not in the same conversation, was it, Mrs. Clements?"

"No, sir; it was in my dining room. She heard that Marable had been caught, and said she hoped he would be shot. She became so excited when she heard the news that she had to be helped out into the fresh air."

It would not do to question a respectable white woman too aggressively; Wise and Flournoy went easy on Pattie Clements, and her time on the stand was short. The prosecution then called Philip Watson, a black farmhand about sixty years old. Watson had not testified at the Lunenburg trials.[25]

On the Sunday after the murder Watson had been hired to help guard the suspects. Early that morning, Watson said, he and the other guards had been told to escort their prisoners from Pollard's over to the Clements place. Hampered by her great weight and short legs, Mary could not walk very fast, so Mary and Phil fell thirty or forty yards behind the others. According to Watson, "Mary said that she remained at the house that day until Miss Lucy said she was going out to set some hens. Mary said that she then went on out of the house with Mrs. Pollard, who had a basket of eggs on her arm. Mary added that as she was leaving she saw a tall man and that she believed that devil was the one who got Mr. Pollard's money, and she thought that he must have caught Mrs. Pollard before she [Mary] got outside of the yard. She said that where she saw that man was by the fence right back of the yard. She stuck to it that she did not have any hand in the killing, saying that when she went home she was busy looking at Mr. Pollard in the field, that he might see that she was not going through his wheat field."

"Did you hear Mary Abernathy make any statement after the arrest of Solomon Marable?"

"Yes, sir," said Watson, "when she heard of it she began to shout, 'Thank God, thank God!' and she fell down on the floor out of the chair where she was sitting."

Two plus two: As the prosecution had it, Mary's fervent thanksgiving, along with her desire to see Solomon shot, added up to an admission of guilt. The villainous Mary Abernathy wanted Solomon dead so that he could not tell on her.

But these calculations would have to wait. Court ended abruptly at 5:00 P.M. when a messenger ran in with a telegram: Judge Crute's son lay dangerously ill with pneumonia. The boy was sixty miles away, in Bedford City, where he attended school. The judge apologized to one and all, then made a dash for the train station.

*   *   *

No one begrudged Judge Crute the journey to his son's sickbed; fifteen-year-old Charlie was his only living child.[26] The next afternoon the judge returned to Farmville on the four o'clock train, reporting his son was no worse.

Court opened minutes after Judge Crute arrived. On this third day of Mary Abernathy's trial, the atmosphere was entirely different, for the insufferable heat had moved on in the night, and in its wake came the classic weather of the Virginia spring, with sun, a bit of breeze, and temperatures topping out in the seventies. It was still too dry to suit the farmers, but for those who spent their days in court it was an immense relief.

Mary Abernathy was delighted to see Alec Guigon come into court. Guigon had spent the last two days in bed, suffering with a headache that had lightened up just enough to allow him to come down from Richmond on the train. Of her three attorneys, Guigon was the one who showed Mary the most personal solicitude. He shook her hand in public—Pokey's too—and asked after her health and the baby's.

"Old Man" Philip Watson was back on the stand. Flournoy would do the heavy lifting for the defense, while an extremely pale Guigon listened and tried not to move his miserable head.

"Did I understand you to say that Mary told you she did not know any more about the death of Mrs. Pollard than you did?" Flournoy asked Watson.

"Yes, sir, she said she was as clear of the death of Mrs. Pollard as the angels in heaven."

Flournoy took Watson back to Mary's account of her departure from the Pollard house. As the lawyer scratched away at Watson's story, almost everything unraveled. It was not in fact clear what Lucy Pollard was doing when Mary left; Lucy had *said* she was going out to set hens, but did she as yet have the eggs in hand? Watson was not so sure. And what of the mysterious man? Which fence was he near? How far away was he, and which way was he headed? Watson was confounded. Still, he stuck to part of his main point, that Mary herself had said she had walked out of the house *with* Lucy and that Mary had seen a man.

The prosecution would have it this way: Lucy Pollard had begun to cross the yard, eggs in hand, on the way to her chickens. Mary Abernathy walked with her, pretending to be headed home. A few feet away lurked her co-conspirator, Solomon Marable. Another moment and Solomon would have Lucy Pollard in his grip while Mary Abernathy flailed at her with the ax. But the prosecution needed firmer evidence that Mary Abernathy had in fact stayed that long.

The prosecution called Henry White, a white man who farmed about two miles from Pollard's. On the Monday after the murder, White claimed, he came to the Pollard place and for a short time served as Mary Abernathy's guard. Mary sat on the ground, leaning against the cornhouse door, according to White, who then testified:

> She said, "When I left Miss Lucy she was in the house at the side table fixing the eggs in a little box. I then went out of the back door for some water and came on around the house, between the chimney and the tree and I looked down along by the fence and I saw Solomon."
>
> I said, "Did you know it was Solomon?" She said, "I know it was Solomon." And she clapped her hands. I said, "Well, Aunt Mary, I heard that you said you saw a man down there with a ragged coat and an old piece of a hat on, and that you could not tell whether it was a white man or a colored man." She clapped her hands and said she knew it was Solomon. She then said, "Do you think I could have the heart to kill a woman and then go and help to shroud her?"

Eggs again: If White could be believed, Mary Abernathy by her own statement had stayed at the Pollard house for a significant interval after Edward went to the field. She had had Lucy Pollard in view just before Lucy headed out to the henhouse with the eggs. Mary had been *in* the house, moreover, having come out the back for water, and that meant she was in the yard just a few steps from the spot where Solomon said he had been waiting.

If White could be believed. On one point he was easily challenged: The Pollards kept their water bucket on the front porch, not in back. White was either confused or making things up. He claimed, moreover, that he had not told anyone his story until very recently, after Solomon had been convicted the second time. This in itself seemed suspicious. The murder was all anyone had talked about for weeks. If White had really possessed this vital information, why had he kept it to himself?[27]

Flournoy rose for the cross-examination and promptly changed the subject. White had been a member of the search party that had combed the woods near the river, looking for clues and the stolen goods. Flournoy asked him: "Did you find anything?"[28]

"We found Solomon's old clothes, his overalls, shoes, hat, socks. We also found his coat hanging up in the old tool house at old Meherrin bridge. I examined the overalls, but found no blood on them as they were too much covered over with turpentine. His coat was examined and was the same way, but we could find no blood at all. This was on Monday morning."

"Wasn't this after the news of the murder was spread throughout the land, and after a company of cavalry was scouring the country for Solomon, and hadn't he been seen at Chase City?"

"Yes."

"Then when you and Mary had that conversation by the Pollard corn house, this information about Solomon was broadcast?"

"Yes, sir."

"What became of those clothes?"

"I don't know."

In fact, the clothes had been turned over to William Neblett, Lunenburg's commonwealth attorney, who had subsequently managed to lose them—a display of flaming incompetence on Neblett's part and another indicator of how badly Solomon had been served by the absence of counsel. In the days immediately after the murder the press had printed the rumors that Solomon's clothes were "covered with blood."[29] But during Solomon's first trial not one word had been said about his discarded clothing. It was not until Henry White took the stand on this day, a full ten months after the murder, that anyone who had seen the clothes described their actual condition.

No blood. With that, the mystery of Lucy Pollard's death became another league deeper.

The prosecution called Lula Knight Abernathy, the day's last witness. The young woman who now approached the stand was a walking symbol of what Mary Abernathy had missed during her ten months in jail. Lula Knight had married Mary's twenty-three-year-old son Willie on Christmas Day. Mary had missed the wedding, of course, just as she had missed birthdays and baptisms and her own wedding anniversary—her twenty-seventh—in February. The great moment for her church meanwhile had come in September, when forty black Baptist pastors had gathered at the Mount Mitchell church for preaching, feasting, and transacting their common business. Hosting them was an honor and a great labor for the members of the church, a once- or twice-in-a-lifetime event. Mary Abernathy had missed that too, along with last year's harvests and half of this year's planting. This spring the hot weather was causing everything green to come on fast; she could see that from the trees leafing out in Farmville's court square.[30]

Lula Knight Abernathy promised to tell the whole truth, but that was the last thing she was allowed to say during this session of court. Both sides were set for a battle royale. In Mary Abernathy's first trial, Lula had quoted Mary Abernathy's five-year-old daughter: "Mama look like she been fighting." Of all the evidence purporting to corroborate Solomon's story, this had been the most damaging.

Judge Crute sent the jury out of the courtroom, and the lawyers argued. At 9:00 P.M. Crute declared he had heard enough. He would rule on the admissibility of Lula Knight Abernathy's testimony in the morning.

Mary Abernathy, the spectators, and the officers of the court went out into a cool, clear night, Flournoy's challenge still in their ears. "If that was not hearsay testimony," Flournoy declared, "I do not know what hearsay testimony is." Did the prosecution seriously propose, Flournoy asked, to make the words of a five-year-old child the "looprope" that would hang the child's own mother?[31]

The life of Mary Abernathy, the reporters thought, depended on the answer to that question.

17

EGG-SUCKING DOG

D ay four of the trial of Mary Abernathy began on another idyllic
spring morning, with Lula Knight Abernathy back on the witness
stand. Robert Southall hauled himself to his feet and began fish-
ing for testimony powerful enough to send Mary Abernathy to her
doom. The young witness, who struck the *Times* reporter as "intelli-
gent-looking," resisted the bait.[1]

"Were you at Mary Abernathy's on the day of the murder?"

"I was there on Friday."

"Did you see Mary Abernathy when she came back?"

"Yes, sir. I woke up just before she got there. She was about as far
from me as across this courtroom when I first saw her." [The courtroom measured forty feet across.] "She came up the path to the house

and got a chair, and went around the corner of the house and sat down. Wilson Abernathy then asked her to fix his suspenders, and she sent one of the children to bring her a needle and thimble and thread."

"What did she say to her husband?"

"She said that while she was up at the house she saw a man coming around the fence. Uncle Wilson said he reckoned it was one of the sawmill hands—Solomon Marable."

"What time was that?"

"I don't know."

So far Southall had nothing. He moved to the central question, first warning his witness not to repeat what Mary Abernathy's child had said until the judge gave his permission: "You say when you first saw Aunt Mary coming from Mr. Pollard's she was about as far from you as across this courtroom. Did you hear a remark made by Aunt Mary's little child about her mother?"

Lula Abernathy admitted that she had.

"How far was she from the child when the child made the remark?"

"The child was on a fence behind the house, and Mary was up in the yard—far enough not to hear what she said." The witness nodded to Austin Clements, who sat in the courtroom about thirty feet away. "Aunt Mary was as far from the child as I am from Mr. Clements."

"How loud did the child speak? Talk just about as loud as she spoke."

"I don't know, sir; I can't talk like a child."

Southall tried again. "Did the child talk loud enough to be heard as far as from here to where Mr. Clements is sitting?"

"I don't know. She didn't whisper. I was sitting right at the child."

Judge Crute was eager to settle the point. "Lula," he interjected, "do you think that child was close enough to Aunt Mary for Aunt Mary to hear what she said?"[2]

"No, sir," said the witness, more definitely than before.

"That being the case," said the judge, "I do not think the witness should be allowed to tell what the child said."

It was a signal victory for Mary Abernathy. The jury would not hear the statement "Mama look like she been fighting." But Southall persisted.

"You saw Aunt Mary that day when she returned from Mr. Pollard's. What was her appearance?"

"She looked just like she always did. I saw no change in her."

"What was the condition of her clothes?"

"I didn't see any difference in her clothes; they looked like they did when she went away."

Lula Knight Abernathy stood down, her testimony a total bust for the prosecution. The prosecution called its last major witness.

Martha Ann Thompson sailed up the aisle, eyes blazing. She was in her sixties and built like a barge. Two of her sons—David James Thompson and Lucius Pettus, the "Winking Man"—had been made notorious by the Pollard case. She thumped down into the witness chair and awaited Southall's first question.[3]

"Did you hear Mary Abernathy say anything about the murder?"

"I did."

"State what it was."

Martha Thompson had gone to the Pollard place on Monday afternoon, three days after the murder. She found Mary Abernathy under guard, sitting on the doorsill of the cornhouse. A manhunt was on for Solomon. Martha Thompson continued her testimony:

> Mary Abernathy had lived at my house for three years; her husband had worked at our place, and that was why I went where she was. I said, "Mary, what are you doing here?" She said, "Miss Martha, save me. I was sick six months at your house, and you saved my life." Mary caught hold of me right around my skirts and held me tight. I said, "What have you done for me to save you?"
>
> She said, "Not guilty. Solomon done it." I said, "Mary, the gentlemen have gone to see if it is Solomon they have caught at South Boston." She said, "I hope they'll shoot that Negro's brains out before they bring him here." It turned out, however, that they had not caught Solomon.[4]
>
> I said to Mary whoever murdered Mrs. Pollard, hanging is too good for them. I told her it was the most brutal murder I ever heard of. I said her arms were held until they

were black, her throat was choked until it was black; there were the prints of the fingers upon her throat as black as they could be. Her forehead was gashed all to pieces, the back of her head was crushed into a jelly; her jawbone was broken; her shoulder was badly broken. Mary said, "Lord have mercy upon me," and she fell over and laid there like a great beef and I left her in that condition.

Flournoy rose to conduct the cross-examination. The prosecution, he saw, would have the jury believe that the words "save me" and "I hope they'll shoot that Negro's brains out" implied guilt. Flournoy of course would contend the opposite, but as a matter of interpretation, this would have to wait for his closing argument. For now Flournoy had to take a different tack. It seemed odd that Martha Thompson had not come forward until this moment. Perhaps she had slanted her story to deflect suspicion from her sons. The lawyer began probing. "Did you ever testify in these cases before?"

"I never did." Martha Thompson looked daggers at him.

"Did you ever talk with anyone about your conversation with Mary Abernathy?"

The highly articulate Mrs. Thompson suddenly knew nothing. "I can't tell you the first time I told of it."

"Well then could you tell how long it was after the murder that you told someone of this conversation?"

"I don't know how long after the murder before I spoke of it."

Around they went, Flournoy the soul of politeness, but finding every way possible to challenge the authenticity of the witness's account. Martha Thompson in turn found every way possible to evade Flournoy's questions. "Don't know . . . don't recollect . . . can't name . . . I told you that before."

For just a moment in the midst of these evasions Martha Thompson turned herself into a character witness for Mary Abernathy: "I want you to understand that Mary Abernathy lived at my house three years and never did anything wrong. She always did what I told her; if she had not she could not have stayed there."

Her answers were otherwise useless except as missiles; she

flung them like stones at Flournoy's head. He turned to his partners in a silent plea for help. Wise and Guigon merely grinned at him and made no move; they were having too much fun watching their colleague get "whupped" by a woman. Flournoy turned back to the iron-clad Mrs. Thompson with further questions, to which she responded with insults and further evasions.

At length George Wise leaned over to Flournoy. "Let her go, Flournoy!" he said in his best stage whisper. "For God's sake let her go!"

Martha Thompson sailed out, beaming in triumph. The people in the courtroom laughed themselves silly, judge and jurors included, and whenever the hilarity began to subside, a gesture of mock humiliation from Flournoy would set them off again. They laughed for a full five minutes. Eventually they managed to compose themselves, and a short time later the prosecution rested.

The midday recess lasted longer than usual, two precious hours in which Mary Abernathy's lawyers refined their strategy for the next segment of the trial.[5] The key issue was whether Mary herself should testify. In the nine months since her initial conviction, Mary Abernathy had won over numbers of men who considered themselves tough-minded and impartial. If she took the stand, she would surely help her cause—as long as her own attorneys were asking the questions. The danger lay in the cross-examination. By reputation, Robert Southall could flummox the steeliest witness.

Would Mary Abernathy's lawyers put an unlettered woman up against one of the best trial lawyers in the state? In fact they would.

*   *   *

"TALK SLOWLY AND distinctly," Flournoy said, "and tell the jury all you know about the killing of Mrs. Pollard."

Mary began, earnest and solemn.[6] "The way I found out that Mrs. Pollard was dead was that Wilson told me." Mary Abernathy told a straightforward story, one that matched Edward Pollard's. Then she came to the moment when Mary Barnes headed out to the vegetable patch to join Edward, leaving Mary Abernathy alone with Lucy. The reporters listened intently to hear how she would account for her movements in the final moments of Lucy Pollard's life.

"How long did you stay after Mary Barnes left?" Flournoy asked.

"Not a minute, hardly."

"What was Mrs. Pollard doing?"

"Sewing buttons on Mr. Pollard's pants. The last talk I had with Miss Lucy was when she said, 'When are you going over to Cousin Martha's?' " This was Martha Thompson, the dowager whose testimony had entertained the court earlier in the day.

"I said, 'In a few days.' She said, 'Tell her howdy, and I am coming to see her soon.' I said, 'Good evening, Miss Lucy,' and I went straight on home."

"What did you do when you got there?" Flournoy was still asking the questions.

"I said, 'Hand me my chair, children,' and Wilson came to me to fix his galluses, and I made the children hand me my needle and thread."

"When did you hear of the murder?" asked Flournoy.

"I heard Mr. Pollard ringing the bell and hollering, and Wilson said, 'Hush, children, hush; I think that is the boss,' and he listened and said, 'I'm going up there to see what's the matter.' He went on and I followed him. When I got half way to the house, I met Wilson coming back. He said, 'Someone has killed ole Miss.' I said, 'Lord, that ain't so, surely.' "

Step by careful step, Flournoy walked Mary Abernathy through the events that followed the death of Lucy Pollard: the gathering of the neighbors in the yard, Mary's initial questioning, her all-night vigil with the corpse, the shrouding, her arrest. She was calm and clear and so far made perfect sense.

Flournoy moved onto thinner ice. It was time to try to neutralize all the odd bits of testimony that might add up to a verdict of guilty. The case against Mary Abernathy had come to this: to snippets of conversations that allegedly took place in the days immediately following the murder. In her first trial it had been different, when Solomon's accusations had steamrollered everyone, flattening Mary Abernathy and the other women in turn. This time there would be no such accusations; no prosecutor in his right mind would put Solomon on the stand, and with no Solomon, the prosecution's case was weaker than ever. No physical evidence connected Mary Abernathy to the murder: no blood, no money, no stolen goods. Nor was there any evidence of bad feeling between Mary and Lucy Pollard. What remained were the bits of talk reported by four witnesses: Pattie Clements, Phil Watson, Henry White, and the redoubtable Martha Thompson.

Flournoy began with Pattie Clements. "What did you do on Sunday morning?" he asked Mary.

"We were taken to Mr. Clements' house. We got there early in the morning."

"Did you converse with Mrs. Clements?"

"Yes, sir. I wanted to walk out and I asked her to go with me." Pattie Clements had testified that Mary Abernathy had spoken as though she had known where the Pollards' money was. Mary saw nothing incriminating in that conversation. "As we were walking she asked me did I know who killed Mrs. Pollard. I said I did not. I said I had never been arrested before in my life, and I did not know anything about courthouses and law, and I wanted her to tell me that if they found the one who got Mr. Pollard's money, what would they do with us. She said she did not know."

Flournoy moved on quickly to Phil Watson. Watson had testified that Mary herself had told him that she and Lucy Pollard had walked out of the house together and that Miss Lucy had a basket of eggs on her arm.

"Did you have any conversation with Phil Watson, when he was walking with you while you were under arrest?"

"Yes, sir. Phil said that murder was a terrible thing, and I said yes, I had never known such a thing to happen in the county before."

"What did you tell him about seeing a man going down the fence, when you were coming away from Mr. Pollard's on the evening of the murder?"

"I told him that when I first went in Mr. Pollard's porch that evening, I saw a man going on out to the big road, but never thought anything of it. When I went home, I did not see a living thing till I got to my house."[7]

"Did you have any conversation with Phil Watson or anyone else about Mrs. Pollard's eggs?"

"I never said anything about eggs," Mary Abernathy replied, "no more than what I said to Mrs. Pollard. My little puppy followed me to the house and went to a coop and scared a hen. Miss Lucy asked me if he would suck eggs. I told her I did not think he would. I went to the end of the porch and called him."

Flournoy: "Did you tell Phil Watson that?"

"I told him that if I told him anything about eggs."

"Did you ever have a conversation with Mr. H. A. White?"

Mary Abernathy disposed of White in one sentence: "I never said a word to him in my life to my knowledge."

While Flournoy had Mary Abernathy on the stand, he wanted her to talk about two incidents, one when she wished Solomon dead and the other when she had rejoiced at the news that Solomon had been caught. "Did you ever have a conversation with Mrs. Thompson?"

"Yes, sir."

"What was said?"

"She told me that anybody who had killed Mrs. Pollard ought to be hung. I said yes, that the one who had done it surely ought to be hung, that it was a terrible thing."

"When did you hear that Solomon had been arrested?"

"At Mr. Clements' house in the dining room. Mrs. Clements came to the door and said, 'You all be still. They have caught the rascal who got Mr. Pollard's money!' I clapped my hands and thanked God. And I do thank him yet."

I do thank him yet. With those words Mary Abernathy became her own star witness.

*   *   *

THE NEXT MORNING it rained all over the Southside. John Mitchell, Jr., was on the train to Farmville, hoping to catch the last day or two of Mary Abernathy's trial. Mitchell stared through the raindrops that scuttled across the windows of the moving train, scarcely noticing the green and blooming countryside beyond. He was depressed beyond speaking.

He had not expected to go to Farmville at all. Despite his intense interest in Mary Abernathy's trial, he had expected instead to be in Staunton, where the Republican party was holding its state convention. In a presidential election year much was at stake, and Mitchell had had his own course planned for many months. First, he would go to the state convention as a delegate from Richmond; that convention in turn would send him to the national convention in St. Louis to help select the Republican nominee for president of the United States. In Republican politics Mitchell was a player, ready for the national stage.[8]

But nothing had gone according to plan. Six months earlier William Mahone had died. A political boss of the first order, Mahone against all odds had held Virginia's fractious Republicans together. With Mahone gone, the party split into two rival factions, each notable for its pigheadedness and ambition. Their rivalry had little to do with policy or principle. It was instead about patronage, the federal jobs and contracts that would be theirs to command if the Republicans won the White House.[9]

In Richmond it was war. Mitchell worked night and day to bring the Richmond party under his faction's control, but his opponents refused to knuckle under. In March, when the city's Republicans were to select delegates to the state convention, each faction held its own meeting and selected its own slate of delegates. The two rival delegations then descended upon the state convention in Staunton, each believing that the credentials committee would send its opponents packing. No one felt more confident than Mitchell.[10]

But he had been outmaneuvered, and here he was on a train for Farmville. On the previous day the convention had opened in Staunton—and promptly tossed him out! It also gave the boot to James Bahen, the white grocer and saloonkeeper who was Mitchell's closest political ally. For both men, Staunton was a numbing defeat.[11]

For several weeks the commotion had absorbed Mitchell so fully that he had given little time to the Lunenburg case. He had missed all of Solomon Marable's trial, which he covered in his weekly *Planet* by reprinting articles from the *Times* and the *Dispatch*, reproducing them without even editing out the *Dispatch*'s racist language. This week's *Planet* was due out in less than twenty-four hours. For Mary Abernathy's trial, borrowed columns would once again have to suffice.

The train reached Farmville shortly after noon. Mitchell made his way to the quaint little courthouse on Main Street and found the courtroom packed. Squeezing into a seat at the table reserved for the press, he was immensely relieved to hear that Mary Abernathy had been a stalwart witness from beginning to end; Robert Southall had cross-examined her the previous evening and again this morning and hadn't tripped her once.

In the waning hours of testimony the defense launched a final assault on the credibility of Cass Gregory. George Wise rose and called H. Claiborne Epps, son and deputy of the Richmond jailer.

"Mr. Epps," said Wise, "Mr. H. C. Gregory has testified that he had never been to the Richmond jail to see the prisoners except when he went there in September. Will you state whether he had ever been to the jail before?"

"Yes, sir," said Epps. "The prisoners were committed to the jail on July 21st and a few days thereafter—I don't remember how many—Mr. Gregory came to the jail about nine o'clock and Captain Cunningham introduced him to me. Mr. Gregory said he wanted to talk to the prisoners. He talked to Marable first, and then asked for Pokey Barnes, saying he thought he could get more out of her than he could out of the old one."

"While we don't ask you what it was, do you remember the conversation he had with Pokey Barnes?"

"Very distinctly," said Epps.

Judge Crute would not let Epps repeat what Gregory had said. Wise, however, was satisfied. It was clear that Gregory had been sniffing around the jail just days after the Lunenburg prisoners had landed there and that he had lied about it—or failed to recollect it, which from the prosecution's point of view was little better.

Wise called a second Richmond deputy, W. D. Weisiger, who confirmed that Cass Gregory had indeed visited the prisoners soon after they were deposited in the Richmond city jail. Weisiger, moreover, had witnessed Gregory's infamous second visit to the jail, the one that took place just days before Mary Abernathy and Pokey Barnes were to have been executed.

"Well, tell what happened," said Wise.

"He said he wanted a private interview with the prisoners. I told him he could have it in the presence of an officer. Mary Abernathy was then called in, and Mr. Gregory told her he had come all the way from South Carolina to save her life. He told her he would take a petition to the governor in her behalf if she would tell him where the money was."

"What did Mary say?"

"She said, 'If you were to put a whole regiment of soldiers in front of me I could not tell you anything about that money, not to save my life. I know nothing about it.'"

Objection! The prosecution wanted Mary's response stricken out. Although common sense suggested that her words provided essential evidence, judges looked askance at such statements. A "self-serving declaration" on the part of the accused normally was not admissible, especially when significant time had elapsed between the commission of the crime and the making of the statement; it was simply too easy for a guilty defendant to cook up a story and become practiced at protestations of innocence. The law was a bit slippery, however, and Judge Crute wanted to study it. He would rule on Mary's statement later. In the meantime the defense could proceed with its attempt to break down Cass Gregory's testimony.[12]

The defense called Captain Frank Cunningham, who had had a busy winter of soldiering, singing, and keeping the secrets of such outfits as the Ancient Arabic Order of Nobles of the Mystic Shrine.[13]

Now Cunningham joined the jailers, placing Cass Gregory at the city jail in July, shortly after the prisoners were transported from Lunenburg. "I had gone down to the jail that day with a newspaper man," the captain explained. There, quite by chance, he had bumped into Cass Gregory. "I spoke to Mr. Gregory cordially, and I think I introduced him to Mr. Claiborne Epps, at the jail door as I was coming out."[14] Cunningham was not able to say if Gregory talked with the women. But by placing Gregory at the jail—at a time when he claimed never to have been there—Frank Cunningham put another hole in Cass Gregory's credibility.

Gregory, however, was unflappable. In the last moments of the trial the prosecution put him back on the stand, and he suddenly remembered having visited the jail in July to question Solomon Marable about a suspected arson near Fort Mitchell. He had absolutely no recollection of talking to the women at that time, but if Mr. Epps said he had done so, he was willing to admit it was true.

* * *

IN FICTION, COURTROOM scenes typically build to climax, the truth bursting out in some last-minute bombshell. In real cases, however, testimony tends to end in a completely different way, the evidence shredding into separate, fine strands, like fringe on a garment. Late on a cloudy Friday afternoon Mary Abernathy's lawyers called their final witnesses. From each they wanted a strand or two, something a juror might grasp and hold on to until he found himself in a state of reasonable doubt.

A Chase City man described Solomon's flight and capture; the defense team made sure the jury registered the contrast between Solomon's attempt to escape and the steady behavior of Mary Abernathy. J. F. Eubank, the magistrate who took charge in the hours immediately following the murder, testified that his guards had been ordered *not* to talk to any of the suspects. So when Mary Abernathy said Henry White had never conversed with her at all, perhaps she spoke truth. Edward Pollard returned to the stand to repeat his testimony about the buttons Lucy had sewed on his pants. He also claimed that no one but Lucy knew where he kept his money, a statement immediately contradicted by Austin Clements.

"The general impression in the neighborhood was that Mr. Pollard kept money in the house," said Clements. "I have borrowed money from him and have seen him go and get it."[15]

And so testimony in the murder trial of Mary Abernathy sputtered to an end. Closing arguments began that night and consumed almost all of Saturday. For Mary Abernathy, Saturday was the hardest yet. Through five days of testimony, her faith had sustained her, and she had held up amazingly well. But the baby had suddenly taken sick—pneumonia, the doctor thought. The country people who crowded the courtroom Saturday morning, most of them on Abernathy's side, now saw her looking "haggard and care-worn."[16]

Her lawyers, by contrast, were bright-eyed, keyed up for big performances. Flournoy, a son of the Southside, spoke for more than two hours. Chief among his targets: Cass Gregory. "I don't propose to impeach Mr. Gregory's veracity," Flournoy declaimed. "I would not accuse a bob-tailed yellow dog of sucking eggs unless I knew he sucked them." Flournoy did charge Gregory with forgetfulness, however, and also with prejudice. "No hungry hog ever wanted an ear of corn as bad as he wants the life of this poor prisoner at the bar." Sly, this Flournoy, leaving Gregory's honor intact (lying was a breach of honor) while associating the man with slavering animals.[17]

Flournoy also argued psychology: Murderers like Solomon Marable ran. Mary Abernathy did the opposite, voluntarily answering Edward Pollard's alarm. Even more telling, Mary Abernathy washed and dressed Lucy Pollard's body for burial. This more than anything proved her innocence, for killers shrank from the sight and touch of their victims. First to last, Flournoy argued, Mary Abernathy's actions bespoke her innocence.

George Wise rose then to close for the defense. Wise left the barnyard metaphors behind, turning to hard reason and the central question of timing. The prosecution claimed that the murder had taken place early, at about four-thirty, very shortly after Edward Pollard left the house for his field. Mary Abernathy, the prosecution was suggesting, walked to the end of the Pollards' front porch to make sure Solomon Marable was ready and waiting; once Edward was out of earshot, they set upon the defenseless Lucy Pollard.

At once passionate and logical, Wise explained that the crime could not have been committed that way. Edward Pollard, by his own testimony, did not leave the house until four-thirty. After he left, his wife sewed five buttons on his pants, and then she went and got the eggs, thirty of them, and marked each one. Together the sewing and the marking of eggs would have taken close to thirty minutes. Lucy Pollard was not killed until five o'clock at least, Wise contended, and by that time Mary Abernathy had returned to her cabin and was sitting on her own porch, placidly mending for her husband.

The prosecutors got the last word, as always, and they were good—better than their witnesses. The *Times* reporter, before he heard their closing speeches, claimed the prosecution had not proved its case beyond a reasonable doubt. After hearing the closing arguments, the same reporter thought the prosecution might at least get a hung jury.

*   *   *

THE JURORS WERE not permitted to go to church on Sunday. Instead they put on clean shirts and conducted a worship service in their hotel; people who strolled by that morning could hear them singing. In the afternoon the jurors returned to hashing over the evidence against Mary Abernathy.[18]

For her attorneys, Sunday was a long, anxious day. Several problems preyed on their minds. One, Mary Abernathy was still the last person known to have seen Lucy Pollard alive. Two, in her earliest examinations, Mary Abernathy had apparently contradicted herself on whether she had seen anyone suspicious around the Pollard place on the day of the murder. A third issue: How long had she stayed at the Pollard house after Edward Pollard and Mary Barnes went out to the field? This past week, when her attorneys put her on the stand and asked her that, she had answered, "Not a minute, hardly." But J. F. Eubank, the justice of the peace who had presided over the initial investigation, testified that Mary had at first said she had stayed ten or fifteen minutes. Judge Crute's instructions to the jury made Mary's attorneys nervous as well. On the most significant issue he sided with the prosecution, ruling out Mary's ringing declaration of innocence, the one she had made in response to Cass Gregory's offer to save her life.[19]

On a cool Monday afternoon the jury sent word that it had reached a verdict. Wilson Abernathy joined the small crowd that gathered in the courtroom. Judge Crute had gone off again to see his ailing son; court began ten minutes after his return on the four o'clock train. Crute immediately sent the jurors to their room to make their final, official finding. They looked grim, and the spectators began whispering that the verdict must be guilty. Mary sat up front, not moving at all.[20]

After five excruciating minutes the jury returned, and the clerk spoke. "Gentlemen of the jury, have you agreed upon a verdict?"[21]

"We have," said the foreman.

"Mary Abernathy, stand up," said the clerk. Mary stood. A reporter noticed she did not look much taller standing up than she had sitting down.

"What say you, gentlemen of the jury?" the clerk asked. "Is the prisoner at the bar guilty or not guilty?"

"Guilty."

The moment was deeply quiet. Mary Abernathy held her head level, held herself in. Her lawyers sat in silence. Guigon was first to shake it off, asking the judge to poll the jurors individually. Judge Crute did so and then asked for further motions. Flournoy arose. "We wish to enter a motion for a new trial and an arrest of sentence." Flournoy was so upset he forgot half of what he was supposed to say. With Wise whispering in his ear, he completed the motion. "On the ground that this verdict is contrary to the law and the evidence."[22]

"Very well," said the judge. Argument respecting a new trial was set for morning, and the court adjourned.

A few minutes later Wilson Abernathy found himself outside on the courthouse green, head in hands, inconsolable. The people around him did not know what else to do for him, so they took up a collection.

CHAPTER

18

TRACKS

The trial of Pokey Barnes opened under "a leaden sky" on a Thursday, the last day in April. The gloom hanging over the courthouse matched the mood of the women's lawyers, still depressed by the conviction of Mary Abernathy three days before. Mary herself was suffering terribly, fretting over her sick baby and sleeping hardly at all. Her ordeal now appeared endless. The one person who seemed immune to the general funk was Pokey, who sat beside her attorneys looking relaxed and cheerful, as though waiting for the curtain to rise at the theater.[1]

Jury selection took all day. At dark another all-white panel of farmers took their places in the jury box, and the prosecution called Edward Pollard.

Edward was wearing out; anyone could see it. His mind remained sharp, though, and once again he gave a coherent account of the day's events. The reporters took no notes; they had heard the story so many times they could write it from memory.

After a break for supper Pollard returned to the stand to be cross-examined by George Wise. Suddenly the reporters sat up and started scribbling. Edward had just said something new, that about a month before his wife's death, he had lent a hundred dollars to a neighbor.

"Who did you lend that money to?"[2]

"I don't know whether it is right for me to tell you that," said Edward. "It has not got anything to do with this case."

"His honor will determine that," Wise said, "and there are three gentlemen on the other side to stop me if I go too far. To whom did you lend that money?"

Edward hesitated. "I lent it to J. H. H. Thompson."

"Who?"

"Herbert Thompson"—the brother and business partner of David James Thompson.

"Did he see the rest of your money?"

"He only saw what he got."

"Did you ever ask Mr. White if he would like to see a thousand dollars in one pile?"

"No, sir." Edward was certain about this. "I wouldn't be as big a fool as that."

"Do you know whether it was known in the neighborhood that you had money?"

"I was accused in the neighborhood of handling a heap of money, but I don't know that anyone had a right to suppose so, as I never told anyone such a thing. I have always been poor, and am now."

Wise let Pollard stand down, satisfied for the present with the implications of his testimony: Everyone in Fort Mitchell thought the Pollards kept a lot of money in their house. In this depression the list of people with a motive for robbing the Pollards would include just about every living soul within the range of local gossip. Still, some of those souls must have been more frantic than others. Who among all those neighbors was the most desperate? Herbert Thompson needed a fast hundred dollars. Perhaps a man who needed to borrow that much might be tempted to help himself to the whole stash.

"The Commonwealth calls Emma Harding."

Court had been in session for more than twelve hours, but the judge wanted to get through one more witness. Emma Harding was someone new. She had not testified in the earlier trials, nor had her name surfaced in the press. The reporters studied her as she settled into the witness chair: a black woman, small and very dark, age difficult to say—possibly thirty. She had a goiter, a huge swelling under her chin that could be neither fixed nor hidden.[3]

Pokey looked at her as if she were homemade slime.

The first question: "Do you know of any difficulty which occurred between Mrs. Pollard and Pokey Barnes at any time previous to the murder?" Before Emma Harding could speak, the defense was making vehement objections. Judge Crute sent the jury out of the courtroom.

Emma Harding opened her mouth and revealed her second affliction. She stuttered, badly. As she struggled to say her piece, an old story emerged: Pokey's quarrel with Lucy Pollard, ten months before the murder. But though the episode was familiar in outline, the Pokey of Emma Harding's rendition was highly profane and unaccountably belligerent. Lucy Pollard had started the conversation.

" 'Ain't this Pokey Barnes?'[4]

"Pokey replied, 'Yes, damn you, this is me.' " As Harding pushed the words out, Pokey's curse rang through the courtroom.

" 'Mr. Pollard has told you to keep off his premises.'

"Pokey said, 'Who in the hell is Old Man Pollard?' Mrs. Pollard turned away, and Pokey said, 'Yes, damn you, if I had a pistol with me I'd shoot your damned heart out.' " Pokey had put her hand down the front of her dress, as though reaching for a weapon.

"Mrs. Pollard then turned and said, 'Pokey, I am going to tell Mr. Pollard that you have threatened my life, just as soon as he comes home tonight.'

" 'Tell him, damn you. I'll kill you if it's the last thing I do.' "

As soon as Emma Harding stood down, Wise and Flournoy jumped up to argue that her story should be disallowed. Judge Crute sat quietly for a moment, the air still blue from Harding's vivid testimony. At length the judge decided to consult some lawbooks. Shortly before ten court adjourned for the night.

* * *

IN THE MORNING court started badly for Pokey Barnes. Judge Crute rapped his gavel promptly at nine and announced that he would admit Emma Harding's testimony. With the jury listening this time, she again told her story, complete with curses.[5]

Flournoy got to his feet for the cross-examination. Emma Harding had not testified in Pokey's first trial; Flournoy wanted to know how she came to be summoned for this trial. Had she told anyone about the incident since Mrs. Pollard was killed?

"I told Mr. Gregory." Scratch any surface, and there was Cass Gregory.

"Where were you when you told Mr. Gregory?"

"I was at his house."

"Why did you go to Mr. Gregory's?"

Emma Harding did not want to answer. "I didn't have any business at Mr. Gregory's house," she said the first time Flournoy asked the question. "I was partly raised with Mrs. Gregory," she said the second time. Third time: "I just went down there to see them. That was all the business I had there."

"Did Mr. Gregory send for you?"

Emma Harding finally answered. Just last week her brother had brought her a note from Cass Gregory, asking her to come see him. It took her a whole day to walk to his place. When she got there, Gregory asked her about the quarrel between Pokey Barnes and Lucy Pollard. Then he had her summoned.

When all the lawyers were through with Emma Harding, George Wise again moved to have her testimony stricken. The motion was promptly overruled, perhaps just as well. Emma Harding had portrayed Pokey as hot-tempered and menacing. But Harding had also introduced a stealthy Cass Gregory, moving quietly in the shadows. Perhaps the jury would sense it. The judge and Asa Watkins, Prince Edward's prosecuting attorney, surely would sense it: There was something creepy about this whole case.

The defense believed that the new evidence against Mary Abernathy, and almost all the evidence against Pokey Barnes, had been elicited, orchestrated, embellished, or even manufactured by Cass Gregory. Hence their attacks on Gregory during Mary Abernathy's trial. For Mary they had failed to get acquittal, but they had put a certain kind of currency in the bank, deposits of doubt meant to suggest to the judge that the state had no case against Pokey Barnes, that all the evidence, such as it was, could be traced back to the highly suspect maneuvers of a single obsessed individual.

Meantime no one denied that Pokey Barnes had quarreled with Lucy Pollard; the prosecution now brought on Susan Thompson for confirmation. Like Emma Harding, "Aunt Susan" had witnessed the quarrel, but in her measured account Pokey's behavior made more sense. Susan Thompson recollected no cursing. She did not recall hearing Pokey threaten Lucy Pollard's life. Pokey had lost her temper, though, when Lucy Pollard accused her of stealing vegetables. After the fight was over, said Thompson, she had scolded Pokey for being so rough on Mrs. Pollard. Pokey admitted that her temper was too high and that she often said things she shouldn't. After that, Pokey laughed it off, and no more was said about it.

Emma Harding had just testified that the three women had said nothing about the incident as they continued down the road. The reporter for the *Times* made a note of the contradiction.

*   *   *

HALF THE ART of trial reporting was listening for contradictions. Midway through this second day of Pokey's trial they got an earful from Ellen Gayle.

Since the day Lucy Pollard was killed, Ellen Gayle had had several moments of fame. She had twice been arrested as a suspect, then released for lack of evidence. She had surfaced again at Pokey's first trial, giving Pokey a large portion of her alibi; Ellen had testified that she had been with Pokey all afternoon. A month later, however, under questioning by Cass Gregory, she had changed her tune.

Ellen Gayle now took the stand, prepared to tell her new story under oath. Everyone listened hard as she described the afternoon's events: "As soon as we got to Pokey's she cooked bread and she asked me to have some. I had the headache mighty bad. She said if

I'd eat some it might help my headache. We ate and then lay down on the floor." After a time Aunt Betsy Ellis and her daughter Mary Crag-head came by and invited Pokey to go with them to the Thompsons' farm to ask for cherries. Pokey invited Ellen to come along too. "Pokey and I walked some of the way, and then we turned back, and we got to a place I did not exactly know."

" 'This don't look like the way we came,' " Ellen had said.

" 'No, it don't,' " Pokey replied.

"We kept going on until we got to an old gate place. I said, 'I'm not going this way.' She said, 'Why?' I said, 'Because I'm not going this way.' She said, 'Well, you hold on for me at the gap. I'm going through here a little way. You wait until I come back.' I waited at the gap, and after a while, I don't know, I guess it was about a half an hour, she came on back. She said, 'If I'd known all this sumac was out here I'd have gathered it last year.'

"Then we went on back to Pokey's house." Ellen's headache was no better. "As soon as we got there I picked up Pokey's child's dress, spread it out on the floor, and lay down on it."

There it was: Pokey Barnes had been out of sight for perhaps thirty minutes, at just about the time Lucy Pollard was murdered. Southall wanted to make sure the jury was getting the picture.

"Ellen, what time did you, Betsy Ellis, and Mary Craghead leave Pokey's house?" asked the lawyer.

"When we got down by the fodder stacks in Mr. Fore's field, the four o'clock train went along."

"Where is that old gate place?"

"It is somewhere back of Mr. Pollard's house, on the north side," said Ellen.

"How far is it from the house?"

"I don't know, but it is not very far."

"Did you see Pokey after you turned back?"

"I looked back and saw Pokey once. She was walking along very slow—walking down toward Mr. Pollard's. She had then crossed over the sunk part of the land in the lane."

"Where did that lane come from and go to?"

"It came from out of the woods, and the other end of it runs right up to Mr. Pollard's stable."

Southall switched gears. "What kind of a dress did Pokey have on that day?" he asked.

"I think it was some kind of an old blue dress."

"How did she look when she got back?"

"She looked tolerable warm," Ellen said. "The weather was hot."

"Did you notice anything about her clothes?"

"There was one snag in her coat. That was all I noticed."

"Why did you turn back?"

"I knew that Mr. Pollard had ordered Pokey not to come through there, and more than that, she had taken some of Mr. Pollard's chickens—and I did not want to go through Mr. Pollard's place with anybody like that."

George Wise rose for the cross-examination. His unusual eyes gave him a certain feline look. Now he pounced.

"Didn't you tell at Lunenburg Courthouse," Wise said, "and didn't you tell two women, before you got to Lunenburg Courthouse, that Pokey was not out of your sight one single instant during the walk that afternoon?"

"If I did it was because I was so much afraid of Pokey," Ellen replied. "She had beat one woman most to death."

"But didn't you tell the court and two women that Pokey was not out of your sight that afternoon?"

"Yes, I did, but it was because I was so afraid of Pokey."

"And so you acknowledge you told a lie under oath."

"If I did it was because I was afraid of Pokey."

"You say you were afraid of Pokey when there was a whole regiment of soldiers to protect you?"

"Soldiers or no soldiers," said Ellen, "all that Pokey wanted was to get loose and get to me."

A stubborn witness, Ellen Gayle. When Wise finished, Guigon and Flournoy each took a turn at breaking down parts of her testimony. They didn't get far, but they accomplished their essential mission: Ellen Gayle had confessed to perjury.

*　　*　　*

THE AFTERNOON WORE on amid humdrum testimony about times, distances, and sightings of Pokey and Ellen coming and going on that hot afternoon. Just west of the Pollard farm lay a cornfield belonging to the Fore family. There Clyde Fore, white and nineteen years old, had been at work with several black field hands, among them David Williams. Pokey's house was easily visible from the men's location. Williams now testified that he had seen Pokey Barnes and Ellen Gayle walking north toward Thompsons' with the other women. Later he saw Pokey and Ellen returning together.

The men were sowing corn in the many spaces where nothing had come up after the first planting—tough, sweaty work in hard ground. When Pokey and Ellen came back, Williams testified, the men had done two sets—down one row and back the next and down and back again. He didn't know how long it took to finish a row, but he thought the women were gone no more than half an hour.

Clyde Fore followed Williams to the stand and confirmed his hand's sense of time: With the corn about a third missing, Fore thought a man would take fifteen minutes to go up one row and down another.

Constable Austin Clements was next, fortified with a hand-drawn map and a batch of precise measurements. How long were the rows in Fore's cornfield? By surveyor's chain, Clements answered, 264 yards.

Pokey's lawyers started: not at the message but at the messenger. In all the other trials this sort of testimony had been given by Cass Gregory, and with good reason. Gregory himself had made the survey and drawn the map, and in each of the previous trials he had spent long stretches on the stand, showing the jury the lay of Pollard's land. But in the latest trial the women's lawyers had turned the tables on Gregory, exposing his leaky memory and dubious motives. This time, evidently, the prosecution meant to protect Gregory by keeping him off the stand.

Constable Clements, the newly anointed expert on distances, went on to describe the landmarks made suddenly significant by Ellen Gayle. You could see the back of the Pollards' house from the old gate place, which lay seventy-four yards to the north. In between was a deep sink. If you walked the lane from the gate place toward the house, you would lose sight of the house while you were down in the sink and not see it again until you climbed up the other side and fetched up in the yard.

Pokey knew the sink from the night of Solomon's capture, when the crowd in Pollard's front yard keened for blood. She had scrambled down there with her mother and Solomon and a squad of farmers turned commandos. The sunken place hid them all and probably saved their lives.

As afternoon stretched into evening, the prosecution called Durelle J. Gregory, Cass Gregory's oldest son. Durelle stayed home and cultivated what was left of the family farm while his father dashed about the country, failing at the tobacco business and playing detective. Robert Southall, asking the questions for the prosecution, elicited young Gregory's story.

On the morning after the murder he had walked up the lane to the old gate place. There, near the draw bars, were three left footprints, two going in toward the Pollard house and one coming out. Whoever made the tracks was barefoot.

"Did you measure those tracks?" Southall asked.

"I did," Gregory responded.

"Did you afterwards measure the foot of any person that corresponded with them?"

George Wise almost shrieked, "Wait one minute! Where is that measure?"

Gregory didn't know. "I took no care of it after the Lunenburg trial," he said.

Three pieces of physical evidence had gone astray since the first set of trials. Lunenburg's commonwealth attorney had misplaced the letter that Solomon Marable had allegedly sent to himself. Gone too were the clothes abandoned by Solomon near the river.[6] And now the stick. Such carelessness itself told a story: After the initial verdicts no one had given Pokey or Solomon or either of the two Marys the remotest chance of mounting successful appeals.

Judge Crute sent the jury out of earshot, and Durelle Gregory elaborated his story. Bill Pettus and Cass Gregory had discovered the three tracks in the early morning. Gregory—*Cass* Gregory—then measured them with a stick. That afternoon the coroner's jury took

Pokey Barnes and Ellen Gayle out to the old gate place and had them make new footprints in the soft dirt at the edge of the lane; so many people had tramped around there that the original tracks were gone. The stick fitted the fresh tracks exactly. Afterward Cass handed the stick to Durelle, who gave it no further thought after the first trials ended. But he thought it might still be in the pocket of his old coat at home.

"Well, then," George Wise said, "let him produce it!"[7] Wise was barely in control of himself. The prosecution was trying to hang his client on physical evidence that was only rumored to exist, that the jury would not see, that no one had seen in months. Wise argued this one with his whole soul, and the prosecution fought back with equal ardor.

Judge Crute wanted to think it over. He called a recess and sent the lawyers out, their hearts still racing, to cool off and get supper.

*   *   *

OVER SUPPER THE prosecuting attorneys decided they did not want to risk an adverse ruling on the admissibility of Durelle Gregory's testimony. When everyone came back for the night session, the prosecutors simply took the issue off the table. They reserved the right to recall Durelle Gregory, however.

Meantime the prosecution called James Eubank, Fort Mitchell's justice of the peace. Eubank now confirmed the discovery of tracks by the old gate place. What was more, Eubank had found evidence nearby that someone had climbed over the fence. He had spotted footprints on the lower rail. On the top rail, a sharp splinter had snagged a small square of blue cloth, possibly torn from a dress.

Defense attorney Alec Guigon approached the witness stand, showed Eubank a piece of cloth and asked him to identify its color. Eubank pronounced it blue.

"It happens to be green," said Guigon in triumph. Little snorts of suppressed laughter bubbled up from all parts of the courtroom. Further questioning revealed that the original square of blue cloth had vanished. It had passed from hand to hand, said Eubank, and had never been returned to him.

So the phantom fabric joined the procession of other lost evidence—the stick, the letter, the suit of clothes. The one piece of physical evidence that had *not* been lost was the murder weapon. Edward Pollard's old meat ax had found a home in the courtroom, on the floor at the reporters' feet. Their wobbly table had driven them to distraction—until some practical soul had the idea of using the head of the ax to shim up one of the legs. There it lay, steadying the reporters' table, blood still on its blade.[8]

*   *   *

THE NEXT MORNING the prosecution rested. Now it was Pokey's hour, and since it was Saturday, the courtroom quickly filled with country people. Pokey's lawyers bent to their first task, demolishing the credibility of Ellen Gayle. They had already scored one victory on this cloudy morning; as soon as Judge Crute opened court, he had ruled out all testimony about the scrap of blue cloth.[9]

The defense called Sergeant Hugh Cardoza of the First Virginia Volunteers Hospital Corps. He was not in uniform; this morning he was dressed like the clerk he was in his civilian life. When the troops first arrived in Lunenburg, Cardoza explained, he had set up a pharmacy in a vacant store. He was in the store when his commanding officer came in with Ellen Gayle and ordered him to take a statement from her.[10]

" 'Pokey come to our house about 11 o'clock and asked for a chicken,' " Cardoza testified, quoting Ellen Gayle. As Cardoza continued his rendition of Ellen's statement, the familiar elements fell in line, from the walk back to Pokey's to the invitation from Betsy Ellis and Mary Craghead to go to Thompsons' for cherries. Then Cardoza came to the key segment of Ellen Gayle's original statement: " 'We went about three-quarters of a mile toward Thompsons' and came back home. This was about four o'clock. I lay down and went to sleep, and don't know where Pokey was while I was asleep. When I woke it was about 6:30. When I lay down it was about 4:30. Pokey was awake when I lay down, and she was awake when I got up.' "

Further questioning brought the point home: Cardoza was certain that Ellen Gayle had told him that she and Pokey walked *together* all the way back from Thompsons'. The sergeant was not the only one to say so. After a long recess for dinner, the defense lined up three additional witnesses, each of whom testified about a conversation with Ellen Gayle. First came Peter Hutson, a white man from Fort Mitchell who had arrested Ellen Gayle shortly after the murder. When he did so, Ellen told him she had been with Pokey all afternoon.

Then came Betsy Ellis, the elder of the two women who had walked toward the Thompsons' place with Pokey and Ellen Gayle on the afternoon of the murder. As the four women approached the Thompson house, she said, *Ellen* had wanted to turn back, fearful that Mr. Thompson would not give cherries to so large a crowd. Later, as they walked to Lunenburg Courthouse to testify, Gayle had told Ellis that she had been in Pokey's company all day. When Ellis stood down, her daughter Mary Craghead took the stand and gave an almost identical account.

Ellen Gayle, the prosecution's star witness, had clearly committed perjury. How could anyone be condemned to death on the word of such a woman? Pokey's attorneys could already hear in their heads the ringing phrases they would use to berate Ellen Gayle in their closing arguments.

* * *

IN THE DIMMING light of a gray afternoon, the defense called its own best witness. Pokey looked out at the spectators. They were mostly her kind of people—washerwomen and farmers, slaves at one time, or the children of slaves. They crowded into one-half of the courtroom, and as they waited for Pokey to speak, they stood still as death. George Wise asked her to state everything that happened on the day of the murder.

Pokey began with her morning hike to Fort Mitchell to deliver clean laundry to the Fore family.[11] "Mrs. Fore commenced counting the clothes, while I stood there at the side of the bed." Most of the women in the courtroom knew the feeling, had stood by while some white woman counted laundry, as though nothing else would stop them from stealing. "I told her that there was a pair of Mr. Fore's pants which I hadn't brought. She told me that she had two more pair that she wanted me to carry down for her and have a crease on the knee. She said, 'Pokey, I want you to scrub some for me. You can scrub today or tomorrow, either you want.' I told her I would scrub for her Saturday.

"I went to Mrs. Bradbury's. She asked me to go up the cherry tree and gather some cherries. I climbed the tree and ate what cherries I wanted and threw her down some."

Pokey's voice was clear, her manner direct, her recollection thorough, as she recounted her famous visit to Ellen Gayle, their bargain, and their return to Pokey's house. New, homely details helped her story ring true: Ellen had put on an old hat, Pokey now added, and when they reached Fort Mitchell, they had stopped in at Mrs. Weatherford's, where Ellen asked to see the new baby and Pokey asked for a bite of bread. By the time Pokey reached the crucial part of her testimony—the part about the aborted walk to Thompsons' for cherries—the courtroom crowd was rapt and entirely in her corner.

> When we got half way—Ellen said it was half way; I had never been to Mr. Thompson's and didn't know how far it was—Ellen said she did not want to go any further. I turned around and came back to my house with her. In going back to the house I went on through a piece of pine, where they had grubbed it and planted corn, and I said, "Humph, Ellen, I won't get any sumac here this year." And as I said this I saw three bunches of sumac, and I stooped down and broke them off.
>
> When I got home, I took the chair and sat down at the window. Rosa went to eating very soon after I got there. Ellen laid down on the floor again and I told her to lay on the bed, but she would not. I sat at the window with Martha Ann laying across my lap. She had fallen down the steps while I had gone. We were talking about the Baptist Association meeting, and about sweethearts and other things. Ellen said she was going to Drake's Branch to buy a set of furniture.

Betsy Ellis and Mary Craghead returned with the cherries, and they all walked out to Pollard's field, where Mary Barnes was at work and much in need of a drink of springwater. Ellen and Mary Barnes then struck the day's last bargain, Ellen offering two chickens for beef that Mary would buy from Lucy Pollard. " 'And don't let her give you bony beef,' " Ellen had said.

Pokey continued:

> Then we went on towards home. I had gotten nearly to my spring when I heard the bell ring three times, and I said to Ellen, Mama did not have long to stay by herself. I thought the bell was ringing for Mama to come to the house. Then the bell commenced ringing again and Mr. Pollard commenced hollowing. I hollowed and asked Mama what he was hollowing for. She said he was calling the cows, she reckoned.
>
> He kept ringing the bell, and kept hollowing, and I told her Mr. Pollard didn't call cows that way, and she had better go and see what was the matter. She dropped the hoe and ran up there. I had to go by my house to go up there. I kept straight up to Mr. Pollard's. When I got to my house I saw Clyde Fore, Charley Bailey, Dave Williams, and Ben Knight, and I kept on up there with them.
>
> When I got there at the gate and looked where he was standing we saw her laying down there, and he said, "Gadfoundit, just look there, somebody has killed my wife!"

Pokey Barnes made the most of her time on the witness stand. She accounted for every minute and every movement on the day of the murder. She told of both arrests. She confessed to having had hot words with Lucy Pollard, ten months before the murder, and recalled being chided by Susan Thompson for her high temper. But just a few days before the murder, Pokey added, Mrs. Pollard had come to her house to return a key to her mother. On that occasion Mrs. Pollard had made peace, said she had no hard feelings, that it was Mr. Pollard who objected to Pokey's coming on the place, and he was old and cranky.[12]

"Did you see Solomon Marable on the day of the murder?" asked Wise.

"I think I saw Solomon when I went to carry the clothes home to Mrs. Fore that morning," said Pokey. "He was standing at Mr. Spencer's store, at Fort Mitchell, talking to Mr. Schofield, Mr.

Spencer's merchant. I had to pass Mr. Spencer's store on my way to Mrs. Fore's."

"Did you see Mary Abernathy on the day of the murder, prior to the killing?"

"I did not see Mary Abernathy that day. I hadn't seen her for a fortnight. The last time I had seen her was at Mrs. Thompson's at a burial."

The youthful Alec Guigon took over for the final questions. "Did you have anything to do with that murder?" he asked.

"I did not," said Pokey.

"Did you know anything about it?"

"I did not," Pokey said again.

"Did you know anything about Mr. Pollard's money?"

"I did not know that he had any money."

Pokey was perfect. SHE WAS A VERY EFFECTIVE WITNESS IN HER OWN BEHALF, declared the *Times* headline. IF AN ACTRESS, A CONSUMMATE ONE. "Many who believed her guilty," the article went on to say, "now proclaim that she is innocent."[13]

Judge Crute had planned to keep court in session until 10:00 P.M., but a juror had taken ill and could scarcely sit up. At 6:30 court adjourned. As it was Saturday night, the afflicted juror would have all Sunday to recover. Robert Southall meanwhile would have all Sunday to prepare a treacherous cross-examination.

*   *   *

WHEN COURT OPENED late on Monday morning, the "prisoner at the bar" was not Pokey Barnes. It was instead Solomon Marable, brought before Judge Crute for sentencing.

In former days Solomon had often appeared in court sporting a bright neckerchief. But Solomon had given up the things of this world and no longer wore vivid colors. His clothes were ragged; he needed a haircut and a shave. He stood motionless beside his attorneys, his eyes wandering around the room. He seemed to hear nothing the judge said.

Judge Crute had plenty to say. In all his years on the bench he had never before pronounced the death sentence, and he felt the need to explain himself. He would set the execution for the last possible date, so Solomon would have opportunity to appeal. Meantime, whenever Solomon asked, the judge would permit a minister of the Gospel or some other Christian man to help prepare his soul for eternity. Barring a successful appeal, sixty days hence Solomon Marable would hang in the Prince Edward County jail.[14]

Half of the courtroom, the half assigned to black people, was filled with spectators. After the judge had spoken, they murmured in wonder: that a man could hear his own death sentence and react not at all.

CHAPTER

19

ONE SHALL BE TAKEN

A lumbering white man, a slender black woman, each with a fine
mind. In a courtroom suffused with pale sunlight, Robert
Southall and Pokey Barnes faced off. Southall meant to show
that Pokey had been close to Mary Abernathy and Solomon Marable,
close enough to suggest conspiracy. How long had it been, he asked,
since she'd visited Mary Abernathy's house?[1]

"I have never been to Mary Abernathy's house since she has been
living there," Pokey answered simply.

How many times had Solomon Marable been to her house?

Twice, Pokey answered: once in the winter, when she gave a
party, and then he came back sometime after that. "He got to talking
his smart talk around there, and I drive him away."

"How long before the murder was it when Solomon was last at your house?"

"I don't know how long it was," said Pokey. "It was a long time."

Did she know that Edward Pollard had money?

"I never seen him have any," said Pokey. "He never paid me none, for all the work I did for him."

Mr. Pollard paid nothing at all?

"He only paid me two pounds of sheep and a peck of meal, and I worked for him over a month."

Edward the Cheap. People would believe Pokey on that point.

When had she last been on Edward Pollard's place?

"I never have been in Mr. Pollard's since he told me not to go on his land."

Pokey admitted to arguing with Lucy Pollard but did not recall cursing her. She had never stolen chickens. She saw no tracks when she was taken to the old gate place the day after the murder. She did not know how far it was to the Thompsons' house; she had never seen it.

This she did know: She knew where she and Ellen Gayle walked after they separated from Betsy Ellis and Mary Craghead. They picked their way back through Thompsons' pinewoods, got over a little ditch and the spring branch at the same place they had crossed going out, and climbed the fence into the Fores' field, the same place they had climbed over on the way out. Southall tried every which way to get Pokey to suggest that she had come back by some other route, but she didn't budge.

William Hodges Mann took over the questioning. Courtly as ever, he asked where she was when the 4:00 P.M. train blew. Pokey said she didn't know exactly.

"Why, Ellen Gayle and Mary Craghead both recollect this," Mann said.

"Ellen Gayle recollects a heap," said Pokey.

Had she been born a century later, Pokey Barnes could have made a fine trial lawyer herself. Mann got no further with her than Southall had. Pokey was simply too smart for them and too sure of herself, delivering her testimony with no hesitations or contradictions. At times she showed her temper, but it was the indignation of the falsely accused. After two hours of fruitless cross-examination Pokey stood down.

Her flawless performance put extra pressure on the prosecution. Although they had already rested their case, they had reserved the right to reopen the issue of the tracks. Four men waited in the wings to testify. Once again the prosecution called Durelle Gregory.

Over the strenuous objections of the defense, Judge Crute now allowed Gregory to tell his entire story to the jury. By the old gate place, Gregory explained, three left footprints had been found on the soft, sandy edges of the path (the center was packed hard and hence no right tracks). The tracks were measured with a stick. Because the original tracks were destroyed in the course of the day, Pokey and Ellen were taken out in the afternoon to make new ones. Pokey's foot was about a sixteenth of an inch longer than Ellen's, and a trifle wider. The stick was then brought out, and the fresh tracks matched right up with the measurements made early that morning.

The tracks had actually been found by Cass Gregory and Bill Pettus, David James Thompson's older half brother and business partner. Now Pettus took the stand to confirm that one track was slightly longer and wider than the other. A notch had been cut on the stick to indicate the wider one.

"Were *two* notches cut?" Alec Guigon asked the questions for the defense.

"No, sir."

"Then how did you find out how the smallest track made in the morning corresponded with the small track made in the afternoon?" Guigon was good on the technical dimensions of things.

"Mr. Gregory held his finger there when he measured it."

"He didn't hold it there all day, did he?"

"No, sir."

"Then how did you know that the small track made the morning and the small one made in the afternoon were identical?"

"I kept it in my eye," said Pettus. "My eyesight is good."

"So you kept it in your eye from early in the morning until late in the afternoon, did you?" asked a skeptical Guigon. If the missing stick were admitted as evidence, the jury would at least understand that the "measurements" were made partly by eyeball.

The prosecution called Howard Fore, station agent at the Fort Mitchell train depot and an heir to the land on which Pokey Barnes had lived. One Saturday night in January he had achieved his own bit of fame after his younger brother Clyde came home drunk, began abusing the whole family, and at length pulled a pistol. In self-defense, Howard grabbed a shovel and struck his brother on the head, knocking him cold and inflicting a four-inch gash that laid the skull bare. The next day young Clyde recovered sufficiently to speak. He didn't remember a thing but said that he didn't blame his brother for having clocked him. The Richmond press ate this up. Ever since Lucy Pollard's murder, any ruckus was newsworthy so long as it happened in Lunenburg.[2]

The day after the murder Howard Fore had gone with the other members of the coroner's jury to the old gate place and watched Pokey Barnes and Ellen Gayle make footprints in the powdery dirt. Thereafter, he now testified, he watched Durelle Gregory fit the stick into the tracks. The stick fitted Pokey's track perfectly.

This time Flournoy handled questions for the defense. How did Fore know that the stick used in the afternoon was the same one used in the morning? Fore had no answer. Flournoy pressed. How much bigger was one track than the other? Fore could not tell. To him, he finally confessed, Pokey and Ellen's tracks looked just alike.

One further question: Could there not have been others who made the tracks? After Edward Pollard had raised the alarm, dozens of people shuttled in and out of the Pollard place, and they came from all directions. Did anyone measure *their* tracks?

Cass Gregory had. Now Gregory was sworn and proceeded to tell the jury that he had seen a number of barefoot women around the Pollard place, on the night of the murder and the day following. He got several of these women to make tracks too and then measured them. None of these footprints matched those made by Pokey and Ellen.

This new information made a striking picture for the mind's eye. Cass Gregory calls forth a woman, kneels in the dirt, measures the print of her left foot, moves on to the next woman. He is the prince in a warped *Cinderella*.

*　　*　　*

SOMETHING WAS UP. In the opening moments of the trial's fifth day all the lawyers disappeared into a private room for a long time. When they filed out, they looked more important than usual.

"May it please the court." Asa Watkins spoke for the first time. As commonwealth attorney for Prince Edward County, Watkins served officially as the lead prosecutor. For four days, however, he had only listened while Robert Southall and William Hodges Mann examined the witnesses.[3]

Now Watkins took charge. He had listened carefully to the prosecution's evidence, he said, and considered the case from every angle. "And now that all the evidence in the possession of the Commonwealth has been given in, I cannot believe that it is sufficient to justify the jury in bringing in a verdict of guilty. I have reached this conclusion without consultation with anyone," Watkins said. "In view of these circumstances, therefore, I ask the privilege of submitting a motion for a nolle prosequi."[4]

Judge Crute spoke from the bench. "I have never insisted upon the continuance of a case when the commonwealth's attorney desired to enter a nolle prosequi, and I shall not do so in this case. The motion is therefore allowed."

Pokey Barnes had a keen mind but knew no Latin and was not certain what had just happened. George Wise leaned over to her.

"Pokey," he whispered, "you are free."

*　　*　　*

HOW LONG DID it take a man to replant two rows of corn in hard ground? How far was it to Thompsons' cherry orchard? When witnesses answered this second question, it had seemed to the reporters a complete sleeper: The newspapers printed neither question nor answer.

How interesting and strange that the case of Pokey Barnes came down to two calculations of distance and time. From the time Pokey left her house with Ellen Gayle to the time of their return, only about thirty minutes elapsed, not enough to walk to Thompsons' and back, through woods and over plowed ground, *and* commit a murder and robbery. For all the high drama about tracks, a scrap of blue cloth, Ellen Gayle's about-face, and Pokey's hot confrontation with Lucy Pollard, Pokey Barnes owed her sudden freedom to numbers of the most mundane kind. The other key factor, as Watkins explained, was the prosecution's failure to show any evidence of conspiracy with the two people already convicted of the crime. Hence his decision to terminate the prosecution, an unusual move and, to all appearances, a stunning act of conscience.[5]

"I walk where I please." So Pokey had once told Lucy Pollard. Now Pokey was legally free to walk anywhere, but she walked first to jail. Word of her release had flashed though Farmville, and predictably, a few soreheads made ugly remarks about what should be done with her.[6] To keep her safe, Pokey's lawyers asked Judge Crute's permission to return her to her cell until they could get her out of town on the 4:08 P.M. train.

In the afternoon Mary Abernathy was called into court. Even though Pokey's acquittal knocked the bottom out of Solomon's original story, Mary Abernathy had been lawfully convicted of murder and must now be sentenced. Pokey Barnes returned to the courtroom to stand with her friend. The clerk spoke. "Mary Abernathy, have you anything to say why sentence should not be pronounced against you?"

"No, sir." Mary clasped the baby to her chest. She looked frightened, but her voice was steady. "No more than this: I am not guilty of killing Mrs. Pollard, and I don't know where that money is, either."

Judge Crute's voice trembled as he scheduled Mary Abernathy's execution. For the past fifteen days his only son had struggled for life, suffering from the same illness that laid waste to Mary's small daughter. Now the judge must pronounce the death sentence on a mother with her baby in her arms. On July 8, five days after the execution of Solomon Marable, Mary Abernathy was to hang in the Prince Edward County jail.[7]

Her lawyers were poised for another appeal by the same process as before: They would first ask the circuit court (and if necessary the Supreme Court of Appeals) for a writ of error and supersedeas; if they got their writ, they would argue for a new trial. If their argument prevailed, Mary would stand trial a third time. She would have to stay in jail all the while, probably for months. But what else could she do?

In the time left to them, Judge Crute wanted Mary Abernathy and Solomon Marable held in a sturdier jail in a safer location. He therefore ordered them transported to the city of Lynchburg.

Come the apocalypse, says the Book of Matthew, "Two women shall be grinding at the mill; the one shall be taken, and the other left."[8]

Pokey Barnes would soon board a train, headed northeast to Richmond and freedom. Mary Abernathy and her baby would ride west, bound for another crumbling jail in another strange city.

*   *   *

THE FIRST TRAIN out of Farmville was the *Cannonball*. Escorted by her father, Joseph Barnes, and lawyers Guigon and Wise, Pokey threaded her way across a platform thronged with happy people, and climbed aboard. The mood was an odd brew of elation and caution. Everyone knew that acquittal could be lethal; the same court order that set the prisoner free might also incite the mob. The lawyers were especially concerned for their client's safety in the towns nearest Farmville. When the train passed through them—Burkeville, Crewe, Nottoway, Blackstone—Joseph Barnes covered Pokey up and made her hunker down between the seats.[9]

The train arrived in Richmond at seven on a summery evening, and Pokey at last breathed free. John Mitchell, Jr., stood beaming on the platform, shook hands with the lawyers, and showed Pokey and her father into a waiting carriage. Off they went on a triumphal tour of black Richmond.

First stop, Mitchell's newspaper office on Broad Street, where Pokey exchanged congratulations with the hardworking staff. They had kept her plight in the headlines for nearly a year, and every Saturday, when the paper came off the press, all hands had pushed the *Planet* out to mailboxes across Virginia and the nation. Pokey had been in the *Planet* office for only five minutes when jubilant people began to close in from every direction. It was no mean feat to get her back in the carriage and on her way.

In the ten months since her conviction in the Lunenburg court, Pokey had had several moments of celebrity, but nothing could have matched the exuberance of black Richmond. Thousands poured into the streets. The carriage rolled slowly through the tonier sections of Jackson Ward, stopping first at the homes of Rosa Bowser and Marietta Chiles, officers of the Women's League and fund raisers extraordinaire. By this time the carriage was mobbed, and it was all the burly driver could do to part the crowd and move the horses on. They stopped again at the black YMCA, whose Ladies' Auxiliary had befriended Pokey and Mary Abernathy during their long incarceration in the Richmond jail. All along the route the people cheered for Mitchell and called down blessings on Pokey, who thanked them and blessed them back, touching the hands of all she could reach. "All the earth is the Lord's," said the *State* the next day, "but Jackson Ward belonged to Pokey Barnes last night."[10]

Pokey was almost home. The carriage made its way past Mitchell's own house and came to a final stop at the home of Bettie Graves, a Women's League activist and a widow with grown sons. Pokey was to live with Mrs. Graves while she decided what to do next. At this moment she knew only that she would never return to Lunenburg.[11] Meantime her public awaited. Hundreds of eager people filled the street outside the Graves house. That night Pokey met them all.

The celebration went on for days. Streams of well-wishers continued to call, and Pokey greeted as many as she could. But after another day of benedictions and congratulations she faced exhaustion, and so did her landlady.[12] The solution: Three nights after Pokey's release, the Fifth Street Baptist Church opened its doors to all comers.

The place was packed "from pit to dome," a significant minority of whites squeezing in with the multitude of African Americans. Pokey Barnes sat up front at a table in the chancel, dressed smartly in black, her hat trimmed in white and a rose in her hair. Up front also sat four preachers, and Mitchell, of course. The service went on for three hours, and afterward hundreds pressed toward the front. They formed a line, two and three deep, Pokey greeting each person as they filed past. Many left contributions, placing their coins on the table or directly in Pokey's lap. So it continued until midnight.[13]

*   *   *

On May 10, the first Sunday after her release, Pokey rode in a carriage with John Mitchell, Jr., to three different churches. The day was bright and hot; the crowded sanctuaries were alive with fluttering fans. By late afternoon Mitchell had spoken to thousands, he had basked in the praises of Richmond's most influential black ministers, and with Pokey's help he brought home almost fifty dollars, precious money for the defense of the two Marys, who had now spent forty-seven Sundays behind bars.[14]

For Mitchell it seemed a stroke of unbelievable luck that Pokey had been released just as his political campaign was getting under way. Elections for city officials were to take place at the end of May, and Mitchell was running for reelection as alderman.

He was nominated on the very night that Pokey Barnes made her triumphal return to Richmond. After Pokey was safely ensconced with Bettie Graves, Mitchell had attended a Republican ward meeting a few blocks away, its purpose to choose a slate for the upcoming election. Mitchell was nominated for alderman, as was his white ally James Bahen, in a high-spirited gathering that went on until three in the morning. "Half of the ward stayed up so late," a reporter quipped, "that when it was going to bed it met the other half getting up."[15]

The slate did not please everyone, however. Jackson Ward's Republicans had been badly factionalized for years, and some of Mitchell's opponents went away disappointed. Some had wanted an all-black ticket; they were especially eager to dump Mitchell's pal Bahen. Others had expected to be nominated themselves.

In short order, they bolted, as they had done in several previous elections. The night after Mitchell's slate was announced, his rivals met to nominate a ticket of their own. Having achieved the release of Pokey Barnes, Mitchell himself was untouchable; as a concession to the inevitable, Mitchell's enemies put him at the head of their ticket. For every other slot, they nominated a challenger.[16] No one knew which faction would prevail, but in heavily Republican Jackson Ward, Mitchell's reelection looked like a sure thing.

*   *   *

THEN AGAIN. THE election came off as scheduled, but not as Mitchell had planned. He lost his bid for reelection to the city council. The day after his defeat a miserable John Mitchell, Jr., found himself on a train to Lynchburg. Had he been a poet, he might have used the ride to compose some lines about the fleeting nature of earthly fortune.

This Lynchburg journey should have been a triumph. Mitchell had agreed to give the commencement address at the Virginia Seminary, a fledgling black Baptist college that he had nurtured since its founding.[17] But it would be at best a bittersweet occasion, as "Alderman" Mitchell was no more.

How could such a thing be? In a word, theft. White Democrats stole the election. When the Republicans put up two rival slates, Democrats sniffed the sweet scent of opportunity. The Democratic party—white virtually to a man—had not won an election in Jackson Ward in more than twenty-five years. But the Democrats now had the law on their side. The Walton Law of 1894 had deliberately made voting complicated; any given election would thus produce many potentially invalid ballots. A panel of election judges—in Richmond, Democratic election judges—then decided which ballots to discard. Since they could toss out as many ballots as they chose, they controlled the outcome.

Besides, the Democrats wrote the book on election theft. Or rather, had there been a book, here is how it might have read for the Richmond municipal election of May 28, 1896:[18]

HOW TO WIN

The first principle is *delay*. Although the law says the polls are to open at sunrise (on May 28, that would be 4:54 A.M.), stall for at least one and one-half hours. By that time the line will be long, and the voters at the back may give up and go to work.

If four voting booths have been erected, knock down three of them.

When the first Republican-looking fellow steps up to the booth, be ready with questions. We suggest the following: "How many children do you have?" "How old is your mother-in-law?" "What was the date of your grandfather's funeral?" "How many times have you been in jail?"

Use your creativity! With practice you will make each voter take up to eighteen minutes to cast his ballot. At sundown, when the polls close, many voters will still be waiting in line. They are out of luck.

The second principle is *close inspection of ballots*. If in your precinct the opposition has a large majority, prepare to throw out *as many as three-quarters* of their ballots.

If you have four precincts, let the opposition win one of them.

Speak feelingly to reporters: What a shame that so many voters mark their ballots improperly!

As the slang had it, John Mitchell, Jr., had been "done up."[19] Mitchell well knew that elections got stolen all the time, but he had presumed himself exempt from such treatment. Even more galling, he had been sabotaged by fellow Republicans—African Americans, no less. The white Democrats, rascally as they were, could not have won Jackson Ward if black Republicans had stuck together. And what irony! Mitchell had been bounced out of office in the hour of his greatest glory.

In a few days he would decide whether to contest the election. In the meantime he prepared for his commitments in Lynchburg. A city of twenty-five thousand, Lynchburg lay a hundred miles west of Richmond. In much of this hilly place the ground was too steep to build upon; the remaining areas tended to be closely built and densely populated. The city jail conformed to the pattern, forty inmates crammed into a gloomy two-story building only seventy-six feet long and fifty-five feet wide. Most inmates lived four or five to a cell. Solomon Marable and Mary Abernathy had cells to themselves, however, high-security, steel-lined chambers on the lower tier. Mary's cell was two doors down from Solomon's, fronting on the same corridor. They could hear but not see each other.[20]

Mitchell was shown in through the main entrance of the old stone structure and descended a few steps to the ground floor. In the dim light he could just make out the gaunt figure of Solomon Marable, framed by his cell door.

"Marable, have you forgotten me?"

"No, sir," Solomon answered.

Mitchell walked down a few steps to greet Mary Abernathy, then returned with pencil and pad at the ready.

"Marable, do you still claim the women are innocent?"

"Yes, sir, Mary Abernathy is innocent." With Mitchell scribbling as fast as he could, Solomon went back to the beginning. "In the morning, I was sitting on Mr. Spencer's porch. I left there and went up the road, going to the sawmill. David James Thompson was standing on the side of the fence on the public road, with his hand leaning on the side of the fence."

Solomon talked for more than an hour. The plot was the same as before, but in this telling Solomon sketched in more details, and with each detail—the placement of Thompson's hand on the fence, for example—the story seemed more authentic. It would make a big article for the next issue of the *Planet*.

Mitchell then stepped over to Mary Abernathy's cell. She wept when she saw him. Mitchell felt like weeping too. They wanted to shake hands, but the iron mesh was too fine to allow a hand through. Mary sat behind the door, holding baby Bessie. The furnishings consisted of one chair, the trunk Mary had received in Richmond, and a mattress on the wooden floor.

After Mary composed herself, they spoke. She had had visitors: Father Welbers, a Baptist minister, and a number of ladies, some of them white.[21] Mary wanted to know all about Pokey and the other Richmond folks. Mitchell filled her in and assured her that her appeal would go forward in a few weeks. For Solomon he held out no hope.

During her long days in jail Mary had stitched two counterpanes, and she now presented them to Mitchell. Without thinking, he said he could not take them, as he had to deliver a speech that night at the Virginia Seminary. Mitchell left five dollars for her, but he might better have found a way to accept her gift.

*　*　*

THE HEADLINES OF late May were dominated by the boisterous campaigns preceding Richmond's election and the many charges of fraud that followed. Barely noticeable was a little item in the *State*:

David James Thompson, the sandy-haired storekeeper from Finney-wood, had filed suit against the *Richmond Times* for libel and defamation. He wanted ten thousand dollars in damages.[22]

Neither the *Times* nor the *Dispatch* breathed a word of this; the high-circulation newspapers evidently did not wish to remind readers that big money could be made by suing them. The complaint Thompson filed with the court, however, told a fuller story. At issue were two articles, both published the previous September. The first had appeared just after Judge Coleman rejected the women's appeal; at that bleak moment it looked as though Solomon, Mary Abernathy, and Pokey all might hang a week hence. With three lives at stake, the *Times* for the first time named David James Thompson as the white man whom Solomon accused of the murder. The article also reiterated Solomon's white man story, giving it greater weight by implying that Solomon had confessed it to Father Welbers.

The second article had appeared ten days later. This one charged that David James Thompson had recently stabbed a black man and to avoid prosecution had paid the victim to leave the state. All this, claimed Thompson, had ruined his reputation among his neighbors, who "wholly refused, and still do refuse, to have any transaction, acquaintance, or discourse with the said plaintiff."[23]

Note the timing. Eleven days before Thompson filed his suit, Pokey Barnes had established her innocence, and with that, Solomon's original tale of a female conspiracy fell to pieces. Who killed Lucy Pollard? The logical course now was to take a harder look at Solomon's white man, David James Thompson.

But not, perhaps, if it cost ten thousand dollars. Thompson's lawsuit lay on the press like a sopping wet blanket. The summer of 1896 brought no resurgence of the energetic investigative reporting that had marked the case's early days, nor did local officials reopen the case. Lunenburg officials did not question the credibility of the four men who had provided David Thompson's alibi, nor did they seem to think their own inaction required any justification. Now the reporters followed in the same train; they simply let the white man angle slide.

Plenty of other stories lay ahead of them. First up, the execution of Solomon Marable, scheduled for July 3. Readers always wanted to know how a condemned man met his doom.

CHAPTER

20

MESSAGES

Stovall, N.C., May 13th, '96

Dear Husband,

I seat myself to write you a few lines to let you hear from me. We are all well at this time and hope that these may find you the same. I got your letter Saturday and was glad to hear from you, saying you were well. I am glad to know that you are still alive, and living on the promises of God.

He has promised to save whosoever put their trust in Him. I am glad to know that you have faith in the Lord, to believe that He can save you. Although you have sinned you must pray that the Lord may forgive you for what you have done, because He is the only one that can save you from ruin. We all pray for you, knowing that you are in the hands of justice. We are all trusting that you may be saved at the last day.

I am glad that you do continue to write to me, and let me know that you are yet alive. The children are all well, Henry and Johnny.

I am still living with mother. We have a nice crop of corn planted and are still planting more. We are doing very well so far. Mother and I take in washing and that helps us much.

Mother and Jackson went down to grandmother's last Sunday. They all were well down at the house. I haven't heard from your mother since I wrote to you last, but I want to go down there as soon as I can to see her. Your brother Tom is married.

I have much to write, but haven't the time this morning. Will write more next time. All send their love to you.

From your wife,

FANNIE MARABLE[1]

May 17, 1896

My Dear Daughter,

I take the opportunity of writing you a kind letter and I hope when you receive my letter it will find you enjoying the best of health, as it leaves me in very good health. We had a grand meeting this morning. We had baptizing, and two persons were baptized. I would be very glad to see you. You must come to see me as soon as you can.

I have been quite sick with that same old misery in my head that I have every Spring. I have been feeling better today than I have been for two months.

We are going to have flower mission over here. Fix me up a box of something to eat and send it to me next week. Be sure and send me a big white apron. Be sure and send me the box by the middle of the week or Friday.

I enjoyed those things which you sent me so much. O, I can't tell you how I do feel in this place. Tell your papa to come over here next week and bring me some money; if he cannot bring any money tell him to bring me a sack of flour and sugar. If you think that it is best to write and see about the children I want you to write, but if you don't think it is best for you to write you better not do so.

This is a beautiful Sunday, and I wish I could be with you. I hope you are enjoying yourself. You must pray for yourself and me. You must pray every day and all the time and the Lord will help you and keep you safe from harm and danger. Trust God and no man can hinder; for God is Lord of all and King of Kings. Only trust Him.

I have not been punished since I have been here. I have been getting along all right with my work. I hope we will see each other and all live together again very soon.

Mr. Burrell has been over to see me and several ladies came with him. All the ladies have brought me nice presents.

Give my best regards to Mr. Mitchell and tell him it is past my mind what to say to him for what he has done. I cannot fix it in words but God will fix all things. I have two good guard masters to work under, and a nice lady that watches over us. I put all my trust in the Lord. Write to me next week and tell Mr. Mitchell to come over and see me next week.

Lizzie sends love to you and is glad to know that you are free again. Be sure to send me something next week.

Tell Mr. Mitchell I feel so grateful to him, and to all others who helped to defend us in this cross.

No more at this time. Write soon. Many kisses. Here is a lock of my hair.

> *Your affectionate old mother,*
>
> MARY BARNES

Lynchburg, Va., May 25, 1896

Mr. Mitchell,

Dear Sir:—I received your kind and welcome letter and I was glad to hear from you. It found us well. If I get a new trial in June I think I will get clear. I wish you would come up here I want to see you. Baby is getting on very well and I wish you could see it.

Give my love to all of my friends. Tell them that I want

to see them all so bad. You must be sure to come up here. Give my love to Pokey. I will close.

Yours truly,

Mary Abernathy

Newport, R.I., June 6, 1896

Mr. John Mitchell, Jr.:

My Dear Brother:—We are always desirous of helping the unfortunate and needy, and have called upon the Young People's Sunday Afternoon Literary connected with the Mount Olivet Baptist Church to aid the unfortunate Mary Abernathy in her great battle for life and I herewith enclose you an express order for the sum $9 in behalf of the Young People's Sunday Afternoon Literary, to aid you in your great work for human life, and may the blessings of God rest upon you and ever keep you.

Respectfully,

W. H. Jackson, Pres.

Bessie H. Brown, Sec'y

New Kent Co., Va. June 8, 1896

Mr. John Mitchell,

Dear Sir:—Enclosed please find $4.00 from Second Liberty Baptist Church to help save poor Mary Abernathy. We send this because we believe she is innocent. Your efforts in the Lunenburg Case have been unparalleled. Such sacrifice of time and means should be commended by enemies as well as by friends. Some of the members of my church are subscribers to the *Planet*, and I hope others will soon subscribe.

May God put it in the hearts of those who have the life of Aunt Mary in their hands to do justice at whatever sacrifice.

May you and the *Planet* live long to defend the right and condemn the wrong.

Sincerely yours,

A. H. Cumber, Pastor

Richmond, Va.

Dear Aunt Mary:—

Your favor received and contents noted. The lawyers have received the record in your case from Farmville, and tomorrow morning will begin the work of preparation of your petition for presentation to Judge Coleman. They are confident of success.

Yours truly,

JOHN MITCHELL, JR.

CUMBERLAND CH, VA. JUNE 24, 1896

TO RICHMOND PLANET, RICHMOND, VA:

WRIT OF ERROR IN CASE OF MARY ABERNATHY GRANTED TO-DAY.

GEORGE D. WISE

RICHMOND, VA. JUNE 24, 1896

TO MARY ABERNATHY

C/O CITY SERGEANT SAM'L JOHNSON, LYNCHBURG, VA.

JUDGE COLEMAN GRANTED A WRIT OF ERROR TO-DAY. THIS STOPS HANGING.

JOHN MITCHELL, JR.

Stovall, N.C., June 28, 1896

Dear Husband:

I seat myself to answer your kind note. I got it yesterday. I was glad to hear from you and still more glad to know that you are still praying. That is the best thing that you could do for yourself, is to pray for the Lord to save you, because He is the only one that has the power to save.

We were all well when I got your note. All send their love to you and they all say that you must still keep praying.

We hope to see you again bye-and-bye, where we will never part no more, but be in a bright, shining world.

Your dear little Henry has not forgotten you yet. He looked at your picture and said, "This is papa," and is all the time asking to see my papa. Where is your trunk?

Henry knows where he left you the last.

We ask him sometimes to see if he remembers it, and he says, "In the road."

He has a very good recollection. So I must close at this. I am still working, trying to take care of the children and myself.

Please write to me and let me hear from you as long as you live. I am glad to hear from you at any time. Write me again as soon as you get this and let me hear.

Your wife,
FANNIE MARABLE

21

SOLOMON'S BODY

How do you hang a tall man in a squat jail?

Inside the Prince Edward County jail nine steps led from the first floor to the second, banister on the left, wall on the right. From the second-story landing a person could look down over the banister and get a clear view to the ground. In this spot Sheriff Dickinson intended to hang Solomon Marable.

The scaffold was a marvel of simplicity, and cheap too—"the cheapest scaffold that was ever erected," according to the *Times*. A wide board about four feet long was attached to the second-floor banister and then hinged to the wall opposite. With a tug on a trip rope, the board would simply drop against the wall. The whole thing, said the *Dispatch*, cost only $1.50. In truth it cost more than

$5, but no one at the courthouse issued a correction.[1]

It cost another forty cents to ship the hanging rope, the same rope that had been sent to Lunenburg in September.[2] After thirteen years of hangings, the rope had taken on an almost magical quality, bringing confidence to the executioner. By the same token, thirteen years was a long time, and Sheriff Dickinson, who had never before executed anyone, wanted to make sure the rope remained strong enough to do its gruesome duty. Above the platform where the condemned man would stand, a hole was cut in the ceiling and the rope attached to the exposed joist, making just enough clearance for a seven-foot drop. Two days before the execution the sheriff and his men dragged a two-hundred-pound sandbag up to the scaffold to test the trap and the rope.

The trap fell, and the rope held. The next day the sheriff and a deputy fetched Solomon Marable from the Lynchburg jail.[3]

*　　*　　*

IN THE EARLY morning of execution day the darkness surrounding the Prince Edward jail was total: no stars, no moon, and no wind at all; just low clouds and steady drizzle. Solomon Marable sat with jailer Edward Matthews, who prayed with him and read from the Bible.[4]

At four in the morning they heard someone hail the deputy at the jail's entrance. John Mitchell, Jr., had arrived on the early train. Thirteen men were to watch Solomon die later that morning, and Mitchell was one of them.

"How are you feeling, Solomon?" Mitchell asked.

"Tolerable," answered Solomon.

"Did you sleep any last night?"

"Yes, sir."

"I expected to come to see you before you left Lynchburg, but could not so arrange it."

"Yes, I looked for you up to the time I left," Solomon answered, and then lifted his voice to another register. "Zion is my home," he declared. "I am going to heaven. I am ready and willing to go. Prayer is the gate, and faith unlocks the door."

The two men talked for a time; then Mitchell headed out to get breakfast. The sky had lightened just enough to reveal a small man approaching the jail. Father Welbers offered Mitchell his hand, then walked on through the drizzle to try to see Solomon. Judge Crute, however, had ordered that no clergyman be admitted unless invited by Solomon himself. This morning Solomon turned the priest away.

Welbers resolved to try again but had little hope. The last time he had seen Solomon was in the Lynchburg jail. Welbers did not believe the white man story and had said as much to Solomon, urging him to come clean. But Solomon had stood firm. Instead of changing his story, he had changed spiritual advisers.

When John Mitchell returned to the jail at seven, the noise coming from inside stopped him in his tracks. The sound came from Solomon: the choked, squealing sobs of a man who must cry but will not give himself up to it. By this time a delegation of men and women from the Baptist church had arrived. They struck up a familiar hymn of comfort, and in a few minutes Solomon was able to sing with them.

Mitchell went in then to take down Solomon's final statement. The jailer placed two chairs outside the cell door. H. D. Perkins, a white reporter for the *Richmond Times*, took one; Mitchell, the other. "Marable," said Mitchell, "we desire to get your last statement concerning the murder of Mrs. Pollard." Still in his shirtsleeves, Solomon began. Perkins and Mitchell kept their jackets and hats on, their straw boaters bent low over their notebooks.[5]

"All I have to say in this world, if I never speak anymore, if my life be taken away from me, it will be taken away from me unjust. David James Thompson is the man who killed Mrs. Pollard."

Was Solomon certain of the name?

"There is no mistake about the name. He is a low, spare made man, got long, curly, sandy-colored hair. He got long sideburns, come down equal to his mouth, and sandy moustache, not so long. He was here during the trial, had on a gray overcoat. He lives at Finneywood. He is called The Boss. He is the depot agent and stays at the post office."

With some prodding from the newspapermen, Solomon gave more detail than ever before:

I left my house about six o'clock that morning, went directly to Fort Mitchell, staying there about two and a half hours, I suppose; then left there, going towards the sawmill to work. On my way I came across Thompson on the roadside. He was leaning on the side of the fence with his elbow resting on the rail and his hand up to his jaw. This was about one hundred yards from the depot.

I walked up to speaking distance. Thompson says, "Good morning, Solomon." I said, "Good morning, Mr. Thompson." He said, "Where you going?" I said I was going to the sawmill. He said, "No you ain't, God damn it, you are going with me," and he jerked out his pistol and said, "You come up beside me."

I went up beside of him and he said, "Do you know anybody at Mr. Pollard's?" I said, "I know some people who work there." He said, "Who are they?" I said, "Aunt Mary Barnes has been working there," and he said, "That all?" I said, "Mary Abernathy works on the place there and Pokey Barnes lives on the line fence."

He said, "That's all I want to know." Then he took me by his side and went through the woods to an old house that was caved in at the spring branch at Mr. Pollard's. He sat down there. After sitting there awhile we heard Mr. Pollard's bell ring.

The reporters wanted to know why the bell rang. "I don't know what it rung for," said Solomon. "After a while the bell rang again. We stayed there a long time after the second bell ring."

Then next I saw Aunt Mary Barnes coming down the spring hill. I said, "Yonder is Aunt Mary Barnes now." He says, "Where is she going?" I said, "I don't know. She has a bucket on her arm. Guess she's going to the spring." He says, "You see anyone else?" I said, "No, sir."

We sat there a good while afterwards and I heard someone talking to a horse, saying "Come up!" And he said, "Do you see anybody?" and I said, "No, sir."

I sat there nigh as I can come at it, a quarter of an hour.

> He got up then and said, "Get up, and come on." And we
> got up and went up the spring hill. He says, "I'm going to
> make a noise at the door and I want you to catch 'em
> when they come out."

The journalists raised their heads and stopped Solomon for a
moment: Whom was Solomon supposed to catch when he or she or
they came out? Solomon answered:

> He made no distinguishing as to who. I said, "Mr. Thomp-
> son, I don't care to have anything to do with them folks.
> They ain't done nothing to me, and I nothing to them."
> He says, "God damn it, that ain't what I told you to do,
> and damn it if you don't do as I told you to do, I'll shoot
> your damn head off." When he got up to the yard fence, he
> repeated the same words over again.
> He went up to the house. He made a noise at the door
> and she came out and saw his shadow as he was going
> around the house, and she looked at it and did not look
> behind her, and commenced walking backward upon me,
> and directly as she stumbled against me I caught her by
> the hands. At the same time Thompson came from behind
> the house. He says, "Do you know me?" She says, "You are
> a white man." She was about to recognize him, I thought,
> when he cut her off by saying, "How long has Mr. Pollard
> been back here?" I disremember whether she said before
> twelve or after twelve o'clock.
> He says, "I came here to kill old Pollard, but as I don't see
> him, I'll just kill you." He picked up the axe and drew back,
> and when he drew back I turned her loose and he said,
> "Where in the hell are you going?" I answered I wasn't going
> anywhere, and he struck her three licks with the helve and
> then he turned the eye of the axe and I don't know how
> many times he struck her. She was on the ground.

The *Times* reporter broke in again. The largest pool of blood had
formed under Mrs. Pollard's head, but more blood had pooled a few
feet closer to the house. Could Solomon account for this? Solomon
replied:

Yes, while the white man was striking her as she lay on the ground, she kept drawing up her feet, digging her heels in the ground, and pushing herself along.

I started away. He said, "Where are you going now?" I replied that I was going home. Thompson said, "No, you ain't; I have got to have more talk with you." He caught me by my arms and carried me on in the house with him. Just as we got in the big part of the house, he went to a trunk and reached his right hand into one drawer and got something and put it in his pocket. I don't know what that something was. He next put his left hand in a lower part and drew out a roll of paper money and put it into his pocket, but how much it was I don't know."

Solomon paused for a moment when one of his lawyers burst in with the final word from Governor O'Ferrall. "I saw the governor in your behalf," said the attorney, breathing hard. "He said that he could not conscientiously interfere. He would not give you any further time. You'll have to hang."

"Yes, sir," said Solomon, as though he had just been informed that the sun rose in the east. He turned back to the reporters. "We went on down to the road which leads from Fort Mitchell to Burnsgate and where another road crosses it. He gave me two twenty-dollar bills. I didn't know what they were then. He told me to go to Chase City and spend it, and not spend it at any of the little stores around there as it might give me away, but spend some of it and have enough to register the letter back in my own name. He said if I got caught to put Mary Abernathy, Pokey Barnes and Mary Barnes in it, and if I didn't do it, he would kill me on next sight. I left there then and went home."

Solomon stuck to his white man story to the last. As Mitchell rose and stretched, he couldn't help being impressed with Solomon's steadiness and consistency. The new details were impressive too. Solomon had just stated that David Thompson had compelled him to walk to the Pollard place through the woods. This made great sense. Not only was this the shortest route from Fort Mitchell, but it also explained why no one had spotted Thompson and Marable together that morning. And how about the image of

Lucy Pollard on the ground, blinded perhaps and only half-conscious, scooting backward to get away from the ax? The image was horrifying. But this too clarified something that had gone unexplained before.

The deputy announced the arrival of Reverend H. H. Mitchell, pastor of Farmville's largest black church, First Baptist. Solomon asked for a moment's delay while he poured water into a basin, washed his face and hands, and put on his jacket and tie. He had gained weight, and when he buttoned his jacket, it pulled across his chest. Reverend Mitchell came in then and commenced a service, the little group from the church singing and praying to prepare Solomon for his journey to the other side.

When the service was over, the ladies left, and Solomon asked for a last private word with John Mitchell, Jr., who stepped up to the grate and gave Solomon his hand. "Give my love to my wife and children," said Solomon. "Tell her good-bye and to meet me in glory. Tell her I am going to heaven. They can take the body, but they cannot kill the soul. Tell her I am trusting in Jesus. Tell her that prayer is the gate to heaven, and faith unlocks the door. Tell her to do the best she can with the children." A tearful Mitchell promised to tell Fannie all these things. He promised too that Solomon's body would be sent home for burial.

"God bless you, Mr. Mitchell! I know you have done all you could for me. God has a crown of glory for you and it will be given you at the last day."

At nine-thirty Sheriff Dickinson appeared at the cell door, paper in hand. Voice trembling, Dickinson read the death warrant. Then he unlocked the door, swung it open, and manacled Solomon's hands behind his back. The jailer had brought him a deluxe breakfast, but it sat untouched on a tray. Solomon had eaten during the night, though, had made his way through a bunch of bananas, brought to him by special request. Now he looked at the men who were about to watch him die. "I know that I feel better even than any one of you who will see me hung."[6]

The sheriff escorted him down the corridor and up the nine stairs, Solomon nodding to those whom he recognized. On the landing Solomon stepped up on a chair and thence to the trapdoor. The top of his head grazed the ceiling. The sheriff and his deputy strapped Solomon's legs together at the ankles and just above the knees.

The sheriff was just about to ask him whether he had anything to say when Solomon spoke out. "Well, gentlemen, you all is strangers to me here. Some of you may know the Lord in the pardoning of your sins and some not. But here is something that will be a warning to you. I have made a true statement just before I came up here to the reporters downstairs, and I again declare it to be true. Jesus is standing by me on the right hand side. I've got a free ticket to glory. Prayer is the gate and faith the key which will unlock the door."

The witnesses shifted on their feet, some standing behind Solomon on the landing, some down on the ground floor, and a few lined up on the stairs along the banister. Solomon preached on: "I will wear a crown of glory. I am speaking to all. Color makes no difference to me. How many can say they are striving for that place? All who are will show it by holding up their hands."

Several hands went up.

"Now, let me see how many sinner men are making their way to hell. It makes no difference about your color. Raise your hands!"

Nobody moved.

"My feet are taken out of the miry clay. This is all I have to say."

The sheriff placed a black hood over Solomon's head. Then he put the noose around Solomon's neck and slipped the knot.

"Does it hurt you?" the sheriff asked.

"Yes, it's rather tight," said Solomon.

"How is that?"

"It pinches my neck."

The sheriff loosened the rope just a bit. Two physicians were present, and one of them spoke up. "You'd better place the cap outside of the rope. Excuse my suggestion." The sheriff did as the doctor said.

"I bid each and every one good-bye," came the voice from under the hood. "May they have the blessing which this world assures. Good-bye to each and every one!"

Reverend Mitchell delivered a final prayer.

The voice came again from under the hood. "I would like for Mr.

Mitchell to take charge of my things, my hat and such, and send them to my wife."

"What Mitchell?" asked the sheriff.

"John Mitchell. Farewell to each and everybody!"

The sheriff gave a sharp pull on the trip rope and Solomon shot straight down. There were two quick convulsions about his neck and chest, and after that no motion but the swinging.

*　　*　　*

IN THE 1880s and 1890s there arose new structures that one day would stand as great hallmarks of modern American life. Among them was bureaucracy.

In Virginia no one asked for it. Political theory, at least among the sorts who landed in the legislature, ran heavily to the famous maxim that the government that governs least governs best. But bureaucracy came to the Old Dominion anyway, mostly by accident or stealth, to wit: the Anatomical Board of Virginia.

The Anatomical Board was created by the legislature in 1884 to collect human bodies and apportion them among the state's three medical schools for dissection. Since the 1840s medical men at the forefront of their fast-developing profession had insisted that doctors in training be instructed in "practical anatomy," cutting into cadavers to see for themselves what lay inside. But where to get the bodies? Nobody volunteered; to most nineteenth-century people, mutilating a body was sacrilege. Accordingly, there developed a bizarre market in human corpses, many of them stolen from new graves by thieves known as resurrectionists and sack-'em-up boys. Most vulnerable were the burial grounds of the poor. And most of the bodies that ended up on the dissecting table were those of black people.[7]

The whole sordid situation was exposed in 1882, when Chris Baker (the black "janitor" at Richmond's Medical College of Virginia), his black assistant, and two white medical students were caught red-handed with a fresh body. Although grave robbery was a crime, Baker and the others were acquitted, and black Richmonders were outraged. Highly embarrassed, the doctors wrote an Anatomical Bill and in 1884 lobbied it through the General Assembly.[8]

Thus was born the Anatomical Board of Virginia, an agency

intended to discourage body snatching while assuring the medical colleges a supply of lawfully acquired corpses. In the new system, deceased prisoners and paupers became Virginia's cadavers of choice. The remains of all convicts who died in jail now belonged to the state, as did those of paupers who died in local poorhouses. Families could try to intervene; if kin claimed a body and could afford to transport and bury it, then the departed inmate might escape the Anatomical Board. Otherwise the remains were to be sacrificed to science.

While the new system was an improvement over the wholesale desecration of graves, no one was really satisfied. As before, most of the bodies delivered to the medical schools were those of African Americans, a source of continuing grief and frustration in black communities. It did not help that the medical schools in question refused to admit black students. Meanwhile the board's members—professors of anatomy in the schools for which the bodies were destined— felt frustrated as well. Even with the law at their backs, they had great difficulty getting jailers and overseers of the poor to send the bodies. The board thus faced perpetual shortages of what it termed anatomical material.

In 1895 the board held its annual meeting and came away with an aggressive collection plan, "the sense of the meeting being that we claim all bodies when needed."[9] The get-tough policy was still in force eight months later, when Solomon Marable was executed.

On July 3, 1896, when the body of Solomon Marable was taken down in the Prince Edward County jail, an agent of the Anatomical Board waited outside with a wagon, a pine coffin, and a big crate addressed to the University College of Medicine in Richmond.[10]

*　　*　　*

THE NEXT DAY, July 4, John Mitchell, Jr., was arrested for abducting the body of Solomon Marable.

The day had begun on a hopeful note. Mitchell was back in Richmond and at 8:00 A.M. set out with three black ministers on a simple mission: to get written permission from the University College of Medicine to take possession of Solomon's body. After calling upon two of the college's officials, Mitchell thought he had what he needed. The ministers then stationed themselves at the college's rear door, ready to intercept the body when it arrived from the railroad station. They had a wagon also and an undertaker standing by to begin the embalming.

Then everything went haywire. The body, Mitchell learned, should not have gone to the University College of Medicine—it was not UCM's turn—but rather to its bitter rival, the nearby Medical College of Virginia.[11] Mitchell set out to find MCV's dean, but it was Saturday, and the man was not in his office. Meantime the crate bearing Solomon's remains had arrived and was loaded on the ministers' wagon. What to do? The corpse would not keep long in the July heat. Mitchell hesitated, then ordered the body delivered to his friend William Selden, the black funeral director whose mortuary was nearby.

Enter William P. Mathews, M.D., secretary of the Anatomical Board and the main engine of its successes. If the board got bodies, it was because Mathews found the agents, paid them well, gave them pep talks, and sent them barrels.[12] Determined that no "anatomical material" should ever elude him, he tended to press the board's legal rights beyond all reason.

Mathews was furious when he learned that Mitchell's gang had intercepted Solomon Marable's body. Quickly he organized his own gang, stormed over to Selden's—and snatched the body back! This time Solomon's remains went to the Medical College of Virginia.

Meanwhile, not satisfied with the mere recovery of the body, Mathews had John Mitchell, Jr., and William Selden arrested, charging Mitchell with abduction and Selden with receiving stolen goods.

Editor and undertaker quickly made bail, and Mitchell set out again with the ministers. For several hours they crisscrossed the city, now in search of legal counsel as well as the elusive dean of the Medical College of Virginia. When at length they found him, he stonewalled them.

Fortunately they found George Wise as well. Wise leaned on his friend the dean and that night brought the other interested parties to the table. Not coincidentally, they convened at the offices of the *Richmond Dispatch*. The very existence of the Anatomical Board depended on avoiding adverse publicity. If Dr. Mathews insisted on cutting up Solomon Marable, the story would be all over the morning papers.

A sullen William P. Mathews kept everyone else waiting until well past dark, but in the end he surrendered. John Mitchell, Jr., offered to pay the shipping charge from Farmville. Then he swallowed hard, apologized verbally and in writing, and came away with a written order for the body of Solomon Marable.[13]

*   *   *

MIDNIGHT, JULY 4, 1896. All was quiet around the Capitol grounds, except for the creaks of two carriages and the slow clip-clop of the horses, pulling hard up the steep grade toward Broad Street. In the carriages rode a posse of black ministers. Ahead of them, hanging from the south face of the New City Hall, loomed the most enormous Confederate flag they had ever seen. For three days past Richmond had hosted a gigantic reunion of Confederate veterans. Sixty-five thousand veterans and spectators had come from all over the South, with a proportional number of reporters, performers, and pickpockets. By now most had gone home, but reminders of the reunion were everywhere. The Capitol lawn was a white sea of wastepaper, peanut shells, and lemon peels.[14]

In a few moments the ministers crossed Broad and alighted at the Medical College of Virginia, a boxy structure built in the Egyptian style. Tonight it looked more than ever like a mausoleum. Reverend James H. Holmes, the gray-bearded senior member of the ministerial party, hammered on the front door. No response. Holmes hammered some more and shouted words not befitting a man of God.

Just then John Mitchell, Jr., arrived, and they heard someone calling from the other end of the building. Mitchell walked around to the back, and there, shoes in one hand and a lantern in the other, sat the infamous resurrectionist Chris Baker—as Mitchell called him, "the colored wizard of this institution."

"Now, if there is any man on earth afraid of the living and at home with the dead," Mitchell wrote, "it is Chris Baker." In Baker's body-snatching days, "colored folks couldn't get into a grave at the colored cemetery before Brother Baker would have them in a bag on the way to this same medical college."[15]

"Is this Mr. Mitchell?" Baker asked.

"Yes."

"Produce the order and you can get the body." William Selden's elegant funeral wagon had just arrived, burning lamps hanging from both sides. Chris Baker disappeared into the building. A short time later he came out again, calling for undertaker Selden. After an hour Selden stuck his head out the door and called Mitchell in.

He soon found himself in a dimly lit dissecting room. In the center of the floor a large barrel lay on its side, and from it protruded the head and arms of Solomon Marable. Earlier in the day Chris Baker had removed the body from its coffin and pushed it into a crouch inside the barrel, throwing in some salt and heaven only knew what else. But then Mitchell had turned up with his order. So for the past hour Baker and Selden had been working to get the body *out* of the barrel.

"One more pull, Selden, come on!" Baker and Selden each grabbed an arm and pulled for all they were worth. The body had swollen and would not budge. The only substances emerging from the barrel were salt and blood, which made a paste on the floor.

"Can't get it out tonight! Can't get it out tonight!" sang Baker as he hopped around the barrel. "Come in the morning! Say what time you'll be here and it'll be all right. Pull any more, burst the kneepans off."

Marable's mouth was slightly open, emitting gas from time to time. "Wait 'til the gas passes off! Can't pull on it any more." When enough gas escaped, Baker thought he could get the body out without damage to the kneecaps. "Let it stay 'til morning!—'Twill be all right. Come here Selden, help get it back in here." With some prying and pushing, they got one arm back in. Then they stood the barrel on end and wrestled the other arm in. Baker bent down, scraped the salt from the floor with his hands, and tossed it into the barrel.

There remained the matter of the head. Baker backed off a few paces, then took a flying leap, landing squarely on top of what remained of Solomon Marable. It worked. The barrel closed.

*   *   *

CHRIS BAKER WAS wrong about the swelling's going down. When Selden returned in the morning, it was worse. Selden and his co-workers sighed and loaded the barrel onto their wagon. After they reached the funeral home, they got the body out by smashing up the barrel.[16]

They labored over the body all day, cleaning it up, reducing its size, and working out the distortions of the face. Then they embalmed it as best they could. After the shrouding, the body was laid in a casket, which was packed in ice and placed in a zinc-lined box.

In the wee hours of Monday morning, Selden's funeral wagon bore Solomon's body to the train station, through streets puddled from evening thunderstorms. Selden was to take the body to North Carolina while John Mitchell, Jr., stayed behind to deal with their legal problems.

Mitchell had sent a telegram to Fannie Marable, and before it could be delivered to the farm where she lived, everyone in the village of Stovall, North Carolina, knew the body was on its way. When the train arrived in midafternoon, the men loitering about the station had a lot of questions for Selden. Was he John Mitchell? Who was he then? How did he get the body? Why didn't they bury the man in Virginia? How come the box didn't smell?

The station agent called to some of the black men gathered at the depot, asking if the grave was ready. It was not, they told him. It had been half dug in the usual burying ground, but then Mr. Stovall had made them stop. Another group of men came up, and the agent put the same question to them. "No, sir," one of them replied. "We thought to have been able to get a grave in another desolated burying ground, but we were objected."

At four o'clock a site was found three miles off on a farm owned by a white man named Cox. Under a menacing sky, five men hurried ahead to dig the grave, while four others lifted the box into a waiting wagon. They had made only half a mile when they were assaulted by a furious rain.

Farmer Cox let them wait inside while a cart was sent for Fannie Marable. She soon arrived with her sisters, and the mourners processed about four hundred yards to the grave site. Selden preached, a local man prayed, and the casket was lowered into the mud, the rain coming down in torrents all the while. When the service was over, Selden paid the wagoneer and the gravediggers and presented Fannie Marable with five dollars that John Mitchell, Jr., had sent for her. Then, everyone soaked to the skin, they turned from the grave.

In Richmond that same day the charges against Mitchell and Selden were dismissed.

CHAPTER

22

COMMON SENSE

To the tobacco farmers of Virginia, July brought suckers and hornworms. The suckers came first, little shoots that if left alone grew into scrawny leaves worth almost nothing. Suckers had to be twisted off, only to reappear every seven days or so. The worms turned up a week or two after the first suckers, and as they ate the precious leaves, they too had to go—squashed on the spot or tossed into gunnysacks for turkey feed or fish bait. All hands turned out for suckering and worming, women and children included.[1]

In any other July, Edward Pollard would have been out suckering and worming with the best of them. But Edward, now seventy-three, had not recovered from the illness that had told on him during the trials in March and April. In early July he became bedridden and wrote his will. His doctor diagnosed "catarrh of the bowels," a condition that in a later time might have been called colon cancer.[2]

For several weeks Edward lay wasting in the feather bed in the big room, surrounded by the objects with which he and Lucy had made a home: the sideboard, his armchair, the dining table, the pictures and trunks. Grain and hay filled his barns. A hundred pounds of bacon hung in the smokehouse. More than forty of his neighbors owed him money, and for the first time in his life he'd put his own money in the bank. He was conscious until the last day and frank to the end. He admitted that he was very much afraid of death.

Edward Pollard died at ten forty-five on the morning of July 30, 1896. He was buried the next day in the orchard next to his late wife Lucy.

*   *   *

MARY ABERNATHY REMAINED in legal limbo throughout July and August. The guards in the Lynchburg jail marveled at her serenity, and indeed a signal blessing had been given her: Each day since June a woman from the black church had come for the baby and taken her out for a long excursion in the fresh air. At eight months Bessie Mitchell Abernathy was thriving. Mary drew strength from her child's robust health and her faith in God and composed herself for whatever might come next.[3]

On September 2 her petition for a new trial came before the cigar-chewing Judge Samuel Coleman in circuit court. The attorneys eased into their familiar places in Prince Edward's picturesque courthouse: Mann, Southall, and Watkins for Lunenburg; Henry Wood Flournoy and Alec Guigon for Mary Abernathy. Because this was an appeal, Mary herself was not present. She would await word from her cell in Lynchburg.[4]

Argument took all morning. Mary Abernathy's team set the terms, working from the bill of exceptions they had filed at the trial's conclusion. Judge Crute's biggest mistake, they argued, concerned the exchange in the Richmond jail, when Cass Gregory had offered to save Mary from hanging if she would tell where the money was. "I know nothing about it," Mary had declared—seemingly airtight proof of her innocence. Judge Crute, however, had instructed the jury to disregard it; he had evidently bought the prosecution's contention that this was a self-serving declaration and therefore inadmissible.

Judge Coleman had the annoying habit of making up his mind before the lawyers finished their arguments. As the last attorney sat down, the seat of his pants had barely brushed the chair when Coleman began explaining his decision. He was not impressed with any of the exceptions. In each instance he sustained Judge Crute.

But one last motion remained. After Mary Abernathy was pronounced guilty, her attorneys had asked Judge Crute to set the verdict aside as contrary to law and the evidence. Lawyers always submitted that motion when they lost; so routine was it that judges rarely paid it any attention. But Judge Coleman did. He had studied the testimony. The defendant had not been proved guilty.

Mary Abernathy was entitled to a new trial.

*　　*　　*

SHE NEEDED LITTLE time to pack; everything she owned was already stored in her trunk. On September 21, three weeks after Judge Coleman had authorized a new trial, the Prince Edward sheriff telegraphed his counterpart in Lynchburg and instructed him to escort Mary Abernathy to the train station.

By early afternoon they were waiting at the Lynchburg station. The train from Farmville was announced, and in a moment Mary Abernathy saw Alec Guigon and John Mitchell, Jr., hurrying toward her. Guigon handed an official-looking piece of paper to the city sergeant. Now three people knew what was happening, but Mary was not one of them. What, she asked Guigon, did he plan to do with her next?

"I'm going to take you to Richmond."[5]

"What for?" The last anyone had told her, she was destined for Farmville and a third trial.

"Because you are free."

She looked from Guigon to Mitchell to the city sergeant, who nodded in affirmation. She cried then, but not for long.

Their train would depart in just ten minutes. Mitchell went off to buy Mary a one-way ticket to Richmond. The city sergeant headed in another direction to see about her trunk. For the first time in fifteen months Mary Abernathy stood free of the custody of an officer of the law.

They took the 2:25 train, baby Bessie looking out the window as they gathered speed. Once they were under way, Guigon and Mitchell explained exactly what had happened that morning. The key decision had been Lunenburg's. With Edward Pollard in his grave, the prosecution had no witness to place Mary at the scene of the murder. Lunenburg's lawyers concluded that they could not get a conviction. A few days before a third trial would have begun, they quietly informed the other side that they would drop the case.[6]

Alec Guigon then set about choreographing Mary's release. Judge Crute had called the case first thing that morning when the September term of the county court began. Asa Watkins then rose to ask for a nolle prosequi, much as he had in the trial of Pokey Barnes. The judge promptly wrote an order discharging Mary Abernathy from custody, and a grinning Guigon headed for the train station. The train arrived with John Mitchell, Jr., already aboard, Guigon climbed on, and the two proceeded to Lynchburg to liberate Mary Abernathy.

Happily for Mary, her return to Richmond included a stop in Farmville. She arrived in late afternoon to the cheers of hundreds. Farmville's black citizenry had worked hard to bring about this day; they had watched in the night, visited by day, prayed at all hours, and kept both Mary and Pokey busy, fed, and respectably dressed. Now their sacrifices were rewarded with a free and joyful Mary Abernathy.

Judge Crute too wanted to be part of this last scene. With Sheriff Dickinson and Jailer Matthews, the judge worked his way through the crowd and went up into the passenger car to shake Mary's hand and wish her well. When the all aboard came, the three men stepped back down to the platform. But Mary reached out the open window and took Judge Crute's hand one more time. "Judge," she said, "God's been talking to you."[7] The judge blushed and melted back into the crowd as the train pulled away, carrying Mary Abernathy to her new life.

*　　*　　*

IN THE FIRST moments of Mary Abernathy's freedom, a reporter asked her how she felt. Eyes brimming, she surprised him by exclaiming, "I feel just as I did before I was ever put in jail!"[8]

And so it proved. Mary emerged from incarceration in fine spirits and remarkably good health, though physically weaker than she at first realized. She had been living in Richmond for about two weeks when a crisp October morning tempted her out for a long walk. She went first to Broad Street to have her portrait taken and then headed down to the jail to pay her respects to her former keepers. She insisted on walking all the way, downhill and up, an effort that would not have taxed her in her days on the farm. After her fifteen months in jail, however, the hike left her exhausted and wondering at her loss of endurance.[9]

In every other visible way she flourished. Life in Richmond brought one euphoric reunion after another. On her first night of freedom who should be waiting for her but her friend Pokey Barnes? The two were to live together in the home of the widow Graves until their new lives took shape.

Mary's eldest and most cosmopolitan child, Samuel, rushed up from Newport News as soon as he heard of his mother's release. Mary ached to see her other children, but letters from Lunenburg told her it was not safe for her to go there; she would have to wait until they could come to her. In the meantime Wilson Abernathy managed to travel up from Lunenburg with their married daughter Amy Gregory. They could stay only one night, but they enjoyed a party and made a plan. At the first of the year, when Wilson's tenant farm contract expired, he was to join Mary permanently in Richmond.[10]

It would be a leap in the dark for Wilson and also for the children, who had never looked upon a city, much less lived in one. It was a shorter leap for Mary, who was touched daily by the warmth of the people who stopped in to congratulate her. These Richmond people were impressive and generous. When she had her chance to honor them in the mass, she took it.

On a Wednesday night in early October, First African Baptist opened its doors for the city's first formal celebration of her freedom.[11] Mary brought the baby, and Pokey came too, along with the usual suspects: John Mitchell, Jr., and a string of ministers, including the church's eminent leader, Reverend James H. Holmes. Pokey had been featured at half a dozen such services after her own release. Hence she understood what she was supposed to do. She would sit up front, where everyone could see her, while the men delivered themselves of two or three hours' worth of oratory. Afterward she touched the people's hands and accepted their donations.

This would not do for Mary Abernathy. In front of a huge crowd in the city's largest black church, she got to her feet and told her own story. When she was through, she looked at Pokey, and Pokey in turn stood up and spoke. They were good, Pokey and Mary, at times breathtaking, their rapt audience hearing the clang of Edward Pollard's farm bell, feeling the heavy sorrow at Lucy Pollard's shrouding, imagining the captives' terror on the night the Pollards' yard filled with the roiling mob.

The ministers were not silenced, of course, but they were completely upstaged. They were even upstaged by nine-month-old Bessie, who spent the evening going happily from lap to lap in the audience. Like her mother, the child wore her celebrity well.

From that night forward Mary Abernathy and Pokey Barnes spoke for themselves, a drawing card that may have accounted for the astonishing crowd that gathered for the next performance on their schedule. The invitation came from the Harrison Street Baptist church in Petersburg. It would be the Lunenburg women's first public appearance outside Richmond, and to say the least, they were eagerly anticipated.

They arrived in Petersburg on a crystalline evening in late October. For two and a half blocks in all directions the streets around the church were packed with people, all of them anxious to get a seat when the doors were opened. No one knew the exact size of the crowd; guesses ranged up to eight thousand. But say it was only half that. There were still five times as many people as the church could hold.[12]

When the doors opened, the crowd surged forward. People were knocked down and stepped on in the stampede, and after the church had filled completely, the multitude on the outside still pressed to get in. Fearing a riot, Mitchell and the ministers canceled the evening's program. They turned off the church lights after things settled down a bit, and the great mass of people went home disappointed and shaken.

Mary Abernathy with nine-month-old Bessie Mitchell Abernathy.
PHOTO FROM THE *RICHMOND PLANET*, 17 OCTOBER 1896,
COURTESY OF THE LIBRARY OF VIRGINIA.

Mary and Pokey were shaken too, hiding out under police protection in a narrow cookshop next door to the church. They stayed in a private home that night and returned quietly to Richmond the next day.

*   *   *

For Mary Barnes, still grinding out her time in the penitentiary, the evening of the near riot went like any other. The bell rang, and eighty women lined up with their tin mugs and pans. As each inmate reached the head of the line, she got coffee in her mug and a square chunk of bread in the pan. That was supper, the same every evening. By dark the women were locked up for the night.

For John Mitchell, Jr., and all the other defenders of the Lunen-burg women, the final project was to get Mary Barnes out of prison. Once Mary Abernathy was set free in late September, Mitchell allowed himself to hope that Governor O'Ferrall would pardon the other Mary in a matter of days. But this governor had a different con-cept of the pardon process.[13]

To Charles O'Ferrall the exercise of executive clemency was a grave and often agonizing responsibility. He would not begin to con-sider a case until he had in hand a petition and ample supporting documents. To pardon Mary Barnes, O'Ferrall needed officials in Lunenburg and Prince Edward to get busy and furnish him with writ-ten proof that the prosecution had presented no evidence of her guilt other than the perjured testimony of Solomon Marable. Those very officials, however—Orgain, Crute, Watkins, and the rest—were con-sumed by the 1896 election, one of the most passionate in history. Bryan vs. McKinley, silver vs. gold: "It was a battle of Ballots," wrote Lunenburg diarist (and creative speller) Robert Allen, "between Wall Street Bankers, & English Bankers & all the Trusts, cyndicates, com-bines, monopolies of every kind, the money power every where, the almost united Press of the whole country, in conspiracy against the mass of the home honest conservitive working people of the coun-try, for life and liberty and it has been the hotest contest ever waged."[14]

The case of Mary Barnes came up at precisely the wrong time and was drowned out by the roar of apocalyptic politics. October turned to November, and November to December, with no pardon in sight.

*   *   *

INSIDE THE PENITENTIARY Sundays brought a change of pace. The shoe factory shut down; the inmates put on clean uniforms and, if they chose, attended an afternoon worship service. Mary Barnes looked forward to Sundays, attended her "meeting" faithfully, and hoped—almost always in vain—that someone would visit her. On the first Sunday in December, she was summoned to the superinten-dent's office.

She found herself in a room with the rawboned superintendent

B. W. Lynn, some guards, and a white woman she did not know, a middle-aged woman wearing a big hat and little spectacles. A guard brought soap and a basin of water and told Mary to start washing. The strange woman wanted to look at her hands, but they must first be very clean.[15]

Her hands?

The woman was introduced as Mrs. Rickey—to be precise, Adele Marie Graef Rickey. German-born and at one time a student of medicine, Mrs. Rickey traveled the nation, visiting prisons and asylums to conduct research on the human hand. Expertly read, argued Mrs. Rickey, the hand was a window into the soul, revealing everything that mattered about an individual: mental and moral characteristics as well as the physical.

"I would not advise a man to marry a girl with long, tapering fingers, if they are smooth," declaimed Mrs. Rickey. "The absence of lines in a hand denotes very little intellectual culture."

Her method, she insisted, bore no resemblance to the hocus-pocus of palm reading. Mrs. Rickey practiced the new science of "manimorphology." "Long, thin, supple fingers are usually those of diplomats, of deceivers, or pickpockets," said Mrs. Rickey, possibly conscious that no employees of the State Department were present. "Very short and very thick fingers are a sign of cruelty. Hands that cannot open wide and are stiff and dry indicate a miserly disposition and void of sympathy."

Mrs. Rickey had only three days in Richmond but quickly won the press's attention by examining famous prisoners. The penitentiary was just then short of celebrities, but the superintendent managed to produce Frank Cole, a white man widely admired for clever burglaries and jailbreaks, and Mary Barnes.

Frank Cole: "Almost a mechanical genius," bubbled Mrs. Rickey. "He is altogether out of his element in his present surroundings."

Mrs. Rickey adjusted her spectacles and squinted at the clean hands of Mary Barnes. "Mary Barnes has a terrible hand," she remarked. But it was a complex case, as she explained to reporters later in the day. "She is very cunning and can be described as belonging to the weasel family. Yet the woman possesses a certain amount of will power, and a faculty for using her companions to carry out her crafty devices. Mary Barnes's fingers are very pointed, which indicates that she is extremely impulsive."

Was she guilty? "The Barnes woman," said Mrs. Rickey, "I do not believe had sense enough to plan the whole murder, but she was capable of contriving the cunning part of the scheme and seeing that others executed it."

Cunning was a low, animal form of intelligence, as opposed to the loftier sort that one would find in, say, a constitutional lawyer or a manimorphologist. While she was at it, Mrs. Rickey examined the hand of Superintendent Lynn and declared him eminently qualified to head such an important institution.

*   *   *

DECEMBER HAD BEEN warm. But just before Christmas the wind turned and blew down from the north, delivering frigid air that quickened steps and froze the edges of the ponds. The sudden chill put Richmonders in a holiday mood, and people with money or credit scuttled out to buy toys and firecrackers for their children.

The governor's mansion overflowed with children, the younger ones the offspring of Charles O'Ferrall's second marriage. ("It is nothing, my dear," he once told his wife when an especially noisy scuffle broke out behind the mansion, "only your children and our children fighting my children.")[16] But the governor's family Christmas would not begin until he had sent his gift to the penitentiary, a packet of pardons for the innocent, the sick, and the guilty who had suffered enough.

Anyone hardy enough to walk in Capitol Square on the night of the twenty-third would have seen the light coming from the governor's office window at the mansion. He was working late. Sometime past midnight he decided to pardon Mary Barnes.[17]

She was pardoned with five other inmates. Four were men who had already served significant time; of these, three were seriously ill. The fifth was Octavia Hodges, a young white woman who had served four years for shooting a sewing machine salesman to death, had blown a hole through his chest when he approached her for something other than a sale.[18] Only in the case of Mary Barnes did the governor deem it necessary to publish an explanation of his reasoning.

"The life or liberty of a citizen, however humble," O'Ferrall concluded, "is too sacred in the eyes of the law or of civilized man to be taken upon the testimony alone of a self-convicted perjurer and murderer, one declared to be so base and degraded as to exclude him as a witness in subsequent trials in a court. Every mandate of justice and dictate of conscience require that the prisoner be restored to her liberty."[19]

Amen to that. By the time Mary Barnes went to trial in Lunenburg Courthouse, Solomon Marable's contradictions had stuck out like Edward Pollard's ears. But "Old" Mary Barnes had been sacrificed anyway. After her conviction she was isolated by her prison sentence from her daughter Pokey and from Mary Abernathy. Beyond the minimum necessary to secure her pardon, no one paid her much attention.

To the end she was the odd woman out. On Christmas Eve, Superintendent Lynn personally handed her the written pardon. She was free to leave the prison then but did not go out that day because she had nothing decent to wear.[20]

On a bright, windy Christmas morning, John Mitchell, Jr., came for her in a carriage, intending to drive her to the place her husband, Joseph, had rented across the river in Manchester. Mitchell arrived shortly after nine to find that Mary Barnes had already walked off. She had made her own living arrangements—for the moment sans Joseph—boarding in north Richmond with a couple named Jackson. An exasperated Mitchell turned the carriage around and went to look for her.

*   *   *

IN LUNENBURG AND all over the South, January was the month of motion and hope.

Croppers and renters bundled up goods and children, piled wagons high, and drove carefully over frozen roads to new places. Most were destined for a version of the rural life they already knew. Others were animated by higher hopes or deeper desperation, and they took bigger chances. They dressed up, packed little, and kept going until they reached a train station. At day's end they were in a town or city, embarked on a new life.

Among the seekers who abandoned the countryside in January 1897 were the Abernathys. They appeared one day on Bettie Graves's doorstep—ten of them! Mary Abernathy was overjoyed. Bettie Graves was overwhelmed. John Mitchell, Jr., once again the fixer, found them a small row house to rent on the northwestern outskirts of the city near the stockyards.[21] Mary and Wilson and their younger children moved in and soon blended into the blue-collar life around them.

Mary returned to the spotlight from time to time. The port city of Norfolk had offered crucial support to the Lunenburg women, its people sending nearly $400 just in time to fund the battle in the Supreme Court of Appeals. Three months after her release Mary Abernathy took the baby to Norfolk. They packed the Bute Street Baptist Church two nights running, saw the ocean, and came home with $150.[22]

Mary Barnes made appearances as well. No one had figured her for an orator, and she drew small audiences on her own. But she added something authentic and touching to the more fluid talk of Mary Abernathy and John Mitchell, Jr. Together they drew big audiences in Hampton and Berkeley in the Tidewater and in Danville to the southwest.[23]

Where meanwhile was Pokey Barnes? Pokey had lit out for the big city. At about the time the Abernathy family moved to Richmond, the *Planet* reported that Pokey Barnes had remarried, moved to New York, and found work.[24] The *Planet* lost track of her after that, save for one article on a glittering evening in Hartford, Connecticut.

"Brethren and sisters, I am Pokey Barnes of Lunenburg County, Virginia, whom you have read so much about." Pokey stood to the right of the altar in Hartford's Union Baptist Church. She wore silk and a black hat trimmed in velvet and ostrich feathers. With the confident diction that she had used so ably on the witness stand, Pokey told her story, a hair-raising tale of lynch mobs narrowly escaped, of handcuffs worn so long that they rusted shut, of a looming scaffold and her yawning grave. Pokey, it was clear, knew how to take a good story and make it better. She held her audience for nearly two hours. Before bidding them good night, she gave them a laugh line to break the somber mood. She was not educated, she said, and had no D.D.'s

Pokey Barnes as she appeared in May 1896.

PHOTO FROM THE
RICHMOND PLANET,
27 JUNE 1896,
COURTESY OF THE
LIBRARY OF VIRGINIA.

or M.D.'s after her name. She was simply "Pokey Barnes, C.S." Pokey Barnes, Common Sense, sent her audience chuckling into the night.[25]

The *Planet* article gave ample evidence of Pokey's talents as a speaker. Perhaps inadvertently it also raised a question about her future as a mother. Embedded in the report like a bit of shrapnel was a sentence indicating that Pokey's daughter, Martha Ann, by this time about six years old, was still in Lunenburg.[26] Free for eight months, Pokey had not gotten her child out. The Hartford church took up a collection to help Pokey move her daughter to "a place of safety," but the documents end there. The morning after her Hartford speech, February 20, 1897, Pokey Barnes took the train back to New York City. It is not known where life took her after that.

CHAPTER

23

THE PITCHER TO
THE WELL

The pitcher may go to the well a long long time, but will
ultimately get broke.

—ROBERT ALLEN, CHRISTMAS 1888

Two months after Edward Pollard died, the neighbors gathered
at his place one last time. The farm was to be broken up, and
everything that could be carried, carted, or led away on a halter
was for sale. More than a hundred people came.

The October weather was brisk, but no matter how bracing the
day, a sale always brought a funereal feeling, intensifying as the
barns and yard emptied. The horses went quickly, a pair of bays and
Edward's famous gray mare. Lucius Pettus bought the six head of
cattle. Stacks of fodder were hauled away, along with barrels of
wheat, bushels of sweet potatoes, a tub of onions. All of Edward's
implements went on the block, and everything in the kitchen. Bas-
kets, bowls, boxes, bottles: All were gone by sundown, dispersed

among seventy-five households. The items were useful and cost little, and because of the murder, they doubled as souvenirs. The farm bell went for $1.25. David James Thompson paid pennies for the pepper box in which the Pollards had kept their keys.[1]

The murder of Lucy Pollard was a story with one grisly beginning and dozens of endings.[2] Except for Solomon Marable and Edward Pollard, all the many players went on with their lives, scattering like Lucy's pots and pans to their separate destinies. Yet in ways barely visible to them at the time, they remained characters in a common large story—not a murder mystery this time but a sad coming-of-age story for Virginia.

*   *   *

JOHN MITCHELL, JR., never did marry Marietta Chiles. She died in 1924, still single. The gravestone put up by her fellow teachers at the Baker School said, "She hath done what she could." Mitchell lived until 1929. A bachelor to the last, he collapsed in his *Planet* office at age sixty-six.[3]

Mitchell was only thirty-three on the day that Mary Barnes walked out of the penitentiary. The Lunenburg case had been an amazing coup, earning him something the white press hardly ever granted black individuals: respectful attention. Among African Americans Mitchell had become a hero of national stature. In black newspapers across the country his name stood for courage and race pride.[4]

It can be a mixed blessing for an ambitious person to peak so early. After he was cheated out of his position on the city council in May 1896, Mitchell promised a thousand cheering supporters that he would regain his council seat if he had to fight all summer. Authority to certify election results, however, lay with the council's sitting members, most of them white Democrats who were only too happy to bid Mitchell adieu. By midsummer the white press was calling him a "sick political kitten."[5]

Dead duck was more like it. Mitchell never regained his seat on the city council, nor in the years left to him would he attain public office of any kind. Like many other men, Mitchell fell victim to the gathering forces of white supremacy. By the opening of the new century no blacks served in the Virginia legislature or on Richmond's city council, a result achieved largely by fraud. Shamed by the magnitude of the corruption—and fearful lest blacks make common cause with populist whites—a critical mass of white Democrats at last succeeded in calling a constitutional convention. Their work, the Constitution of 1902, disfranchised more than 80 percent of black men and a great many whites, so many that the framers did not dare submit their work to the voters for ratification. Instead they simply proclaimed it the new law of the commonwealth. Local politicos then moved to clean out any remaining pockets of black activism. In Richmond, Jackson Ward was gerrymandered out of existence in 1903.[6]

As time passed, John Mitchell, Jr., grew heavier around the midriff and jawline, and harder of heart, his cynicism deepening with each new assault on the rights of black Virginians. He had championed Richmond's black militia companies; they were abolished in 1899. The General Assembly segregated the railroads in 1900 and streetcars in 1904. In 1911 Richmond adopted racial zoning, an attempt to segregate residential neighborhoods further. In the 1920s, no longer content to follow the lead of other states, Virginia moved into the "racial integrity" vanguard. In 1924 the General Assembly implemented the "no trace" rule: Only those with *zero* discernible African or Asian ancestry qualified as "white." (In deference to those who claimed descent from Pocahontas, many of them members of the elite, a person with up to one-sixteenth American Indian ancestry also qualified as white.) Everyone else was lumped together as colored, and marriages between members of the two groups were forbidden.[7]

Few white people stood with Mitchell against the accelerating juggernaut of white supremacy. *Father Lambert Welbers*, a fearless and forthright opponent of segregation, was the exception. Unfortunately for Virginia, Father Welbers was transferred to a Delaware parish in September 1896. In a parting gesture, he brought a guest pastor to Richmond, Father Charles Uncles, one of only four black Roman Catholic priests in the United States. On the final Sunday that Welbers spent with his Richmond congregation, the towering Uncles celebrated the mass. The diminutive Welbers assisted him, an act that spoke volumes.[8]

In the new century John Mitchell, Jr., made do with grimier white allies. At age sixty-six, attorney *George Douglas Wise* won a seat in the constitutional convention of 1901–02. Since the close of the Lunenburg case Wise had continued to represent black clients in criminal trials, and he ran for the convention as a dissident, promising to fight the wholesale disfranchisement of black men. This he proceeded to do, but he also demonstrated how much racism could be packaged in a course of ostensible moderation. In advocating measures that would have disfranchised comparatively few voters, Wise cranked up the rhetoric, venting sentiments normally associated with white race radicals. No matter who voted, he told his all-white colleagues, Caucasians were naturally superior and therefore would rule. And suffrage was a short-term problem anyway. Two such drastically different races could not coexist forever; eventually, Wise argued, "the African will have to go."[9]

As Wise spoke, African Americans were already going—though not toward the oblivion of Wise's fantasy. They were moving from the South's farms to its towns and cities; many also moved to the burgeoning industrial centers of the North and West, a phenomenon that after 1915 became known as the Great Migration. They were pushed out by the prolonged depression in agriculture; rural counties like Lunenburg had no work for most of their young and had been exporting them, white as well as black, ever since the Civil War. But the relentless pressure of white supremacy pushed especially hard on black southerners. With the way opened by kin, they moved north in record numbers when World War I created an urgent need for workers. Altogether, between 1890 and 1920, hundreds of thousands of black Virginians sought opportunity outside the places they had been born; in 1920, for the first time, Lunenburg had fewer black residents than white.[10]

John Mitchell, Jr., soldiered on in Richmond, coming into his prime just as Jim Crow took its mature shape. Like many of his contemporaries, Mitchell devoted his energies increasingly to business, one of the few avenues of distinction still open to black men and women. Along the way the *Planet* lost its edge, its content having less to do with the struggles of black Americans as a group and more with the personal fortunes of John Mitchell, Jr. Some issues read like extended advertisements, for Mitchell's bank, Mitchell's fraternal order, and Mitchell's real estate offerings (homes for the living, cemetery plots for the dead).[11]

He still wrote some forceful editorials, and at times the *Planet* helped mobilize the whole community, as in 1904, when black Richmonders boycotted the newly segregated streetcars for nearly a year.[12] But neither journalism nor business quite satisfied Mitchell's desire to be in the center of things. John Mitchell, Jr., was made for politics. White supremacy deprived him of the job he did best and loved most, one more testament to the colossal waste of talent that blighted Jim Crow America.

*   *   *

THE POST-LUNENBURG career of Governor *Charles O'Ferrall*, like that of John Mitchell, Jr., was essentially tragic. Like Mitchell, he loved politics. Like Mitchell also, O'Ferrall was sidelined from 1896 on.

O'Ferrall's ruin began that summer, when the Democratic National Convention went for free silver, voting to knock gold off its pedestal as the sole standard of value and to elevate silver, which was to be coined as fast as miners could dig it out of the ground. More, the convention nominated William Jennings Bryan, the young silverite from Nebraska. Bryan's acceptance speech was to become one of the most famous in history. "You shall not press down upon the brow of labor this crown of thorns," he thundered, "you shall not crucify mankind on a cross of gold."[13]

The convention was electrified. The governor of Virginia was appalled. O'Ferrall believed free silver was lunacy, believed it so firmly that he bolted his party, throwing his support behind a dissident ticket of "gold Democrats." Having learned from experience that faithfulness to principle won him respect, if not always agreement, O'Ferrall was dumbfounded by what happened next. Newspapers across the state exploded in outrage at his stance. Richmond's largest Democratic club summarily stripped him of his membership. All over Virginia local Democrats passed venomous resolutions and called on their governor to resign.[14] O'Ferrall the politician was finished, crucified on a cross of silver.

In his last gloomy year as governor he was troubled more deeply still by the return of lynching to Virginia. O'Ferrall had begun his term intent on eradicating mob violence, and at the dawn of 1897 it looked as though he had done it. After the troops left Lunenburg Courthouse in July 1895, eighteen months went by without a single call for the militia.[15] To the degree that lynching could be ended by leadership from the top, O'Ferrall seemed to have ended it.

The problem of course was the failure of leadership at the other end. On April 24, 1897, word reached Richmond that a young black man had been lynched in Alexandria. Charged with sexual assault on a white girl, Joseph McCoy had been placed in the town jail. In the middle of the night five hundred men and boys stormed the jail, seized McCoy, and hanged him from a lamppost.[16]

O'Ferrall was baffled. How could someone be lynched in a town with a professional police force and a company of militia? Information gathered over the next few days revealed a classic case of cowardice, possibly collusion, on the part of the authorities. The mayor claimed to have been lost in slumber when the lynching took place. Several policemen had been roughed up by the mob but afterward could not identify their assailants. Some of the militiamen were thought to have joined the mob. Not one person would name the ringleaders.

Lest potential lynchers be emboldened by the Alexandria case, O'Ferrall looked to make a show of arms. A few days after the McCoy lynching, mob violence threatened to erupt in nearby Fairfax. The sheriff did not think he needed troops, but the governor sent them anyway and afterward twisted the sheriff's arm until he "asked" for military help. No lynching took place in Fairfax.

After his term as governor ended, O'Ferrall struggled with political exile. His health was poor, in part because of old war wounds, but he returned to the practice of law and in 1904 published a memoir, a genial book that helped rehabilitate his reputation. A year after the book appeared, O'Ferrall died at age sixty-five. In his funeral procession walked a riderless horse, symbol of the fallen hero.[17]

O'Ferrall was handsomely eulogized, the press emphasizing his valor in battle. His most significant achievement, however, had come during his term as governor when Virginia turned the corner on mob violence. For this O'Ferrall took ample credit. "I had broken down almost entirely the spirit of lynching," his memoir claimed. O'Ferrall had in fact had plenty of help, from the acutely sleep-deprived white men who hustled the Lunenburg prisoners out of the county, for example, and from the chronically sleep-deprived black men who guarded them for weeks while they were jailed in Farmville. Still, O'Ferrall's role had been pivotal. Every subsequent Virginia governor took it as his duty to intervene whenever a lynching seemed imminent.[18]

*   *   *

FRANK CUNNINGHAM, militia captain, tenor, and man-about-town, died of kidney disease in 1911. On the day he was buried, many thousands—white people and black—turned out to mourn him. Those who crowded into the church heard much touching music, including one vocal number played on the gramophone. Captain Frank got his last wish: He sang at his own funeral.[19]

Among his honorary pallbearers was *William Hodges Mann,* once the architect of the legal case against the Lunenburg women, now the governor of Virginia. Mann had labored long and hard for the Democratic party, but his ascent to high office had been delayed by his staunch opposition to the liquor traffic. After free silver faded as an issue, however, prohibition was the next wave, voters blaming the world's woes on drink instead of the gold standard. Democrats found it expedient to go from wet to damp to very nearly dry, and in 1909 Mann got the nod for governor. Mrs. Mann took it as an omen that the punch bowl broke on the very day they moved into the Executive Mansion.[20]

Sworn in at age sixty-six, Mann was the last of the Virginia governors to have served in the Civil War. With his silvery white hair and goatee, he looked every inch the old-time Virginia gentleman, a curious look considering the times. Outside the South it was a heady, high-energy period of reform. Virginia had its reformers too, many of them women, black and white, who emerged in numbers to try to empower other women and speed Virginia's hesitant entry into the modern world.

One such reformer was *Rosa Dixon Bowser,* still active in the organization that succeeded the Richmond Women's League. The league had come into being to raise money for Pokey Barnes and the two Marys, and in this inaugural mission they outdid themselves. Pledging five hundred dollars at first, they eventually raised almost seven hundred dollars, much of it coming five and ten cents at a time from Richmond's domestics and washerwomen.

That enormous total suggested how profoundly they identified with the accused women from Lunenburg, perhaps how endangered they themselves felt. The Richmond Women's League expanded in the decade after 1896 but was deliberately vague in its public pronouncements, camouflaging its programs in chirpy phrases like "uplifting influence" and "little deeds of kindness." It also changed its name, abandoning League, which implied an energetic presence in politics, and adopting the less provocative Richmond Mothers' Club.[21]

The work went on more visibly after 1908, when local organizations formed a statewide network, the Virginia State Federation of Colored Women's Clubs. The federation took as its special charge the reclamation of troubled adolescent girls, but few causes went untouched. Education, public health, prison reform, interracial cooperation: In the early twentieth century, civic-minded black women launched dozens of campaigns, not least of which was the effort to make what difference they could through electoral politics. In 1920, after the Nineteenth Amendment was ratified (no thanks to Virginia), more than two thousand black women in Richmond registered to vote.[22]

The Mann administration was scarcely touched by this ferment. Virginia's female reformers generated some marvelous debate, in which the governor did not generally participate, and they proposed many new laws, most of which he opposed or ignored; the exceptions were some modest additions to public health and welfare agencies. Mann funneled most of his own reform energies into scientific agriculture.[23]

Though more sluggish than some, Mann's term as governor was not so different from those of the younger men who succeeded him. With the electorate docile and small, politics became dull by design, the machine specializing in maintaining its power and conducting

government on the cheap. The interesting stuff of Virginia life mainly happened elsewhere, its drama in the longings of thwarted vision-
aries, its poetry in the rhythms of everyday life.

*   *   *

FOUR MILES FROM the village of Stovall, North Carolina, at the end
of a rocky road, a broad cornfield met a stand of woods. Here stood
a cornhouse, a cow barn, and a two-room log dwelling, the refuge of
Fannie Marable.[24]

Fannie had been only twenty when her husband, Solomon, was
executed. Afterward she resumed her maiden name and continued
to live with her mother, Belle Morton, growing corn and taking in
washing. Theirs was another big family in a small house; Fannie had
six younger brothers and sisters, several of whom were old enough
to help with the chores and with her little boys, Henry and Johnny.

Fannie remarried in 1899. Sam Watkins was twelve years her
senior, a widower with three teenage daughters. Before long Fannie
and Sam had two more daughters. If it was a happy marriage, it was
not to last. Fannie died in about 1903, not yet thirty years old. The
orphaned Henry and Johnny went to live with their grandmother,
Belle Morton, who saw to it that they attended school. Fannie's two
small girls remained with their father, who soon remarried.

*   *   *

AND WHAT OF *Mary Abernathy* and *Mary Barnes*? They are harder
to see; even when the press was most intensely interested in their
case, the accused women often faded from view. This had everything
to do with the fact that men did all the writing; not surprisingly, the
men tended to think the Lunenburg story was about *them.* Much of
the time, of course, the story *was* about men; it could hardly have
been otherwise when women were systematically excluded from the
legal system, from government, from the militia and the newspaper
business. And thank goodness for the men's involvement. Had men
like Mitchell and O'Ferrall not stood boldly for justice and due
process, Mary Abernathy and Pokey Barnes would surely have
hanged.

Still, we could wish that the men had hogged the spotlight less.

We could wish equally that the press had taken an interest in the women's lives after the murder story was over. Just two small notices, both about the Barnes family, appeared in 1897 and 1898. The *State* and the *Planet* deemed it mildly newsworthy when Mecklenburg County authorities finally found a criminal charge that would stick to Rosa Barnes, who was convicted of arson after a neighbor's house had burned down. Six months after her mother, Mary Barnes, came out of the penitentiary, twenty-two-year-old Rosa went in, her two-year-old son in tow.[25]

A year later the *Planet* announced that Joseph Barnes had enlisted in the army. In the spring of 1898 Congress called for troops to fight the Spaniards in Cuba. Claiming to be only forty, Joseph enrolled in the Sixth Virginia Infantry, a regiment built upon the black militia units founded in Richmond in the 1870s. The Sixth Virginia was sent to staging areas in Tennessee and then Georgia but did not see military action. The men endured plenty of conflict, however, especially over their demand that they be commanded by black officers, a demand endorsed resoundingly by the *Planet*. The conflict was abruptly resolved by the disbanding of the regiment only six months after its formation.[26]

Aside from these fragments, the press no longer covered the Lunenburg women or their families. But like other ordinary people, the women left just enough tracks in census records and city directories to let us see the outlines of their lives.

The two Marys both settled permanently in Richmond, living out their days at opposite ends of Jackson Ward. (Although no longer a political entity after 1903, Jackson Ward retained its name and its status as the symbolic center of black Richmond.) Mary and Joseph Barnes landed in Shockoe Bottom in one of the city's worst slums, a long block from the railroad tracks and a short block from the old city jail. Mary and Wilson Abernathy lived on higher ground, moving every few years but always finding a rental among the row houses on Moore Street or nearby Catherine Street. As they aged, Mary and Wilson were surrounded by children and grandchildren, some living with them, others next door or down the block.[27]

Both the Barnes and Abernathy families lived in neighborhoods inhabited almost entirely by black people; Richmond was segregated on a scale not thinkable in the countryside. In Lunenburg, people lived near their fields, a practical necessity that kept white households dispersed among those of their more numerous black neighbors. One result was a great deal of humdrum interaction between blacks and whites. Think of the hours before Lucy Pollard's death, before anyone knew it would not be an ordinary day. Mary Abernathy chatted with the Pollards about ridding cabbages of bugs; Pokey Barnes was in and out of two white families' houses (and up and down another white family's tree); Mary Barnes and Ellen Gayle planned a three-way transaction with Lucy Pollard involving two chickens, two pounds of beef, and a quarter of a dollar. The substance of these encounters was highly variable and did not always imply that blacks had to do the bidding of whites. It was the farm wife's duty, for example, to provide the midday meal to any hands working on her place. The last meal Lucy Pollard cooked she served first to her husband and Austin Clements and then to Mary Barnes.[28]

This was not the whole story, of course. Forms of address made it clear that blacks were to defer to whites, and younger people to their elders. (Lucy, who was called Mrs. Pollard or Miss Lou, called the two Marys Aunt Mary or Auntie. Pokey was just plain Pokey.) Moreover, within hours of Lucy's death it became clear that casual conversation could be displaced almost instantly by suspicion and the threat of lethal violence. But the countryside probably provided a fuller range of interracial interaction than Richmond, where segregation grew more pronounced by the day. As more miles of electric streetcar track radiated from the city center, hundreds, then thousands of white Richmonders moved to new, segregated suburbs. The housing they left behind quickly filled with black tenants, many of them migrants fresh from Virginia's farms and small towns.[29]

For a person like Mary Abernathy, now living in Richmond and working at home, it became possible to live in a virtually all-black world. She could buy food from a black grocer or fishmonger or confectioner. She could order coal from a black fuel dealer. She could take her worn shoes or her broken umbrella to a black repairman. She could put her savings in a black bank and, when she felt sick, consult a black doctor, even a black woman doctor.[30] She could also choose among a dazzling array of organized social events. Richmond's black churches (two dozen and counting), fraternal organizations, and mutual benefit societies looked after their members' needs for community and fun as well as their spiritual and financial ones; the calendar was studded with pageants, dances, parades, debates, theatricals, lectures, and excursions. A few years after the Abernathy and Barnes families had settled in Jackson Ward, a commercial entertainment sector developed along North Second; black Richmonders went to "Two Street" to catch vaudeville acts and eventually movies.

Mary Abernathy's social world probably centered on her porch and yard; houses were crowded, and most of the neighborhood's informal social life took place outdoors, where social life and work flowed together. Cramped though her family already was, Mary took in boarders. She also took in washing, an option most black mothers preferred to domestic service. Though arduous and badly paid, laundry work offered the dignity of self-employment, as well as the chance to keep tabs on children and to socialize with neighbors—no small thing for a lover of talk like Mary Abernathy. House lots were narrow on her block; boiling clothes in her yard, Mary could easily keep up a running conversation with the woman next door.[31]

Her only other occupational option was domestic service. Although Richmond supported an impressive contingent of black professionals and entrepreneurs, there was just a little room at the top. The vast majority of poor migrants from the countryside could find employment only as domestics or laborers. Mary Barnes worked as a domestic. Joseph Barnes called himself a minister when he joined the army, but the city directories never listed him as anything more exalted than a "laborer." Laborers did whatever work came to hand—often heavy, dirty, or dangerous work—and were subject to spells of unemployment. Wilson Abernathy, also listed as a laborer, told the census taker in 1900 that he had been out of work for two months out of the previous twelve.

Their children and grandchildren could do better, in terms of both education and occupation. Unlike their older siblings, who had spent their childhood days on the farm, Ida, Jesse, and Bessie Mitchell Abernathy went to school and stayed there long enough to learn to read and write before joining the labor force in their teens.

The same was true of Frank and Lucy Barnes, Mary and Joseph's Richmond grandchildren.[32] As for work, the young men were able to move a rung or two above the catchall category of laborer. The young women had fewer choices, but the city did offer one important option: the chance to escape domestic service and its attendant problems—long hours, loneliness, sexual danger. Bessie Abernathy and Lucy Barnes were the first women in their families to find jobs in factories.

Wilson Abernathy did not live long enough to see his youngest come of age. He died at about sixty, probably in 1909. Mary lived a few years longer, continuing to earn her living by taking in laundry.[33]

She must have had few idle moments. When the census taker came around in 1910, shortly after Wilson had died, he found Mary Abernathy living in a very populous household. Four of her grown children lived with her. Twenty-six-year-old Ida had married Willie Epps, who tended steam engines in a factory; they had four small children. Amy Gregory, Mary's eldest daughter, had left her husband in Mecklenburg more than ten years earlier and now worked as a laundress in a private family. Son Jenning, single and twenty-four, hauled bricks for a builder, and son Jesse, age twenty, was a meat cutter in a butcher shop. The household also included two of Mary's other grandchildren—six grandchildren altogether, ranging in age from six months to nine years. Add one lodger (another butcher), and the house on Moore Street sheltered a total of thirteen people.

There must never have been a time when Mary Abernathy was alone. She died on June 18, 1915, after a short bout with pleurisy.

To the census taker who canvassed Shockoe Bottom in 1920 we are indebted for a final portrait of the Barnes family. Mary was at least seventy by then and employed as a cook in a private family. Joseph, also about seventy, was not employed. After serving nearly five years in prison, their daughter Rosa had been discharged and found work in Richmond as a domestic, at times living with her employers. In 1920, by this time in her forties and still single, she lived with her parents; she evidently looked after Joseph, who may have been disabled, and took charge of the household while the other adults went out to earn wages. Two grandchildren lived there as well: Frank Barnes, age twenty-three (and probably Rosa's son), drove a wagon for a commission merchant. The other grandchild, Lucy Barnes, was twenty-seven and worked in a tobacco factory. They had a female boarder also, a tobacco factory sweeper and possibly a friend of Lucy's. The littlest member of the household was great-grandson Joseph, four months old and probably Lucy's child.

Mary and Joseph Barnes, both born in slavery, lived into the Jazz Age. Joseph died in about 1924, having made it to nearly seventy-five. Mary, small and tough, lived to about eighty, doing domestic work for others until almost the very end. She died of a cerebral hemorrhage on October 21, 1928.[34]

24

WHO KILLED
LUCY POLLARD?

T he money was never found—not for lack of looking, of course. After the adults gave up, generations of Fort Mitchell's children squinted down hollow logs and dug under sagging cabins, imagining that they might find the treasure that had eluded everyone else. They perhaps found all manner of interesting things, but so far as anyone knows, they did not find the Pollards' money.

All the more reason to think that the money departed the Pollard house in the way Solomon Marable said: in someone's pockets, within minutes of the murder. Reason too to suspect a white man or at any rate a person whose occupation enabled him to launder considerable cash.

Who killed Lucy Pollard? More than a hundred years after the fact, her murder remains unsolved. Because local officials simply dropped the case, no paper trail leads directly to a suspect. We are left to make what we can of the tangled, fragmentary evidence left lying around by accident.

Let's proceed on the supposition that Solomon Marable told the truth, or a near version of it, when he accused David James Thompson. When Solomon implicated the women (at least eight times over a period of five weeks), every rendition was different. The white man story, by contrast, was consistent all the way through. Nine versions of the white man story were recorded over a period of eleven months. From the first halting rendition in Lunenburg court to Solomon's dying declaration almost a year later, the basic story remained the same, with no fatal contradictions.[1]

The problem with the white man story, of course, was that David James Thompson produced a strong alibi; four men swore that on the day of the murder he had been at his place of business at all hours. Is there any way to reconcile their contentions with Solomon's?

There is—*if* we suppose that Solomon Marable gave a faithful account of the action but named the wrong perpetrator. No one ever testified to the whereabouts of Herbert (J. H. H.) Thompson, David's shadowy older brother.

Try this: Herbert Thompson killed Lucy Pollard, Cass Gregory engineered the cover-up, and for both men, the motive was money. Let's begin there. While murderers do not always leave a trail, debtors usually do. We turn to the sorry financial history of the Thompson brothers.

* * *

FOR MANY YEARS James L. ("Jimmie") and Martha Ann Thompson were the leading citizens of Finneywood, Virginia. In 1883 a railroad and depot were built on their land, energizing trade at their post office and general store; that was when Jimmie brought their younger son, David, from the farm to learn the mercantile business. His mother's fair-haired boy and his father's right-hand man, David James Thompson came into adulthood at medium height, with a wiry build and sharp facial features—"foxey-looking," in the uncharitable words of the *Richmond Times*, "with a hatchet face, and yellow whiskers."[2]

When Jimmie Thompson died in 1893, David and his older brother, Herbert, inherited several farms, with marketable timber as well as cropland and pasture. They got the Finneywood store too, and twenty-six-year-old David soon assumed his father's mantle as postmaster and station agent. Both positions were salaried; even in the hard times of the middle 1890s so many enterprises should have enabled the Thompson sons to make a decent living. But trouble set in early. Even before his father died, David racked up disquieting numbers of debts to wholesalers, stocking the store with a high volume of goods purchased on credit. He spent even more heavily after his father's death, doing business under the name of Thompson & Pettus, a three-man firm made up of David himself, his brother, Herbert, who mainly handled timber, and their older half brother Bill Pettus, who mostly farmed. David was the most active partner, and with each passing month, the debts mounted.[3]

In April 1894 the county sheriff appeared in Finneywood bearing a legal summons from a supplier of "fancy" groceries. Thompson rushed to Richmond and threw himself on the mercy of the manager, who agreed to give him more time to pay his $130 debt. Six months later the bills still were not paid, and in November 1894 the lawsuit was renewed.[4] By this time six different companies had lined up to get the court's help in collecting from Thompson & Pettus.

Some of David Thompson's purchases—two new iron safes and a set of oak furniture—may have been intended to impress potential in-laws. In any case, in a double ceremony on November 14, 1894, David James Thompson and his half brother Bill Pettus each took a young wife. Now twenty-eight, David married eighteen-year-old Mattie Lee Adams, daughter of a substantial farmer.[5]

Many miseries awaited the new Mrs. David James Thompson. Less than a month after the wedding the sheriff returned, this time under orders to seize property, sell it, and distribute the proceeds to Thompson & Pettus's creditors. David managed to put him off, claiming that everything on the place belonged to the estate of his deceased father. On this visit the sheriff got nothing, but the creditors persisted, and their numbers grew. A seventh creditor sued

Thompson & Pettus in January 1895, an eighth in February, the ninth in March, the tenth and eleventh in May. In that month Herbert Thompson borrowed one hundred dollars from his brother-in-law and another hundred from Edward Pollard. By the middle of June, Thompson & Pettus owed more than three thousand dollars.[6]

Lucy Pollard was murdered on June 14.

That same day Thompson & Pettus borrowed sixty-six dollars from a neighbor, a white farmer named Robert Langford. This transaction would not be worthy of special notice except that they promised to repay Langford in twenty-four hours.[7]

*   *   *

DO THE RECORDS show any evidence of an infusion of cash after June 14? The Thompsons' financial history in the year after the murder is interesting both for its initial period of quiet and for the tumult that came later. For seven months after the murder and robbery, Thompson & Pettus held off its creditors. No new lawsuits were filed, and no legal action taken on the old ones.

The Pollard money may well have made this possible, but given the magnitude of the Thompsons' debts, eight hundred dollars–plus was not enough to render them solvent for long. The dike burst in February 1896, when three wholesalers sued Thompson & Pettus and won. Others soon followed. By summer the firm of Thompson & Pettus was under court order to pay seven new creditors a total of more than fifteen hundred dollars—this on top of the old debts, which also remained unpaid.[8]

David James Thompson played for time. Finally, in October 1896, an exasperated judge moved aggressively on behalf of the creditors, dissolving the firm of Thompson & Pettus, ordering some of its assets sold at auction, and placing the land in the hands of a commissioner, who over the next five years rented it to several tenants and used the proceeds to pay down the debts.

Herbert Thompson died in 1898 at only thirty-six. (The cause of death was not recorded.) David spent the next several years in a humiliating struggle to hold on to his inheritance; to continue running his store, he had to rent the space from the court-appointed commissioner.[9] It is not known when he started beating his wife,

Mattie. She first had him arrested in February 1907, charging that he "did unlawfully throw her down, and violently choke her, and has at divers previous times drawn a pistol on her the said Mrs. M. L. Thompson, and threaten to kill her." In October 1908 Mattie threw him out. A separation agreement specified her terms: For the time being they would live apart, with Mattie managing her own property. David for his part promised to leave her alone. "If he conducts himself in a sober and proper manner, and it is so known to the people associating with him and the public generally then in a year or more a reconciliation may possibly be made with the consent of Mrs. Thompson, but the abandonment of use of intoxicating liquors must be total, permanent and known publicly."[10] In June 1909 Mattie had David arrested again, charging that he "did beat her, and do her serious bodily harm."

In about 1910 David turned over a new leaf. Mattie took him back, and they moved to a hamlet called Briery in Prince Edward County. There they lived on two acres, purchased by Mattie, and again ran a post office and store. In these years Mattie kept David on a short leash, and the family suffered no embarrassing run-ins with creditors. But Mattie died in 1917, succumbing to tuberculosis, and David quickly reverted to the style to which he had once been accustomed. Less than six months after Mattie's death, the first creditors took David to court. By 1922 they were lined up eighteen deep. A document filed with the court in 1930 termed him "penniless and entirely dependent on his children for support." He died in 1931, age sixty-four, of "cancer of the Liver."[11]

*   *   *

IT IS TIME to sort through the evidence respecting the Thompsons. A few incriminating facts are already on the table. David and Herbert both had a powerful motive for robbery and took a twenty-four-hour loan on the day of the murder. In later life David had a drinking problem and battered his wife. Ambiguous evidence is also on the table, most notably the affidavits of four men who swore that David Thompson was about his place of business the entire day. Let's take a closer look at the affidavits, at David Thompson's libel suit against the *Richmond Times*, and at the behavior of the larger family.

From this distance, unfortunately, the affidavits' truthfulness cannot be determined. One of the men who gave a statement was the Thompsons' cousin. Another was David Thompson's clerk. A third, a black man who worked for the Thompsons as a farmhand, lived on David Thompson's place with his large family. He could not read and would not have been able to tell whether the statement he made was the one written down. The fourth, a railroad employee, lived nearby. All four probably had accounts at the store, meaning they owed Thompson & Pettus money.[12] In other words, all had incentives to cover for the Boss. Still, a man would typically be loath to risk his reputation on an outright lie.

What about the libel suit? In May 1896, two weeks after Solomon Marable was sentenced to death for the second time, David James Thompson sued the *Richmond Times*, claiming his business and reputation had been badly damaged by two articles. One had named him as the man Solomon Marable accused of murder; the other charged that he had stabbed a black man and then paid him to leave the state. The case came to trial in June 1897, and Thompson won, although the jury awarded him only a thousand dollars, one-tenth of what he had asked for. There is no record of what was said in that courtroom.[13]

On its face, Thompson's victory would appear to argue for his innocence. But the law of defamation was a peculiar beast. Say that you call me a horse thief and I sue you for defamation. If I win, does this mean I am innocent of stealing horses?

In fact, no. Virginians could bring defamation suits under either of two sets of law. One tradition had developed in the campaign against dueling. To encourage men to use the courts instead of pistols to resolve affairs of honor, the General Assembly had authorized Virginians to sue those who insulted them. These lawmakers took an interesting page from English jurists with respect to truth and falsehood. Throwing the ugly truth in someone's face was the sort of insult most likely to provoke a fight and thus disturb the public peace. For our purposes, the point is that one need not be *falsely* accused to win a defamation suit. I can sue you for calling me a horse thief even if I ride to court on the horse I stole from you.[14]

A defamation suit could also be brought under the common law, another English import. In this tradition truth mattered; a statement was defamatory only if untrue. But the defendant bore the burden of proof. After you call me a horse thief and I sue you, it is your job to show that I actually stole the horse. If you cannot prove me guilty, then you have defamed me and must pay damages to compensate me for the injury you have done my good name.

David Thompson thus had the law entirely on his side. Murderer or no, Thompson was safe in suing the *Times* because the newspaper could not prove his guilt. From other evidence, meanwhile, it looks as though the lawyers decided that the murder was better left alone. Virginia law provided the *Times* one out: If a timely retraction and apology were published, the jury was to consider assessing lesser damages.[15] Accordingly, the *Times* did use its editorial page to apologize to David James Thompson—but only for the story that had accused him of stabbing a man and then paying him to leave Virginia. Had Thompson's attorneys intended to hash out the murder accusation in court, the *Times* would presumably have apologized for that story as well.

The *Times* paid promptly, all in a lump. What happened to that thousand dollars is hard to say. The records do indicate that David Thompson paid the interest on a large sum owed to one of his neighbors, and he paid off one debt completely, the sixty-six dollars Thompson & Pettus had borrowed from Robert Langford on the day of Lucy Pollard's murder. Why would Thompson pay this debt and none of his many others? Certainly Langford knew something—perhaps too much—about Thompson's whereabouts on the day of the murder.[16]

The most interesting wrinkle in the defamation suit, meanwhile, appeared in a single sentence in the *Planet*. The assault at issue had indeed taken place, the *Planet* said, but according to David Thompson, it had been committed by his brother, Herbert.[17]

A mysterious figure always, Herbert Thompson left few traces in the records. Two scraps of official paper confirm that he was arrested twice in 1894, once on an unspecified charge and once for assault. When summoned to testify in his brother's defamation suit, he failed to appear.[18]

Did Herbert Thompson kill Lucy Pollard? The one-day loan suggests the Thompsons were especially desperate. Say Herbert secures the sixty-six dollars from Langford in Finneywood and then heads to Fort Mitchell to pay some of what he owes Edward Pollard. (Or it could have worked the other way around, with Thompson intending to ask Pollard for an additional loan to repay Langford.) On the way, Thompson gets to thinking about the thousands the Pollards supposedly have cached in their house. Just then Solomon Marable walks up. Thompson knows Marable, who works for him off and on at the sawmill. From there the action unfolds more or less as Solomon later claims.

Of course it is possible that the white man was not a Thompson at all. But a series of actions on the part of the larger Thompson-Pettus family suggests they were protecting someone. On the night of the murder, Edward Pollard sent for Martha Ann Thompson, Herbert and David's mother, to come take charge of the house. Martha Thompson was kin by marriage to Lucy Pollard, and as her behavior at Mary Abernathy's trial showed, she was good at taking charge of things. On the night of Lucy's death, however, she sent word that she was unable to come (staying home, one wonders, to buck up? sober up? console? extract the truth from? her agitated son). In her place Martha Thompson sent Bill Pettus, one of two sons from her first marriage and the third partner in Thompson & Pettus.[19]

The next morning Herbert Thompson came to the Pollard place and was appointed to the coroner's jury along with Bill Pettus: better to ask the questions than have to answer them. With Cass Gregory, Bill Pettus said he found tracks by the old gate place. Bill's brother, Lucius Pettus, was also at Pollard's that morning. The day Solomon was caught, Lucius rode with the posse that returned him to Pollard's; along the way Lucius heard Solomon's very first confession implicating the women. (Solomon later claimed he was told to confess or hang on the spot; thinking Lucius knew everything, Solomon followed the killer's earlier orders and implicated the women.)[20] During the trials in Lunenburg Courthouse Lucius Pettus became famous as the Winking Man, inducing Solomon to abandon the white man story. Nell Pettus (Bill's wife) soon took a role as well, as scribe of the "tell-tale letter" in which Joseph Barnes accused Mary Barnes of murder and lesser sins. Other witnesses to the letter were Bill Pettus and Martha Thompson, who had her bigger moment of fame when she testified in Mary Abernathy's second trial. On cross-examination she named no one to whom she had told her story, and she refused to say why she had not come forward earlier; the attorneys for the defense thought her testimony fabricated. Altogether the Thompson-Pettus family compiled an impressive record of public activity in the case, most of it contributing to the conviction of Solomon and the three women.

But two questions arise, one obvious and one nagging. The obvious question: If Herbert Thompson committed the murder, why didn't Solomon just say so? To this we return in a moment. The nagging question comes from a detail in Solomon's white man story. In six of the nine recorded versions, Solomon had the white man speaking to Lucy Pollard and Lucy speaking back. "Do you know me?" the white man had asked. Lucy had responded, "You are a white man." In Solomon's last three confessions, he added that in a second or two Lucy did recognize the man, or seemed to; that was when the man picked up the ax and started swinging.

"You are a white man." The statement is just strange enough to ring true. What takes explaining is Lucy Pollard saying it to Herbert Thompson or to David, either of whom she should have recognized. Lucy had probably lived in the Thompson household years before; David would have been about fourteen at the time and Herbert nineteen. Since marrying Edward Pollard, Lucy had visited back and forth with their mother, Martha.[21]

Any of several factors could account for Lucy's failure to recognize the white man instantly. She had just emerged from the comparative darkness of the house; facing the white man, she would have been looking west into the sun. The man may have changed his looks (shaved a beard or grown one) or pulled his hat over his eyes. Lucy herself wore spectacles, which may have helped her see close objects (she had been marking eggs), while blurring more distant ones.

Let's pick up the bigger question: Why would Solomon name the wrong Thompson? To answer this we need to look at timing and the odd behavior of Cass Gregory.

*　　*　　*

THOMPSON, DAVID, JAMES. The names came out in three installments, in that order. "Thomason" was the name Solomon Marable
gave Frank Cunningham in Lunenburg Courthouse during a recess in
Pokey Barnes's first trial. While no name appeared in the press at
this time, "Thompson" probably went out on the Lunenburg
grapevine within minutes.[22]

On Sunday, July 21, 1895, Solomon, Mary Abernathy, and Pokey
Barnes were deposited in the Richmond city jail. Three days later, on
July 24, Solomon switched back to the white man story for good.
Speaking to jail officials and reporters that afternoon, he named
"David Thomas or Thompson," adding (accurately) that this Thomp-
son had a young-looking wife.[23] Nine months later it was revealed
that Cass Gregory had visited Solomon that morning.

The name James emerged on August 10, when the *Planet* made it
clear that Solomon Marable was accusing the David Thompson of
Finneywood. The *Planet* did not name its source. But it was perhaps
not a coincidence that the day before this issue of the *Planet* went to
press, Cass Gregory was back in Richmond.[24]

Why would Gregory induce Solomon to name David James
Thompson? The short answer is that Gregory found a way to make it
profitable. For the longer answer, read on.

*　　*　　*

FROM THE FIRST hours after Lucy Pollard's death, Cass Gregory
locked on to the case in an extraordinary way, his involvement even
wider and deeper than the foregoing chapters have suggested. Here,
in order of their occurrence, is a list of his moves, those not yet
brought forward in this account.

On the Sunday after the murder Gregory took the train to Chase
City to join the manhunt for Solomon Marable. A week before the
first trials began in Lunenburg Courthouse, Fannie Marable was
ordered arrested; Gregory traveled with the constable to North Carolina to make the arrest and return her to Lunenburg. The next
week, when it came time for the sheriff to bring Solomon Marable,

Mary Abernathy, and Pokey Barnes back to Lunenburg for trial, Cass Gregory was one of the two guards who went with him. After Rich- monders raised doubts about the fairness of the trials, Gregory sent a long anonymous letter to the *Dispatch*, outlining his reasons for believing the women guilty. In February, in anticipation of new trials, he visited at least a dozen houses in Fort Mitchell in an attempt to dig up additional evidence (or, as the women's lawyers suggested, to manufacture evidence). In March, when Solomon Marable was tried the second time, Gregory testified at length; one night he leaked a rumor that Marable was about to switch back to the story accusing the women.[25]

Altogether Gregory made a remarkable showing. What drove him? Clearly, he wanted to lead and be noticed. His life story also suggests we look wherever significant money might be at stake. Like the Thompson brothers, Cass Gregory was plagued by indebtedness, both chronic and acute. The way he handled those debts reveals something of his character.

Gregory blamed a freak storm for the start of his financial strug- gles. In 1878 he had begun trading tobacco in Keysville. One night in 1882 the roof blew off his tobacco warehouse and crashed into the building next door. Gregory was thirty-seven then, with a wife and four children, and the destruction of the warehouse pitched him into a crisis.[26]

In 1882–83 the construction of the long-awaited Keysville & Durham Railroad created a sudden demand for crossties and bridge timbers. Although he had little capital himself, Gregory had a gift for talking other people into risking theirs. With the Hanmer brothers, he bought 263 timber-rich acres lying less than a mile from the new track bed; the Hanmers put up two-thirds of the purchase money, but only Gregory's name went on the deed. In a second enterprise, Gre- gory put up no money at all. When his friend Tom Spencer found a sawmill and engine for sale at seventeen hundred dollars, they bought them with Spencer's money. Gregory was to pay his half from his share of the lumber they sold.

Both deals quickly soured, and everyone wound up in court. The Hanmers sued Gregory, claiming he had sold timber from their 263 acres without telling them and then sold the land itself, neither informing the Hanmers nor paying them their share of the purchase price. Gregory's partnership with Tom Spencer meanwhile ended like a bad marriage, each party blaming the other and both feeling cheated and used. Spencer claimed that Gregory never paid for his share of the sawmill. He further claimed that Gregory had collected most of the payments due their company but either did not keep books or would not show them; the strong implication was that Gregory was skimming from their timber operation to pay his other creditors. A dozen other charges provoked a dozen counter-charges.[27]

In all this the most interesting fact was that Gregory, not Spencer, initiated the lawsuit. Despite his manifestly shady business practices, Gregory believed that he was fundamentally right and that the court would take his side. Cass Gregory walked the earth with an almost magical self-confidence. Despite the danger signs, people tended to trust him.

Gregory and his wife, Ella, were never really solvent after their crisis of 1882–84, and in the spring of 1895, not long before Lucy Pollard's death, they experienced another financial emergency. Cass had spent the winter as a tobacco broker in Roxboro, North Carolina. In April, as the tobacco-buying season neared its end, Gregory took out two five-hundred-dollar loans from the Farmers Bank of Roxboro. The loans were due on June 22 and July 2, and if the Gregorys could not pay, they stood to lose all their personal property.[28]

Lucy Pollard was killed on June 14. Is there evidence that any of the Pollard money ended up in Cass Gregory's pockets? The months immediately following the murder saw some transactions of interest. Gregory did not repay the thousand dollars he owed the Farmers Bank, but for the first six months he paid the interest, at 8 percent not a trivial sum. More intriguing was the repayment of a sizable debt—to Sheriff M. C. Cardozo, no less. One of the county's most active moneylenders, Cardozo had helped Ella Gregory buy part of the farm on which she had been raised, advancing her four hundred dollars when the place was sold for debt in 1892. In January 1896, about seven months after the murder of Lucy Pollard, Ella Gregory managed to pay what she owed to Cardozo.[29]

It was a brief respite in a long downhill slide. When Cass and

Ella attempted to consolidate their debts late in 1896, the paper work revealed that they owed more than four thousand dollars.[30] How they stayed afloat is not clear. In 1900 they turned up in Brunswick, another county in the Virginia Southside. Cass worked as a real estate agent, did some surveying, and became a notary public. By 1910 it appears Ella had died; Cass was boarding with a family named Lewis who lived on the industrial side of Lawrenceville near the railroad yards.[31]

At age eighty-three, Cass Gregory made his last significant transaction, bilking his landlady out of four hundred dollars. He told her he would invest her money in Liberty bonds, but when he died two years later, no Liberty bonds were found among his effects. Nannie Lewis sued his estate. The court awarded her the two town lots Gregory had owned, together worth about fifty dollars, but her four hundred dollars were gone for good.[32]

*　　*　　*

COULD CASS GREGORY have killed Lucy Pollard? This seems too crude for an operator like Gregory, who down to his old age demonstrated remarkable aptitude for talking other people into taking risks for his benefit. Also, nothing in the public record suggests him capable of homicidal violence.

Since Gregory was master of the indirect and the covert, we should look for something more complex from him. Let's look again at the events of July 22 to 24, 1895. The day after Solomon Marable, Pokey Barnes, and Mary Abernathy were placed in the Richmond city jail, a reporter interviewed Solomon in the presence of Frank Cunningham. Solomon once again pinned the murder on the women. But Cunningham believed the trials had not proved the women guilty, and the next morning, Tuesday, the *Dispatch* reported that Cunningham was pushing Marable to implicate a white man once again. The *Times* ran a story as well, for the first time publishing the name of the white man Solomon had implicated in Lunenburg Courthouse: Thomas or Thomason.[33]

By Tuesday afternoon the reports were causing a sensation in Lunenburg. On Wednesday morning Cass Gregory appeared at the Richmond jail. He talked his way in and was allowed to speak with

Solomon Marable. That afternoon Marable changed his story for the last time. In the presence of several reporters and jail officials, Solomon named David Thompson as Lucy Pollard's killer.[34]

Gregory's conversation with Marable may be the key to everything, but we have no reports about what was said. Gregory did not even admit he had made the visit until nine months later, when George Wise smoked him out during Mary Abernathy's second trial.

Two scenarios seem plausible, one simple, the other complex. The simple one: David James Thompson was the killer; whatever Gregory had to say that day, Solomon decided to tell the truth. The complex one: When Gregory saw the newspapers, he was struck by the thought that Solomon was about to erupt; Gregory feared that Frank Cunningham and the reporters would badger Solomon until he exposed the killer. Thanks to the *Times*, the Thompson name was already in play. For reasons we'll take up shortly, Gregory instructed Solomon to name *David* Thompson—the Finneywood David Thompson—as the killer, and Solomon obliged him, perhaps because Gregory promised him something, perhaps because Gregory threatened his family. Recall that Gregory had gone to North Carolina to arrest Fannie Marable; he knew exactly where Solomon's wife and children lived.

Let's stay with this second idea, that Cass Gregory induced Solomon Marable to implicate David James Thompson. What would that gain Gregory?

Perhaps in the beginning Gregory acted in good faith; like most of Fort Mitchell's white people, he believed Solomon and the women guilty, and it made sense to get them convicted, especially if they could lead him to the money. Heaven knew (though the public did not) he needed the money himself. This would explain his early intense activism, his arrest of Fannie Marable, for example, and his guarding Solomon, Pokey, and Mary Abernathy when they were returned to Lunenburg Courthouse for trial. Besides, the county paid his expenses for these journeys, plus seventy-five cents a day—a little walking-around money that helped him appear the gentleman despite his actual insolvency.[35]

Suppose that in the course of his investigation he learned who the killer was, someone other than David James Thompson. Suppose, further, that Gregory approached the killer and promised to shelter him from prosecution in exchange for a chunk of the stolen money.

How to pull that off? With two strategies at once. First, Gregory would make it look as though he believed with all his heart that the women murdered Lucy Pollard. This would account for his highly publicized September visit to the Richmond jail, when he offered to get their lives spared if they would reveal the location of the money. It would account too for his war on the women; not only did he orchestrate evidence against them, but he also fed the press highly quotable statements disparaging the white man story. To wit: "The white-man story is known by the people of this community to be utterly false in every particular, and is so preposterous and far-fetched as to not cause a single serious thought in the mind of any intelligent man."[36]

The slicker move was to get the papers to pursue the *wrong* white man—namely, David James Thompson. Thompson would be able to establish an alibi, of course, but that was perhaps the point. Thompson would not suffer in the long run, and Solomon Marable would again be exposed as a liar; nothing he said from that moment on would be believed. In any case, from the vantage point of late July, it looked as though the decoy would not have to serve for very long. Everyone believed Solomon Marable would be executed on September 20. Once Marable was out of the picture, the white man would be in the clear.

As it turned out, of course, there was something in it for David Thompson as well, the thousand dollars in damages paid him by the *Richmond Times*. In retrospect, the *Times* had been rash to print the rumor that Thompson had stabbed a man and then paid him to leave the state, but the editor had thought himself on solid ground, his source "a well-known citizen of Lunenburg."[37] Here too the word of Cass Gregory? In league with David Thompson? What better way to set up a profitable defamation suit than to plant damning disinformation in Lunenburg's least favorite newspaper?

Someday, perhaps, the crucial evidence will come to light, at last allowing us to solve the mystery of who killed Lucy Pollard. In the meantime this murder story must have a different sort of ending, one about race and remembrance.

AFTERWORD

F ort Mitchell is not on the map, but it's still there: the old depot, the post office and store, a scattering of houses, and the Mount Mitchell Church, along with Salem Christian Church, built in 1906.[1] A mile to the east lies the Pollard farm. At this writing in 2002, the house still stands. The barn fell in a few years ago; across the road from its ruins is the tiny cemetery where Lucy and Edward Pollard were laid to rest, materials all for a meditation on what endures and what passes away.

Why was the Lunenburg case forgotten?

We confront the intriguing, often mysterious process by which current events are transformed into written history—or consigned to oblivion. In any given place and time (since the advent of the newspaper at any rate), scores of stories are deemed sufficiently note-worthy to be written up in the media. Other events fail to qualify as news, but someone commits them to paper or passes them down as spoken stories. All things preserved, artifacts included, carry poten-tial for study by historians, who in each generation decide anew what matters enough to be written into history. As a practical matter, much must always be left out. But some omissions are more instruc-tive than others, and they invite special scrutiny. What was it about the Lunenburg case that made it unmentionable as history?[2]

Or perhaps the question should be reversed: What was it about history that made the case unmentionable? Historians of things Vir-ginian have most often been drawn to times when the fate of the nation played out on Virginia turf: Jamestown in 1607, the American Revolution and the launching of the new Republic, and the Civil War above all. Any traveler will find the revolutionary era and the Civil War (and increasingly Jamestown) amply enshrined in Virginia's bat-tlefields, monuments, and museums. Travelers won't notice much from the 1890s. The seemingly unlovely decades after the Civil War, tarnished by poverty, election fraud, and the near absence of Virginia from the national stage, inspired few memorials and attracted few historians.[3]

The neglect of the entire period, in other words, reduced the chances that Lunenburg would find its way to the published page. But this can be only part of the explanation. In that same neglected period the Richmond press made hay of three other sensational mur-der stories, all with a young white man suspected of killing his (white) wife or lover. All three earned permanent places in local lore, popping up in memoirs, steaming up the pages of local histories, and reprised for periodic rehashing in the press.[4]

Consider the possibility that the memory of the Lunenburg case was actively repressed. Of all the players in the Lunenburg drama, only William L. Royall and Charles O'Ferrall published memoirs, and neither mentioned Lunenburg.[5] This is unremarkable in Royall's case; although Royall wrote many editorials about the Pollard mur-der and served briefly as Solomon Marable's counsel, Lunenburg was a short side trip in a career devoted mostly to advocacy of the gold standard and full payment of the public debt.

That O'Ferrall should leave out the Lunenburg case, on the other hand, is amazing. Lunenburg was the most dramatic story of his term as governor, and it had deep substance as well as drama. Not least, the Lunenburg case gave O'Ferrall the opportunity to make his most powerful stand against lynching.

Nevertheless, he left it out. O'Ferrall wrote in a time of swelling Confederate nostalgia and, like other white men of his generation, he wanted most to tell war stories. He opened his book not with his birth or the arrival of his ancestors in America, but with John Brown's raid at Harpers Ferry. Brown's raid, "the match that ignited the fire of secession," also initiated the eighteen-year-old O'Ferrall into military action.[6] In his memoir O'Ferrall went on to devote twenty chapters, half his book, to secession and the four years of war. He wrote just one chapter about his four years as governor.

Still, that chapter could have made room for the Pollard case. O'Ferrall spent several pages on crimes, punishments, and his agonies over petitions for pardon. He also proudly recounted his stance against lynching. Either section would have made a good place for the Lunenburg case, the foremost criminal case of his term and the pivotal episode in his antilynching crusade. Why leave it out?

An answer is suggested by a story O'Ferrall did tell, the case of a tall, light-skinned, and very unfortunate African American named Nannie Woods. One October night in 1889 a tobacco warehouse and several dwellings in the town of Rocky Mount burned to the ground. A black man named George Early was arrested on suspicion of arson. Spirited out of town for fear of a lynching, Early was pressured to confess and said he had been lurking near the scene of the crime but had only stood in the shadows while the warehouse was torched by two other black men. In a subsequent confession Early enriched his story by implicating nineteen-year-old Nannie Woods, who allegedly had held up her apron to keep the fatal match from going out. At the trials Early was convicted of arson and sentenced to hang, as was one of the other men. Nannie Woods was tried without counsel and also sentenced to hang. The sole evidence against her was George Early's testimony. Early, however, changed his story and from the gallows proclaimed Nannie Woods innocent. Governor Philip McKinney then intervened, giving Woods eighteen years in the penitentiary instead of death. She had served five years of her sentence when Charles O'Ferrall became governor. O'Ferrall granted her a full pardon early in 1895.[7]

The Nannie Woods case bore an eerie resemblance to Lunenburg, but the racial dynamics in the wake of her conviction were entirely different. When O'Ferrall pardoned Woods, he evoked the ancient tradition of noblesse oblige, acting the well-worn part of the gentleman who bestowed charity upon the underprivileged. "She was a negro and friendless," he wrote, neglecting to mention the twenty-one leading citizens of Rocky Mount who had endorsed her petition. He also exaggerated the abjectness of her situation. Woods had spent five years in prison; O'Ferrall remembered the number as twelve. In his telling, the case of Nannie Woods was about mercy, not politics—a safe race story for the era of Jim Crow.[8]

By 1904, when O'Ferrall published his book, the rhetoric of race had become so toxic that noblesse oblige was about all that was left of white progressivism on the race issue. By the same token, the Lunenburg story seemed to belong to some other country. Consider what the Lunenburg case had that the Nannie Woods story did not: a united and highly mobilized African American citizenry, formidable African American leadership, and a critical mass of whites and blacks who worked in concert to the same end. At times they worked as equals. At times the whites were subordinate; George Wise and his legal team, after all, worked for John Mitchell, Jr. And the outcome: Black people, as a people, won this one.

The Lunenburg case also called forth highly unusual reporting from the white press, which under ordinary circumstances treated black Virginians with indifference or contempt. After the first set of trials, white reporters became intrigued by the case, but the women initially did not interest them much. The reporters focused instead on the actions of other white men—on Lunenburg officialdom, the White Man, the Winking Man—and, as the appeals process gathered momentum, on the virtuosity of the lawyers. But in time the women got through to them. White reporters came to know Pokey Barnes and Mary Abernathy as distinct individuals, began to fear for their safety, and came to care about their fate. Eventually even Solomon Marable won reporters' admiration with his courage on the scaffold.

HE MET HIS AWFUL FATE CALMLY, said one headline. MEETS DEATH FEAR-LESSLY, said another.[9]

White men not only paid attention to the Lunenburg prisoners, meanwhile, but at times put themselves at great risk for them. Think of the posse that sneaked Solomon and Pokey and Mary Barnes out Edward Pollard's back door and hid them all night as they made their way through the woods to the courthouse. Think of O'Ferrall himself when he threw over the constitution to keep Solomon, Pokey, and Mary Abernathy out of Lunenburg Courthouse. His attorney general, a circuit court judge, and the officials of the city jail stuck their necks out as well. These were noble deeds, but these men did not own them. The triumph of white supremacy somehow transformed their heroics into something suspect and unseemly, as though risking one's skin for darker people shamed the risk taker himself.

We have asked how current events are made into history. It is likewise worth asking how history is implicated in current events, how history can be deployed for political ends. From the early 1890s on, as we have known for some time, the forces of white supremacy made a concerted effort, through both fraud and the law, to eradicate black political power. We are now beginning to appreciate the intellectual and cultural dimensions of this effort: One way white supremacy was established and maintained was by erasing the memory of a powerful and responsible black citizenry, by excising the history of whites and blacks working together on more or less equal terms. These erasures, conscious or not, had the effect of making white supremacy seem natural, inevitable, rock solid by virtue of having been in place forever. The effect also was to make it more difficult for dissenters to imagine alternatives.

Erasing was easy, vastly easier than disfranchising voters or segregating passengers on streetcars. All it took was selection, leaving out whatever felt uncomfortable, putting in stories that posed no threat to the new order. It also mattered that men like O'Ferrall took part in this process. Those who wrote the first historical accounts of the times in which they had lived influenced everything written thereafter.

If the memory of Lunenburg was suppressed in a larger effort to

discourage dissent, it stood to reason that the case would be redis-
covered when the tables turned and the dissenters began to receive
their due. Thank goodness for the archivists, librarians, county
clerks, the clerks' clerks, and packrats of all descriptions, who collected the original documents and kept them from harm. Because of
their work, the documents were waiting when the civil rights movement brought down Jim Crow and inspired a profound rethinking of
the American past. Following leads suggested two decades earlier by
the first generation of academically trained African American historians, numerous scholars from the 1950s forward turned a fresh eye
on the previous century, restoring black Americans to history and
searching for the roots of twentieth-century protest.[10]

In 1973 Ann Field Alexander completed an eye-opening dissertation on the early career of John Mitchell, Jr. Here at last was a context for the Lunenburg case, and Alexander featured it as an
important victory for Mitchell and the cause of racial justice in Virginia. Samuel Pincus followed in 1978, including Lunenburg in a dissertation on the (surprisingly fair) treatment of African Americans in
the Supreme Court of Appeals. In the 1990s the case at last emerged
in print, reflecting the growing depth and range of African American
history, as well as mushrooming interest in the history of women.
W. Fitzhugh Brundage explored lynching and Virginia's comparative
success at stopping it. Elsa Barkley Brown found in the Lunenburg
case evidence of the increasing salience of gender and class issues
within black public life. Most recently, Michael Trotti's 1999 dissertation took the Pollard murder in an entirely different direction, credit-
ing John Mitchell, Jr., with the development of a distinctive genre of
sensational crime reporting.[11]

These works together suggest the wide range of issues touched
by the Lunenburg case; they also suggest the contours of a larger
reinterpretation of the southern past now in progress. In recent
scholarship on the late nineteenth-century South, extralegal violence, economic discrimination, disfranchisement, legally mandated
segregation, and a virulent strain of racism loom large; by 1910 or so
America's own system of apartheid was clearly in place. But we are
taking a closer look at what it took to establish that system, and
what we increasingly see is ferment and improvisation, some of it

running against the grain of white supremacy. For the roughly forty years between emancipation and disfranchisement, our southern story must include considerable division and ambivalence among whites, a hundred forms of resistance among blacks, and at times coalition across the race divide.[12]

This is the large story contained in the smaller package of the Pollard murder case. After the arrests of Mary Barnes, Pokey Barnes, and Mary Abernathy, almost anything could have happened, including lynching, legal execution, or condemnation to three life-times in prison. That the Lunenburg women ultimately went free was not quite a miracle, but it took an unusual convergence of groups and individuals who for a time rose to extraordinary deeds; had any of them failed to act, the women's cause would probably have been lost. From the women themselves it took faith, fortitude, and high intelligence on the witness stand. It also took the concerted efforts of a huge community. Nothing predetermined that Afro-Virginians would launch a campaign on behalf of the Lunenburg women, nor was it foreordained that they would succeed. Given the frequency with which blacks paid the price for crimes they did not commit, it would have been understandable had black Virginians fallen into cynicism or despair. Given the factionalism that plagued Republican politics, it would have been no surprise had the movement to free the Lunenburg women fractured along the same lines. Instead the movement flourished, first to last exhibiting uncommon unity and spirit.

The Lunenburg women also owed their ultimate freedom to the decisions of key white men who at critical moments transcended the race prejudice in and around them. They could easily have done nothing. They could have done evil and would not have suffered for it. Instead they put their highest priority on basic fairness and the rule of law. In the end, after a long ordeal, the Lunenburg women got something like justice.

Although Fort Mitchell is not on the map, a road sign points the way. Head south from Keysville on Highway 360 about nine miles. Near Old Friendship Church—Lucy Pollard's church—you'll see the sign for Fort Mitchell. Turn east on Route 630; when you cross the tracks, you've arrived.

In this community more than a hundred years ago, stricken neighbors tried to comprehend what had happened to Lucy Pollard. We may yet learn more. A courthouse, an archive, a shoebox in the attic could be holding crucial documents. When they surface, there is just a chance they will tell us who killed Lucy Pollard; more likely they will show us something important and new about that time and place. Either way, it will be time to tell the Lunenburg story again. With luck, it will be a good story, another transcendent tale that helps us remember what matters and speak what's true.

ACKNOWLEDGMENTS

H ere is one last clue. On the one hundredth anniversary of the
Lunenburg murder, Sandy Treadway, Brent Tarter, and Julie
Campbell drove with me to the Pollard place, where we hoped
to find an answer to a question posed by the *Richmond Times* in
1895. If Lucy Pollard was already dead when Edward Pollard and
Austin and Willie Clements came through the front gate, could they
have failed to see her body lying in the yard? Our ambiguous conclusion: It was just possible, though highly unlikely. Like reporters
before us, we reached this conclusion after taking turns lying in the
grass a few feet from the northeast corner of the chimney. Not too
long after that, we found ourselves crawling with wood ticks. I'm not
sure how I can repay this particular debt, but it's a pleasure to

acknowledge the generosity of the many people who have contributed to this project.

In Lunenburg the late Estelle Ashworth Whirley allowed us to tramp over the Pollard farm. Pat Ashworth Doutt took me inside the Pollard house and with Ken Doutt shared what she knew of the property. W. Carter Thompson of Fort Mitchell and Reginald H. Pettus of Keysville imparted their knowledge of local history. At the courthouse, Circuit Court Judge William L. Wellons allowed me into the Lunenburg courtroom and filled me in on its past. Grace Marshall and Gordon Erby, clerks of the Lunenburg court, responded readily to my questions; I am especially grateful to Mr. Erby for allowing me to study freshly processed chancery records. I am also much indebted to the county clerks of Mecklenburg, Prince Edward, Charlotte, Nottoway, and Brunswick (all in Virginia) and Person County, North Carolina.

Many of the essential documents are housed in Richmond in the Library of Virginia, a place blessed with an extraordinary collection of local records and an equally extraordinary staff. State Librarian Nolan T. Yelich saw to the timely processing of the library's Lunenburg holdings, and I thank Conley Edwards, Minor Weisiger, and the entire archival staff for exemplary work on dozens of occasions. I am grateful also to Frances Pollard of the Virginia Historical Society and to archivists and librarians at the Medical College of Virginia, the University of Virginia, the Southern Historical Collection of the University of North Carolina at Chapel Hill, Duke University, the North Carolina State Archives, the Archives of the Josephite Fathers, and the National Archives and Records Administration.

Many of this book's illustrations come from rare and fragile newspapers; Audrey C. Johnson and Pierre Courtois, both of the Library of Virginia, made their reproduction possible. Fannie Sims Godley and Lillian W. Lovett graciously provided portraits of their kinswoman Marietta L. Chiles, and Paula Giddings led me to a rare portrait of John Mitchell, Jr. Connie Smith of Connie Smith Design, Seattle, converted my amateurish maps into art.

In the conduct of research, I generally subscribe to the mother-please school (I really *would* rather do it myself), but living a long way from my sources, I have called on others for help. Jennifer Davis McDaid applied her amazing research skills to scores of questions. Also pitching in were Elizabeth Rose, Vesta Gordon, Julie Campbell, Jennifer Ritterhouse, G. C. Waldrep III, Karla Kelling, and Susan Bragg. All along Brent Tarter and John Kneebone have contributed astute research advice, and I especially appreciate Kneebone's letting me tag along on a visit to Woodland and Greenwood cemeteries. My son Michael McCormick came along on my initial trip to Fort Mitchell (he had his first ice cream cone in Chase City). He was eight months old at the time; now he helps me with my computer. So does my daughter Betsy McCormick, who wrote some hilarious parodies of my prose and offered sound advice about the opening. Sandra Gioia Treadway has done me more good turns than I can count; to Sandy and to John Treadway, who for many years have provided my home away from home, thanks again, and don't change the locks!

I have had very significant institutional as well as individual support. The idea for this book first crystallized while I held a fellowship from the John Simon Guggenheim Memorial Foundation. A fellowship from the John D. and Catherine T. MacArthur Foundation underwrote most of the research and much of the writing. During the years in which this project has taken shape, it has been my privilege to serve on the faculties of three great institutions of higher learning: Rutgers, the State University of New Jersey; the University of North Carolina at Chapel Hill; and the University of Washington. All three have materially supported my research; they have also afforded me wonderful students and colleagues and, in each wider community, cherished friends.

For responses to this book's first chapters I thank Stephanie Camp, Madeleine Yue Dong, Pat Ebrey, Susan Glenn, Uta Poiger, Lynn Thomas, Anne Firor Scott, and Kate Swatek. And I am extremely grateful to everyone who read the entire manuscript: to Julie A. Campbell, Paul Clemens, Jacquelyn Dowd Hall, Jana Harris, Susan Jeffords, Katheryne McCormick, Dick McCormick, Jennifer Ritterhouse, Julie K. Stein, and Brent Tarter. Allan Doyle, Elizabeth Escobedo, and Karla Kelling helped immensely with intense, eleventh-hour proofreading. At W. W. Norton, Edwin Barber and Amy Cherry offered candid comments, useful deadlines, and superb editing.

Finally, I have immeasurable debts to the people whose lives are at the center of this book. I hope I have begun to repay them by telling their stories as best I know how.

SUZANNE LEBSOCK
Seattle
July 2002

NOTES

A Note on Sources

Unless otherwise noted, county records cited in the endnotes are the originals, located in the offices of the county clerks of Lunenburg, Mecklenburg, Prince Edward, Charlotte, Nottoway, and Brunswick. The great majority of county records located outside of the counties are in the Library of Virginia, herein abbreviated LVA. The Prince Edward Loose Court Papers were located in the Prince Edward courthouse when I read them; they have since been transferred to the Library of Virginia.

1. The Populist drama was the pivot of C. Vann Woodward's *Origins of the New South, 1877–1913* (Baton Rouge: Louisiana State University Press, 1951), which remains the single most influential book in southern history. Populism has been less central in most of the published histories of Virginia politics, but I think it is due for a comeback.

2. The standard works in Virginia political history for this period are William DuBose Sheldon, *Populism in the Old Dominion: Virginia Farm Politics, 1885–1900* (Gloucester, Mass.: Peter Smith, 1967, reprint of 1935 edition, originally published by Princeton University Press); Allen W. Moger, *Virginia: Bourbonism to Byrd, 1870–1925* (Charlottesville: University Press of Virginia, 1968); Raymond H. Pulley, *Old Virginia Restored: An Interpretation of the Progressive Impulse, 1870–1930* (Charlottesville: University Press of Virginia, 1968). So far as I am aware, the first mention of the Lunenburg case in a work of history was in Ann Field Alexander's unpublished Ph.D. dissertation, "Black Protest in the New South: John Mitchell, Jr., (1863–1929) and the *Richmond Planet*" (Duke University, 1973). Samuel Norman Pincus followed with his dissertation, "The Virginia Supreme Court, Blacks, and the Law, 1870–1902" (University of Virginia, 1978), pp. 412–47; this dissertation was published by Garland in 1990. More recently, a few brief treatments of the case have appeared in print, reflecting a new interest in the history of women and African Americans. See Suzanne Lebsock, *"A Share of Honour": Virginia Women 1600–1945* (Richmond: Virginia Women's Cultural History Project, 1984), p. 125; W. Fitzhugh Brundage, *Lynching in the New South: Georgia and Virginia, 1880–1930* (Urbana: University of Illinois Press, 1993), pp. 173–76; Elsa Barkley Brown, "Negotiating and Transforming the Public Sphere: African American Political Life in the Transition from Slavery to Freedom," *Public Culture*, 7 (1994), pp. 141–44. A more extended treatment of the case appears in Michael Ayers Trotti, "Murder and the Modern Sensibility: Sensationalism and Cultural Change in Richmond, Virginia, from the Victorian Era to the Age of Ragtime," unpublished Ph.D. dissertation (University of North Carolina at Chapel Hill, 1999). Alexander's biography of Mitchell, *Race*

Man: The Rise and Fall of the "Fighting Editor," John Mitchell Jr., is forthcoming from the University Press of Virginia.

3. Quoted in Ann Field Alexander, " 'Like an Evil Wind': The Roanoke Riot of 1893 and the Lynching of Thomas Smith," *Virginia Magazine of History and Biography*, 100 (April 1992), p. 202.

4. *Richmond Planet*, 14 December 1895.

CHAPTER 1: "MURDER MOST BRUTAL"

1. The conversation was recounted by Mary Abernathy; the wording comes from the *Richmond Times*, 24 April 1896, and the Mary Abernathy Trial Transcript (hereinafter MATT), p. 65, Prince Edward County Court Papers, LVA. Further evidence given by Mary Abernathy is in the *Petersburg Index-Appeal*, 21 June 1895, and the *Richmond Planet*, 27 July 1895. Wilson Abernathy's corroborating testimony appeared in the *Times*, 16 July 1895, 18 March 1896. The *Times*, 11 August 1895, pegged the distance from the Abernathy house to the Pollard house at 660 yards. MURDER MOST BRUTAL was the headline of the first newspaper article to report the crime: *Dispatch*, 16 June 1895.

2. Mary Abernathy quoting Edward Pollard, *Index-Appeal*, 21 June 1895. Testimony of Cass Gregory, MATT, p. 37; *Times*, 14 July 1895.

3. Descriptions of the body appeared in MATT, pp. 27–28, 37, 43; Pokey Barnes Trial Transcript, p. 4, in Mary Barnes Pardon Papers (24 December 1896), Secretary of the Commonwealth, Executive Papers, LVA (hereinafter PBTT); *Dispatch*, 12 July 1895, 17 March 1896; *Times*, 17 March 1896; *Charlotte Gazette*, 27 June 1895.

4. *Dispatch*, 6 August 1895; testimony of Edward Pollard, MATT, p. 27, and PBTT, pp. 3, 6.

5. PBTT, p. 6.

6. Documentation of the life of Mary Abernathy is below in Chapter 6.

7. Testimony of Mary Abernathy, MATT, p. 65; testimony of Cass Gregory, *Times*, 22 April 1896. Mary Abernathy's statement of June 14 was not recorded. What appears here is a paraphrase of several statements she gave at later times, the first printed in the *Index-Appeal*, 21 June 1895; Justice Eubank testified (MATT, p. 82) that

with one exception Abernathy's June 14 statement was consistent with those she made later at the magistrate's hearing and at her trial in county court. Her statement was corroborated by Edward Pollard, *Dispatch*, 6 August 1895; MATT, pp. 25, 31–32; PBTT, p. 6.

8. Testimony of Edward Pollard, PBTT, p. 6.

9. *Planet*, 10 August 1895; testimony of Edward Pollard, PBTT, p. 6; *Times*, 2 and 5 May 1896.

10. Virginia, *The Code of Virginia: With the Declaration of Independence and the Constitution of the United States; and the Constitution of Virginia* (Richmond: James E. Goode, 1887), pp. 244–81, secs. 790–944, spells out the duties of local officials. The amounts come from E. A. Clements's claims in the Lunenburg Court Papers, LVA (hereinafter LCP, LVA).

11. The order is in LCP, LVA.

12. MATT, pp. 27–28; PBTT, pp. 4, 7; *Dispatch*, 8 August 1895.

13. MATT, pp. 34, 65.

14. On bruises: MATT, pp. 27, 43; *Times* and *Dispatch*, both 17 March 1896. On the calico dress: *Dispatch*, 3 August 1895.

15. MATT, p. 33; PBTT, p. 3; *Dispatch*, 6 August 1895. The *Dispatch* article said the loft was in disarray, but as no other source confirms this, I think this is embellishment on the reporter's part.

16. MATT, pp. 28, 29, 33; PBTT, pp. 3, 5, 10.

17. MATT, p. 30; PBTT, p. 7.

18. MATT, pp. 27–28, 76, 84; PBTT, pp. 4, 10; *Times*, 14 July 1895.

CHAPTER 2: CHASE CITY

1. *Oxford* (N.C.) *Public Ledger*, 21 June 1895; *Times*, 11 July 1895; *Presented by the Chase City Calcium Water Company, Chase City, Va.* (Weldon, N.C.: Harrell's Printing House, 1910); Douglas Summers Brown, *Chase City and Its Environs: The Southside Virginia Experience, 1765–1975* (Chase City: Publication Committee, 1975), pp. 153, 160, 165–67; Susan L. Bracey, *Life by the Roaring Roanoke: A History of Mecklenburg County, Virginia* (printed in Richmond for the Mecklenburg County Bicentennial Commission, 1978), pp. 321–22. Weather courtesy of Robert Allen Diary, Allen Family Papers, Virginia Historical Society; unless otherwise noted,

all information on weather comes from this source. On town life: Edward L. Ayers, *The Promise of the New South: Life after Reconstruction* (New York: Oxford University Press, 1992), pp. 55–103.

2. A sketch of the restaurant: *Planet*, 16 May 1896. Marable's visit was described by Mary and Jennie Wootten, MATT, pp. 64–65; *Times*, 14 July 1895, 17 March 1896; *Dispatch*, 17 March 1896. Solomon's similar account: *Times*, 28 July 1895, and the *Planet*, 21 September 1895.

3. Marable's accounts of his visit to Clarke's store: *Times*, 14 September 1895; *Planet*, 6 June 1896; *Marable* v. *Commonwealth*, pp. 3–4, a printed petition in the Library of the Supreme Court of Appeals of Virginia in Richmond. I thank Terry Long for her help in locating this and other Supreme Court documents. Clarke's accounts: MATT, p. 63 (which gives the letter's text); *Times*, 18 March 1896 (Jones quotation); *Dispatch*, 18 March 1896. The sequence of events varies somewhat from one account to another, but Marable and Clarke both agreed that Marable made purchases, that Clarke wrote the letter, and that Marable at first put two bills in the envelope and then removed one.

4. For the train schedule: *Chase City Progress*, 20 September 1895.

5. Pokey Barnes's testimony: *Times* and *Dispatch*, both 20 July 1895. Ellen Gayle's account: *Times* and *Dispatch*, both 18 July 1895. Further details on Ellen Gayle's initial statement: *Times*, 3 May 1896. A plat in the Prince Edward Loose Court Papers says Pokey's house was 275 yards from Pollard's.

6. The search warrants and arrest records are in LCP, LVA. Searches were described in MATT, pp. 38, 45; *Dispatch*, 22 April 1896.

7. Ages of Fannie Marable and her sons are from the 1900 Census, Granville County, ED 61, sheet 16, North Carolina. All references to the census are to the United States Manuscript Census Schedules (hereinafter MCS), available on microfilm in the National Archives and Records Administration, Washington, D.C., and many other research libraries. Solomon's accounts of their flight: *Marable* v. *Commonwealth*, p. 4; *Times*, 28 July, 14 September 1895; *Planet*, 21 September 1895, 6 June 1896. Fannie's account: *Times*, 24 October

1895. Other testimony: MATT, pp. 64, 81; *Times*, 18 March 1896. The *Times*, 20 June 1895, said that Mary Wootten notified authorities of Solomon's return.

8. *State* v. *Solomon Marable*, Granville County Criminal Actions, North Carolina State Archives. Newspaper accounts appeared in the *Oxford* (N.C.) *Public Ledger*, 12 and 19 January, 2 February 1894; *Times*, 24 October 1895. Solomon and Fannie's marriage license, dated 4 June 1892, is noted in the Granville County Marriage Register, 1884–1893, North Carolina State Archives. On Granville: Laura F. Edwards, *Gendered Strife and Confusion: The Political Culture of Reconstruction* (Urbana: University of Illinois Press, 1997); Sharon Ann Holt, *Making Freedom Pay: North Carolina Freedpeople Working for Themselves, 1865–1900* (Athens: University of Georgia Press, 2000).

9. This dialogue was recollected by Solomon and printed in the *Planet*, 6 June 1896.

10. *Code of Virginia* (1887), secs. 3704–07, pp. 885–86. John Mitchell, Jr., frequently cited cases of disproportionate sentencing in the pages of the *Planet*.

11. On taking versus stealing, and for a complex analysis of theft and resistance in slavery, see Eugene D. Genovese, *Roll, Jordan, Roll: The World the Slaves Made* (New York: Pantheon Books, 1974), pp. 599–609; Lawrence W. Levine, *Black Culture and Black Consciousness: Afro-American Folk Thought from Slavery to Freedom* (Oxford: Oxford University Press, 1977), pp. 121–33; Edward L. Ayers, *Vengeance and Justice: Crime and Punishment in the 19th-Century American South* (New York: Oxford University Press, 1984), pp. 124–30. Theft and related crimes against property were the most frequently prosecuted crimes in the nineteenth-century United States. See Lawrence M. Friedman, *Crime and Punishment in American History* (New York: BasicBooks, 1993), p. 109. On violent crime: Roger Lane, *Murder in America: A History* (Columbus: Ohio State University Press, 1997).

12. There is a large literature on southern African Americans in the postwar period. Two recent, concise starting points are Noralee Frankel, "Breaking the Chains: 1860–1880" and Barbara Bair,

"Though Justice Sleeps: 1880–1900," both in *To Make Our World Anew: A History of African Americans*, ed. Robin D. G. Kelley and Earl Lewis (Oxford: Oxford University Press, 2000), pp. 227–80, 281–344. For more detail, see Leon F. Litwack, *Been in the Storm So Long: The Aftermath of Slavery* (New York: Random House, 1979). On the Southside: Lynda J. Morgan, *Emancipation in Virginia's Tobacco Belt, 1850–1870* (Athens: University of Georgia Press, 1992), pp. 127–227. Jeffrey R. Kerr-Ritchie, *Freedpeople in the Tobacco South: Virginia, 1860–1900* (Chapel Hill: University of North Carolina Press, 1999). On the altered world of former slaveholders: James L. Roark, *Masters without Slaves: Southern Planters in the Civil War and Reconstruction* (New York: W. W. Norton, 1977); Genovese, *Roll, Jordan, Roll*, pp. 97–112.

13. Ayers, *Vengeance and Justice*, pp. 167–184, 250–52, discusses theft after the Civil War and notes a crime wave throughout the South in the late 1880s and early 1890s. As far as I'm aware, this psychic hypothesis about why whites punished alleged black thieves so harshly is mine. It seems to me that the growing white obsession with rape in this period grew out of the same mentality, a comparable anxiety that black men were taking what belonged to white men.

14. For dress, laundry, and accusations of theft, as well as a larger history of domestic workers, see Tera W. Hunter, *To 'Joy My Freedom: Southern Black Women's Lives and Labors after the Civil War* (Cambridge: Harvard University Press, 1997). Stephanie M. H. Camp's forthcoming book on women's everyday resistance to slavery analyzes the role of dress in slaveholders' attempt to degrade enslaved women and the women's resistance to that attempt.

15. *Dispatch*, 1 August 1895; *Index-Appeal*, 21 June 1895.

16. The testimony of Edward Pollard and Mary Barnes jibed on this point, except that Barnes said she stooped down by the body while Edward Pollard claimed he told her to turn around and run to the neighbors' as soon as she came in the front gate. Edward's recollection of the hours immediately following the murder was somewhat fuzzy, so I believe Mary Barnes on this one. *Dispatch*, 28 July, 6 August 1895. The arrest warrants are in LCP, LVA. According to the

Dispatch, 16 May 1896, Rena Barnes said she had visited the Marables' house the morning after the murder; the authorities may have thought her part of a conspiracy.

17. PBTT, p. 6.

18. The summons to the coroner's jury is in LCP, LVA.

19. All the arrest and search warrants concern African American suspects. Nothing in any of the newspaper accounts or reported trial testimony suggests that any whites were treated as suspects.

20. Quotations from testimony of Phil Watson and Mary Abernathy: MATT, pp. 49, 67. Pattie Clements (MATT, p. 46) testified that a rumor that an unnamed man had been captured reached the Clements farm at about 1:00 P.M. Watson confirmed this, though he said the message was delivered by Pattie Clements's mother; other witnesses said the messenger was Pattie Clements. Other accounts of events on this day: *Dispatch*, 17 July 1895; *Times*, 17 July, 20 August 1895; MATT, pp. 45–48, 66. Recollections of Pokey Barnes: *Planet*, 27 June 1896.

21. Cass Gregory reported he caught the train with eight or ten others, and once in Chase City they joined the search on foot. Gregory also reported that fifty Chase City men, some on horseback, were involved in the search: MATT, pp. 38, 45. The *State*, 17 June 1895, reported the staking out of bridges and ferries.

22. Durelle Gregory's age is from the Gregory Family Bible Record, 1765–1896, LVA. The sense that he was steady and a good farmer is derived from his later success in acquiring real estate in the area. His role in the investigation: *Times*, 2 and 5 May 1896. The report of the coroner's jury (in LCP, LVA) shows he was a member of that body. Events of this night were reported in MATT, p. 48; *Planet*, 27 June 1896.

23. *Dispatch*, 16 June 1895.

CHAPTER 3: FLIGHT

1. A New York agent advertised European tours ranging from $135 to $565 and a tour to Palestine for $650: *Dispatch*, 4 January 1896.

2. On the impact of the panic and depression: Moger, *Virginia:*

Bourbonism to Byrd, pp. 145–65; Sheldon, *Populism in the Old Dominion*, pp. 15–21.

3. Hundreds of thousands of these papers have been preserved, many of them in the Library of Virginia and many in county courthouses. Specific examples follow in later chapters.

4. So Gregory testified: MATT, p. 37.

5. Gregory's age: Gregory Family Bible Record, 1765–1896, LVA. Edna Crenshaw Craig, *Its Waters Returning* (Charlotte, N.C.: Delmar Company, 1989) calls Gregory a civil engineer. References to his surveying: Brunswick County Fiduciary Accounts, vol. 4, p. 366; Brunswick County Civil War Pensioners, Act of 1902, LVA. His timbering and tobacco businesses: *Hanmer* v. *Gregory*, Mecklenburg Chancery Papers, File 131, LVA; *H. C. Gregory* v. *W. T. Spencer*, Lunenburg Papers, Chancery File 131, *Roxboro* (N.C.) *Person County Courier*, 9 January, 1 May 1895.

6. Allen Diary, 13–20 June 1895.

7. I am grateful to E. Jackson Gregory for showing me a photograph of Cass Gregory.

8. Gregory's whereabouts were briefly noted in MATT, pp. 37–38, 43, 65; *Times*, 2 May 1896.

9. *Richmond Planet*, 7 September 1895. This conversation was recalled by Edward Pollard in MATT, p. 36.

10. Testimony of H. A. White, MATT, p. 52.

11. Mary Abernathy was the source of this quotation, in MATT, p. 67. Sources on the proceedings (all sketchy) include MATT, pp. 43–44, 67–68, 82; *Times*, 25 April 1896; *Planet*, 27 June 1896. Orders convening the coroner's jury and dismissing the women from custody are in LCP, LVA.

12. This was Pokey Barnes's account: *Planet*, 27 June 1896. It refers only to "Mr. Hudson," so it is possible the Hutson named here was someone other than Peter.

13. The *Times*, 30 June 1895, described the scene. On the bloodstains: *Charlotte Gazette*, 27 June 1895.

14. Accounts of Marable's arrest: *Times*, 19 June 1895; *Dispatch*, 20 June 1895, 18 March 1896.

15. The *Times*, 19 June 1895, said that "a negro" (unnamed) brought the news to Chase City. The *Dispatch*, 3 August 1895, reported

that Ben Daniel contacted a white neighbor named James Winn. The conversation between Ben Daniel and Solomon Marable was given on the witness stand by Daniel himself and reported in the *Dispatch*, 18 March 1896, and in the *Times* of the same date.

16. The other William Henry Marable appeared as a two-year-old in the 1880 MCS, Clinton Township, Sampson County, N.C., ED 189, sheet 2.

17. Testimony of Walter Gregory: *Times*, 18 March 1896. Warrants for the women's arrest were issued before the posse returned to Fort Mitchell with Solomon.

18. *Planet*, 27 June 1896. The arrest warrants are in LCP, LVA.

19. *Dispatch*, 20 June 1895.

20. The *Star*, 19 June 1895, said two hundred. The *Times* of the same date said four or five hundred.

21. The *State*, 19 June 1895, and the *Petersburg Index-Appeal*, 21 June 1895, praised the authorities for withholding the allegedly bloody clothes, thereby removing one incentive to mob violence. The *Dispatch* reported that the clothes were bloody on 18, 19, and 20 June 1895, as did the *Times* on 20 June 1895. The presence of ropes: *Dispatch*, 20 June 1895. The actual condition of the clothes: MATT, p. 50.

22. Pollard's staring down the suspects: *Times*, 30 June 1895.

23. Neblett's birth and death dates: Bell, *Old Free State*, vol. 2, p. 324. His presence at Pollard's: *Charlotte Gazette*, 27 June 1895; *Planet*, 27 June 1896.

24. An arrest warrant and subsequent notation of Ellen Gayle's release for lack of evidence are in LCP, LVA.

25. On Clements's stalling the crowd: *Index-Appeal*, 20 June 1895; *Marable v. Commonwealth*, p. 5. The *Times*, 30 June 1895, said the commonwealth attorney made the long speech.

26. *Planet*, 27 June 1896.

27. Quoted by Pokey Barnes, ibid.

28. The wait until dawn: Ibid. The fear of encountering "a force of men determined to take the prisoners" was reported in the *Index-Appeal*, 21 June 1895. LCP, LVA contains Deputy Sheriff E. H. Bacon's claim for reimbursement for the breakfast. The Lunenburg Courthouse is still standing.

29. A report by Robert Allen et al., 13 June 1896, LCP, LVA describes the jail, which no longer stands.

30. MATT, pp. 67–68; *Planet*, 27 July 1896. The warrant is in LCP, LVA, as are two related documents: the justice of the peace's binding Abernathy over for "tryal" and Harding's claim for reimbursement for guards, meals, horse hire and feed.

31. *Star*, 21 June 1895; *Times*, 22 June 1895.

32. *Dispatch*, 21 June 1895. It is not clear why Sheriff J. W. Ellis was not in charge of this, though Ellis's claims for reimbursement suggest he had gone to southern Mecklenburg County to search there. Ellis's term as sheriff was to expire on July 1. The county court judge was away visiting friends in a difficult-to-reach location in Amelia County. Documents in LCP, LVA show that Bacon sent a courier to the judge, who then drove to Blackstone to telegraph Petersburg authorities, asking them to take the prisoners into the Petersburg jail. Other accounts are in the *Times*, 21 and 22 June 1895; *Dispatch*, 28 July 1895.

33. *Times*, 21 and 22 June 1895; *Dispatch*, 20 and 21 June, 28 July 1895; *Planet*, 27 June 1896.

CHAPTER 4: INDEPENDENCE DAY

1. Allen Diary, 4 July 1895; I corrected one spelling ("robing"). The *Charlotte Gazette*, 27 June 1895, and the *Petersburg Index-Appeal*, 3 July 1895, also commented on the demise of old-time July Fourth celebrations.

2. Cardozo claimed expenses for train and buggy fare on July 4: LCP, LVA. The newspapers usually spelled his name "Cardoza," suggesting the way it was pronounced. Handwritten documents in Lunenburg Courthouse consistently show the spelling as Cardozo. For lynching predictions: *Dispatch*, 19 and 20 June 1895; *Times*, 20 and 21 June 1895; *State*, 19 June 1895; *Star*, 21 June 1895. Most unnerving was a *Dispatch* report, 21 June 1895, that on the night the prisoners were taken out of Lunenburg, a hundred men had massed near the courthouse, sending a squad of masked men to scout the prisoners' location. Reports of continued bitterness: *Times*, 23 June 1895; *Index-Appeal*, 27 June, 5 July 1895; *Dispatch*,

29 June, 10 July 1895. "Blood hot": Allen Diary, 22 and 25 June 1895.

3. Cardozo's age is calculated from the 1880 and 1900 MCS, Lewiston District, Lunenburg County (respectively, ED 136, sheet 2 and ED 37, sheet 18). His activity in the Republican party is documented in letters to party boss William Mahone, 1 and 3 November 1892, Mahone Papers, Duke University, and in a later letter to W. F. Wickham, 23 October 1897, Republican Party of Virginia Papers, Virginia Historical Society, as well as the *Times*, 25 March 1896. On voting laws: Moger, *Virginia: Bourbonism to Byrd*, pp. 56, 97–98, and 163 for the Walton Act of 1894, which made balloting more complex and fraud easier to commit. For a fresh perspective on Southside politics: Harold S. Forsythe, "'But My Friends Are Poor': Ross Hamilton and Freedpeople's Politics in Mecklenburg County, Virginia, 1869–1901," *Virginia Magazine of History and Biography*, 105 (Autumn 1997), pp. 409–38.

4. On Cardozo's unseating of incumbent J. W. Ellis: Allen Diary, 23 May 1895. Judge George C. Orgain was in debt to Cardozo more or less continuously from 1882 on, as documented by the following, all in Lunenburg Courthouse: Deed Book 40, p. 2 (1878); Deed Book 41, p. 181 (1883), p. 353 (1883), p. 431 (1884), p. 480 (1884); Deed Book 42, pp. 73–74 (1885), p. 133 (1885), p. 236 (1885); Deed Book 43, p. 90 (1887), p. 127 (1888), p. 465 (1889); Chancery Order Book C, p. 642 (1882); Fiduciary Book 9, p. 81 (1901).

5. The quotations are respectively from the *Times*, 18 June 1895; *Star*, 18 June 1895; *State*, 18 June 1895; *Dispatch*, 22 June 1895; *Charlotte Gazette*, 27 June 1895.

6. Quoted in Alexander, " 'Like an Evil Wind,' " p. 202. For more detailed statistics, as well as a close study of Virginia and Georgia, see Brundage, *Lynching in the New South*. Stewart E. Tolnay and E. M. Beck, *A Festival of Violence: An Analysis of Southern Lynchings, 1882–1930* (Urbana: University of Illinois Press, 1995) found that in ten states (not including Virginia) just under 3 percent of all lynch victims were women. According to Crystal Nicole Feimster, "'Ladies and Lynching': The Gendered Discourse of Mob Violence in the New South, 1880–1930," unpublished Ph.D. dissertation (Princeton University, 2000), 148 women were lynched in the United States from 1880 to 1930; 120 of them were African Americans.

7.   Charles T. O'Ferrall, *Forty Years of Active Service* (New York: Neale Publishing Co., 1904), p. 184 (quotation). My account of O'Ferrall's career is drawn from this autobiography and from Minor T. Weisiger, "Charles T. O'Ferrall: 'Gray Eagle' from the Valley," in *The Governors of Virginia, 1860–1978*, ed. Edward Younger and James Tice Moore (Charlottesville: University Press of Virginia, 1982), pp. 135–46. Swem Library, College of William and Mary, holds a small collection of O'Ferrall manuscripts. The Library of Virginia holds the executive papers of all the governors; the collection for O'Ferrall is very thin.

8.   The numbers are from Brundage, *Lynching in the New South*, pp. 281–82. Tolnay and Beck, *A Festival of Violence*, p. 30, chart the increase elsewhere in the South.

9.   This account of the Roanoke riot and lynching is based on Alexander, " 'Like an Evil Wind.' "

10. For categories of lynchings see Brundage, *Lynching in the New South*, pp. 17–45. For the contention that spectacle lynchings were a modern invention linked to consumer culture, see Grace Elizabeth Hale, *Making Whiteness: The Culture of Segregation in the South, 1890–1940* (New York: Pantheon Books, 1998), pp. 199–239.

11. George M. Fredrickson, *The Black Image in the White Mind: The Debate on Afro-American Character and Destiny, 1817–1914* (New York: Harper & Row, 1971); Joel Williamson, *A Rage for Order: Black-White Relations in the American South since Emancipation* (New York: Oxford University Press, 1986), pp. 70–151, 181–91. Williamson substitutes "retrogression" for "degeneracy."

12. As Jacquelyn Dowd Hall suggests, "the emotional circuit between interracial rape and lynching lay beyond the reach of factual refutation. A black man did not literally have to attempt sexual assault for whites to perceive some transgression of caste mores as a sexual threat." " 'The Mind That Burns in Each Body': Women, Rape, and Racial Violence," in *Powers of Desire: The Politics of Sexuality*, ed. Ann Snitow, Christine Stansell, and Sharon Thompson (New York: Monthly Review Press, 1983), p. 334. In addition to works by Brundage, Feimster, Hale, and Tolnay and Beck cited above, recent scholarly works elucidating lynching and nineteenth-century understandings of lynching include Ayers, *Vengeance and Justice*, pp.

237–55; Jacquelyn Dowd Hall, *Revolt against Chivalry: Jessie Daniel Ames and the Women's Campaign against Lynching*, rev. ed. (New York: Columbia University Press, 1993); W. Fitzhugh Brundage, ed., *Under Sentence of Death: Lynching in the South* (Chapel Hill: University of North Carolina Press, 1997); Christopher Waldrep, "Word and Deed: The Language of Lynching, 1820–1953," in *Lethal Imagination: Violence and Brutality in American History*, ed. Michael A. Bellesiles (New York: New York University Press, 1999), pp. 229–58; Bertram Wyatt-Brown, *The Shaping of Southern Culture: Honor, Grace, and War, 1760s–1890s* (Chapel Hill: University of North Carolina Press, 2001), pp. 283–95; Nell Irvin Painter, " 'Social Equality' and 'Rape' in the Fin-de-Siècle South," *Southern History across the Color Line* (Chapel Hill: University of North Carolina Press, 2002), pp. 112–33. On the perception of whites as savages: Mia Bay, *The White Image in the Black Mind: African-American Ideas about White People, 1830–1925* (New York: Oxford University Press, 2000), pp. 95–111. On the antilynching campaigns of Ida B. Wells, see Chapter 11 below. In recent years some scholars have proposed that rape was commonly used as a comparable weapon of terror against southern black women. See Darlene Clark Hine, "Rape and the Inner Lives of Black Women: Thoughts on the Culture of Dissemblance" in *Hine Sight: Black Women and the Reconstruction of American History* (Brooklyn, N.Y.: Carlson Publishing, 1994), pp. 37–47; Nell Irvin Painter, "Soul Murder and Slavery: Toward a Fully Loaded Cost Accounting," in *U.S. History as Women's History: New Feminist Essays*, ed. Linda K. Kerber, Alice Kessler-Harris, and Kathryn Kish Sklar (Chapel Hill: University of North Carolina Press, 1995), pp. 125–46.

13. Alexander, " 'Like an Evil Wind,' " p. 202. Brundage, *Lynching in the New South*, p. 282, does identify one lynching in Scott County in May 1894. A *Dispatch* editorial, 22 June 1895, however, stated flatly: "There has not been a lynching in Virginia since Colonel O'Ferrall became Governor." Either the *Dispatch* was unaware of the Scott County lynching, or the killing was not classified as a lynching at the time. In any case, O'Ferrall's reputation was still intact.

14. William H. Gaines, Jr., "Courthouses of Lunenburg and Meck-

lenburg Counties," *Virginia Cavalcade*, 20 (Winter 1971), p. 29.

15. *Report of the Adjutant-General of the State of Virginia for the Year 1895* (Richmond: J. H. O'Bannon, Superintendent of Public Printing, 1895), pp. 64–65. There was at least one drummer of the percussionist kind. "Drummer" was also a synonym for salesman, of whom there were at least three in the regiment. The men's names, ranks, ages, and terms of service are listed in the Muster Rolls in the Archives, LVA. I found occupations for many of them in J. H. Chataigne, comp., *Chataigne's Directory of Richmond, Va., 1895–96* (n.p.: n.p., 1896).

16. Lunenburg Order Book 37, p. 205, contains Judge Orgain's order to have the prisoners returned from Petersburg. LCP, LVA contains Cardozo's claim for transportation for himself and two guards. There are also claims for wages from the two guards. The *Times* and *Dispatch*, 12 July 1895, give information on the Petersburg–Richmond leg of their journey.

17. The two-dollar figure comes from a letter of Joseph Bryan to "all unsalaried correspondents of The Times who receive the Daily paper," Letterbook, 15 April to 21 December 1895, p. 363, Joseph Bryan Papers, Virginia Historical Society. The *Dispatch*, 3 August 1895, said that the men who covered the trials were "local correspondents, gentlemen who are next-door neighbors of our Lunenburg friends." The articles referred to in the paragraphs that follow were printed in the *Times* and *Dispatch*, 12 July 1895.

CHAPTER 5: SOLOMON ON TRIAL

1. Arrival and departure times: *Report of the Adjutant-General*, p. 65. Weather report: *Dispatch*, 13 July 1895. References to the hotels and general stores, typically notations of payments made to them for goods or services to the county, are scattered through LCP, LVA, as are references to the Masonic Hall, applications to sell liquor, and a repair to the public well. The *Dispatch*, 17 July 1895, mentioned the falling of the well sweep. Churches: *Times*, 18 July 1895, and *Star*, 18 December 1895.

2. Gaines, "Courthouses of Lunenburg and Mecklenburg Counties," pp. 22–33; John O. and Margaret T. Peters, *Virginia's Historic*

Courthouses (Charlottesville: University Press of Virginia, 1995), pp. 53–54.

3. *Dispatch*, 13 July 1895, 24 January 1896.

4. Fannie's journey home: *Times*, 24 October 1895. Records concerning her arrest are in LCP, LVA, as is a form listing the jail's inmates with dates of their incarceration.

5. *Times*, 13 July 1895. Marable was indicted the previous day. Lunenburg Order Book 37, p. 204; *Dispatch*, 12 July 1895.

6. G. L. Sherwood and Jeffrey C. Weaver, *20th and 39th Virginia Infantry* (Virginia Regimental Histories Series), p. 63, give Orgain's birth date as 6 November 1838, but according to the 1900 MCS, Lewiston District, Lunenburg, ED 37, sheet 9, Orgain was born in October 1836; the 1900 census also said that his wife, Rebecca, had given birth to thirteen children, ten of whom were still living in 1900. At the time of the trials the Orgains' children ranged in age from twelve to thirty-two. Orgain's military experience is outlined in Bell, *Old Free State*, vol. 1, pp. 590–94. Milestones in his legal career are in Lunenburg Order Book 31, pp. 292, 319; Book 36, p. 317. Documents concerning Orgain's debts were recorded in the following Lunenburg Deed Books: Book 38, p. 139; Book 40, p. 2; Book 41, pp. 48, 124, 181, 182, 353, 431, 480, 498, 524; Book 42, pp. 73, 74, 133, 165, 166, 236, 536; Book 43, pp. 90, 127, 465, 495, 587; Book 44, pp. 110, 347; Book 48, pp. 142, 145, 148. Also on debts: Lunenburg Fiduciary Book 9, p. 81; Lunenburg Chancery Order Book C, p. 642, and Book D, p. 240. A portrait of the judge hangs in the courtroom.

7. I. B. Bell, who appears to have been Lunenburg's leading attorney, declined the invitation to defend Marable, claiming he could not spare the time. *Times* and *Dispatch*, 13 July 1895.

8. Pincus, "The Virginia Supreme Court, Blacks, and the Law," pp. 49–66, is the only work to examine the composition of Virginia juries in depth. On the Readjusters' role: James Tice Moore, *Two Paths to the New South: The Virginia Debt Controversy, 1870–1883* (Lexington: University Press of Kentucky, 1974), p. 103; Jane Dailey, *Before Jim Crow: The Politics of Race in Postemancipation Virginia* (Chapel Hill: University of North Carolina Press, 2000), pp. 1, 53–54, 64, 86, 153.

9. Lunenburg Order Book 37, p. 207. The *Times*, 13 July 1895,

said two of the jurors were black. Robert Allen's diary, 13 July 1895, said four jurors were black.

10. Neblett's portrait: *Dispatch*, 28 November 1895. Robert Allen thought Neblett incompetent (diary, 23 May 1895), an opinion apparently shared by Edward Pollard, who hired a second attorney to assist the prosecution.

11. Each reporter who covered the trial produced his own version of Solomon's statement; although these versions vary, they do not conflict except in the instance explained in Note 24 below. The version printed here is a composite pulled together from the *Dispatch*, the *Times*, and the *Index-Appeal*, all 13 July 1895, plus the *Charlotte Gazette*, 18 July 1895.

12. These principles were spelled out in Orgain's instructions to the jury in Mary Abernathy's trial: *Abernathy* v. *Commonwealth*, p. 17, Library of the Supreme Court of Appeals of Virginia.

13. The newspaper articles on Marable's trial reported Edward Pollard's testimony only in the sketchiest way. What follows in the text is the first detailed version of Pollard's story to be published, *Dispatch*, 6 August 1895, a borrowing that seems justified by the fact that his story was consistent from one published telling to the next. The names Robertson and Robinson were often confused by nineteenth-century people (one guesses that Virginians typically swallowed the middle syllable). In this article "Robinson" was used, but I have changed it for the sake of consistency. Trudier Harris, "Porch-Sitting as a Creative Southern Tradition," *Southern Cultures*, 2 (1996), pp. 441–60, muses on the porch as a space that could be inhabited by blacks and whites at the same time.

14. *Dispatch*, 13 July, 28 July 1895; *Times*, 23 July 1895.

15. Allen Diary, 12 July 1895. The diary, 23 May 1895, mentions his election to his twentieth term as justice. A published but unidentified obituary is in Section 22, Allen Family Papers.

16. Allen Diary, 13 July 1895.

17. The diaries of the late 1860s are full of complaints about free labor; Allen wrote an essay on the subject on 11 December 1867. On blacks' and whites' divergent beliefs about labor after emancipation: Jacqueline Jones, *Labor of Love, Labor of Sorrow: Black Women, Work, and the Family from Slavery to the Present* (New York: Ran-

dom House, 1986), pp. 44–78; Eric Foner, *Reconstruction: America's Unfinished Revolution, 1863–1877* (New York: Harper & Row, 1988), pp. 102–10, 124–75; Morgan, *Emancipation in Virginia's Tobacco Belt*, pp. 127–59, 187–96; Kerr-Ritchie, *Freedpeople in the Tobacco South*, pp. 31–69.

18. *Times*, 14 July 1895; *Index-Appeal*, 14 July 1895.

19. Lunenburg Order Book 37, p. 207; *Index-Appeal*, 14 July 1895; *Times*, 14 July 1895.

20. *Times* and *Dispatch*, 14 July 1895.

21. Quoted in the *Times*, 14 July 1895.

22. *Index-Appeal*, 14 July 1895. The *Times* of the same date says that Marable called Rena Barnes and Lizzie Bragg, Pokey's eldest sister, to the stand, but the drift of their testimony is not clear.

23. Quoted in the *Dispatch*, 14 July 1895.

24. The account of Solomon's opening statement in the *Dispatch*, 13 July 1895, had him saying that Mary Abernathy reached in "her pocket"—evidently meaning Lucy Pollard's pocket—and handed a key to Mary Barnes. The inclusion of Mary Barnes here was probably a mistake on the part of the newspaper. The same reporter wrote an article published several days later (July 18) in the *Charlotte Gazette*, but this article had Mary Abernathy reaching down to get the key (presumably from Lucy Pollard); it did not mention Mary Barnes. The *Index-Appeal*, 13 July 1895, had Mary Abernathy handing keys to Pokey Barnes. The *Times* of the same date did not mention keys.

25. *Dispatch*, 14 July 1895.

26. Ibid.

27. *Times* and *Dispatch*, both 14 July 1895. In both papers "something serious" was a paraphrase and not a quotation.

28. *Times*, 14 July 1895.

CHAPTER 6: QUICK WORK

1. Allen produced two diaries for this period; one was perhaps a draft and the other slightly more polished. The quotation here combines the two, adding punctuation for greater clarity.

2. *Times*, 14 July 1895 (quotation); *Dispatch*, 14 July 1895; Lunenburg Order Book 37, p. 208.

3. *Times* and *Index-Appeal*, both 14 July 1895.

4. *Dispatch* and *Times*, both 16 July 1895.

5. References to Frank Cunningham's activities appear in many sources, including the *Star*, 23 October, 9 November, 20 December 1895, the *State*, 3 September 1895, and the *Times*, 18 August, 7 September 1895; Joseph Bryan to F. W. Cunningham, 2 February 1893, Letterbook b28, Joseph Bryan Papers; a clipping in the Bagby Family Papers, Virginia Historical Society, contains resolutions of respect from the Colored Baptist Ministers' Conference of Richmond in recognition of Cunningham's singing at many black funerals. I am grateful to the staff of the *Dictionary of Virginia Biography* for the following additional references: George W. Rogers, "Ward Clubs Once Had Lively Time in Richmond Politics," *Richmond News Leader*, 1 June 1954; Vera Palmer, "The Consoling Voice of 10,000 Funerals," *Richmond Times-Dispatch*, 20 October 1935; *Times-Dispatch*, 5 December 1959 (suggesting that Cunningham intended to sing at his own funeral); Elizabeth Copeland Norfleet, "Frank Ward Cunningham," *Richmond Quarterly*, 8 (Fall 1985), pp. 40–44.

6. Landon C. Bell, *Southsider, a Lawyer's Life: Law, Lumber and Coal* (Richmond: Richmond Press, 1954), pp. 109–21.

7. Unless otherwise noted, this day's court proceedings are from the *Times* and *Dispatch*, both 16 July 1895 (all quotations are from these newspapers), and Lunenburg Order Book 37, p. 210. The condition of the courtroom comes from a proposal to the Board of Supervisors to fix it up; LCP, LVA.

8. Allen Diary, 23 May 1895. County court judges were chosen by the General Assembly. Perry served from 1870 to 1891: Bell, *Old Free State*, vol. 1, p. 342.

9. Wilson Abernathy was able to come up with only $2.50: *Times*, 26 July, 18 September 1895. Perry may also have been unwilling to engage Neblett in another unfair fight.

10. *Dispatch*, 16 July 1895 (quotation). Lula Knight's age comes from the 1900 MCS, Lunenburg, ED 40, sheet 17 (she might have still been sixteen, as she had a July birthday). She married William Abernathy on Christmas Day 1895: Lunenburg Marriage Register, 1853–1929, p. 67.

11. The gentlemen were not named, nor was their testimony given. *Index-Appeal*, 16 July 1895 (quotation).

12. Such petitions are scattered through the Lunenburg and Mecklenburg Court Papers, LVA.

13. I have been unable to learn anything about the family in which Mary Abernathy grew up. Wilson was raised on a farm a few miles from the courthouse; until 1865 he was owned by Mary T. Abernathy, a single woman who shared a household with her two single siblings, Jesse D. and Lucy P. Abernathy: *Mary T. Abernathy* v. *D. B. Bragg*, Lunenburg Ended Chancery Cases, 1873-014. Wilson and Mary's marriage was recorded in the Lunenburg Marriage Register, 1853–1929, p. 17. Births of children were recorded in the Lunenburg Register of Births, pp. 143, 155, 182, 200, 231, LVA. Birth dates for the other children were calculated from information given in the 1880 MCS, Lunenburg, ED 139, sheet 18 and the 1900 MCS, Richmond City, ED 59, sheet 8. Wilson appeared in the Lunenburg Personal Property Books in the years 1871–74, 1876–79, 1881–85, 1887, 1889–91, 1893, 1895. The first Abernathy child to be married was Amy, who married James Gregory, a farmhand from Mecklenburg, in 1893. Son William married Lula Knight late in 1895, and Charner married Grace Knight in 1900. The three weddings are recorded in the Lunenburg Marriage Register, 1853–1929, pp. 64, 67, 76. Unlike their parents, Amy and William were married by an African American minister, Isaac Craghead. The only legal action I have found concerning anyone in the family was a small debt case involving Wilson in 1871 (Lunenburg Court Records, 16 January 1871, VHS); such cases were commonplace and did not imply a bad reputation in the neighborhood.

14. Kerr-Ritchie, *Freedpeople in the Tobacco South*, pp. 209–33, points to impressive gains in black landholding in the 1890s; from state tax records for 1900 he finds 458 black landholders in Lunenburg. These gains, he argues, were due in part to the extensive outmigration of older children, who then sent money back to parents to help them purchase land. At the same time black landholdings tended to be relatively small and poor. The *Dispatch*, 30 December 1896, gave figures for the value of real estate holdings (land and buildings) based on taxes paid; in Lunenburg the real estate owned by blacks

accounted for only 7.3 percent of the assessed value of real estate in the county. For a careful analysis of how blacks in a similar county acquired land and other resources, see Crandall A. Shifflett, *Patronage and Poverty in the Tobacco South: Louisa County, Virginia, 1860–1900* (Knoxville: University of Tennessee Press, 1982).

15. The pregnancy was announced eight days later in the *Dispatch*, 23 July 1895; it seems more than reasonable to suppose that Mary Abernathy had been aware of her condition for some time.

16. *Times*, 20 August 1895. E. H. Bacon's claim for supper and lodging for the jurors on this date: LCP, LVA.

17. Neblett quotation: *Dispatch*, 17 July 1895. Marable's reply is a composite of similar quotations in the *Dispatch* and *Times*, both 17 July 1895. Shorter and somewhat different versions were printed in the *Index-Appeal* on the same day and in the *Dispatch* on 8 August 1895.

18. Lunenburg Order Book 37, p. 210; *Times* and *Dispatch*, 17 July 1895. The *Times* also reported that "several people tried to monkey with the guard" but gave no details.

19. *Times*, 17 July 1895; *Report of the Adjutant-General* (1895), p. 65.

20. *Times*, 14, 16, 17, and 18 July 1895; *Dispatch*, 16 and 17 July 1895.

21. Pattie Clements quotations are composites from the *Dispatch*, 17 July 1895 and the *Times*, 17 July, 20 August 1895.

22. So Pattie Clements told the *Times*, 4 August 1895.

23. This is a composite of statements printed in the *Times* and the *Dispatch* on 17 July 1895.

24. Quotations from the closing arguments come from the *Times*, 17 July 1895.

25. The instructions were printed in *Abernathy* v. *Commonwealth*, pp. 16–18.

26. The action of the black juror, Junius Bagley, was mentioned by a white juror, who also told the *Times*, 3 August 1895, that he himself was ready to convict after five minutes' deliberation. E. H. Bacon's claim for feeding and lodging the jurors: LCP, LVA. On scout patrols: *Dispatch*, 18 July 1895.

27. On reinforcements: *Report of the Adjutant-General* (1895),

p. 65; *Dispatch* and *Times*, both 17 July 1895. The morning's proceedings were outlined in the *Dispatch* and *Times*, both 18 July 1895.

    28. *Abernathy* v. *Commonwealth*, p. 15.

    29. Allen Diary, 17 July 1895.

CHAPTER 7: THE PRINCE OF LIARS

    1. The first night's proceedings: *Times* and *Dispatch*, both 18 July 1895.

    2. According to Marie Jenkins Schwartz, *Born in Bondage: Growing Up Enslaved in the Antebellum South* (Cambridge: Harvard University Press, 2000), slave children were set to productive labor at five or six and subjected to harsh punishments at the same age. See also Wilma King, *Stolen Childhood: Slave Youth in Nineteenth-Century America* (Bloomington: Indiana University Press, 1995).

    Daughter of Mary and Wallis (names given in the Mecklenburg Marriage Licenses, 1870–72, 1 July 1871, LVA), Mary Barnes was evidently owned until 1865 by George W. Burwell, whose papers are in the Southern Historical Collection, University of North Carolina—Chapel Hill. I am grateful to Roslyn Holdzkom and Jill Snider for their timely processing of this collection, which contains mentions of a Mary, a Wallis, and, in 1872 and 1873, Joseph Barnes. Enslaved people are often difficult to trace because the census schedules did not give the names of individual slaves, nor typically did they list slaves in family groups; they did give each person's sex, age, and color (black or mulatto). In the 1860 Slave Schedule, Mecklenburg County, p.43 Mary was possibly the person listed as "11 F B"—eleven-year-old female, black. The birth year of her first child is calculated from the 1870 MCS, Christiansville District, p. 39, Mecklenburg; the child's color ("light ginger") and her mother's height were given in the Register of Inmates, 1894–1902, Virginia State Penitentiary, Department of Corrections, LVA. Joseph Barnes told the *Planet*, 19 October 1895, that he had belonged to Repps Barnes. The 1860 Slave Schedule, Charlotte County, pp. 7–8, shows Repps Barnes as the owner of thirty-eight slaves; Joseph may have been the one listed as "13 M B." Joseph's height comes from his service records in the Spanish-American War, National Archives and Records Administration, Washington, D.C.

3. For Joseph Barnes's reputation among whites: *Times* and *Dispatch*, both 26 July 1895. Ages of the Barnes sisters calculated from the 1880 MCS, Lunenburg, ED 136, sheet 47. The first known arrest of Lizzie (full name Mary Elizabeth Bragg) was on 14 October 1890, LCP, LVA. The Mecklenburg Court Papers, LVA, show that she was tried in that county for petty larceny on 28 May 1894. They also contain a claim for warranting and trying Rena Barnes for petty larceny, 3 January 1895. Several documents concerning the breaking and entering charge against Lizzie Bragg are in LCP, LVA. Lunenburg Order Book 37, p. 233, notes her conviction in the August term of county court. The Register of Inmates, 1894–1902, p. 30, records her arrival in the penitentiary, adding that she claimed to be pregnant ("says she is Enciente"). Judge Orgain mentioned Rosa Barnes's pregnancy in a letter printed in the *Dispatch*, 28 July 1895.

4. Mecklenburg Marriage Register, Book 1, p. 367. My earlier research turned up a few examples of women, widowed or divorced, who resumed the use of previous surnames after the dissolution of a marriage: Suzanne Lebsock, *The Free Women of Petersburg: Status and Culture in a Southern Town, 1784–1860* (New York: W. W. Norton, 1984), pp. 71, 73. Elsa Barkley Brown and Gregg D. Kimball, "Mapping the Terrain of Black Richmond," *Journal of Urban History*, 21 (March 1995), pp. 333–34, and Scott C. Davis, *The World of Patience Gromes: Making and Unmaking a Black Community*, 2nd ed. (Seattle: Cune, 2000) argue that respectability was a fluid concept among black Richmonders; the same was likely true among rural people. On the political dimensions of respectability: Evelyn Brooks Higginbotham, *Righteous Discontent: The Women's Movement in the Black Baptist Church, 1880–1920* (Cambridge: Harvard University Press, 1993), esp. pp. 185–229.

5. *Dispatch*, 12 July 1895.

6. This exchange was quoted in the *Times*, 18 July 1895, which conveyed some (though not all) of Solomon's replies in broad, stereotypical dialect ("Yes, I saw you dar" . . . Up at de house . . . I'se telling the truth now"), which I have modified. The *Times* did not use dialect in quoting Pokey.

7. Affidavit of F. W. Cunningham, *Marable* v. *Commonwealth*, p. 22.

8. The 1900 MCS, Charlotte County, ED 39, sheet 13 showed Ellen Gayle, born 1860, in a household with her seven children, the youngest born in 1898. Ellen was listed as single and as a "Laborer Any Kind."

9. The newspapers (*Times*, *Dispatch*, *Index-Appeal*, all 18 July 1895) did a particularly bad job of reporting Gayle's testimony; the reports were skimpy and contradicted one another. Fortunately, she also told her story to a sergeant in the military, who then took down Pokey's story and found no material difference between the two. What appears here comes from the sergeant's recollection of Gayle's story, published in the *Times*, 3 May 1896, with some additional details supplied by Gayle in the *Times* and *Dispatch*, both 2 May 1896. The sergeant scrambled some pronouns and made mistakes on some names; I fixed these.

10. The Ellis family appeared in the 1870 and 1880 MCS, Rehoboth District, Lunenburg. In 1870 Betsy Ellis appeared as the twenty-six-year-old mother of four, including Mary M. Ellis, then five months old.

11. Their testimony and that of Ben Knight below are derived from very inadequate summaries in the *Times* and *Dispatch*, both 18 July 1895.

12. Lunenburg Order Book 37, pp. 213–14; *Dispatch*, 1 August 1895. Time of adjournment: *Times*, 18 July 1895.

13. The *Dispatch* and the *Index-Appeal*, both 18 July 1895, reported that the judge and prosecutors brought out evidence for both sides but did not specify how they assisted Pokey. Frank Cunningham's affidavit in *Marable* v. *Commonwealth*, pp. 24–25, said that "there was a good deal of muttering and discontent and criticism of the Commonwealth's Attorneys by people who were complaining that they were acting as counsel for the prisoners."

14. *Dispatch*, 18 and 19 July 1895; *Times*, 18 July 1895.

15. Allen Diary, 18 July 1895.

16. Neither the *Times* nor the *Dispatch* of 19 July paid much attention to Grace Knight's testimony, and both garbled it; the version here is the best I can do, but it may be flawed.

17. Lunenburg Order Book 37, p. 214.

18. *Dispatch*, 19 July 1895.

19. *Dispatch*, 1 August 1895.

20. Cunningham's speech and Marable's response were recalled in Cunningham's affidavit, *Marable* v. *Commonwealth*, p. 23.

21. *Dispatch*, 1 August 1895; Lunenburg Order Book 37, p. 212, shows Gregory's appointment as a deputy on July 16. The state of the soil—"as dry as fresh burnt ashes"—was reported in Allen Diary, 19 July 1895.

22. *Marable* v. *Commonwealth*, p. 23; *Dispatch*, 20 July 1895; *Times*, 20 and 26 July 1895; *Index-Appeal*, 20 July 1895.

23. *Times*, 18 July 1895.

24. Newspaper accounts of Susan Thompson's testimony were sketchy; I imported the "slick path" quotation from the *Times*, 3 May 1896. Pokey's responses were given by Thompson: *Dispatch*, 20 July 1895. The "high temper" statement originally appeared as a paraphrase in the *Times*, 20 July 1895. Additional brief reports of Thompson's testimony: *Index-Appeal*, 20 July 1895; *Dispatch*, 8 August 1895.

25. *Times*, 20 July 1895. The *Dispatch* version was much shorter and gave a different sense of the timing of that last walk.

26. This speech is a composite of the *Times* and *Dispatch* versions, both 20 July 1895.

27. This rendition of the white man story is a composite of *Times* and *Dispatch* versions of 20 July 1895. The newspapers rendered Marable's speech (inconsistently) in dialect; I have substituted standard spellings for the reporters' "de," "dis," "den," "wid," and "gwine." The sequence of courtroom events comes from the *Index-Appeal* of the same date. An affidavit by one of the soldiers, printed in the *Dispatch*, 15 September 1895, was also helpful.

28. *Marable* v. *Commonwealth*, p. 25 (quotation); *Dispatch*, 20 July 1895.

29. *Dispatch*, 20 July 1895.

30. Ibid. Neblett's opening sentence appeared in the original as a paraphrase. My interpretation below, emphasizing the difficulties white men faced in protecting their families, parallels that of Joel Williamson, as he explores why many men turned from conservatism to race radicalism: *Rage for Order*, p. 182.

31. This is a composite of the quotations in the *Dispatch* and *Index-Appeal*, both 21 July 1895.

32. Allen Diary, 4 August 1895.

33. The judge's instructions and the sentence are in *Mary Barnes* v. *Commonwealth*, pp. 11–15, Library of the Supreme Court of Appeals. Additional information on her trial is in the *Times* and *Dispatch*, 21 July 1895; *Report of the Adjutant-General* (1895), p. 66.

34. Quotations are from the *Dispatch*, 21 July 1895. The reporters amused themselves this day by (some of the time) writing black speech in dialect; I have changed "wid" to "with" and "de" to "the."

35. A major discrepancy appeared between Solomon's account and that of Edward Pollard. According to the *Dispatch*, 8 August 1895, after Solomon said he had seen Mary Barnes chopping bushes on the day before the murder, Edward Pollard was recalled and said this was not possible, for Mary Barnes had worked with him all that day in the tobacco field.

36. Lunenburg Order Book 37, pp. 216-18; *Planet*, 27 June 1896. Quotations of officials pronouncing sentences: *Mary Barnes* v. *Commonwealth*, p. 13; *Marable* v. *Commonwealth*, p. 31.

37. *Report of the Adjutant-General* (1895), p. 66; *Times*, 23 July 1895.

CHAPTER 8: "MIRABILE MARABLE"

1. A very useful description of the jail appeared in the *Times*, 18 August 1895. "Mirabile Marable" was the title of a *Dispatch* editorial, 23 July 1895.

2. Fiske Kimball, *The Capitol of Virginia: A Landmark of American Architecture* (Richmond: Virginia State Library and Archives, 1989); see also the articles by F. Carey Howlett, James E. Wootton, and Selden Richardson in *Virginia Cavalcade*, 51 (Winter 2002).

3. On Mitchell, see two works by Ann Field Alexander, "Between Two Worlds: John Mitchell's Richmond Childhood," *Virginia Cavalcade*, 40 (Winter 1991), pp. 120–31, and "Black Protest in the New South." I thank Professor Alexander for allowing me to read

portions of *Race Man*, her forthcoming biography of Mitchell. On Mitchell's antilynching campaign, see two works by W. Fitzhugh Brundage, *Lynching in the New South*, pp. 164–76, and " 'To Howl Loudly': John Mitchell Jr. and His Campaign against Lynching in Virginia," *Canadian Review of American Studies*, 3 (Winter 1991), pp. 325–41. On Mitchell's political career: Michael B. Chesson, "Richmond's Black Councilmen, 1871–96," in *Southern Black Leaders of the Reconstruction Era*, ed. Howard N. Rabinowitz (Urbana: University of Illinois Press, 1982), pp. 191–222. A helpful Web site was posted in 1997 by the Virginia Newspaper Project, Library of Virginia, "'Born in the Wake of Freedom': John Mitchell, Jr., and the *Richmond Planet*," www.lib.virginia.edu/cataloging/vnp/planet/pref.htm.

4. The ninety-two-thousand figure includes the ten thousand residents of Manchester, across the James River, at that time a separate city. The official opening of the Confederate Museum (now part of the Museum of the Confederacy) did not take place until February 1896, but the project had been conceived in 1890 and was well along by July 1895; see John M. Coski and Amy R. Feely, "A Monument to Southern Womanhood: The Founding Generation of the Confederate Museum," in *A Woman's War: Southern Women, Civil War, and the Confederate Legacy*, ed. Edward D. C. Campbell, Jr., and Kym S. Rice (Richmond and Charlottesville: Museum of the Confederacy and the University Press of Virginia, 1996), pp. 131–63. For Mitchell's hostile response to the unveiling of the Lee monument: Marie Tyler-McGraw, *At the Falls: Richmond, Virginia, and Its People* (Chapel Hill: University of North Carolina Press, 1994), p. 209; *Planet*, 31 May 1890.

5. For a fuller economic history of Richmond in this period: Virginius Dabney, *Richmond: The Story of a City* (Garden City, N.Y.: Doubleday, 1976), pp. 220–66; Michael B. Chesson, *Richmond after the War, 1865–1890* (Richmond: Virginia State Library, 1981), pp. 145–206; Leon Fink, *Workingmen's Democracy: The Knights of Labor and American Politics* (Urbana: University of Illinois Press, 1983), pp. 149–77; Peter Rachleff, *Black Labor in Richmond, 1865–1890* (Urbana: University of Illinois Press, 1989); Tyler-McGraw, *At the Falls*, pp. 184–217.

6. On the creation of Jackson Ward: Chesson, *Richmond after the War*, pp. 157–59. On Jackson Ward and other black neighbor-

hoods (some below Broad Street): Brown and Kimball, "Mapping the Terrain of Black Richmond." A map of Richmond's wards is in Tyler-McGraw, *At the Falls*, p. 197.

7. According to 1895 statistics, *Times*, 1 January 1896, the average number of white women in the city jail at any given time was 2. The comparable number of African American women was 32. The numbers for white men and African American men were 32 and 117 respectively. Howard N. Rabinowitz, *Race Relations in the Urban South, 1865–1890* (Urbana: University of Illinois Press, 1980), p. 43, gives comparable figures on arrests for several southern cities.

8. *Planet*, 27 July 1895; for clarity I substituted some proper names for pronouns.

9. *Chataigne's Richmond City Directory, 1895–1896*, pp. 795–96, listed seven attorneys who were "colored persons." Joseph Gordon Hylton, "The African-American Lawyer, the First Generation: Virginia as a Case Study," *University of Pittsburgh Law Review*, 56 (Fall 1994), pp. 107–64, reports thirty-eight black lawyers in Virginia in 1890, 2.3 percent of the total. On Wise: *Eminent and Representative Men of Virginia and the District of Columbia of the Nineteenth Century* (Madison, Wis.: Brant & Fuller, 1893), p. 599; *Times-Dispatch*, 4 February 1908. Mitchell's call on Wise: *Times*, 24 July 1895; *Planet*, 27 July 1895.

10. *Richmond Elite Directory (Blue Book), Society and Club Lists* (Richmond: J. L. Hill Printing Co., 1893); Alexander Brown, *The Cabells and Their Kin: A Memorial Volume of History, Biography, and Genealogy* (Harrisonburg, Va.: C. J. Carrier, 1978), p. 395; Mecklenburg County Marriage Licenses, 1870–1872, LVA; *Star*, 24 July 1895; *Times*, 15 March 1896.

11. *Dispatch*, 23 July 1895; *Star*, 24 July 1895; *State*, 25 July 1895.

12. *Dispatch*, 27 July 1895. John B. Minor, "Alexander Barclay Guigon," *Proceedings of the Thirty-fourth Annual Meeting, the Virginia State Bar Association* (1923), pp. 72–75.

13. For a history of the penitentiary: Paul W. Keve, *The History of Corrections in Virginia* (Charlottesville: University Press of Virginia, 1986), pp. 28–98. Newspaper articles detailing penitentiary life include *Times*, 10 November 1895, 14 January, 24 May, 23 December

1896; *Dispatch*, 14, 19, and 26 January, 24 December 1896; *State*, 17 January 1896. The profile of female inmates is derived from Register of Inmates, 1885–1894 and Register of Inmates, 1894–1902. Mary Barnes appears on p. 29 of the second register. Records of food purchased for prisoners are in this collection, in the Minutes of the Board of Directors.

14. Superintendent B. W. Lynn's advocacy of flogging: *Times*, 29 September 1895; *State*, 17 January 1896; B. W. Lynn to Henry George, 19 November 1894, Superintendent's Correspondence, Virginia State Penitentiary, Department of Corrections, LVA. Lynn claimed that prisoners were whipped only after a trial, and never in anger, with a maximum of thirty-nine lashes that did not break the skin. Evidence on the flogging of a woman: *Times*, 12 December 1895.

15. Cunningham's opinion: *Dispatch*, 23 July 1895. On the history of the Richmond press: Earle Dunford, *Richmond Times-Dispatch: The Story of a Newspaper* (Richmond: Cadmus Publishing, 1995).

16. This interview was published in the *Planet*, 27 July 1895. The *Times*, 25 July 1895, summarized Marable's new story. The questions put by reporters were implied but not explicitly given in the *Planet* account. Because the *Planet* was not published until Saturday, it is not known whether all this detail was given in the Wednesday interview or Mitchell acquired some of it later in the week. The matter of naming is especially important. The *Times*, 25 July 1895, printed the day after the Wednesday interview, gave only the surname Thompson, and for this reason, in the first sentence quoted, I have plugged in the *Times* language. The *Planet* story, published Saturday, gave the name "David Thomas or Thompson."

17. Quotations: *Dispatch*, 23 July 1895; *Times*, 20 and 21 July 1895.

18. *Times*, 25 July 1895. The story below comes from the *Times*, 24 and 25 July 1895; *Dispatch*, 25 July 1895; *State*, 26 and 27 July 1895. Dern quotations: *Times*, 24 July 1895.

19. The *Dispatch, Planet, Star*, and *State* all called for new trials on Saturday, July 27. The *Times* did so on July 26 and reprinted a similar editorial from the *Charlottesville Progress*. On the continuing Dern saga: *Dispatch*, 2 and 23 August 1895; *Times*, 31 July, 1, 4, and

10 August 1895; *Star*, 18 October 1895; *Oxford* (N.C.) *Public Ledger*, 19 July 1895.

CHAPTER 9: THE RISE OF EDWARD POLLARD

1. *Chase City Progress*, 3 April 1975. I am grateful to W. Carter Thompson for sharing this article with me. See also Craig, *Its Waters Returning*, p. 49.

2. *Chase City Progress*, 3 April 1975; Bracey, *Life by the Roaring Roanoke*, pp. 227–28. The train station is pictured in Donald R. Traser, *Virginia Railway Depots* (Richmond: Old Dominion Chapter, National Railway Historical Society, 1998), p. 160. Liquor licenses granted to Paul Fore from 1873 to 1892 are in LCP, LVA.

3. The *Planet*, 10 August 1895, identified Justis as author of the *Times* articles. The nickname Billy was given in John H. Gwathmey, *Legends of Virginia Lawyers: Anecdotes and Whimsical Yarns of the Old Time Bench and Bar* (Richmond: Dietz Printing Co., 1934), p. 49.

4. *Times*, 1 August 1895.

5. Justis's initial visit to the Pollard farm: *Times*, 28 July 1895. Line drawings of the Pollard house appeared in the *Times*, 4 August 1895, and the *Dispatch*, 8 August 1895.

6. Plats of the Pollard farm were printed in the *Times*, 14 and 28 July, 1 August 1895, and in the *Dispatch*, 8 August 1895; these differed somewhat from one another, and Edward Pollard later said that none was wholly accurate. A hand-drawn plat is located in the 1896 Prince Edward Loose Court Papers.

7. Justis made a major issue of this in the *Times*, 28 July, 1 August 1895. A tramp around the property confirms Justis's observation.

8. *Times*, 1 August 1895.

9. Willie Clements interview: *Times*, 4 August 1895. Willie's age: MATT, p. 44.

10. A sketch of the Pollards was first printed in the *Times*, 30 June 1895. I am grateful to Reginald H. Pettus of Keysville, Virginia, for sharing with me the original photograph from which the published engraving was copied. Trotti, "Murder and the Modern Sensi-

bility," pp. 58–60, 107–10, studies other sensational murders, finding a similar uninterest in the lives of female victims.

11. I reconstructed the Fowlkes family from Bell, *Old Free State*, vol. 2, p. 407; Lunenburg Will Book 10, pp. 70, 107; Lunenburg Deed Book 35, p. 648; *Emma L. Quarles* v. *Truly Garnette Fowlkes*, Nottoway Ended Chancery Cases, No. 1176; Nottoway Will Book 1, p. 51; Manuscript Census Schedules for Nottoway, 1850–1880; Nottoway Marriage Register, 4 February 1885, 17 February 1886, 3 August 1887; Prince Edward Marriage Register 1, p. 35 (1876). The Fowlkes home is pictured in W. R. Turner, *Old Homes and Families in Nottoway*, 3d ed. (Salem, W.Va.: Walsworth Don Mills, 1982).

12. The Fowlkes financial history is reconstructed from the following Nottoway records: Land and Personal Property Books, 1823–73; Will Book 4, p. 44; Book 5, p. 300; Deed Book 1, pp. 191, 201, and 207; Book 9, p. 211; *H. B. Fowlkes* v. *Sarah C. Fowlkes*, Ended Chancery Cases, No. 249. Quotation from 1870 MCS, Haytokah Township, p. 25, Nottoway County.

13. Lunenburg Marriage Register, 1853–1926, p. 41. The 1880 MCS, Mecklenburg County, ED 144, sheet 40, listed a Lucy A. Fowlkes in the Thompson family (a different set of Thompsons from those into which Edward Pollard had married). The middle initial *A.* was wrong, but the age (forty) was close, and her marital status (single) and her relationship to the head of the household (cousin) were correct.

14. A. B. Cummins, *Nottoway County Virginia: Founding and Development with Biographical Sketches* (Richmond: W. M. Brown & Son, 1970); Turner, *Old Homes and Families in Nottoway*; Nottoway Deed Book 10, p. 369 (1840). Patrick Pollard appeared in the Nottoway land books as owner of this property until 1859, when he disappeared.

15. The year of Edward's leaving home was figured from the Nottoway Personal Property Books, which show that from 1846 on, Patrick Pollard paid a head tax on one male above the age of sixteen (himself); for the previous several years he had been paying on two males above sixteen.

16. The marriage license is in Lunenburg Will Book 13, p. 220 (1848).

17. The MCS for Rehoboth District, Lunenburg, listed Frances in 1850, 1860, and 1870, respectively placing her birth year as 1810, 1800, and 1796. The Thompson children were named in Lunenburg Order Book 29, p. 132 (1844). Records concerning their guardianship and inheritances are in Lunenburg Order Book 29, pp. 105, 124, 452, 459.

18. A survey of the Robert Thompson farm after its division among heirs is in *George Shorter* v. *Robert Thompson's Administrator*, Lunenburg Ended Chancery Cases, 1858-011. Edward Pollard first appeared in the Lunenburg Land and Personal Property Books in 1849. After the state began keeping birth records in 1853, Edward reported the births of three slave children: Lunenburg Register of Births, 1853–1888, pp. 41, 49, 66.

19. Evidence that Edward skimped on improvements to Frances's farm comes from an 1873 lawsuit, which said the farm had "very ordinary land with very old improvements, which are much out of repair." *Pollard* v. *Thompson*, Lunenburg Ended Chancery Cases, File 9. Edward bought eighty-five acres in 1850 and eighty-seven acres in 1858. Charlotte Deed Book 28, p. 69; Lunenburg Deed Book 36, p. 300.

20. Compiled Service Records (Confederate), Roll 1050, National Archives and Records Administration microfilm in LVA. From 1861 to 1863, while the taxation system was still functioning, the personal property books showed no falling off in livestock production on the Pollard farm.

21. The 1870 MCS, Rehoboth, p. 8, listed in the Pollard house two black boys, one fourteen years old and blind and one a ten-year-old who "labors on the farm." The forty-year-old black woman living next door was possibly the boys' mother; her household also included a sixteen-year-old white boy, a farm laborer who may have worked for the Pollards. The 1880 MCS, Lunenburg, ED 139, p. 11, listed an eight-year-old white boy as a "servant" in the Pollard household; the child was also Edward's ward: Lunenburg Order Book 33, p. 464. Robert Allen Account Book, 1893–1900, Allen Family Papers, VHS, showed that in 1894 Allen paid women twenty to twenty-five cents a day for work in his garden, while paying men fifty cents. Such wage disparity was nationwide and permeated every occupa-

tion open to women: Alice Kessler-Harris, *A Woman's Wage: Historical Meanings and Social Consequences* (Lexington: University Press of Kentucky, 1990).

22. Lunenburg Marriage Register, 1853–1929, p. 23. Betsy Lewis's reported birth year varied wildly from one census to the next. Because she first appeared in the Charlotte Personal Property Book in 1831, I am betting on 1810.

23. Betsy Lewis inherited sixty-four acres from her father through her brother, who died in 1873. Edward and Betsy used an old legal device to give Edward full control of this property, selling it and then buying it back the same day for the same price. Charlotte Deed Book 34, p. 113. Betsy also owned personal property, including four head of cattle, suggesting a dairying operation. Charlotte Will Book 11, p. 301; Charlotte Personal Property Books, 1855–1863. Edward's land purchases: Lunenburg Deed Book 38, p. 617; Deed Book 40, pp. 100, 133.

24. The photograph may have been a wedding portrait. Analyzing Lucy's clothing, Julie Campbell of the Library of Virginia believes the portrait was taken in the 1880s. Evidence of illiteracy for Frances Thompson and Betsy Lewis: 1860 MCS, Lunenburg, Dwelling 48; Charlotte Deed Book 34, p. 113; Lunenburg Deed Book 40, p. 133.

25. One of Edward's forms is preserved in Judgments, LCP, LVA. In the 1870s Edward sued for amounts of ten, twenty, and twenty-five dollars: Lunenburg County Court Records, 1856–1885, VHS. In the late 1880s he continued to bring actions for modest amounts, but also won at least two judgments for more than one hundred dollars: Lunenburg Circuit Court Order Book 4, p. 481; Charlotte Chancery Orders, No. 6, p. 47.

26. In the year after Edward married Lucy, he was taxed for the first time on over $1,000 worth of stocks, bonds, and money out at interest: Lunenburg Personal Property Book, 1883. In 1855, when Lucy was still a minor, she and her four full siblings sold a tract apparently inherited from their mother. Lucy's share was $125; if safely invested, it would have grown considerably by the 1880s. Lunenburg Deed Book 35, p. 648. It is also possible she received an inheritance from her father that was not processed through the regular probate system. On women gathering sumac for sale and their

other means of earning money: *Gee's Executor* v. *Robert Moore*, Lunenburg Ended Chancery Cases, 1895-031. On rural women's productivity: Lu Ann Jones, "Re-visioning the Countryside: Southern Women, Rural Reform, and the Farm Economy in the Twentieth Century," unpublished Ph.D. dissertation (University of North Carolina, 1996.)

27. PBTT, p. 11.

28. The two lawsuits are noted in the LCP, LVA.

29. *Planet*, 10 August, 19 October 1895.

30. According to the 1850 MCS for Lunenburg, sixteen-year-old Bill Thompson was not living with his mother and her new husband. Thompson had successfully sued Pollard in 1866, but in an unusual move Pollard appealed and won: Lunenburg County Court Records, 1856–1885, VHS; Lunenburg Order Book 32, p. 85. Thompson's stubbornness I infer from the Friendship Baptist Church Minutes, vol. 1, pp. 44, 48, 51, 55, which indicate the failure of repeated attempts to settle a dispute between Thompson and another church member. I am grateful to Mrs. Nancy Berkley of the new Friendship Baptist Church, Drakes Branch, Virginia, for allowing me to study the church's records. Road orders are in Lunenburg Order Book 35, p. 218, Book 37, pp. 54, 77, 94, 99.

31. *Dispatch*, 3 August 1895 (quotation). Five committee members sued Pollard in magistrate's court in January 1895: LCP, LVA.

32. *Dispatch*, 6 August 1895.

33. Ibid.

34. Edward's admission that he had sent Lucy to order Pokey off his land: *Times*, 1 May 1896. Lucy was received "upon her experience," suggesting she had been baptized earlier in life: Friendship Baptist Church Minutes, vol. 1, pp. 252, 286.

35. *Dispatch*, 6 August 1895.

36. Since its inception in the North in the 1830s, the penny press had sensationalized murder. Trotti, "Murder and the Modern Sensibility," p. 81, identifies the *Dispatch*, founded in 1850, as Virginia's first penny paper. On the press and crime sensations, see Andie Tucher, *Froth & Scum: Truth, Beauty, Goodness, and the Ax Murder in America's First Mass Medium* (Chapel Hill: University of North Carolina Press, 1994); Amy Gilman Srebnick, *The Mysterious*

Death of Mary Rogers: Sex and Culture in Nineteenth-Century New York (New York: Oxford University Press, 1995); Patricia Cline Cohen, *The Murder of Helen Jewett: The Life and Death of a Prostitute in Nineteenth-Century New York* (New York: Random House, 1998); Karen Halttunen, *Murder Most Foul: The Killer and the American Gothic Imagination* (Cambridge: Harvard University Press, 1998).

CHAPTER 10: THE THIRTEENTH JUROR

1. *Code of Virginia* (1887), sec. 928, p. 278. Orders respecting the cleanup are in LCP, LVA.

2. Both stories appeared 23 July 1895.

3. *Star, Dispatch*, and *Times*, all 2 August 1895.

4. The interview was published in the *Planet*, 27 July 1895. I have condensed it, made small alterations for clarity (substituting names for pronouns), and corrected spellings of names (Fore for Ford). The detail about the child's dress as part of the bargain I imported from the *Times*, 3 May 1896, adding it here to help make the point about the invisible economy. On rural women's economic roles and options: Jacqueline Jones, *Labor of Love*, pp. 79–109; Lu Ann Jones, "Re-visioning the Countryside."

5. *Dispatch*, 6 August 1895. The same article pointed out that Ellen's original story—that she fell asleep after their return to Pokey's—was contradicted at the trial by both Lula Knight (it was actually Grace Knight) and Rosa Barnes, but Ellen was not put back on the stand to clarify what happened. Gregory did not admit until many months later that he had taken the *Dispatch* reporter to Ellen Gayle's; MATT, p. 42.

6. *Times*, 7 August 1895; *Index-Appeal*, 7 August 1895. Comments on Pokey's appearance were in that week's *Planet*, 10 August 1895.

7. *Dispatch*, 8 August 1895. Records of the arrest and disposition of the case are in LCP, LVA; although Pokey was charged with assault and fined two dollars, a note says the case was "compromised & settled," which suggests she may have had a justifiable grievance. I have been unable to learn anything further about Cora Knight's death.

8. *Dispatch*, 3 August 1895 (quotations). The indictment and judgment are in LCP, LVA. The *Times*, 16 August 1895, reported her commitment to the penitentiary.

9. *Dispatch*, 8 August 1895 (quotation). Ben Knight was a widower; according to the 1880 MCS, Lunenburg, ED 139, p. 15, his first wife's name was Hellen. It is not clear if he was related to Cora Knight.

10. *State*, 8 August 1895. The *Index-Appeal*, 9 August 1895, said Gregory had brought the letter to Richmond.

11. The summonses were issued on July 2 and are in LCP, LVA. Rumors of more arrests: *Charlotte Gazette*, 4 July 1895.

12. A TELL-TALE LETTER was in the *State*'s August 8 headline. The same article included an interview with Joseph Barnes that made no reference to the letter. It is also interesting that the letter's authenticity was not publicly challenged. My sense is that no one had an interest in extending the letter's life: The supporters of the accused women would not want to give additional play to a text that portrayed Mary Barnes as a faithless wife and negligent mother, and neither the *State* nor the *Dispatch* would be eager to admit it had been bamboozled. One other factor suggesting forgery is that the letter was not introduced as evidence in Mary Barnes's trial (if it was, the news reports failed to mention it).

13. *Dispatch*, 9 August 1895 (quotation); *Times*, 17 August 1895.

14. Lunenburg Order Book 37, pp. 235–36.

15. *Times*, 17 August 1895. Hazlewood's account helps explain why black jurors would go along with the verdict. It may also have been that these particular jurors were called because in previous jury service they had shown themselves unlikely to rock the boat.

16. Quoted in the *Times*, 18 August 1895.

CHAPTER 11: TAKING SIDES

1. Veronica Alease Davis, "Rosa L. Dixon Bowser," in *Dictionary of Virginia Biography*, ed. Sara B. Bearss et al. (Richmond: Library of Virginia, 2001), vol. 2, pp. 160–62. Not nearly enough is known about Bowser, but for the larger context: Stephanie J. Shaw, *What a Woman Ought to Be and to Do: Black Professional Women*

Workers During the Jim Crow Era (Chicago: University of Chicago Press, 1996).

2. I do not wish to weigh in here on the much-debated issue of whether these people continued the old plantation aristocracy or were an essentially new class; I merely want to contrast their social and political centrality with the comparative marginality of white supremacists of the 1990s. There is a large literature on white supremacy; some thoughtful points of entry include George M. Fredrickson, *White Supremacy: A Comparative Study in American and South African History* (New York: Oxford University Press, 1981); Barbara J. Fields, "Ideology and Race in American History," in *Region, Race, and Reconstruction: Essays in Honor of C. Vann Woodward*, ed. J. Morgan Kousser and James M. McPherson (New York: Oxford University Press, 1982), pp. 143–77; Williamson, *Rage for Order*; Glenda Elizabeth Gilmore, *Gender and Jim Crow: Women and the Politics of White Supremacy in North Carolina, 1896–1920* (Chapel Hill: University of North Carolina Press, 1996); and Stephen Kantrowitz, *Ben Tillman and the Reconstruction of White Supremacy* (Chapel Hill: University of North Carolina Press, 2000).

3. On Wells: Hazel V. Carby, *Reconstructing Womanhood: The Emergence of the Afro-American Woman Novelist* (New York: Oxford University Press, 1987), pp. 95–120; Gail Bederman, *Manliness & Civilization: A Cultural History of Gender and Race in the United States, 1880–1917* (Chicago: University of Chicago Press, 1995), pp. 45–76; Linda O. McMurry, *To Keep the Waters Troubled: The Life of Ida B. Wells* (New York: Oxford University Press, 1998); Feimster, " 'Ladies and Lynching,' " pp. 164–234; and Patricia A. Schechter, *Ida B. Wells-Barnett and American Reform, 1880–1930* (Chapel Hill: University of North Carolina Press, 2001). On the early national federations of African American women's organizations: Paula Giddings, *When and Where I Enter: The Impact of Black Women on Race and Sex in America* (New York: William Morrow, 1984), pp. 89–117; Stephanie J. Shaw, "Black Club Women and the Creation of the National Association of Colored Women," *Journal of Women's History*, 3 (Fall 1991), pp. 10–25; Deborah Gray White, *Too Heavy a Load: Black Women in Defense of Themselves, 1894–1994* (New York: W. W. Norton, 1999), pp. 21–55.

4. *Planet,* 17 August 1895; quotation in Rosa Bowser letter of 20 July 1896, pp. 85–87, of the Minutes for 1896, Papers of the National Association of Colored Women's Clubs. I am grateful to Sarah Wilkerson-Freeman for providing me a copy of this letter.

5. On Richmond's African American organizations: Elsa Barkley Brown, "Womanist Consciousness: Maggie Lena Walker and the Independent Order of Saint Luke," *Signs: Journal of Women in Culture and Society,* 14 (Spring 1989), pp. 610–33; Rabinowitz, *Race Relations in the Urban South,* pp. 140–43, 226–54; James D. Watkinson, "William Washington Browne and the True Reformers of Richmond, Virginia," *Virginia Magazine of History and Biography,* 97 (July 1989), pp. 375–98. Rachleff, *Black Labor in Richmond,* names dozens of organizations—male, female, and mixed.

6. According to Trotti, "Murder and the Modern Sensibility," p. 273, the *Planet* published its first halftones in December 1894, with the *Times* following in 1901 and the *Dispatch* in 1902.

7. The mistaken date appeared in both the *Times* and the *Dispatch,* 8 August 1895.

8. Gregory's rendering of this episode in the August 8 *Dispatch* was condensed, its meaning difficult to discern. The quotations are taken from a fuller version written by Gregory, *Dispatch,* 1 August 1895.

9. Here again an earlier rendition is fuller than the committee's report. The quotation is from the *Dispatch,* 6 August 1895. Wilson's explanation: *Times,* 11 August 1895.

10. *Planet,* 3 August 1895.

11. On this and other images of black womanhood: Trudier Harris, *From Mammies to Militants: Domestics in Black American Literature* (Philadelphia: Temple University Press, 1982); Deborah Gray White, *Ar'n't I a Woman?: Female Slaves in the Plantation South* (New York: W. W. Norton, 1985), pp. 46–61; Elizabeth Fox-Genovese, *Within the Plantation Household: Black and White Women of the Old South* (Chapel Hill: University of North Carolina Press, 1988), pp. 291–92; Patricia Morton, *Disfigured Images: The Historical Assault on Afro-American Women* (New York: Praeger, 1991); Cheryl Thurber, "The Development of the Mammy Image and

Mythology" in *Southern Women: Histories and Identities*, ed. Virginia Bernhard et al. (Columbia: University of Missouri Press, 1992), pp. 87–108; M. M. Manring, *Slave in a Box: The Strange Career of Aunt Jemima* (Charlottesville: University Press of Virginia, 1998), pp. 18–59.

12. *Planet*, 31 August 1895.

13. *Dispatch*, 10 August 1895; *Star*, 8 August 1895; *Times*, 11 August 1895. The *Planet*, 10 August 1895, was also highly critical of the committee's report, but there is no evidence that these Lunenburg citizens paid attention to the *Planet* at this time.

14. *Times*, 8 August 1895.

15. The resolutions were printed with slight variations in both the *Times* and the *Dispatch* of August 13; this quotation is from the *Times*. "Indignation Meeting" is from Allen Diary, 6 August 1895.

16. Of course it was more complicated than that. See Bertram Wyatt-Brown, *Southern Honor: Ethics and Behavior in the Old South* (New York: Oxford University Press, 1982) and *The Shaping of Southern Culture*; Ayers, *Vengeance and Justice*, esp. pp. 9–33, 266–76; Kenneth S. Greenberg, *Honor & Slavery: Lies, Duels, Noses, Masks, Dressing as a Woman, Gifts, Strangers, Humanitarianism, Death, Slave Rebellions, the Proslavery Argument, Baseball, Hunting, and Gambling in the Old South* (Princeton: Princeton University Press, 1996).

17. *Times*, 8 August 1895. On urbanites' (largely thwarted) attempts to activate the state: William A. Link, *The Paradox of Southern Progressivism, 1880–1930* (Chapel Hill: University of North Carolina Press, 1992). On increasing intrusions of the state in private life: Peter W. Bardaglio, *Reconstructing the Household: Families, Sex, and the Law in the Nineteenth-Century South* (Chapel Hill: University of North Carolina Press, 1995).

18. *Dispatch*, 11 August 1895, which unfortunately gave none of the song's lyrics.

19. *Dispatch*, 3 August 1895.

20. Miller's affidavit was taken on August 21 and published in the *Times*, 15 September 1895. Marable's statements respecting Pettus: *Times*, 28 July, 2 October 1895.

21. *Dispatch*, 31 July (quotation), 1 August 1895.

CHAPTER 12: BAPTISMS

1. "Ordo Baptismi Adultorum," *Collectio Rituum Pro Diœcesibus Civitatum Fœderatarum Americœ Septentrionalis* (New York: Catholic Book Publishing Co., 1964), pp. 138–39, 143 (quotations); Baptismorum Registrum, St. Joseph's Catholic Church, LVA.

2. Welbers to E. R. Dyer, 9 August 1893, Josephite Archives, Baltimore, which also holds a typescript chronology of Welbers's career. See also Stephen J. Ochs, *Desegregating the Altar: The Josephites and the Struggle for Black Priests, 1871–1960* (Baton Rouge: Louisiana State University Press, 1990); Nessa Theresa Baskerville Johnson, *A Special Pilgrimage: A History of Black Catholics in Richmond* (Richmond: Diocese of Richmond, 1978); and Francis Joseph Magri, *The Catholic Church in the City and Diocese of Richmond* (Richmond: Whittet & Shepperson, 1906), pp. 119–20.

3. The quotation is from Matthew 25:40. On the sisters in the jail mission (in this case Henrico County's jail): *Dispatch*, 23 July 1895.

4. Welbers's talk with the governor and Marable quotation: *State*, 13 September 1895. On Peter Claver: John J. Delaney, *Dictionary of Saints* (Garden City, N.Y.: Doubleday, 1980), pp. 150–51; *New Catholic Encyclopedia* (New York: McGraw-Hill, 1967), vol. 3, pp. 922–23.

5. *Planet*, 27 July (Mitchell quotation), 7 September (Fannie Marable letter) 1895.

6. The quotes are from a sermon Welbers preached the Sunday after he baptized Marable. *State*, 16 September 1895.

7. *Planet*, 10 and 31 August, 14 September 1895.

8. *State*, 18 September 1895 (Flournoy quotation). The other quotations are from the *Planet*, 14 September 1895, and the *Dispatch*, 12 September 1895. The *State* version is probably fictionalized but gives an interesting account of Pokey's theology: "Solomon, you say God done forgive you. Well, if dat is so, it do'[don't] make no difference if I do'[don't] forgive you; and if I forgive you and God ain't forgive you dat ain't gwine to help you none. But I is gwine to forgive you."

9. William H. Gaines, Jr., "Courthouses of Amelia and Dinwid-

die Counties," *Virginia Cavalcade*, 18 (Winter 1969), pp. 17–28; Thomas Whitehead, *Virginia: A Hand-Book* (Richmond: State Board of Agriculture, 1893), pp. 200–02; *Planet*, 26 October 1895 (quotation).

10. *Planet*, 14 September 1895 (quotation). The day's proceedings were also reported in the *Planet*, 21 September, 26 October 1895; *State*, 12 September 1895; *Times*, 13 and 15 September 1895; *Dispatch*, 13 and 14 September 1895.

11. William A. Rhodes, "William Hodges Mann: Last of the Boys in Gray," in *Governors of Virginia*, pp. 182–94. Another attorney, Robert G. Southall, also appeared for Lunenburg but appears from the news reports not to have taken a major part in the proceeding.

12. The *Dispatch*, 13 September 1895, reported Guigon as the reader of these two documents; their texts are excerpted from *Marable* v. *Commonwealth*, pp. 15, 27.

13. This is an excerpt from the speech printed in the 14 September *Planet*. The *Dispatch*, 13 September 1895, enumerated the errors alleged by the women's lawyers.

14. The speech given here is excerpted from the *Planet*, 14 September 1895, and the 13 September *Dispatch* with some imports from the *Times*, 13 September 1895.

15. *Planet*, 26 October 1895.

16. This was Coleman's entire speech: *Times*, 13 September 1895.

CHAPTER 13: WHITE MAN STORIES

1. *Planet*, 21 September 1895 (quotation); *Times*, 14 September 1895.

2. *Planet*, 21 September 1895. Pokey would actually have turned twenty-four. On the note being dictated: *Planet*, 9 May 1896.

3. The *Times*, 15 September 1895, reported that after the hearing, Coleman told the women's lawyers that the Lunenburg trials had been "a disgrace and a stain." The *Dispatch*, 14 September 1895, suggested that Coleman wanted the petitions heard by a higher court.

4. The *Sumter* (S.C.) *Watchman and Southron*, 4 September 1895, reported that Gregory had attended the opening of the Sumter Tobacco Warehouse on August 29. Gregory's visit to Richmond was

reported in the *State, Times,* and *Dispatch,* all 18 September 1895.

5. The exchange between Gregory and Pokey Barnes was closely paraphrased in the *Times* and *Dispatch,* both 18 September 1895, as well as the *Planet,* 27 June 1896. I have spliced these paraphrases together and converted them into dialogue.

6. This dialogue was reported by Gregory, in the *Times* and the *Dispatch,* 22 April 1896, and by the deputy, MATT, p. 78.

7. Pincus, "The Virginia Supreme Court, Blacks, and the Law," pp. 25–26; *Times,* 15 and 17 September 1895; *Star,* 16 September 1895.

8. *Planet,* 21 September 1895.

9. *Star,* 17 September 1895; *Dispatch* and *Times,* both 18 September 1895.

10. *State,* 18 September 1895; *Dispatch,* 19 September 1895; *Planet,* 21 September 1895.

11. *Dispatch,* 14, 20 September 1895. Cardozo's expenses for the hanging were itemized in LCP, LVA. On the abolition of public hangings: Louis P. Masur, *Rites of Execution: Capital Punishment and the Transformation of American Culture, 1776–1865* (New York: Oxford University Press, 1989); Friedman, *Crime and Punishment,* pp. 75–76, 168–71; and Trotti, "Murder and the Modern Sensibility," pp. 303–21. On the cultural transformation behind the banning of public executions: Karen Halttunen, "Humanitarianism and the Pornography of Pain in Anglo-American Culture," *American Historical Review,* 100 (April 1995), pp. 303–34.

12. Invoices in LCP, LVA give information on the deputies and vehicles and also stipulate that they were prepared to convey all three prisoners back to Lunenburg.

13. *Times* and *Dispatch,* both 19 September 1895; *Planet,* 21 September 1895 (quotation).

14. The governor did not make a detailed public statement about his reasons for respiting Marable, but the *Dispatch,* 19 September 1895, gave suggestions for his reasoning.

15. *State,* 19 September 1895.

16. *Dispatch,* 20 September 1895.

17. *State,* 19 September 1895; *Charlotte Gazette,* 19 September 1895; *Dispatch,* 20 September 1895.

18. *Times*, 15 September 1895.

19. William L. Royall, *Some Reminiscences* (New York: Neale Publishing, 1909); John Stewart Bryan, *Joseph Bryan: His Times, His Family, His Friends* (Richmond: privately printed, 1935).

20. Allen Diary, 8 November 1870. At this early date Virginia politicians who aligned with the national Democratic party called themselves Conservatives.

21. On disqualification of voters: *Code of Virginia* (1887), sec. 62, pp. 80–81. On election fraud (which was also a national problem): Moger, *Virginia: Bourbonism to Byrd*, pp. 56, 97–98, 163–64; Pulley, *Old Virginia Restored*, pp. 27–31, 45–47, 56, 75–77; Sheldon, *Populism in the Old Dominion*, pp. 53–60, 71–72, 92, 106–08, 111–13. On railroad influence: Scott Reynolds Nelson, *Iron Confederacies: Southern Railways, Klan Violence, and Reconstruction* (Chapel Hill: University of North Carolina Press, 1999).

22. Allen Diary, 7 November 1893. A statistical analysis by Robert Saunders, "Charles T. O'Ferrall: Truncated Modernist" (unpublished paper in the files of the *Dictionary of Virginia Biography* project, LVA), pp. 5–6, confirms that fraud was involved in O'Ferrall's 1893 victory.

23. *Index-Appeal*, 29 September 1895; *Dispatch*, 2 October 1895; *Times*, 8 October 1895.

24. This account is from the *Planet*, 21 September 1895, with a few words cut in from *Marable* v. *Commonwealth*, p. 3; these appear to be slightly different renditions of the same confession.

25. *Times*, 24 September 1895; *Planet*, 28 September 1895. The *Planet* added that Thompson had been tried and acquitted; the indexes to Halifax County records show no evidence of a Thompson's being charged with or tried for this crime.

26. On Thompson's looks: *Times*, 17 March 1896. Although the *Planet* identified the two David Thompsons on 10 August 1895, specifying that Marable had accused David James Thompson of Finneywood, the *Times* did not catch on until September 14, and the *Dispatch* did not acknowledge the existence of two David Thompsons until October 3.

27. *Times*, 28 September 1895. A letter from a neighbor of Thompson's reiterated the respectability defense, terming Thompson

"a man of family, with high respectability, and a property-owner." *Dispatch*, 3 October 1895.

28. The affidavits were published in the *Dispatch*, 3 October 1895.

29. *State*, 7 October 1895 (quotation).

30. The letter was reproduced in the *Planet*, 12 October 1895. The speculation that the thieves were looking for the Pollard money is mine, not Fannie Marable's.

31. *Planet*, 12 October 1895.

CHAPTER 14: NUNC PRO TUNC

1. This contribution and the letters above appeared in the *Planet*, 21 September 1895.

2. *Planet*, 7 and 28 September 1895. On Hampton as "a propertied community": Robert Francis Engs, *Freedom's First Generation: Black Hampton, Virginia, 1861–1890* (Philadelphia: University of Pennsylvania Press, 1979), pp. 161–82.

3. These were some of the contributing organizations listed in the *Planet* through September 28; more were to come. The *Planet*, 24 August 1895, said Mitchell had organized the men into a Planet Relief Club, but this seems not to have persisted as an organization.

4. Documents concerning the hiring of Mann are in LCP, LVA.

5. Mann explained his strategy to Orgain, Neblett, and the clerk John L. Yates in letters of 11 and 14 October 1895: William Hodges Mann Letterbooks, University of Virginia. These letters are too fragile to be photocopied; I thank Vesta Gordon for transcribing them.

6. *Planet*, 7 September (quotation), 28 September 1895. Samuel's surname was Jones; I have not been able to find out enough about Mary Abernathy's early life to learn why he had a different last name.

7. *Planet*, 19 October 1895; Virginia Scott Jenkins, *Bananas: An American History* (Washington: Smithsonian Institution Press, 2000).

8. *Times*, 19 and 20 October 1895 (quotation); *Dispatch*, 20 October 1895.

9. *Dispatch*, 22 October 1895.

10. *Dispatch*, 23 October 1895.

11. *Times*, 22 October 1895; *Planet*, 27 April 1895 (quotation). The *Planet*, 19 January 1895, cited a *Chicago Tribune* article reporting that in 1894 a total of 187 men and 3 women had been lynched. On women as lynching victims, see Brundage, *Lynching in the New South*, pp. 80–81; Feimster, " 'Ladies and Lynching,' " pp. 235–326.

12. *Times*, 21 September 1895; *Star*, 21 September 1895 (quotation). Jennie Watts swore out two peace warrants against the assailants: LCP, LVA. J. Flavious Ashworth was indicted for the assault on Watts, but according to a document dated 1 May 1897, LCP, LVA, skipped the county. Wade Hardy, one of the men who had assaulted German immigrant John Dern, was simultaneously under indictment on a federal moonshining charge. By the time his trial came up in the Watts case, Hardy was serving a sentence in federal prison. Richard Ashworth was sentenced to a year in the penitentiary for the Watts assault: *Dispatch* and *Star*, both 18 October 1895.

13. *Star* and *Dispatch*, both 5 September 1895; *Times*, 8 September 1895. Justice Eubank's notation of the hearing is in LCP, LVA.

14. *Times*, *Dispatch*, *Index-Appeal*, all 10 November 1895. The *Dispatch*, 22 October 1895, quoted Cardozo on the continuing ill feeling toward Cunningham.

15. *State*, 30 October 1895.

16. *Times*, 10 November 1895 (first quotation); *Planet*, 16 November 1895 (second quotation).

17. The women's lawyers had immediately petitioned Judge Orgain, waiving their clients' rights to appear at the nunc pro tunc hearing. Orgain did not reply, but a local correspondent reported that the judge would not grant the petition. With time running out, the lawyers appealed to the state attorney general, who on November 8, with the sheriff en route to Richmond, gave the governor his opinion that the prisoners' presence was not necessary. *Dispatch*, 23 October, 8 November 1895; *State*, 7 November 1895; *Times*, 7 November 1895; *Planet*, 16 November 1895.

18. *Times*, 10 November 1895.

19. This scene was described in the *Planet*, 16 November 1895.

20. Fortunately for Cardozo, the presence of the horses and wagons was not reported in the Richmond press. The men who supplied them filed claims for expenses: LCP, LVA.

21. Bell, *Old Free State*, vol. 1, p. 579. For a scholarly history of early Lunenburg, including white citizens' adoption of a southern, eventually secessionist identity: Richard R. Beeman, *The Evolution of the Southern Backcountry: A Case Study of Lunenburg County, Virginia, 1746–1832* (Philadelphia: University of Pennsylvania Press, 1984).

22. Lunenburg Order Book 37, pp. 268–69. For the first time Orgain also ordered Mary Barnes to Lunenburg. Attempting to fetch her the next day, Cardozo was stonewalled by the penitentiary's superintendent, who took his orders from the governor. The attorney general argued that inasmuch as she was already serving her sentence, Mary Barnes had passed out of Lunenburg's jurisdiction; Mann then decided to leave Mary Barnes alone. *Times* and *Dispatch*, both 14 November 1895; *Annual Report of the Attorney-General to the Governor of Virginia for the Year 1895* (Richmond: Superintendent of Public Printing, 1895), pp. 26–27. City Sergeant Charles Epps was later tried in Lunenburg for contempt of court and fined twenty-five dollars. *Times*, 23 and 24 November 1895; *Dispatch*, 23 November 1895.

23. Attorneys for the women and for Solomon had gotten Judge Beverly Randolph Wellford of the Richmond Circuit Court to issue and then extend a writ of habeas corpus, ordering the prisoners to *his* courtroom, thus keeping them out of Lunenburg. Lunenburg countered with a motion to the Supreme Court of Appeals for a writ of mandamus (rhymes with "famous" and translates from the Latin for "we order") to compel City Sergeant Epps to do his duty and give up the prisoners. The women's lawyers also petitioned the Supreme Court of Appeals to take possession of the prisoners. The lawyers' many moves and arguments were detailed in the *Times* and *Dispatch*, 10–28 November 1895; *Planet*, 9 November–7 December 1895; *Annual Report of the Attorney-General*, pp. 5–13.

24. Prior to taking custody of the prisoners, the Supreme Court ruled that custody belonged to Judge Orgain. It also ruled that the governor had no power to nullify Judge Orgain's orders, that Judge Wellford had no jurisdiction, and that (on technical grounds) Lunenburg could not have a writ of mandamus. *Times* and *Dispatch*, both 22 November 1895.

25. *Times* and *Dispatch*, both 27 and 28 November 1895; *Planet*, 7 December 1895. On the judges' consulting room: *Times*, 18 September 1895.

26. *State*, 5 December 1895; *Star*, 6 December 1895; *Planet*, 7 December 1895.

27. Both the *Times* and the *Dispatch*, 13 December 1895, printed the opinion in full.

28. Quotations come from *Barnes* v. *Commonwealth*, in Martin P. Burks, *Reports of Cases in the Supreme Court of Appeals of Virginia*, 92 (Richmond: J. H. O'Bannon, Superintendent of Public Printing, 1896), pp. 796, 807. Legal citation is 92 Va. 794 (1895).

29. *State*, 12 December 1895; *Planet*, 14 December 1895 (quotations).

CHAPTER 15: NEW LIFE

1. *State*, 2 January 1896; *Times* and *Dispatch*, both 3 January 1896; *Planet*, 4 January 1896. Mary Abernathy at first meant to name her baby Frances but later, possibly in consultation with her husband, settled on Bessie Mitchell: *State*, 6 February 1896; *Times*, 20 March 1896.

2. The belief that the three would be transported together: *State*, 23 January 1896; *Times*, 24 January 1896.

3. *Times*, 23 January 1896 (quotation). Other accounts of the journey to Lunenburg appeared in the *Times*, 24 January 1896; *Dispatch*, 23 and 24 January 1896; *Index-Appeal*, 23 January 1896; *Planet*, 7 March, 27 June 1896. Cardozo's expenses are in LCP, LVA.

4. *State*, 23 January 1896; *Times*, 24 January 1896 (quotation); *Dispatch*, 24 January 1896; *Planet*, 25 January 1896. On Pokey's illness: *Times*, 31 January 1896. According to an account in LCP, LVA, Dr. John Couch visited her five times.

5. *State*, 6 February 1896; *Star*, 6 February 1896; *Dispatch*, 7 February 1896; *Times*, 9 February 1896; *Planet*, 7 March 1896. Cardozo's claim for expenses is in LCP, LVA.

6. *State*, 6 February 1896.

7. *Star*, 22 November 1895; *Times*, 15 December 1895. LCP, LVA contains invoices for new carpet and spittoons, along with two doc-

uments describing needed repairs. On the proceedings this day: *Times* and *Dispatch*, both 11 February 1896.

8. Events of this day: *Times* and *Dispatch*, both 12 February 1896. Bagley's service as deputy: *Dispatch*, 16 July 1895; *Times*, 17 July 1895. For attorneys' questions, Bagley's replies, and those of Cardozo below, I have changed the *Dispatch* reporter's paraphrases into quotations.

9. L. P. Winn had guarded Pokey and Solomon on their return from Richmond and was currently a jail guard: *Times*, 24 January 1896; LCP, LVA. W. J. Bragg had helped transport the militia: LCP, LVA. E. H. Bacon had spirited the prisoners to Petersburg after Solomon's arrest: *Dispatch*, 21 June 1895; *Times*, 22 June 1895. John Bragg had been deputized to fetch recalcitrant witnesses: Lunenburg Order Book 37, p. 212.

10. *Times* and *Dispatch*, both 13 February 1896. The bill for Solomon's shoes is in LCP, LVA. The judge's orders: Lunenburg Order Book 37, p. 309.

11. *Planet*, 7 March 1896, which also described the Prince Edward jailer Edward Matthews as a "colored gentleman."

12. Among the methods were violence, buying votes, and diverse methods of stuffing ballot boxes: Herbert Clarence Bradshaw, *History of Prince Edward County, Virginia, from Its Earliest Settlements through Its Establishment in 1754 to Its Bicentennial Year* (Richmond: Dietz Press, 1955), pp. 436–41. The *Farmville Herald* expressed fellow feeling for Lunenburg's white citizens and officials: 10 and 24 August, 28 September, 30 November 1895. But it also urged restraint on Lunenburg: 26 October 1895.

13. W. E. B. Du Bois, "The Negroes of Farmville, Virginia: A Social Study," *Contributions by W. E. B. Du Bois in Government Publications and Proceedings*, ed. Herbert Aptheker (Millwood, N.Y.: Kraus-Thomson, 1980), pp. 5–44, described Farmville's economy after conducting a two-month study there in the summer of 1897. See also H. Clarence Bradshaw, *History of Farmville, Virginia, 1798–1948* (Farmville: *Farmville Herald*, 1994); Charles Edward Burrell, *A History of Prince Edward County Virginia, from Its Formation in 1753, to the Present* (Richmond: Williams Printing, 1922), pp. 293, 302–05.

14. The courthouse was pictured in the *Farmville Herald*, 20

March 1896; William H. Gaines, Jr., "Courthouses of Prince Edward and Nottoway Counties," *Virginia Cavalcade*, 20 (Autumn 1970), p. 46; Bradshaw, *History of Farmville*, p. 46.

15. Du Bois, "Negroes of Farmville, Virginia," pp. 21–26, 40–41. I have been unable to learn how Matthews came by his appointment as jailer.

16. *Farmville Herald*, 2 November 1895 (quotation). The women's quarters were described in the *Dispatch*, 13 February 1896, and the *Planet*, 7 March 1896, their cell's dimensions given in a report in the Loose Court Papers for 1896. In the same file was an invoice for new beds and mattresses dated February 13.

17. *Times*, 5 December 1895. The central sanction of O'Ferrall's antilynching bill was economic. A city or county that failed to prevent a lynching would be required to raise taxes to pay a heavy fine to the state. Sheriffs and jailers who failed to do their utmost to prevent a particular lynching would be suspended from their posts and could be sued by the heirs of the person lynched. In his legislative message O'Ferrall explained that two-thirds of lynchings involved no charges of sexual assault; he also said that lynching was *never* justified, even for the "crime too horrible to mention." At the same time, he evidently believed that the severest possible penalties for sexual assault would also help curb lynching; his bill called for the death penalty for rape and *attempted* rape. To speed trials, any rape case would move to the top of the docket. It is possible O'Ferrall got his numbers on sexual assault and lynching from literature produced by Ida B. Wells; however, O'Ferrall had been outraged at Wells's suggestion that some rape accusations were concocted by white women who had had consensual sex with black men. See McMurry, *To Keep the Waters Troubled*, pp. 226–27.

18. The General Assembly and most newspapers opposed this proposal, believing it might lead to a police state. *Dispatch*, 19 December 1895; *Times*, 21 December 1895; *Star*, 21 December 1895; *State*, 23 and 26 December 1895.

19. *Times*, 21 December 1895; *Dispatch*, 14 January 1896 (quotations).

20. Allen Diary, 19 February 1896; *Dispatch*, 20 February 1896; *Farmville Herald*, 21 February 1896.

21. *Dispatch*, 20 and 21 February 1896; *Farmville Herald*, 28 February 1896; *Planet*, 7 March 1896.

22. *Dispatch*, 21 February 1896; *Planet*, 7 March 1896.

CHAPTER 16: "A GONE CASE"

1. The *Times* and *Dispatch*, 17–19 March 1896, reported the trial. The record is in Prince Edward County Court Order Book (1891–1898), 16–18 March 1896. The lawyers were Courtney Franklin of Appomattox and William Lancaster of Cumberland. John Mitchell, Jr., may have hired them or acted as agent for someone else: The *Farmville Herald*, 6 March 1896, reported that he had spoken to Franklin about defending Marable, and the *Planet*, 7 March 1896, was the first paper to report Franklin had taken the case.

2. *Times*, 18 March 1896.

3. William E. Neblett quoted in the *Times*, 17 March 1896.

4. *Planet*, 7 March 1896; *Times*, 15 and 22 March, 4 and 19 April, 1896; *Dispatch*, 15 and 29 March 1896.

5. Allen Diary, 18 April 1896.

6. A portrait appeared in the *Farmville Herald*, 3 July 1896. Dickinson's age comes from the 1900 MCS, Prince Edward, ED 76, sheet 8. The trip to round up witnesses: *Times* and *Dispatch*, 18 and 19 April 1896; *Charlotte Gazette*, 23 April 1896. The sheriff's claim for expenses is in the Prince Edward Loose Court Papers, May, 1896.

7. *Dispatch*, 18 April 1896. The Mecklenburg Court Papers, LVA, contain documents concerning these misdemeanors. Rena Barnes's pregnancy is documented in LCP, LVA, as she gave birth in the Lunenburg jail on May 2.

8. *Dispatch*, 1, 15, and 17 March 1896; *Times*, 15 March 1896 (quotation); invoice dated 14 March in Prince Edward Loose Court Papers, 1896.

9. *Times*, 21 April 1896.

10. A biographical sketch of Judge Crute appears in Bradshaw, *History of Farmville*, p. 280. A portrait appeared in the *Dispatch*, 18 February 1896.

11. Watkins was mentioned in Bradshaw, *History of Prince*

Edward County, pp. 439–42, 625. His age is from the 1900 MCS, Prince Edward, ED 74, sheet 14.

12. The *Times* (quotation) and *Dispatch*, both 21 April 1896, gave brief accounts of jury selection; the jurors were pictured in the *Times*, 23 April 1896.

13. *State*, 7 April 1896; *Times*, 4, 7, and 21 April 1896; *Dispatch*, 8 and 21 April 1896; *Farmville Herald*, 24 April 1896.

14. *Dispatch*, 12 February 1896; H. H. Watson, "Judge Robert G. Southall," *Proceedings of the Thirty-sixth Annual Meeting, the Virginia State Bar Association* (1925), pp. 196–99; Gwathmey, *Legends of Virginia Lawyers*, pp. 92–93. Unless otherwise noted, quotations of the testimony are from the Mary Abernathy Trial Transcript (MATT). This is the only extant complete transcript of any of the Lunenburg trials; evidently the lawyers paid to have it made in case of appeal. It is "complete" in that it covers the testimony from beginning to end. It gives only the testimony of the witnesses, however, and does not give the questions asked them by the attorneys, nor does it ordinarily include interventions by the judge. I am working from the typed transcript located in the Prince Edward Court Papers, LVA.

15. This question and the answer come from the *Times*, 21 April 1896.

16. A copy of the warrant, dated 14 June 1895, is in LCP, LVA.

17. The question and the answer are from the *Times*, 21 April 1896.

18. This exchange was quoted in ibid.

19. Ibid.

20. *Times*, 22 April 1896.

21. The "merriment" created by Pollard's method of telling time: Ibid.

22. *Index-Appeal*, 22 April 1896; MATT, p. 37 (quotation). Gregory's testimony is from MATT, pp. 37–41, the *Times*, and the *Dispatch*, both 22 April 1896.

23. *Times*, 17 March 1896. The original quotation was in the plural, Cardozo lumping Solomon and Mary together as "gone cases, sure."

24. This exchange was reported in the *Times*, 22 April 1896.

25. MATT, pp. 47–48.

26. Judge Crute had lost an infant son in July 1895: *Farmville Herald*, 4 January 1896. The 1910 MCS, Prince Edward, ED 101, sheet 9, reported that Judge Crute's wife had borne two children, one of whom was living.

27. The map in the Prince Edward Loose Court Papers suggests that Mary's lawyers went to great pains to point out the location of the water bucket, as a thick *X* marked the spot on the front porch where the bucket stood. Cass Gregory by his own testimony had interrogated White in February, suggesting that White's testimony may have been crafted to suit Gregory.

28. The question is from the *Dispatch*, 23 April 1896. White's testimony is also from MATT, pp. 51–53.

29. *Dispatch*, 19 June 1895.

30. Lunenburg Marriage Register, 1853–1929, p. 67; *Minutes of the Twenty-fourth Annual Session of the Bluestone Baptist Association . . . 1895* (American Baptist Historical Society Microfilm R-78K).

31. *Dispatch*, 23 April 1896.

CHAPTER 17: EGG-SUCKING DOG

1. Lula Abernathy's testimony is from the *Times* and *Dispatch*, 24 April 1896, as well as MATT, pp. 56–58. Unless otherwise noted, the testimony that follows also comes from these three sources. The *Times*, 23 April 1896, reported that on this morning three black men—Daniel Ellis, Joe Wootten, and Ben Daniel—informed Judge Crute that they had been threatened by "negroes" with a whitecapping if they testified against Mary Abernathy or Pokey Barnes. Whether those who made the threats were from Fort Mitchell or Farmville or elsewhere was not specified. Crute vowed to get to the bottom of the matter, but nothing further appeared in the newspapers or court documents.

2. The *Dispatch*, 24 April 1896, had the judge saying "Lulu"; the press often was confused about this name.

3. Martha Thompson's testimony is taken from the *Times*, 24

April 1896, the *Dispatch* of the same date, and MATT, pp. 60–61. As with Lula Knight Abernathy's testimony, the three sources frequently give differing wordings, but the substance is the same.

4. On June 17 a man had been apprehended in South Boston, about twenty-five miles from Fort Mitchell. He was let go after the men who came to identify him found he was not Solomon Marable. *Times*, 20 June 1895.

5. The detail about the timing of the recess was given in the *Index-Appeal*, 24 April 1896.

6. Before Mary Abernathy took the stand, several others were called: Mary Wootten and her daughter Jennie recounted Solomon Marable's appearance in their restaurant; Floyd Clarke from the Chase City dry goods store told of the money Solomon had spent and also of the letter he had dictated; Margaret Bailey testified that Mary Abernathy had behaved normally during the shrouding.

7. The *Dispatch* version of this testimony had Mary Abernathy saying that she saw Solomon when she left the Pollard house. MATT, p. 66, and the *Times* agreed that Abernathy said she saw Solomon when she first entered the porch.

8. Mitchell's arrival in Farmville: *Times*, 25 April 1896. On disputes among Richmond Republicans: Chesson, "Richmond's Black Councilmen," pp. 204–07.

9. Or so it seems from our present knowledge. On Mahone, see Moger, *Virginia: Bourbonism to Byrd*, pp. 8–15, 47–71, and passim; Pulley, *Old Virginia Restored*, pp. 27–45, 62, 70; Moore, *Two Paths to the New South*; and Nelson, *Iron Confederacies*, pp. 81–88. Dailey, *Before Jim Crow*, gives a more nuanced view of patronage.

10. *Times*, 19 and 21 March 1896; *Dispatch*, 20 March 1896.

11. The *State*, 25 April 1896, reported Mitchell as "speechless" at his ouster. The testimony of Epps and Weisiger below: *Times* and *Dispatch*, 25 April 1896; MATT, pp. 76–78.

12. This is my best guess concerning the grounds for the prosecution's objection, which were not explained in the sources. If we assume the legal issue here concerned self-serving declarations, the essential question was whether Mary's statement was spontaneous or in some way premeditated, whether she made it "under circum-

stances which preclude the idea of design. The test is, were the declarations the facts talking through the party, or the party's talk about the facts?" Francis Wharton, *A Treatise on the Law of Evidence in Criminal Issues*, 8th ed. (Philadelphia: Kay and Brother, 1880), p. 554. For example, B shoots C, and B is immediately heard to shriek in horror, "I didn't know it was loaded!" In this instance B's statement might well be admissible. The same words uttered several hours later might not be admissible.

13. *Times*, 18 August 1895; *Star*, 23 October, 2 December 1895, 7 March 1896.

14. Quotations from MATT, p. 81.

15. Clements quotations: Ibid., p. 84.

16. "Careworn" and the baby's illness: *Times*, 26 April 1896. "[H]aggard and care-worn": *Dispatch*, 29 April 1896.

17. Except for the hungry hog statement (*Dispatch*, 26 April 1896), Flournoy quotations are from the *Times*, 26 April 1896. (Arguments were not included in the trial transcript.) The adversarial trial, a comparatively new form of judicial proceeding, typically brought forth a welter of chaotic, contradictory evidence. It was thus up to the lawyer, in the closing argument, to reshape the evidence into a compelling, coherent narrative: Halttunen, *Murder Most Foul*, pp. 100–107.

18. *Times*, 28 April 1896.

19. The instructions were filed with MATT and printed in the *Times*, 25 April 1896. The sources do not explain Crute's reasoning.

20. Brief descriptions of Monday's events appeared in the *Times* and the *Dispatch*, both 28 April 1896.

21. This exchange was quoted in the *Dispatch*, 28 April 1896.

22. *Times*, 28 April 1896.

CHAPTER 18: TRACKS

1. Mary Abernathy's attorneys had spent most of a day arguing that the verdict should be set aside, but Judge Crute denied their motion: *Times* and *Dispatch*, both 29 April 1896. April 30 weather: *Times*, 1 May 1896 (quotation).

2. This exchange comes from the *Times*, 1 May 1896, and from the partial trial transcript, abbreviated here as PBTT.

3. This may have been the Emma Harden who appeared in the 1910 MCS, Mecklenburg, ED 55, sheet 16 B. This Emma Harden was listed as a cook in a private family and had eight children, at least four of whom would have been born before 1896. At the time of the trial she would have been about thirty.

4. Emma Harding's appearance was described in the *Times*, 2 May 1896. The *Times* and *Dispatch* of 1 May 1896 gave only sketchy accounts of Harding's testimony on the first night of the trial. Harding testified again the next morning; the *Times* and *Dispatch*, 2 May 1896, gave fuller accounts of her morning testimony, and that is what I use here.

5. Unless otherwise noted, the testimony given on May 1 comes from the *Times* and *Dispatch* of 2 May 1896.

6. The *Times*, 3 May 1896, reported that a man was dispatched to Lunenburg to fetch Solomon Marable's clothing and returned with it on the morning of May 2, this report confirmed by a notation in the Prince Edward Loose Court Papers, May 1896. The clothes were not produced in the trial, however, and neither source says who had been keeping them.

7. I changed a paraphrase in the *Dispatch*, 2 May 1896, into this quotation. According to the *Dispatch*, 6 August 1895, the prosecution had attempted to introduce evidence about tracks in Pokey's first trial, but Judge Orgain ruled it out. Newspaper reports of Pokey's first trial did not mention this.

8. *Times*, 6 May 1896.

9. Unless otherwise noted, all information on this day's proceedings is from the *Times* and *Dispatch*, both 3 May 1896.

10. The commanding officer, J. H. Derbyshire, also testified this day, but after two hours of argument, most of his testimony was disallowed.

11. The newspapers paraphrased Pokey Barnes's testimony but did not quote her in the first person. I have therefore used the first-person account in the *Planet*, 27 June 1896, with a few phrases from the *Times*, 3 May 1896.

12. This portion of the testimony, and the question and answer sequence following, were reported in the *Dispatch*, 3 May 1896.

13. *Times*, 3 May 1896.

14. Sentencing was described briefly in the *Times* and *Dispatch*, both 5 May 1896, and the *Farmville Herald*, 8 May 1896, and recorded in the Prince Edward County Court Order Book, 1891–1898, p. 429. The *Code of Virginia*, sec. 4051, p. 947, provided that the death sentence be carried out after the next term of the court of appeals, but within thirty days of that term's first day.

CHAPTER 19: ONE SHALL BE TAKEN

1. The responses of Pokey Barnes were given, in somewhat differing language, in the *Times* and *Dispatch* of 5 May 1896, and the *Farmville Herald*, 8 May 1896, which constitute all the sources for this day's proceedings.

2. *Dispatch*, 14 January 1896.

3. William Neblett had gone home over the weekend and not returned: *Times*, 3 and 5 May 1896. For this day's proceedings: *Times* and *Dispatch*, both 6 May 1896; *Farmville Herald*, 8 May 1896.

4. *Farmville Herald*, 8 May 1896 (quotations). The other attorneys followed with brief speeches.

5. Watkins may have had other motives, but the sources shed no light on this.

6. *Dispatch*, 6 May 1896.

7. *Times* and *Dispatch*, both 6 May 1896; Prince Edward County Court Order Book, 1891–1898, p. 431. Abernathy's attorneys had made another attempt to have the verdict overturned, presenting affidavits from four citizens showing that the jury had not been kept together at all times. Judge Crute, however, concluded that no jury tampering had taken place. The sources conflict on Pokey's presence during Abernathy's sentencing, one saying Pokey was present, another saying that sentencing took place at four-thirty, at which time Pokey would already have been on the Richmond train. Judge Crute's son recovered from his illness and grew up to become a physician: Bradshaw, *History of Farmville*, p. 280.

8. Part of this quotation from Chapter 24, Verse 41 appeared in the *Planet*, 9 May 1896.

9. On Pokey's triumphal return to Richmond: *Dispatch, Times,* and *State,* all 6 May 1896; *Planet,* 9 May 1896.

10. *State,* 6 May 1896.

11. On Bettie Graves: *Planet,* 12 October 1895, 21 March 1896, 7 September 1897. Pokey's intent to stay out of Lunenburg: *Times* and *Star,* both 6 May 1896.

12. Newspaper accounts differ on how Pokey Barnes fared the day after her return. The *Star,* 6 May 1896, said she continued to receive visitors that morning. The *Dispatch,* 7 May 1896, said she was exhausted and compelled to spend the day in bed. The *Index-Appeal,* 8 May 1896, said she was receiving a thousand visitors a day.

13. *Planet,* 23 May 1896 (quotation); *Times, Star,* and *State,* all 9 May 1896.

14. *Index-Appeal,* 10 May 1896; *Planet,* 16 and 23 May 1896. Two out-of-town newspapers, Petersburg's *Index-Appeal,* 10 May 1896, and Lynchburg's *News,* 9 May 1896, suggested that Mitchell was exploiting Pokey Barnes for political gain. The Richmond press did not take this angle, and nothing in Pokey's behavior suggested she felt exploited.

15. *State,* 6 May 1896.

16. *State,* 6, 8, and 29 May 1896; *Dispatch,* 7 May 1896. On Republican factionalism: Chesson, "Richmond's Black Councilmen," pp. 204–07.

17. The Virginia Seminary began offering courses in 1890: Emily J. Salmon and Edward D. C. Campbell, Jr., eds., *The Hornbook of Virginia History: A Ready-Reference Guide to the Old Dominion's People, Places, and Past,* 4th ed. (Richmond: Library of Virginia, 1994), p. 268. Mitchell was a founder and gave the school a good deal of positive coverage in the *Planet.*

18. Reports on the conduct of the election: *State,* 29 May 1896; *Planet,* 6 June 1896.

19. *State,* 29 May 1896.

20. On Lynchburg: Steven Elliott Tripp, *Yankee Town, Southern City: Race and Class Relations in Civil War Lynchburg* (New York: New York University Press, 1997). The jail was described in two

Lynchburg newspapers, the *News*, 11 September 1896, and the *Daily Advance*, September 1896. Locations of Mary and Solomon's cells: *News*, 10 May 1896; *Planet*, 6 June, 25 July 1896. Quotations below are from the *Planet*, 6 June 1896.

21. *News*, 10 May 1896; *Planet*, 6 June 1896.

22. *State*, 20 May 1896; *Planet*, 30 May 1896.

23. Declaration, 1 June 1896, *David James Thompson* v. *The Times Co.*, Richmond City Court of Law and Equity Cases, 1897, Box 11, LVA.

CHAPTER 20: MESSAGES

1. Fannie Marable letters: *Planet*, 20 June, 25 July 1896. Mary Barnes and Mary Abernathy letters: *Planet*, 30 May 1896. Letters from donors: *Planet*, 13 and 20 June 1896. Mitchell letter: *News*, 14 June 1896; I added a salutation and signature because these were not published. Telegrams: *Planet*, 27 June 1896. Since the three women could not write, their letters were doubtless dictated.

CHAPTER 21: SOLOMON'S BODY

1. *Times*, 2 July 1896; *Dispatch*, 2 July 1896. The Prince Edward Loose Court Records, July 1896, contain a claim for $5.25 "in making scaffold, &c." The *Planet*, 25 July 1896, printed two line drawings of the hanging scene.

2. On the rope: *Farmville Herald*, 26 June 1896; *Times*, 30 June, 2 July 1896; *Dispatch*, 2 July 1896; *Planet*, 11 July 1896. Shipping charges: Prince Edward Loose Court Records, July 1896.

3. *News*, 3 July 1896; Prince Edward Loose Court Records, July 1896.

4. The *Planet*, 11 July 1896, gave the most detailed account of this day's events. For other accounts: *Planet*, 25 July, 1 and 8 August 1896; *Times*, 4 July 1896; *Dispatch*, 4 July 1896; *Farmville Herald*, 3 July 1896.

5. In his last weeks Marable gave three statements, the first to Mitchell in the Lynchburg jail on May 26, published in the *Planet*, 6 June 1896. He gave the second statement the night before the hanging to the *Dispatch*, published 4 July 1896. The third is described here

and was published in the *Times*, 4 July 1896, and the *Planet*, 11 July 1896. This last version is the most complete, and that is largely what appears here. I have cut in sentences and phrases from the other statements where they add significant detail or clearer language.

6. *Dispatch*, 4 July 1896. All other quotations from Marable's last moments are from the *Planet*, 11 July 1896. The death warrant is in the Prince Edward Loose Court Records, April 1896.

7. James O. Breeden, "Body Snatchers and Anatomy Professors: Medical Education in Nineteenth-Century Virginia, *Virginia Magazine of History and Biography*, 83 (July 1975), pp. 321–45. For a fictional treatment, see Ann McMillan, *Dead March* (New York: Penguin Books, 1998).

8. *Acts and Joint Resolutions Passed by the General Assembly of the State of Virginia during the Session of 1883–84* (Richmond: R. U. Derr, Superintendent of Public Printing, 1884), pp. 61–63. Minutes, Anatomical Board of Virginia, Tompkins-McCaw Library, Medical College of Virginia, Virginia Commonwealth University. Black officials' efforts to address the problem are mentioned in Chesson, "Richmond's Black Councilmen," pp. 212–13. The *Virginia Star*, an African American newspaper published in Richmond, printed a pointed editorial on the subject on 16 December 1882; a copy is in the "Body Snatching" file, Tompkins-McCaw Library.

9. Minutes, Anatomical Board of Virginia, 11 October 1895.

10. *Planet*, 1 and 8 August 1896.

11. The founding of the University College of Medicine three years earlier had been a thumb in the eye of the venerable Medical College of Virginia; their ferocious rivalry ended only with their merger in 1913. Dabney, *Richmond*, pp. 249–51. UCM's Paulus Irving had once practiced in Farmville and probably induced Farmville undertaker W. T. Doyne to ship him Marable's body; the MCV faculty may have thought UCM had tried to steal MCV's "anatomical material."

12. According to the Anatomical Board's minutes, agents were paid fifteen dollars per body. Events of this day were recorded in the greatest detail in the *Planet*, 11 and 25 July 1896. When other sources are used, they are noted below. The UCM officials consulted by Mitchell were Dr. Paulus Irving and the nationally known physician Hunter Holmes McGuire.

13. Only in the *Times*, 5 July 1896, was it clear that Mitchell apologized. Mitchell's *Planet* articles were unusually vague in some respects, with a good deal of passive construction and considerable confusion on the sequence of events, which may suggest that Mitchell was not entirely confident of the righteousness or legality of his behavior. The short reports in the *Times* and *Dispatch*, 5 July 1896, were sympathetic to him, however.

14. On Confederate reunions: Gaines M. Foster, *Ghosts of the Confederacy: Defeat, the Lost Cause, and the Emergence of the New South, 1865 to 1913* (New York: Oxford University Press, 1987), pp. 133–44. For the Richmond reunion, both the *Times* and the *Dispatch* published special editions, 30 June 1896. The number sixty-five thousand was given in the *Times*, 3 July 1896; some estimates went higher. The *Star*, 7 July 1896, reported that a number of professional "crooks" had been apprehended by a special police force.

15. The scenes outside MCV and inside the dissecting room were described in the *Planet*, 11 July 1896, and again, with illustrations, 1 August 1896. All quotations are from those two issues.

16. Accounts of this day's events appeared in the *Planet*, 11 July, 1 August 1896. The quotation below comes from the 11 July edition.

CHAPTER 22: COMMON SENSE

1. Nannie M. Tilley, *The Bright-Tobacco Industry, 1860–1929* (Chapel Hill: University of North Carolina Press, 1948), pp. 33–87. On Robert Allen's farm, according to his 1896 diary, suckering began on July 7 and worming on July 20, with cutting and curing occupying the second half of August.

2. On Pollard's decline: *Times*, 21 and 31 July 1896; *Dispatch*, 23, 26, and 31 July 1896; *Star*, 25 July 1896; *Charlotte Gazette*, 30 July (quotation), 6 August 1896. Robert Allen cataloged Pollard's possessions and the debts due him; Allen Family Papers. On money in the bank: *Times*, 25 August 1896. The will is in Lunenburg Will Book 14, p. 367. Pollard left most of his estate to Lucy's half brother, with other legacies to his sisters, nieces, and nephews. He also gave one hundred dollars to Lucy's church, which was evidently applied to a debt on the building: Friendship Baptist Church Minutes, vol. 1, pp. 43, 51, 52.

3. *Times*, 28 June 1896; *News*, 6 August 1896.

4. The proceeding was described briefly in the *Times* and *Dispatch* of 3 September 1896 and the *Farmville Herald*, 4 September 1896.

5. Events of this day were reported in confusing ways in the *Lynchburg Daily Advance*, 21 September 1896, the *Times* and *Dispatch* of 22 September 1896, *Farmville Herald*, 25 September 1896 (quotations), and the *Planet*, 26 September 1896. The order discharging Mary Abernathy was recorded in the Prince Edward County Court Order Book, 1891–1896, pp. 452–53.

6. *Dispatch* and *Index-Appeal*, both 30 July 1896; *Times*, 1 August, 3 September 1896.

7. *Planet*, 3 October 1896.

8. *News*, 22 September 1896.

9. *Planet*, 10 October 1896.

10. *Planet*, 17 October 1896. According to the *Planet*, Wilson Abernathy did not know of his wife's release until four days after it occurred; he learned of it when another black man overheard a white man reading the story in the newspaper. For several days after that Wilson did not know where Mary was. Mitchell had sent the news to Fort Mitchell, but Wilson had moved to a little place called Arvin, and the message evidently was not forwarded to him there. After Wilson wrote to Mitchell asking about Mary's whereabouts, the confusion was cleared away and a visit arranged.

11. *Planet*, 10 October 1896.

12. *Index-Appeal*, 21 October 1896; *Dispatch*, 21 October 1896; *Planet*, 24 October 1896.

13. *Planet*, 3, 10, 17, and 24 October 1896; O'Ferrall, *Forty Years of Active Service*, pp. 239–47.

14. Allen Diary, 3 November 1896.

15. Accounts of this episode: *Evening Leader*, 5 December 1896; *Times* and *Dispatch*, both 6 December 1896 (all quotations are from these articles). The soap and water detail is borrowed from the *Evening Leader*'s account of Rickey's earlier visit to the Henrico County jail. Late 1896 saw a shakeup in Richmond's newspaper scene. The *State* bought out the *Star* in October but was soon put out of business itself by the *Evening Leader*, a new paper launched

406 · NOTES TO PAGES 300–303

by Joseph Bryan to make money. His *Times* was losing money, in part because of its unpopular campaign for the gold standard. *Times*, 24 October 1896; Bryan, *Joseph Bryan*, pp. 254–56, 263.

16. Quoted in John A. Cutchins, *Memories of Old Richmond (1881–1944)* (Verona, Va.: McClure Press, 1973), p. 30.

17. *Evening Leader, State,* and *Times,* all 24 December 1896.

18. The *Dispatch*, 25 December 1896, implied that two of the pardoned men were black and two white; the *Evening Leader*, 26 December 1896, said all four were black. On Octavia Hodges: *Times*, 25 December 1896.

19. The full text appeared in the *Evening Leader*, 24 December 1896; *Dispatch*, 25 December 1896; *Planet*, 2 January 1897. The pardon papers are in the papers of the Secretary of the Commonwealth, Executive Papers, LVA. They include a transcript of Edward Pollard's testimony in the second trial of Pokey Barnes, showing that Mary Barnes was in the field with Edward at the time the murder was thought to have been committed. As far as I have been able to discover, this is the only portion of Pokey Barnes's trial for which a transcript was made. Producing the transcript took time and probably contributed to the delay in presenting the case to the governor.

20. Accounts of the departure of Mary Barnes: *Dispatch*, 25 and 27 December 1896; *Planet*, 2 January 1897.

21. *Planet*, 27 January 1897.

22. *Planet*, 14 December 1895; *Norfolk Landmark*, 8 and 9 December 1896; *Norfolk Dispatch*, 8 December 1896; *Norfolk Public Ledger*, 8 December 1896.

23. *Planet*, 16 January, 13 February, 13 March 1897.

24. *Planet*, 16 January 1897.

25. *Planet*, 6 March 1897. This speech is also treated in Brown, "Negotiating and Transforming the Public Sphere," p. 143. The *Planet*, 17 October 1896, said Pokey told the story of looking in her open grave the first time she spoke in public in Richmond. It made quite a sensation and seems to have become a standard feature of her presentation; it was noted again in the *Planet*, 24 October 1896. The Lunenburg records clearly indicate that a grave was dug for Solomon Marable, but show no evidence of graves for Pokey Barnes or Mary

Abernathy. It appears that Pokey was embellishing the story; it is also possible that someone in Lunenburg told her that a grave dug for someone else was meant for her.

26. The sentence read, "She told of her child who was in Virginia, and that she would not be surprised to hear that it had been lynched." (The use of "it" instead of "she" was commonplace in nineteenth-century parlance.) According to the *Planet*, 27 July 1895, Pokey said that after her arrest "a woman at Finneywood" had taken charge of her daughter. The 1900 MCS, Mecklenburg, ED 45, sheet 30 listed a Pattie Barnes, age eleven, living in the county almshouse. She may have been Pokey's daughter; Pattie was a nickname for Martha, and the age was about right. She may also have been Mary and Joseph Barnes's youngest child, or there may have been no kinship; Barnes was a common name in the area.

CHAPTER 23: THE PITCHER TO THE WELL

1. Thompson paid six cents for the box and a bowl. The record of the sale is in the Allen Family Papers.

2. Fellow admirers of the work of Judy Walkowitz may recognize this echo of her sentence: "The club had two beginnings, and as we shall see, multiple endings." Judith R. Walkowitz, "Science, Feminism and Romance: The Men and Women's Club 1885–1889," *History Workshop Journal*, 21 (Spring 1986), p. 38.

3. Chiles's grave is in Woodland Cemetery, Richmond. On Mitchell's later life: Alexander, "Black Protest in the New South"; Brundage, " 'To Howl Loudly,' " pp. 332–38; Trotti, "Murder and the Modern Sensibility," pp. 222–39; Virginia Newspaper Project, "*Born in the Wake of Freedom.*"

4. Mitchell was not bashful about reprinting congratulations from other newspapers; see the *Planet*, 16, 23, and 30 January 1897. Partly for that reason, he was not universally beloved among black newspaper editors, some of whom wearied of his self-promotion. Others criticized him on particular issues, like his attacks on W. W. Browne, the conservative and charismatic leader of the True Reformers, a temperance organization turned financial empire. See Brundage, " 'To Howl Loudly,' " pp. 333–34.

5. *Index-Appeal*, 9 July 1896; the original quotation read "James Bahen and John Mitchell are two sick political kittens." On Mitchell's political struggles: *Times* and *Star*, both 3 June 1896; *State*, 12, 13, and 22 June 1896. The *Index-Appeal*, 14 June 1896, said Mitchell had hoped to be a delegate to the Republican National Convention but gave up upon learning that the party would seat his rivals.

6. Andrew Buni, *The Negro in Virginia Politics, 1902–1965* (Charlottesville: University Press of Virginia, 1967); Wythe W. Holt, Jr., "The Virginia Constitutional Convention of 1901–1902: A Reform Movement Which Lacked Substance," *Virginia Magazine of History and Biography*, 76 (January 1968), pp. 67–102; J. Morgan Kousser, *The Shaping of Southern Politics: Suffrage Restriction and the Establishment of the One-Party South, 1880–1910* (New Haven: Yale University Press, 1974); Beth Barton Schweiger, "Putting Politics Aside: Virginia Democrats and Voter Apathy in the Era of Disfranchisement," in *The Edge of the South: Life in Nineteenth-Century Virginia*, ed. Edward L. Ayers and John C. Willis (Charlottesville: University Press of Virginia, 1991), pp. 194–218. Michael Perman, *Struggle for Mastery: Disfranchisement in the South, 1888–1908* (Chapel Hill: University of North Carolina Press, 2001), p. 223, argues that of all the southern states, Virginia "produced the most regressive formula for disfranchisement."

7. Ann Field Alexander, "No Officers, No Fight! The Sixth Virginia Volunteers in the Spanish-American War," *Virginia Cavalcade*, 47 (Autumn 1998), p. 190; Tyler-McGraw, *At the Falls*, pp. 214–15, 227, 229–31. Brown and Kimball, "Mapping the Terrain of Black Richmond," p. 308, note that after their militia units were dissolved, black Knights of Pythias "reuniformed" themselves and marched in the city's streets. In 1904 the General Assembly made it lawful to segregate streetcars; a law of 1906 made streetcar segregation mandatory. Richard B. Sherman, " 'The Last Stand': The Fight for Racial Integrity in Virginia in the 1920s," *Journal of Southern History*, 54 (February 1988), pp. 69–92; Peter Wallenstein, "Law and the Boundaries of Place and Race in Interracial Marriage: Interstate Comity, Racial Identity, and Miscegenation Laws in North Carolina, South Carolina, and Virginia, 1860s–1960s," *Akron Law Review*, 32 (1999), pp.

557–76; J. Douglas Smith, "The Campaign for Racial Purity and the Erosion of Paternalism in Virginia, 1922–1930: 'Nominally White, Biologically Mixed, and Legally Negro,' " *Journal of Southern History*, 68 (February 2002), pp. 65–106. On the larger southern picture: Leon F. Litwack, *Trouble in Mind: Black Southerners in the Age of Jim Crow* (New York: Alfred A. Knopf, 1998).

8.   *State*, 27 August 1896; *Star*, 31 August 1896. The *State* claimed there were only two black priests in the United States, but Ochs, *Desegregating the Altar*, suggests there were four, though only two had been ordained in the United States. See Ochs also for more on Uncles. In February 1896 Welbers wrote several letters to the *Times* arguing against railroad segregation. He went on to a long, productive, at times controversial career. After falling out with his superiors in 1905, he was sent to a poor parish in San Antonio, Texas. He died in 1946 at eighty-four and was buried in St. Peter Claver cemetery in San Antonio. Typescript Chronology, Josephite Archives.

9.   *Report of the Proceedings and Debates of the Constitutional Convention, State of Virginia*, 2 vols. (Richmond: Hermitage Press, 1906), vol. 2, p. 3144 (quotation). Wise's campaign pledges: *Norfolk Virginian-Pilot*, 7 April 1901; *Times*, 12 June 1901. In the former article, Wise declared himself against wholesale disfranchisement, because it violated both the Fifteenth Amendment to the U.S. Constitution and the principle of no taxation without representation. His remarks in the convention were contradictory and defy easy summary; he may have been using the attorney's strategy of trying every possible argument in hopes that one or two would stick with each juror. His obituary: *Times-Dispatch*, 4 February 1908. On race radicalism: Williamson, *Rage for Order*, pp. 70–151.

10. Spencer R. Crew, *Field to Factory: Afro-American Migration 1915–1940* (Washington: Smithsonian Institution, 1987); Earl Lewis, "Expectations, Economic Opportunities, and Life in the Industrial Age: Black Migration to Norfolk, Virginia, 1910–1945," in *The Great Migration in Historical Perspective: New Dimensions of Race, Class, and Gender*, ed. Joe William Trotter, Jr. (Bloomington: Indiana University Press, 1991), pp. 22–45; for a national perspective, see this entire volume. On migration out of the Southside: Kerr-Ritchie, *Freedpeople in the Tobacco South*, pp. 233–45.

11. Brown and Kimball, "Mapping the Terrain of Black Richmond," p. 316, remind us that "black Richmonders often represented individual achievement as collective prosperity, not only removing the logic behind their social subordination in the larger society but also providing for each other 'a new visual landscape of possibility.' " On dilemmas facing the black intelligentsia, including Mitchell, under the pressures of Jim Crow: Kevin K. Gaines, *Uplifting the Race: Black Leadership, Politics, and Culture in the Twentieth Century* (Chapel Hill: University of North Carolina Press, 1996). Bay, *White Image in the Black Mind*, pp. 187–217, also cites the greater conservatism of some black thinkers in the early twentieth century. At the same time, she suggests on p. 188 that the Jim Crow system "began to crumble even as it was being completed . . . when racism began to lose the authority of science and African-Americans began to organize themselves for the long, hard struggle that would ultimately lead to the civil rights movement." My guess is that further study will reveal more ferment in the early twentieth century than most historians currently appreciate.

12. August Meier and Elliott Rudwick, "Negro Boycotts of Segregated Streetcars in Virginia 1904–1907," *Virginia Magazine of History and Biography*, 81 (October 1973), pp. 479–87.

13. Quoted in Paolo E. Coletta, *William Jennings Bryan: Political Evangelist 1860–1908* (Lincoln: University of Nebraska Press, 1964), p. 141.

14. In Minor Weisiger's elegant phrasing, "Flying into the whirlwind of Bryanism, the Gray Eagle crashed to earth." Weisiger, "Charles T. O'Ferrall," p. 146. The *Dispatch*, 13 and 15 October 1896, reported anti-O'Ferrall resolutions in Lunenburg and Mecklenburg. Alec Guigon also became a prominent gold Democrat, serving as counsel to Richmond's Sound-Money League: *Dispatch*, 20 October 1896. After 1896 Guigon continued to practice law, representing one of Richmond's major streetcar companies. He died of cancer in 1923. Minor, "Alexander Barclay Guigon"; Anne Hobson Freeman, *The Style of a Law Firm: Eight Gentlemen from Virginia* (Chapel Hill, N.C.: Algonquin Books, 1989), pp. 131–32, 255–56.

15. Brundage, *Lynching in the New South*, p. 269.

16. Executive Papers, 23–28 April 1897, LVA; *Planet*, 1 May

1897; Brundage, *Lynching in the New South*, pp. 42, 46, 60, 155, 173.

17. Weisiger, "Charles T. O'Ferrall," p. 145; *Times-Dispatch*, 23–25 September 1905; *Farmville Herald*, 29 September 1905.

18. O'Ferrall, *Forty Years of Active Service*, pp. 235–36 (quotation); Brundage, *Lynching in the New South*, pp. 169–78.

19. *Times-Dispatch*, 30 April, 2 May 1911; *News-Leader*, 1 May 1911; *Planet*, 6 May 1911.

20. Etta Donnan Mann, *Four Years in the Governor's Mansion of Virginia, 1910–1914* (Richmond: Dietz Press, 1937), p. 51. On Mann's career: Rhodes, "William Hodges Mann."

21. "The Richmond Mothers' Club," Peabody Clippings, Hampton University.

22. The 2,410 African American women who registered to vote in Richmond represented about 12 percent of the black adult female population of the city; just under 15 percent of Richmond's black men were registered. Suzanne Lebsock, "Woman Suffrage and White Supremacy: A Virginia Case Study," in *Visible Women: New Essays on American Activism*, ed. Nancy A. Hewitt and Suzanne Lebsock (Urbana: University of Illinois Press, 1993), pp. 82–90. Other works on Virginia black women's activism in this period include Brown, "Womanist Consciousness"; Davis, "Rosa L. Dixon Bowser"; Muriel Miller Branch and Dorothy Marie Rice, *Pennies to Dollars: The Story of Maggie Lena Walker* (North Haven, Conn.: Linnet Books, 1997); Anne Firor Scott, "Janie Porter Barrett," *Dictionary of Virginia Biography*, vol. 1, ed. John T. Kneebone et al. (Richmond: Library of Virginia, 1998), pp. 357–59.

23. Rhodes, "William Hodges Mann," pp. 189–93. Works on women's activism in addition to those cited above: Anne Hobson Freeman, "Mary Munford's Fight for a College for Women Co-ordinate with the University of Virginia," *Virginia Magazine of History and Biography*, 78 (October 1970), pp. 481–91; Lebsock, *"A Share of Honour,"* pp. 122–39; Marjorie Spruill Wheeler, *New Women of the New South: The Leaders of the Woman Suffrage Movement in the Southern States* (New York: Oxford University Press, 1993); Sandra Gioia Treadway, *Women of Mark: A History of the Woman's Club of Richmond, Virginia 1894–1994* (Richmond: Library of Virginia, 1995), pp. 34–66; Elna C. Green, *Southern Strategies: Southern*

Women and the Woman Suffrage Question (Chapel Hill: University of North Carolina Press, 1997). Political histories and biographies for this period of Virginia history give virtually no ink to women's political work, although newspapers and other "traditional" sources contain ample evidence.

24. The *Times*, 24 October 1895, described the farm. Fannie used the name Morton when she married Watkins: Granville County Marriage Register, 1884–1905, 22 February 1899, North Carolina State Archives. The families are reconstituted from the 1900 MCS, Granville, ED 61, sheet 16, and from the 1910 MCS for the same location, ED 89, sheets 14B, 18B. Fannie's death is surmised from census information that Sam Watkins remarried in 1904.

25. The indictment is in Mecklenburg Court Papers, LVA. Rosa Barnes's arrival at the penitentiary was noted in the *State*, 30 June 1897, and the *Planet*, 3 July 1897. The Register of Prisoners, 1894–1902, notes her incarceration, 26 June 1897, and discharge, 29 October 1901. Keve, *History of Corrections*, p. 200, quotes a letter from the prison superintendent to the Mecklenburg judge, inquiring about the court's intentions with respect to the child. It is not clear what happened next.

26. *Planet*, 23 July 1898. Barnes's military record is in the Compiled Service Records, War with Spain, National Archives and Records Administration, Washington, D.C. On the Sixth Virginia: Alexander, "No Officers, No Fight!"

27. The Barnes family is more difficult to trace than the Abernathys because the Barnes name was much more commonplace. In many years, city directories listed at least two black men named Joseph Barnes and two black women named Mary Barnes; women tended not to be listed at all unless they were single, widowed, or heads of households. The Barnes family did appear in the 1920 MCS, Richmond City, ED 152, sheet 16. The Abernathys were in the 1900 MCS, Richmond City, ED 59, sheet 8, and the 1910 MCS, Richmond City, ED 104, sheet 6B. On their Richmond context: Brown and Kimball, "Mapping the Terrain of Black Richmond"; Davis, *The World of Patience Gromes*.

28. On Lucy's serving dinner to Mary Barnes: *Dispatch*, 28 July, 6 August 1895. The sources are fuzzy, but Lucy evidently ate with the

men before serving Mary. On segregation as a modern, largely urban form of racial control: C. Vann Woodward, *The Strange Career of Jim Crow*, 3d rev. ed. (New York: Oxford University Press, 1974); John W. Cell, *The Highest Stage of White Supremacy: The Origins of Segregation in South Africa and the American South* (Cambridge: Cambridge University Press, 1982). Intensified segregation in cities would seem to have meant that ordinary black-white interactions shriveled among women and became more one-sided and one-dimensional. The typical encounter pitted a black domestic or laundress against a white authority figure—employer, landlord, policeman, or streetcar conductor (to whom, after 1904, fell the unlovely task of enforcing the new segregation ordinances). Under such circumstances, I'm guessing, negative racial stereotypes abounded and hardened.

29. Brown and Kimball, "Mapping the Terrain of Black Richmond," pp. 302–04; Tyler-McGraw, *At the Falls*, pp. 200–06; Christopher Silver, *Twentieth-Century Richmond: Planning, Politics, and Race* (Knoxville: University of Tennessee Press, 1984), pp. 17–52.

30. The 1895 city directory named significant proportions of black businesspeople in each of these occupations. The black woman physician was Sarah G. Jones, who earned her M.D. from Howard University in 1893 and who, according to the *Planet*, 26 January 1895, was "the first woman to pass the Medical Examining Board of Virginia."

31. On occupational options: Jones, *Labor of Love*, pp. 110–51; Hunter, *To 'Joy My Freedom*, esp. pp. 26–31, 50–65, 74–97, 103–14, 131–36. It appears that many laundresses maximized their productivity and limited their contacts with their clients by sending their children to pick up and deliver: Branch and Scott, *Pennies to Dollars*, pp. 15–17; Hunter, *To 'Joy My Freedom*, p. 57.

32. Public schools in Lunenburg and Richmond were segregated from their inception just after the Civil War. According to the Lunenburg school superintendent, 47 percent of black children ages five to twenty-one were reported enrolled; fewer than half of the enrolled students actually attended on any given day. Among whites, 60 percent were enrolled, with a little more than half attending on any

414 · NOTES TO PAGES 316–320

given day. Annual Report of the Superintendent of Schools, Lunenburg, 1895, Superintendent of Public Instruction, LVA. On the limitations of rural schooling: William A. Link, *A Hard Country and a Lonely Place: Schooling, Society, and Reform in Rural Virginia, 1870–1920* (Chapel Hill: University of North Carolina Press, 1986).

33. To cut costs, Virginia localities stopped keeping birth and death records from 1896 to mid-1912; Wilson's disappearance from the city directories suggests he died in 1909, as does the fact that Mary was listed beginning in 1910. The Virginia Bureau of Vital Statistics holds a record of Mary Abernathy's death; she was buried in Greenwood Cemetery.

34. The year of Joseph Barnes's death is surmised from his disappearance from the city directories. The Virginia Board of Vital Statistics does have a death record for Mary Barnes, who was buried in Greenwood Cemetery.

CHAPTER 24: WHO KILLED LUCY POLLARD?

1. Versions implicating the women: *Dispatch*, 20 June, 12, 13, 14, 16, and 21 July 1895; *Times*, 20 June, 12, 13, 14, 16, 18, and 21 July 1895. Versions implicating the white man: *Marable* v. *Commonwealth*, pp. 2–4, 23–24; *Times*, 20 and 25 July, 14 September 1895, 4 July 1896; *Dispatch*, 20 July 1895, 4 July 1896; *Planet*, 27 July, 3 August 1895, 6 June, 11 July 1896.

2. *Times*, 17 March 1896 (quotation). Thompson gave his biography in a letter to the *Times*, 28 September 1895. His credit history is pieced together from a very large number of court papers. *Charles Davenport* v. *Thompson & Pettus*, Mecklenburg Chancery Papers, File 147, LVA, is the single most informative group of documents on Thompson's struggles in the 1890s. For the later period the richest case is *Stella M. Thompson* v. *D. J. Thompson*, Mecklenburg Chancery Papers, File 153, LVA. Other records containing debt actions against Thompson include Circuit Court Judgments, Circuit Court Executions, and Justice of the Peace Civil Warrants and Executions, all for Mecklenburg County, LVA. A few debt actions are in the Lunenburg records: Circuit Court Common Law Order Book 5, pp. 16, 17, 20.

3. A court later exempted Bill Pettus from liability for the firm's debts because he drew no income from the mercantile business.

4. *Wirt E. Taylor* v. *Thompson & Pettus*, Mecklenburg Circuit Court Judgments, LVA.

5. Charlotte County Marriage Register No. 3, p. 100. Pettus, age thirty-eight, married Nell Hanmer, age twenty, daughter of one of the Hanmers who appear below in a lawsuit against Cass Gregory. On furniture: *William Daffron* v. *Thompson & Pettus*, Mecklenburg Chancery Causes 25-28, LVA.

6. Pollard's loan is documented in PBTT, p. 10. The loan from J. V. Nichols (brother of Herbert's wife) to Herbert and David James Thompson jointly is documented in *Davenport* v. *Thompson & Pettus*.

7. Mecklenburg Justice of the Peace Warrants, 1892–1900, LVA.

8. With each judgment, the court sent the sheriff to Finney-wood to seize property, and each time David Thompson dodged, claiming that all the property belonged to the estate of his deceased father. David was the estate's administrator, and he should have long since settled it. In defiance of the court, however, he had refused to do so; once the estate was settled, the property that passed to David and Herbert would be fair game for their creditors. The cat and mouse game between Thompson and the court respecting administration of James L. Thompson's estate is amply documented in *Davenport* v. *Thompson & Pettus*.

9. I have not been able to find any obituaries for Herbert Thompson; his birth and death dates are in Munsey A. Moore, *Cemetery and Tombstone Records of Mecklenburg County, Virginia* (Chase City: Munsey Moore Publishing, 1982), vol. 1, p. 78. After four years elapsed, the debts still were not paid in full, so in 1900 the court took the next legal step, selling off several tracts of land, along with the big house and general store in Finneywood. David Thompson fought back, hiring an attorney who invoked the homestead law, a statute that exempted two thousand dollars' worth of property from seizure for debt. The court—a friendlier one this time—voided the earlier land sales, and for the moment Thompson was saved. The experience did nothing for his ethics, however, for he refused to pay the attorney who had rescued his property! The attorney turned around and joined Thompson's other creditors in the long-standing

lawsuit that had caused the lands to be auctioned in the first place. Petition of W. E. Homes in *Davenport* v. *Thompson & Pettus.*

Law and local custom tended to favor local landholders over distant creditors; after much ado, most of the land in question eventually returned to the Thompson-Pettus family, the Finneywood property to Martha Ann Thompson and the most valuable Lunenburg land to Bill and Lucius Pettus. The Pettus brothers had a substantial inheritance from their father, which helped them weather the hard times and eventually buy out their kinfolks.

10. The documents concerning the assaults and separation are in Mecklenburg Justice of the Peace Warrants and Commonwealth Warrants, 1907 (first quotation), 1909 (third quotation), LVA; Mecklenburg Deed Book 70, p. 422 (second quotation).

11. Martha Ann Thompson, David's formidable mother, died in 1909. With a substantial inheritance from her, David discharged many of his outstanding debts, some creditors settling for twenty-five or fifty cents on the dollar. David Thompson's financial dealings in this period are most clearly laid out in *Stella M. Thompson* v. *D. J. Thompson.* On the Briery years: Prince Edward Deed Book 62, p. 43; *Morris & Co.* v. *D. J. Thompson; Lindsey, Robinson & Co.* v. *D. J. Thompson; Littlefield-Shepperd Co. Inc.* v. *D. J. Thompson*, all in Law File 52, Prince Edward Courthouse; Prince Edward Common Law Order Book 6, p. 365. David also bought land, which was repossessed for lack of payment: Prince Edward Deed Book 69, p. 285; Book 70, p. 61; Book 72, p. 11; Book 81, p. 1. Quotation on David's pennilessness: Prince Edward Fiduciary Account Book 3, p. 19. Mattie's will: Prince Edward Will Book 17, p. 204. Mattie's and David's death records: Certificates of Death Nos. 13089, 31287, Bureau of Vital Statistics, LVA. The graves are behind the Mount Pleasant United Methodist Church, just off Route 15 in Prince Edward County. I thank W. Carter Thompson for information on the grave site.

12. On the relationship to J. B. Davis: *Jennie E. Pettus* v. *W. W. Pettus*, Mecklenburg Chancery Papers, File 179, LVA. A document in *Davenport* v. *Thompson & Pettus* says that on 1 October 1896 Davis owed Thompson & Pettus $49.23 but does not say when the debt was contracted. Ellis's inability to read and write was reported in the

1880 MCS, Lunenburg, ED 139, p.31. Ellis was subpoenaed to testify in the defamation suit below, but by June 1897 he had evidently moved off the Thompson place. Betsy Ellis, who was with Pokey Barnes on the day of the murder and helped shroud Lucy Pollard's body, was Daniel's wife.

13. *David James Thompson* v. *The Times Company*, Richmond City Court of Law and Equity Cases, 1897, Box 11, LVA; Richmond Court of Law and Equity Order Book 3, p. 18 (1897), John Marshall Courts Building, Richmond, Virginia. The *State*, 25 June 1897, mentioned that the case was in progress; Petersburg's *Index-Appeal*, 26 June 1897, mentioned the verdict, as did the *Planet*, 3 July 1897. The major dailies (the *Times*, the *Dispatch*, and, a new paper, the *Evening Leader*) said nothing about the case, though all three reported other cases decided that week in that same court.

14. A useful introductory text is Laurence Howard Eldredge, *The Law of Defamation* (Indianapolis: Bobbs-Merrill, 1978). For the nineteenth century: Samuel Merrill, *Newspaper Libel: A Handbook for the Press* (Boston: Ticknor and Company, 1888). Among the cases decided by the Supreme Court of Appeals of Virginia, the most informative on the evolution of defamation and libel is *Chaffin* v. *Lynch*, 1 South Eastern Reporter 803 (1887).

15. *Code of Virginia* (1887), p. 803, sec. 3375. In *Thompson* v. *Times*, the judge specifically instructed the jury on this provision. The *Times* apologized on 23 September 1896.

16. The payments are documented in *Davenport* v. *Thompson & Pettus*, as are Thompson's continuing difficulties with creditors and rent payments. Among his other fast moves, David James Thompson in 1897 put all his personal property in his wife's name, the better to protect it from seizure for his debts: Mecklenburg Personal Property Books, 1897–1909, LVA.

17. *Planet*, 30 May 1896. The *Planet* of this date said mistakenly that Thompson sued over a report that "he had at the point of a revolver forced a colored man to drink whiskey until he dropped insensible and died from the effects of it." This rumor had indeed appeared in print, not in the *Times* but rather in the *Planet*, 28 September 1895, which also reported the alleged cutting incident.

18. Brief notations of the arrests are in the Mecklenburg County

Court Papers, Box 1893–1895, LVA. The subpoena, served 14 June 1897, is filed in *Thompson* v. *Times*. That Herbert Thompson was at home to receive a subpoena in a debt case on 9 April 1897 (filed with *Stella M. Thompson* v. *D. J. Thompson*) lends plausibility to the hunch that he skipped the county temporarily to avoid testifying in his brother's libel suit.

19. Edward Pollard's mention of sending for Martha Thompson is in PBTT, p. 6.

20. *Marable* v. *Commonwealth*, p. 4.

21. Mary Abernathy twice reported that her last conversation with Lucy Pollard involved visits to Martha Thompson. *Planet*, 27 July 1895: "Mrs. Pollard was talking to me about Mrs. Thompson. I told her I hadn't been, but I would go as soon as I could. She said she wanted to go too, but Mr. Pollard looked as though he could not do without her then." MATT, p. 65: "Mrs. Pollard said, 'When are you going over to Cousin Martha's.' I said 'In a few days.' She said, 'Tell her howdy, and I am coming to see her soon.' "

22. In an affidavit given on 23 August 1895, Cunningham recalled his initial conversation with Marable about the white man. "I asked him the name of the white man—if he knew him, and he said he did not—that he had never seen him before, but that the man said his name was Thomason." *Marable* v. *Commonwealth*, p. 24. If Solomon told the truth about not knowing the man, David and Herbert Thompson would be in the clear since Solomon clearly knew them. It seems more likely that Solomon lied on this occasion because he was still in Lunenburg and very much afraid of an assassin or mob. Solomon's answer made sense for a man who longed to name the killer but feared the consequences.

23. *Planet*, 27 July 1895.

24. Gregory was in Richmond to present the findings of the Committee on Facts.

25. Papers regarding arrests and conveyances of prisoners are in LCP, LVA. The anonymous letter: *Dispatch*, 1 August 1895. Evidence on his house-to-house canvass: MATT, p. 41. The rumor that Solomon would abandon the white man story: *Times*, 18 March 1896.

26. The destruction of the warehouse was reported in the *Charlotte Gazette*, 18 May 1882, and recalled by Gregory in answer to

questions about his financial history in *H. C. Gregory* v. *W. T. Spencer*, Lunenburg Ended Chancery Cases. The 1880 MCS, Lunenburg, ED 139, p. 31 shows Cass and Ella Gregory with four children ranging from ages three to twelve. In this crisis Gregory's unlikely white knight was Edward Pollard, who had recently begun lending money on a large scale. Pollard made several loans to Gregory, totaling more than a thousand dollars. When the loans came due, Gregory was stuck. Having no other way to pay, Cass and his wife, Ella, conveyed their home place—a farm Ella's parents had given Cass when he and Ella were first married—to Edward, who held the deed for several months while the Gregorys scrambled. They sold land Cass had inherited from his father. They mortgaged Ella's interest in a tract she expected to inherit from her mother. Edward also proved willing to compromise. In 1884 he deeded the farm to Ella alone, to help insulate it from Cass's creditors. No sooner did she get the property back, however, than she mortgaged it to secure one of Cass's debts. Lunenburg Will Book 14, p. 275; Lunenburg Deed Book 37, p. 575; Book 38, p. 568; Book 41, pp. 419, 424, 533, 534. The deeds to and from Edward Pollard do not mention the loans; that information is from *Gregory* v. *Spencer*, as is Gregory's admission of his long-term insolvency.

27. The judge voided the sale to the Baltimore purchaser (who testified that Gregory had not told him of others' interest in the property) and ordered a second sale, the proceeds to go to the Hanmers. *H. D. Hanmer & J. E. Hanmer* v. *H. C. Gregory*, Mecklenburg Chancery Papers, File 131, LVA; *Gregory* v. *Spencer*.

28. To secure the second loan, Cass and Ella Gregory put up as collateral a horse, cart, buggy, wagon, and all their household furnishings. *Farmers Bank* v. *H. C. Gregory & Others*, Person County Superior Court, 1896, North Carolina State Archives; Person County Record of Deeds, Book OO, p. 259, Register of Deeds Office, Roxboro, North Carolina. In the *Person County Courier*, 1 May 1895, an ad for Gregory's Farmers Warehouse included a notice from the Tobacco Board of Trade that business would continue at the warehouse, irregularities concerning a local bank having been corrected; I have been unable to learn more about this suspect situation.

29. *Farmers Bank* v. *H. C. Gregory*. As in the 1884 conveyance

to Edward Pollard, the Gregorys sometimes used ordinary conveyances, deeds that looked like routine land sales, to record what were in fact debt actions, so it is difficult to track their transactions with precision. Since the early 1880s, however, an important theme in their financial history was the ongoing struggle to hold on to land Ella had brought to the marriage. Ella's mother died in 1888, and 1,060 acres descended to Ella and to the estate of her recently deceased brother. He had died in debt, however, and his half was ordered sold to pay his creditors. Ella's half was already mortgaged to cover debts that Cass had contracted earlier (Lunenburg Deed Book 41, pp. 485, 534), but she evidently hoped to hold on to her share and to redeem her brother's share as well. With the four hundred dollars advanced her by Cardozo, she managed to buy her brother's half of the farm (Lunenburg Deed Book 44, pp. 567, 568; payment of the debt was noted in a marginal note saying "Satisfied to me" in Cardozo's hand dated 18 January 1896). It is remotely possible that Cardozo forgave the debt in exchange for Gregory's sleuthing on behalf of the county. However, Cardozo was punctilious about claiming reimbursement for the services he rendered as sheriff, and thus it seems unlikely that he would use his personal assets to fund the Pollard investigation.

30. Lunenburg Deed Book 46, p. 428.

31. 1900, 1910, 1920 MCS, Brunswick (respectively, ED 15, sheet 5; ED 17, sheet 207A; ED 17, sheet 31); Gregory was listed as an "engineer" in 1910 and a "civil engineer" in 1920. He qualified as a notary public in 1914 and 1922; Brunswick Circuit Court Order Book 7, p. 404, and Book 11, p. 126. Other sources for this last segment of Gregory's life include Civil War Pensioners, Act of 1902, Brunswick County, LVA, and Brunswick Fiduciary Accounts, vol. 4, p. 366.

32. *N. A. Lewis* v. *H. C. Gregory's Administrator*, Brunswick Ended Chancery Cases, File 305; Brunswick Circuit Court Order Book 14, pp. 453, 456.

33. *Times* and *Dispatch*, both 23 July 1895.

34. The stir in Lunenburg: *Dispatch*, 26 July 1895. Gregory's jail visit: MATT, p. 84.

35. Claims for these services are in LCP, LVA.

36. *Dispatch*, 1 August 1895.

37. *Times*, 24 September 1895. The *Times* said knowledge of the stabbing had come to light on 23 September. Gregory was in South Carolina then, but on 21 September sent a letter to the *Dispatch*, which evidently arrived on the twenty-third; the *Dispatch* printed it on the twenty-fourth. Two issues: First, one wonders whether Gregory enclosed in the *Dispatch* letter (or wrote separately to the *Times*) an off-the-record tip about the alleged stabbing incident. Second, Gregory's published letter contained some very odd statements that might represent unintended leakage. The *Dispatch*, 19 September 1895, had reported Lunenburg people as highly critical of Gregory's having offered life sentences to Pokey Barnes and Mary Abernathy in exchange for their revealing the location of the money. In his letter of 21 September Gregory defended himself, saying he had meant to dispel some Lunenburgers' belief that the military had made off with the money. His plan had backfired, and he now found himself under suspicion that he was "a partner in the deal. Well, of one thing the stake-holder (whoever he may be) is certain, and that is that H. C. Gregory has not yet drawn his part of the funds. Jesting aside, I do believe that some white man is handling the stolen money, and if so, he may look out, for if life and health and strength last I mean to know who he is."

AFTERWORD

1. I am grateful to W. Carter Thompson for giving me the unpublished "History of Salem Christian Church" (1979).

2. There is a mushrooming literature on historical memory. Some useful starting points for the South and for African American history are James M. Lindgren, *Preserving the Old Dominion: Historic Preservation and Virginia Traditionalism* (Charlottesville: University Press of Virginia, 1993); Nell Irvin Painter, *Sojourner Truth: A Life, a Symbol* (New York: W. W. Norton, 1996), pp. 258–87; Jacquelyn Dowd Hall, " 'You Must Remember This': Autobiography as Social Critique," *Journal of American History*, 85 (September 1998), pp. 439–65; W. Fitzhugh Brundage, ed., *Where These Memories Grow: History, Memory, and Southern Identity* (Chapel Hill: University of North Carolina Press, 2000) and "White Women and the

Politics of Historical Memory in the New South, 1880–1920," in *Jumpin' Jim Crow: Southern Politics from Civil War to Civil Rights*, ed. Jane Dailey, Glenda Elizabeth Gilmore, and Bryant Simon (Princeton: Princeton University Press, 2000), pp. 115–39; David W. Blight, *Race and Reunion: The Civil War in American Memory* (Cambridge: Harvard University Press, 2001).

3. Brent Tarter, "The New Virginia Bookshelf," *Virginia Magazine of History and Biography*, 104 (Winter 1996), pp. 7–102, provides a learned survey of what was then known and not known about the state's history. In the same issue, Karen Ordahl Kupperman, James P. Whittenburg, Jane Turner Censer, Edward L. Ayers, James Tice Moore, and Robert A. Pratt give enlightening responses to Tarter's essay.

4. Trotti, "Murder and the Modern Sensibility," pp. 333–34.

5. Royall, *Some Reminiscences*; O'Ferrall, *Forty Years of Active Service*. Newspaper obituaries of O'Ferrall, George Wise, and Frank Cunningham failed to mention the Lunenburg case. The one mention of Lunenburg I have seen in an obituary is in Minor, "Alexander Barclay Guigon."

6. O'Ferrall, *Forty Years of Active Service*, p. 11.

7. O'Ferrall, *Forty Years of Active Service*, pp. 245–46. My narrative is taken from the Nannie Woods pardon papers, Secretary of the Commonwealth, Box 192, Executive Papers, 1895, LVA, and John S. Salmon and Emily J. Salmon, *Franklin County Virginia 1786–1986* (Rocky Mount, Va.: Franklin County Bicentennial Commission, 1993), pp. 327–31.

8. Unlike Lunenburg, the Nannie Woods case had legs. Virginius Dabney mentioned it in *Virginia: The New Dominion* (Garden City, N.Y.: Doubleday, 1971), p. 414. Dabney evidently picked it up from Charles E. Wynes, *Race Relations in Virginia 1870–1902* (Charlottesville: University of Virginia Press, 1961), pp. 114–15; Wynes evidently got it from Herbert Aptheker's multivolume *A Documentary History of the Negro People in the United States*, vol. 1 (New York: Citadel Press, 1969), pp. 748–49.

9. *State*, 3 July 1896; *Dispatch*, 4 July 1896.

10. The interpretation of southern history that dominated the mainstream academy until the 1950s was challenged from the begin-

ning by W. E. B. Du Bois and Carter G. Woodson, who were joined by a somewhat younger generation that included Luther Porter Jackson and Rayford W. Logan.

11. Full citations appear above in Note 2 to the Prologue.

12. Williamson, *Rage for Order*, p. 155, suggested there had been a "second Reconstruction" in the upper South in the 1880s and 1890s. For samples of recent work, see the essays in Dailey et al., *Jumpin' Jim Crow*.

INDEX

Page numbers in *italics* refer to illustrations.

objectivity vs. sensationalism in, 18
see also specific newspapers
New York City, 302, 303
Nineteenth Amendment, 311
nolle prosequi, 261, 294
Norfolk, Va., 302
North Carolina, 35, 38, 50, 94, 149, 180, 215, 331
Fanny Marable's return to, 70
Solomon Marable's body delivered to, 289–90
Nottoway County, Va., 56, 126–27, 128, 166, 263
nunc pro tunc order, 187, 188, 191, 389*n*

Odd Fellows, 186
O'Ferrall, Charles Triplett, 138, 173, 281, 312
background of, 61
death of, 309–10
in election of 1893, 61, 179
Lunenburg case omitted from memoirs of, 334, 335–36
lynching opposed by, 18, 60–62, 204–5, 309–10, 335, 358*n*, 393*n*
Mary Barnes pardoned by, 298, 300–301
physical appearance of, 62, *62*
post-Lunenburg career of, 308–10
prisoner transfer refused by, 191–93, 337
Solomon Marable's reprieve and, 162, 175–77
troops ordered by, 60, *62*, 65, 188, 190–93
Orgain, George C., 60, 169, 178, 200–202, 204, 298, 359*n*
background of, 70, 360*n*
debt of, 70, 356*n*
Mary Abernathy's first trial and, 84–85, 88, 89, 91
Mary Barnes's trial and, 106, 107
nunc pro tunc order and, 187, 188, 190, 389*n*
Pokey Barnes's first trial and, 93, 94, 99, 100, 103, 104, 399*n*
prisoners ordered to return to Lunenburg Courthouse by, 188, 190, 193, 195, 196–97, 390*n*
sentencing by, 108
Solomon Marable's first trial and, 70–73, 77, 78, 81, 82
special grand jury convened by, 145
Orgain, Rebecca, 360*n*

panic of 1893, 45
pardons, 138, 170, 173, 298, 300–301, 336
Perkins, H. D., 278
Perry, William H., 84–85
Neblett's relationship with, 84, 363*n*
Petersburg, Va., 56, 65, 71, 190
jail in, 57, 77, 87, 96, 355*n*
near riot in, 296–97
Petersburg *Index-Appeal*, 141
Pettus, Lucius, 304, 325, 416*n*
Pollard's problems with, 131, 159
as winking man, 158–59, *159*, 228, 325
Pettus, Nell Hanmer., 143, 325–26, 415*n*
Pettus, W. W. (Bill), 106, 143, 159–60, 249, 259, 320, 325–26, 415*n*, 416*n*
Philadelphia, Pa., 186
photographs, halftone, 152–53
Pincus, Samuel, 338
Pocahontas, 306
politics, 41, 59–62, 203, 305–12
in Prince Edward County, 210
in Richmond, 110–14, 234, 265–68, 305–8, 401*n*
see also elections; *specific political parties*
Pollard, Betsy Lewis, 129, 130, 134–35, 377*n*
Pollard, Edward S., 24–27, 29–31, 53, 102, 121–35, 206, 374*n*–79*n*
alarm sounded by, 13, 24, 25, 42, 76, 87, 94, 98, 102–3, 139, 231, 238, 254, 260, 296
attorney hired by, 71, 361*n*
ax of, *see* meat ax
background of, 126–29
Bill Thompson's hatred of, 128, 133–34, 211–12, 213, 378*n*
Cass Gregory's visits to, 45–48, 214–15, 217, 219
Charlotte farm of, 121, 133, 212
death of, 292, 294, 304, 305, 404*n*
grave of, 292, 333
health problems of, 210–11, 215, 291–92
land purchased by, 128–29
lending practices of, 13, 74, 75–76, 130–31, 211, 212, 237, 242–43, 321, 419*n*
Lucius Pettus's problems with, 131, 159
as Lucy Jane's alleged killer, 125, 134–35
Lucy Jane's death discovered by, 13, 76, 123, 124, 216